Defining Shugendō

Also Available from Bloomsbury

Mountain Mandalas, Allan G. Grapard
The Sea and the Sacred in Japan, Fabio Rambelli
Spirits and Animism in Contemporary Japan, Fabio Rambelli

Defining Shugendō

Critical Studies on Japanese Mountain Religion

Edited by
Andrea Castiglioni, Fabio Rambelli, and Carina Roth

BLOOMSBURY ACADEMIC
LONDON • NEW YORK • OXFORD • NEW DELHI • SYDNEY

BLOOMSBURY ACADEMIC
Bloomsbury Publishing Plc
50 Bedford Square, London, WC1B 3DP, UK
1385 Broadway, New York, NY 10018, USA
29 Earlsfort Terrace, Dublin 2, Ireland

BLOOMSBURY, BLOOMSBURY ACADEMIC and the Diana logo
are trademarks of Bloomsbury Publishing Plc

First published in Great Britain 2020
This paperback edition published in 2022

Copyright © Andrea Castiglioni, Fabio Rambelli, and Carina Roth, 2020

Andrea Castiglioni, Fabio Rambelli, and Carina Roth have asserted their rights under the
Copyright, Designs and Patents Act, 1988, to be identified as Editor of this work.

For legal purposes the Acknowledgments on pp. xii–xiii constitute
an extension of this copyright page.

Cover design by Ben Anslow
Artwork © Sandra Roth

All rights reserved. No part of this publication may be reproduced or transmitted in any
form or by any means, electronic or mechanical, including photocopying, recording, or
any information storage or retrieval system, without prior permission in writing from the
publishers.

Bloomsbury Publishing Plc does not have any control over, or responsibility for, any third-
party websites referred to or in this book. All internet addresses given in this book were
correct at the time of going to press. The author and publisher regret any inconvenience
caused if addresses have changed or sites have
ceased to exist, but can accept no responsibility for any such changes.

A catalogue record for this book is available from the British Library.

A catalog record for this book is available from the Library of Congress.
Library of Congress Control Number: 2020945423

ISBN:	HB:	978-1-3501-7939-4
	PB:	978-1-3501-9158-7
	ePDF:	978-1-3501-7940-0
	eBook:	978-1-3501-7941-7

Typeset by Integra Software Services Pvt. Ltd.

To find out more about our authors and books visit www.bloomsbury.com
and sign up for our newsletters

Contents

Illustrations — vii
Contributors — ix
Acknowledgments — xii
Notes for the Reader — xiv

Introduction: Shugendō and Its Metamorphoses *Andrea Castiglioni, Carina Roth, and Fabio Rambelli* — 1

Part One Intellectual History of Shugendō Studies

1 A Critical History of the Study of Shugendō and Mountain Beliefs in Japan *Suzuki Masataka* — 33

Part Two Constructed Topologies and Invented Chronologies

2 Shugendō within Japanese Buddhism: Considerations on the Formation of Shugendō *Hasegawa Kenji* — 63
3 Imagining an Ancient Tradition: Eighteenth-Century Narratives of Shugendō at Mount Togakushi *Caleb Carter* — 75
4 Otake Dainichi Nyorai and Haguro Shugendō: Unearthing a Lost History *Gaynor Sekimori* — 87
5 Shugendō and Modernity Face to Face: The Daigoji Case *Hayashi Makoto* — 103

Part Three Imagining En no Gyōja and Fictionalizing Shugendō

6 Between Companionship and Worship: A Reflection on En no Gyōja Statuary Past and Present *Carina Roth* — 123
7 En no Gyōja's Legitimization in the Context of Japanese Esoteric Buddhism *Kawasaki Tsuyoshi* — 137
8 The Description of Mountains in *Minoodera engi* *Niki Natsumi* — 145
9 Images of the *Shugenja* in Edo Popular Fiction *William D. Fleming* — 153

Part Four Materiality and Visual Culture

10	The Cult and Statuary of Zaō Gongen *Fujioka Yutaka*	167
11	Religious Culture in Transition: Mt. Fuji *Janine T. Anderson Sawada*	187
12	The Shape of Devotion: Mounds, Stelae, and Empowering Ritual Fasting in the Early Modern Cult of Mount Yudono *Andrea Castiglioni*	205
13	Shugendō as Social Practice: Kumano Talismans and Inscribed Oaths in Premodern Japan *D. Max Moerman*	219

Notes	231
Bibliography	254
Index	280

Illustrations

Figures

1.1	The multidimensional relationship between kami and buddhas	35
3.1	The mountains of Togakushi (right) and Nishidake (left) above the pond of Kagami. Photograph by Caleb Carter	76
3.2	Kuzuryū no Ōkami, Meiji-period *ofuda*. Courtesy of Futazawa Hisaaki (private collection)	81
4.1	*Shugenja* revering the Otake Dainichidō. August 2008. Photo by Gaynor Sekimori	88
4.2	The *honjibutsu* of Dewa Sanzan. Center: Dainichi (Yudonosan); left Kannon (Hagurosan); right Amida (Gassan). Photo by Sekimori collection	90
4.3	Illustration of drainboard, *Ogen Otake monogatari*. Courtesy of the Ideha Cultural Museum. Photo by Gaynor Sekimori	93
6.1	En no Gyōja statue at the oratory of Gyōsen no shuku, Wakayama prefecture. Statue of Jitsukaga on the right. May 2017. Photo by Carina Roth	127
6.2	Map of the Kii Peninsula, with relevant topographical markings along the Ōmine Okugake route	128
6.3	Restored statue of En no Gyōja with votive text by Miyagi Tainen. Courtesy of Shōgoin	131
10.1	Zaō Gongen mirror icon, 1001, Tokyo. Courtesy of Sōjiji Temple	174
10.2	Zaō Gongen mirror icon, twelfth century. Kyoto National Museum Collection. Photographic credit: Mainichi Shinbunsha	175
10.3	Gilt bronze statue of Zaō Gongen, twelfth century, Nara, Ōminesanji. Photo by Fujioka Yutaka	183
11.1	*Fuji sankei mandara*. Hanging scroll, color on silk. 186.6 by 118.2 cm. Sixteenth century. Courtesy of Fujisan Hongū Sengen Shrine, Fujinomiya-shi, Shizuoka	192
11.2	*Fuji sankei mandara*. Hanging scroll, color on silk. 91.5 by 67.3 cm. Sixteenth century. Courtesy of Fujisan Hongū Sengen Shrine, Fujinomiya-shi, Shizuoka	193

11.3	*Sanzon kuson zu*. Woodblock print on paper. 38 by 27.5 cm. Edo period. Courtesy of Fujisan Myūjiamu (Fujiyoshida-shi Rekishi Minzoku Hakubutsukan), Fujiyoshida-shi, Yamanashi	196
11.4	*Hachiyo kuson zu*. Woodblock print on paper. 40.5 by 28 cm. 1680. Courtesy of Fujisan Myūjiamu (Fujiyoshida-shi Rekishi Minzoku Hakubutsukan), Fujiyoshida-shi, Yamanashi	198
11.5	*Ominuki*. Hanging scroll, ink on paper. 1620. Source: Murakami Shigeyoshi and Yasumaru Yoshio, eds., *Minshū shūkyō no shisō*, 483	201
11.6	*Getsugan ominuki*. Hanging scroll; ink and color on paper. 92.0 by 32.0 cm. 1680. Courtesy of Fujisan Myūjiamu (Fujiyoshida-shi Rekishi Minzoku Hakubutsukan), Fujiyoshida-shi, Yamanashi	202
12.1	Stele of Dainichi Sanzon-zō. 1639. Mitsukaidō, Chūtsuma, Ibaraki prefecture. Photo by Tokuhara Satoyuki	210
13.1	1609 oath signed by Ryūkyū King Shō Nei. Tōkyō Daigaku Shiryō Hensanjo	226

Tables

1.1	Founder traditions and modern commemorative events	41
1.2	Founders and foundation years	42
1.3	Writings and capital transfer in the Nara period	43
5.1	Timeline of the main events of modern Shugendō	108
10.1	Principal written sources on Zaō Gongen from the Heian to the Nanbokuchō period	169
10.2	Techniques and bronze components of the Zaō Gongen gilt bronze statues excavated around the main hall of Ōminesanji	178

Contributors

Caleb Carter is an assistant professor in the Faculty of Humanities at Kyushu University. He specializes in Japanese religions within the broader scope of Buddhist studies and East Asian cultures. His interests include issues related to space and place, narrative and folklore, women and gender, and ecology. Carter is currently completing a book manuscript on the historical formation of Shugendō through a case study of Mount Togakushi (Nagano). Recent publications include "Power Spots and the Charged Landscape of Shinto" (2018) and "Constructing a Place, Fracturing a Geography: The Case of the Japanese Tendai Cleric, Jōin" (2017).

Andrea Castiglioni is a senior lecturer at Nagoya City University, specialized in early modern Shugendō history and ascetic movements. Recent publications include "Devotion in Flesh and Bone: The Mummified Corpses of Mount Yudono Ascetics in the Edo Period" (2019), "From *Your Name.* to *Shin-Gojira*: Spiritual Crisscrossing, Spatial Soteriology, and Catastrophic Identity in Contemporary Japanese Visual Culture" (*Spirits and Animism in Contemporary Japan*, Bloomsbury, 2019), and "Shika, sekibutsu, engi ga kataru Yudonosan shinkō: Muromachi makki kara Edo shoki made [The Faith in Mount Yudono Through Poems, Stone-buddhas, and *Engi* from the End of the Muromachi Period to the Early Edo period]" (2017).

William D. Fleming is Assistant Professor of East Asian Languages and Cultural Studies at the University of California, Santa Barbara. He is currently completing a book manuscript titled *Strange Tales from Edo: Rewriting Chinese Fiction in Early Modern Japan*.

Fujioka Yutaka is a professor at Ōsaka University, specialized in East Asian Buddhist sculpture. He is the author of "Yachūji Miroku Bosatsuzō ni tsuite: Keikō Xsen bunseki chōsa wo fumaete" [On Yachūji's Miroku Bosatsu Image, on the Basis of an X-Ray Fluorescence Analysis and Survey] (2014) and "Zaō Gongen, sono seiritsu to tenkai" [Zaō Gongen, Formation and Evolution, 2004].

Hasegawa Kenji is Deputy Director of the Prefectural Museum of Tokushima and specializes in Shugendō history and literature. He is the author of *Shugendō soshiki no keisei to chiiki shakai* [Formation of Shugendō organizations and regional society] (2016) and "Shugendō shi kenkyū no ayumi [Steps in the Study of Shugendō History]" (2015).

Hayashi Makoto is a professor at Aichi Gakuin University. He specializes in Onmyōdō and Shugendō institutional history. He is the author of *Buddha no henbō* [The

Metamorphosis of the Buddha] (2014) and *Tenmonkata to Onmyōdō* [Astronomers and the Way of Yin and Yang] (2006).

Kawasaki Tsuyoshi is a professor at Shūjitsu University and specializes in Shugendō literature. He is the coeditor with Heather Blair of "*Engi*: Forging Accounts of Sacred Origins" (2015), and the author of "The Invention and Reception of the *Mino'odera engi*" (2015).

D. Max Moerman is Professor in the Department of Asian and Middle Eastern Cultures at Barnard College, Columbia University and Co-Chair of the Columbia University Seminar on Buddhist Studies. His research interests are in the visual and material culture of pre-modern Japanese religions. He is the author of *Localizing Paradise: Kumano Pilgrimage and the Religious Culture of Premodern Japan* (2005) and *The Japanese Buddhist World Map: Religious Vision and the Cartographic Imagination* (forthcoming).

Niki Natsumi is an assistant professor at the National Institute of Technology, Akashi College. She specializes in Japanese Literature. She is the author of "Jusha no ie ni okeru kasetsu no denju: Hironari-ryū tennō hōju no rekishi wo chūshin ni [Transmission of Scholastic Traditions in Confucian Families, Centering on the History of Emperor Education According to Hironari-ryū]" (2014) and "Takaosan-zō Takatsukasa Kanehira kanshi nishu ni tsuite [On Two Chinese Poems by Takatsukasa Kanehira Held on Mt. Takao]" (2008).

Fabio Rambelli is a professor of Japanese religions and cultural history, as well as ISF Endowed Chair in Shinto Studies at the University of California, Santa Barbara. His books include *Buddhas and Kami in Japan* (with Mark Teeuwen, 2002), *Buddhist Materiality* (2007), *The Sea and the Sacred in Japan* (Bloomsbury, 2018), and *Spirits and Animism in Contemporary Japan* (Bloomsbury, 2019).

Carina Roth is a research and teaching fellow at La Maison de l'histoire, University of Geneva. She specializes in Shugendō history and textual tradition. She is the author of "Essays in Vagueness: Aspects of Diffused Religiosity in Japan" (2019) and "En no Gyōja" (2019).

Janine T. Anderson Sawada is Professor of Religious Studies and East Asian Studies at Brown University, specializing in the religious and intellectual history of early modern Japan. She is the author of *Practical Pursuits: Religion, Politics, and Personal Cultivation in Nineteenth-Century Japan* (2004) and *Confucian Values and Popular Zen: Sekimon Shingaku in Eighteenth-Century Japan* (1993).

Gaynor Sekimori is a research associate at the Centre for the Study of Japanese Religions, SOAS. She specializes in Japanese religions (Shugendō). Her books include *Shugendō: The Culture and History of a Japanese Religion* (with Bernard Faure and

D. Max Moerman, 2009) and *The Mandala of the Mountain* (2005), an edited translation of the work of Miyake Hitoshi.

Suzuki Masataka is a professor emeritus at Keiō University and president of the Association for the Study of Japanese Mountain Religion. He specializes in Shugendō history and Japanese ethnology. He is the author of *Sangaku shinkō: Nihon bunka no kontei wo saguru* [Mountain Beliefs: Exploring the Roots of Japanese Culture] (2015) and *Myao-zoku no rekishi to bunka dōtai: Chūgoku nanbu sanchimin no sōzōryoku no hen'yō* [The Movements of the History and Culture of the Miáo Ethnic Group: Transformations of the Imagination of Mountain People in Southern China] (2012).

Acknowledgments

On the surface of things, Shugendō appears to be an almost forgotten strand of Japanese religious tradition, led to near extinction by the religious policies of the Meiji Restoration. However, when paying closer attention, Shugendō or Shugendō-related practices and traditions appear at many unsuspected corners. The primary goal of this book is to present an up-to-date collection of studies on Shugendō from both Japanese and non-Japanese scholars. Its explicit aim is to show how Shugendō, similarly to Shinto, spans over a wide and complicated array of religious and cultural modes and activities. This book joins the ranks of two past edited collections of studies on Shugendō, one in the *Japanese Journal of Religious Studies* (Tyler and Swanson, eds., 1989) and the other in *Les Cahiers d'Extrême-Asie* (Faure, Moerman and Sekimori eds. 2011). Like these previous collections, our book does not provide a single synthetic view or offer an overall grasp on Shugendō. To readers familiar with Shugendō studies, this will be nothing new: the subject is so intricate, complex, and diversified that it would be preposterous to pretend to cover every aspect of it in one single volume. The very elusiveness of Shugendō makes much of its allure, the flip side of this being its slipperiness.

It is true that there are few scholars, in Japan and elsewhere, who focus their research on Shugendō. However, since Shugendō can be approached from a wide array of angles and perspectives, it features as a more or less prominent "sidekick" in a great number of studies. Moreover, in the past few decades, research on Japanese religions has changed in character, resulting in more inclusive, and less sectarian, or unilateral, approaches. Shugendō being, as it is, a movement at the crossroads of many other religious traditions, it has gained a much more positive image and a more benevolent scholarly treatment.

Our greatest hope for this collection is for it to inspire future research in a subject all three of us have been fond of, and fascinated by, for many years.

Like many projects, this book has its origin in happenstance (or maybe not?). What are the odds for three scholars interested in Shugendō studies to be simultaneously present at the same university for a prolonged period of time, especially outside Japan? As luck would have it, all three editors of this book were at the University of California, Santa Barbara between 2016 and 2018, when Kawasaki Tsuyoshi floated the idea of co-organizing an international workshop on recent developments in Shugendō studies. The initial idea evolved into an intense two-day conference at the University of California, Santa Barbara in June 2017, the results of which constitute the starting point of the present volume. Of course, the conference papers have been thoroughly revised and reshaped in order to give this volume structure and a certain degree of coherence.

Acknowledgments

We would like to express our gratitude to the many people and organizations that made this book possible. First of all, Allan Grapard, who has been a continuous source of inspiration for all of us. We would also like to thank the Japanese Ministry of Education and Scientific Research for the grant that allowed our initial conference to happen, together with the Northeast Asia Council (Association for Asian Studies), and, at the University of California, Santa Barbara, the Shinto Studies endowment, the Department of East Asian Languages and Cultural Studies, the Department of Religious Studies, the College of Letters and Science, and the East Asia Center. In Switzerland, we would like to thank the Swiss National Science Foundation and the Maison de l'histoire (University of Geneva). The editors are grateful to Iwata Shoin, Tokyo, for granting them permission to translate and publish Hayashi Makoto's chapter, the Japanese original of which has been published by them in 2015. Similarly, we wish to thank University of Hawai'i Press for the permission to use Janine Sawada's chapter due to be published as part of a monograph in 2020. Finally, this book would not have happened without the passion of our editor at Bloomsbury, Lalle Pursglove, the enthusiasm and suggestions of three external reviewers, and the hard work of the entire editorial team.

Notes for the Reader

Japanese names and terms have been romanized according to the common modified Hepburn system; the Pinyin system has been used for Chinese; and the standard transliteration system for Sanskrit. Japanese personal names are written in the traditional order, with the family name first.

In dates, years prior to 1873 (when Japan adopted the standard Western calendar) have been converted to the Western Gregorian calendar.

This book follows the standard periodization of Japanese history (in which the premodern era refers to everything before 1868):

Jōmon period: 14,000–300 BCE
Yayoi period: 300 BCE–250 CE
Kofun period: 250–538
Asuka period: 538–710
Nara period: 710–794
Heian period: 794–1185
Kamakura period: 1185–1333
Muromachi period: 1336–1573
Azuchi-Momoyama period: 1573–1600
Edo (Tokugawa) period: 1600–1868
Meiji period: 1868–1911
Taishō period: 1911–1926
Shōwa period: 1926–1989
Heisei period: 1989–2019
Reiwa period: 2019–present

In the References, some classical texts (*Kojiki*, *Nihon shoki*, etc.) are listed in different modern editions according to the preferences of the contributors to the volume.

Introduction: Shugendō and Its Metamorphoses

Andrea Castiglioni, Carina Roth, and Fabio Rambelli

Shugendō 修験道 is the name given to a Japanese religious tradition centering on ascetic practice in the mountains. Taken literally, Shugendō means "the Way to achieve miraculous powers through practice." Unfortunately (or fortunately), there exists no convenient or standard translation for this expression, and you will find in this book a variety of different interpretations for it, depending on what aspect of the tradition is emphasized. Beyond its enigmatic denomination, Shugendō may, however, be described quite readily. On the one hand, it places natural environment at the core of its practices, with ritualized "mountain entries" (*nyūbu* 入峰) as its most defining feature. On the other hand, Shugendō focuses on the acquisition of special powers (results) aimed at both attaining spiritual advancement and ensuring a livelihood through healing and exorcisms, as well as more standard religious services. *Shugen* practices may be traced to the end of the Heian period (twelfth century), and a wide range of austerities and religious activities in the mountains could be identified in the broad sense of Shugendō, perhaps even defined as a kind of "proto-Shugendō." However, as a discrete and independent religious movement, Shugendō emerged toward the end of the thirteenth century. From its inception to this day, it bears strong doctrinal links to Shingon and Tendai Buddhism, the two main traditions of Esoteric Buddhism in Japan. Another defining characteristic of Shugendō is the fact that it incorporates practices, rites, and deities from the whole spectrum of Japanese religions.

Hence, like Zen or Pure Land schools, Shugendō is best considered a sectarian movement that developed within the broad panorama of medieval Japanese Buddhism toward the end of the thirteenth century. Compared to their Zen and Pure Land counterparts, however, Shugendō practitioners (*shugenja* 修験者), institutions, and religious activities tended to have a higher symbiotic relationship with similar elements in the exo-esoteric Buddhist system (*kenmitsu taisei* 顕密体制) that was pervasive in medieval Japan. For example, Shugendō institutions and *shugenja* often created collaborative and synergic networks with Buddhist monks, other groups of ascetics, and religious confraternities of lay devotees (*kō* 講). This porous and flexible structure, which came to be juridically regulated only at the beginning of the seventeenth century, has been the cause of its near-total erasure from most of the academic narratives about mainstream Japanese religious traditions—narratives that privileged clear-cut and easily definable institutions and teachings. In other cases, Shugendō was simply relegated to the indefiniteness of interpretative labels such as "folklore studies" or "popular religions."

This book presents a collection of Shugendō studies written by a pool of Japanese and Euro-American scholars who share new interpretative visions about Shugendō history, culture, and religious heritage. Because this text is not an introduction to Shugendō per se, it seems appropriate to provide the reader with some key concepts about Shugendō terms, logic, and practices to better interact with the contents of the following pages. Before the thirteenth century, the term *yamabushi* 山伏—"those who lie down in mountains"—denoted a vast range of religious professionals who may or may not have had specific institutional affiliations and who mastered a variety of rituals such as healing ceremonies, purification procedures, and exorcisms. Pre-thirteenth-century *yamabushi* did not specifically conceive of mountains as elective sites for their practices and were, on the contrary, extremely active among members of the lesser urban aristocracy of the imperial capital. From the second half of the thirteenth century, the performance of ascetic practices in the mountains and the importance of religious specialists such as *shugenja*—"those who achieve [supernatural] results through [ascetic] practices"—who increasingly linked their socioreligious charisma to these types of austerities, became a predominant trend. Therefore, the general but vague term *yamabushi* began to be conflated with *shugenja* and mountain asceticism in particular (Hasegawa 1991: 23–4, as well as his chapter in this book).

It is impossible to provide an exhaustive description of the ritual procedures and doctrinal discourses that characterized the mountain-entry rituals performed by *shugenja* during the seasonal self-seclusion periods on a given mountain before the fifteenth century. In general, during the mountain-entry rituals, the geophysical body of the mountain was conceived as a mandalic landscape, while the act of ascending or descending it corresponded to equal progressions or regressions within the ten realms (*jikkai* 十界) of the Buddhist cosmology. The foot of the mountain hosted hells, whereas the top was visualized as the entrance into the realm of the buddhas. The soteriological target of Shugendō, which was reified through the mountain-entry rituals, was to allow *shugenja* to realize perfect buddhahood and non-duality with the body of the cosmic Buddha Dainichi Nyorai 大日如来 while penetrating the inner space of the mountain. From an institutional point of view, the participation in mountain-entry rituals guaranteed *shugenja* career promotions within the Shugendō ranking system and, at the same time, an individual process of empowerment (*genriki* 験力), which produced social capital for legitimizing the religious status and efficacy of Shugendō rituals among lay devotees and patrons.

The arrival of "modernity" proved a disastrous event for Shugendō, which was officially banned by the Meiji government in 1872 within the context of religious reforms aiming at the separation of *kami* and buddhas (*shinbutsu bunri* 神仏分離). Because the doctrinal logic and worship practices of Shugendō tradition were based on combinatory paradigms between (foreign) Buddhist deities and local gods (*kami* 神), Meiji oligarchs perceived it as a threat to the new national polity, the authority of which was entirely centered on *kami*-related discourses. The result was a legalized ostracism and a forced eradication of Shugendō, which was consequently stigmatized as a deleterious heap of anti-modern and obscurantist superstitions. Initially, Shugendō institutions and practitioners were deeply impacted and *shugenja* apparently disappeared from the religious panorama of the Meiji period (1868–1911). Nevertheless, as Suzuki Masataka 鈴木正崇 and Hayashi Makoto 林淳 both point out in the first and fifth chapters of this book, the suppression of Shugendō was never carried out systematically. Even during the Meiji period, *shugenja* and other groups of professional ascetics kept providing lay devotees with their religious services. They merely used religious titles and institutional affiliations that were different from the outlawed Shugendō ones and continued organizing pilgrimages toward numinous mountains. At the same time, the Meiji period marked the beginning of a newly coined identity for Shugendō. At the time in which Shugendō was formally doomed as an actively practiced religious tradition, it was resuscitated and reinvented through academic writings and Buddhist editorial projects. These endeavors contributed to keeping alive its textual and doctrinal heritage until Shugendō was eventually rehabilitated after the Second World War. Nevertheless, when Shugendō was reinstated, upon the promulgation of the new Constitution in 1946, it was but a shadow of its former self. Yet, it remains a living tradition to this day. In fact, it is currently gaining new momentum, thanks to the growing interest, both in Japan and internationally, for eco-spiritual concerns, a fertile crossroads for Shugendō.

The following introductory pages are an attempt at providing a critical analysis of the most relevant formative processes of Shugendō studies, by taking into consideration the agendas of the hermeneutical discourses produced by generations of Shugendō scholars in Japan and abroad.

The Second Wave of Shugendō Studies in Japan

If every end can be considered a new beginning, the 1872 legislative banishment of Shugendō and the following crisis, which shook the entirety of its institutions and practitioners, became the trigger for a radical metamorphosis of this religious tradition. Shugendō as an assemblage of ritual practices, doctrinal transmissions, and performers in flesh and bone temporarily withdrew into the recesses of society while a new form of Shugendō came to light, first as a canonized collection of texts and later as an object of academic research. The abolition of Shugendō followed the *kami-*buddhas clarification edits (*shinbutsu hanzenrei* 神仏判然令) aiming at establishing new modes of worship based on the separation of *kami* and buddhas (*shinbutsu bunri*) in 1868. This prohibition did not have a simple obliterating effect; rather, it instilled in certain social actors the urgency and necessity of preserving Shugendō as an essential and unique example of Japanese-made religious discourse. For instance, in 1879, Umiura Gikan 海浦議観 (1855–1921), who was the head priest of Engakuji and had a historic Shugendō affiliation in Aomori prefecture, started gathering scattered Shugendō doctrinal texts and ritual manuals in a preliminary collection of about fifty volumes. Umiura managed to have his collection of Shugendō texts included in the *Japanese Buddhist Canon* (*Nihon daizōkyō* 日本大蔵経), thanks to the help of its main editor Nakano Tatsue 中野達慧 (1871–1934). From 1917 to 1920, Umiura's work was published in three volumes collectively known as *Shugendō Commentaries*

(*Shugendō shōso* 修驗道章疏). The first of these volumes is dedicated to Tōzan-ha 当山派 (Shingon-style Shugendō) scriptures, the second to Honzan-ha 本山派 (Tendai-style Shugendō) scriptures, and the third to all other Shugendō groups, with special attention being paid to Hagurosan Shugen 羽黒山修驗 and Hikosan Shugen 英彦山修驗 (Miyake 2000).

Thanks to the pioneering works of Buddhist monks such as Umiura and the first generation of Japanese ethno-folklorists such as Yanagita Kunio 柳田國男 (1875–1962) toward the end of the Meiji and in the Taishō (1912–26) period, a revival of Shugendō occurred. This renaissance concretized itself in terms of mountain pilgrimages, which were organized by *shugenja* on behalf of the lay members of religious confraternities, as well as by way of scholarly research and editorial projects. For example, two journals, *Jinben* 神変 (first issue published in 1909) and *Shugen kenkyū* 修驗研究 (first issue in 1921), both entirely dedicated to Shugendō matters, saw the light in those years. In the first two decades of the Shōwa period (1926–45), a further intellectual reframing of Shugendō took place, which was then conceptualized as the most authentic form of Japanese Buddhism as well as an embodiment of both the austere strength that permeated Japan as a modern nation and the spiritual uniqueness of the Japanese people. This ethnocentric and nationalistic view of Shugendō was transmitted by the works of influential scholars such as Uno Enkū 宇野圓空 (1885–1949), the father of folklore studies (*minzokugaku* 民俗学) and ethnology (*minzokugaku* 民族学) in Japan. Others, such as Murakami Toshio 村上俊雄 (b. 1906), Wakamori Tarō 和歌森太郎 (1915–77),[1] and Murayama Shūichi 村山修一 (1914–2010),[2] followed suit. Umiura's intention had been to secure a niche for Shugendō within the mainstream of Japanese Buddhist studies by including Shugendō texts in the *Nihon daizōkyō*. In a different way, in the Shōwa period, Uno's depiction of Shugendō as an ethno-localized form of Buddhism contributed to placing research on Shugendō under the umbrella of folklore and ethnic studies. Uno's interpretative approach also had a considerable impact on post-1945 scholarship, which tended to portray Shugendō as a static receptacle of prehistorical worshiping practices for mountain veneration (*genshitekina sangaku shinkō* 原始的な山岳信仰). Yanagita Kunio, Hori Ichirō 堀一郎 (1910–74), Gorai Shigeru 五来重 (1908–93), and Miyake Hitoshi 宮家準 can be considered the major protagonists of this first phase of Shugendō studies, each one with specific methodological and analytical perspectives.

In the first and fifth chapter of this book, Suzuki Masataka and Hayashi Makoto fully analyze the intellectual approaches of the above-mentioned authors in shaping the cultural perception of Shugendō from the Meiji to the Shōwa period. The present section of our introduction focuses on what we term the second wave of Shugendō studies. Showing its first signs in the mid-1960s, it is mainly characterized by a transition of the analytical approach to Shugendō from the sphere of folklore studies and ethnology to that of history. Shugendō doctrines, practices, and institutions gradually stopped being interpreted as immutable vestiges of a static mountain religion that constituted the seemingly ahistorical religious milieu of the common people (*jōmin* 常民), and acquired dynamism and complexity by being embedded in specific sociohistorical contexts.

Suzuki Shōei 鈴木昭英 was one the first scholars to begin this research trend. He published a series of seminal articles on the religious practices and institutional structures of the "associations of leaders" (*sendatsushū* 先達衆), that is, self-administrated groups of heterogeneous *shugen* practitioners, in the medieval period until their definitive convergence under the control of Daigoji Sanbōin 醍醐寺三宝院 and their ultimate absorption within Tōzan-ha in the early seventeenth century (Suzuki 2003).³

In 1984, Miyamoto Kesao 宮本袈裟雄 (1945–2008) identified the origins of Shugendō in the encounter between ancient mountain beliefs and practices as performed by Buddhist and Onmyōdō 陰陽道 specialists on the one side, and similar mountain worshiping practices by "village *shugenja*" (*sato shugenja* 里修験者) on behalf of ordinary people (*shomin* 庶民) in rural communities on the other side. This second element, which Miyamoto defined as "village *shugen*" (*sato shugen* 里修験), specifically attracted the interest of the author, who created a fourfold categorization of *shugen* practitioners. According to Miyamoto's schema, there were: (1) Buddhist monks who secluded themselves on mountains (*sanrō* 山籠) to strictly observe self-discipline (Skt. *dhūta*, Jp. *tsuta* 斗藪); (2) itinerant holy men (*hijiri* 聖), who constantly wandered across sacred mountains located in various provinces (*kaikoku* 廻国); (3) *oshi* 御師, who played the role of intermediaries and agents between *shugenja* and lay people in the organization of pilgrimages; and (4) *shugenja* who resided in villages (*sato shugenja*). Recluse monks (*intonsha* 隠遁者) and *hijiri* were itinerant religious professionals, whereas *oshi* and *sato shugenja* were settled in rural communities (Miyamoto 2010). Another relevant point of Miyamoto's research is that he relied on a variety of Edo period (1600–1868) historical documents to describe the activities of the *sato shugenja* and, in so doing, he brought to the attention of other scholars the necessity to rethink the early modern period as a crucial moment in the formation of Shugendō institutions and practices. Nevertheless, a problematic aspect of Miyamoto's analysis of Edo period Shugendō is that it cannot be simply reduced to the sphere of the village but should be analyzed in relation to the political, administrative, and cultural strategies adopted by the Tokugawa shogunate and other ruling elites to expand their authority in multiple sectors of society.

In 1981, Kuroda Toshio 黒田俊雄 (1926–93) elaborated a new theory about the social actors who contributed to the formation of Shugendō in an article dedicated to the religious structures that characterized Mt. Hakusan 白山 in the medieval period (Kuroda 1995).⁴ For Kuroda, the set of mountain beliefs and practices that constituted the religious tradition of *shugenja* did not derive from the religious practices of mountain populations (*sanmin no shinkō* 山民の信仰), but came instead from the cultic hybridity fostered by farming populations (*nōkōmin* 農耕民) who inhabited the plains. Whenever members of farming groups had the opportunity to access mountains, they tended to reproduce the religious practices of the mountain populations, inserting some of these elements within the standard ritual and doctrinal structures of exo-esoteric Buddhism (*kenmitsu bukkyō* 顕密仏教) (Kuroda 1995: 307). Although Kuroda does not substantiate this theory with specific examples, it is interesting to underline the effort to create an alternative interpretation from the views of Gorai and Yanagita, who invariably saw in the hunting populations of the mountains (*shuryōmin* 狩猟民) the predecessors of *shugenja*.⁵ In contrast, Kuroda describes medieval *shugenja* as religious specialists who were different from hunters and other mountain inhabitants, but were able to mix religious practices of the mountain populations with exo-esoteric Buddhist doctrines and ritual procedures.

In 1990, Kuroda wrote two articles on the socioreligious elements that characterized the Buddhist exo-esoteric system (*kenmitsu taisei*) in medieval society, and analyzed the role of Shugendō within this broad panorama (Kuroda 1995).⁶ For Kuroda, medieval society was dominated by the dynamic interactions of three power blocs (*kenmon* 権門), namely (1) the imperial court; (2) the main religious institutions, such as the ancient Buddhist temples in Kyoto and Nara; and (3) the warrior class. These three dominating clusters, which represented the center of society, were able to maintain their authority and legitimacy by establishing continuous interactions with peripheries. *Shugenja*, *hijiri*, recluse monks, ordained priests leading a family life (*hansō hanzoku* 半僧半俗), and lay members of religious confraternities (*kōshū* 講衆) played an essential connective role between the three power blocs and the rest of society. Together with other religious professionals, *shugenja* were among the major promoters of popularized versions of exo-esoteric Buddhism, which allowed Buddhist institutions to stretch their influence to the remotest areas of the archipelago. Thanks to this power mechanism, *shugenja* legitimated themselves in front of lay people as intermediaries between subaltern classes and the ruling elites.

In the wake of Kuroda's contextualization of Shugendō within the larger historical and cultural frame of medieval Japan, subsequent research underlines the necessity to draw a clear-cut distinction between those religious practices such as the self-seclusion retreats (*sanrō*), which were performed *on* mountains (as spatial locations) by Buddhist monks and hermits until the eleventh century, and the ascetic practices (*shugyō* 修行), which were specifically performed by mountain ascetics (*yamabushi*) since the end of twelfth and thirteenth centuries.⁷ For medieval *yamabushi*, the mountain landscape shifted from merely providing a space where standard Buddhist rituals were performed, to the ultimate geophysical source of legitimization for their religious activities and their authority within society. Standard Buddhist monks used mountains and forests (but also rivers and seashores) as suitable backgrounds to detach themselves from society (what is known as "Buddhism of mountain forests," *sanrin bukkyō* 山林仏教) and focus on meditation (*zenjō* 禅定), while thirteenth-century *yamabushi* held their retreats on sacred mountains to characterize the specificity of their own ascetic practices and later on identified the very act of climbing the mountain as equivalent to meditation (Tokieda 2005: 26). In other words, the meaning of the mountain changed from a secluded site for religious practices that remained distinct from the site itself, to a natural element that was essential for the realization of correlated ascetic practices, which were directed toward and motivated by the mountain itself.

Post-Kuroda studies also emphasize that Shugendō came to be institutionalized toward the second half of the Kamakura period (1185–1333) and shared many aspects with other Buddhist reformation movements (*bukkyō kakushin undō* 仏教革新運動) of the same age. The precepts restoration movements (*kairitsu fukkō undō* 戒律復興運動), for instance, stressed the necessity for monks to respect monastic regulations as the only available practice in the age of the degeneration of the Dharma (*mappō* 末法). Groups of recluse monks (*tonsei shūdan* 遁世集団) looked for salvation by repudiating the mundane world. *Shugenja* similarly transformed the performance of ascetic practices on mountains into a trademark for their soteriological recipe and emerging religious tradition. The late Kamakura period was the time in which *shugenja*—again, in line with the general trend of other Kamakura Buddhist schools—elaborated the figure of a semi-historical patriarch, En no Gyōja 役行者 (mid-seventh to mid-eighth centuries), established lineages (*kechimyaku* 血脈), and began imagining a set of distinctive practices to differentiate themselves from religious competitors.

One of the most recent methodological developments to Shugendō studies is the research by Tokunaga Seiko 徳永誓子, who problematizes the use of the terms *shugen* 修験 (literally, "the marks [*shirushi* 験] of the practice [*osameru* 修]") and *geza* 験者 (literally, "person with powers") in the written sources of the Heian period (794–1885). For example, the oldest occurrence of the term *shugen* can be found in an entry of the *Nihon sandai jitsuroku* 日本三代実録 (finished in 901), dated 868, seventh month, ninth day. This passage reports that the Buddhist monk Dōju 道珠 entered a mountain when he was young and never came down. One day Emperor Seiwa 清和 (reign 850–880) heard that Dōju had powers (*shugen ari* 修験有り) and summons him to the court (see Chapter Two of this book).[8] Tokunaga points out that in this context the term *shugen* is used in its attributive value and does not qualify a Shugendō practitioner, but simply a Buddhist monk (*shamon*) who acquired powers by performing religious practices in the mountains. In other words, the *Nihon sandai jitsuroku* entry does not say that Dōju was practicing mountain asceticism but simply that he had secluded himself on a mountain to perform Buddhist rituals, which were characterized neither by the site where they were performed nor by the intention to worship the mountain itself (Tokunaga 2015: 86). In the ninth century, the semantic range of the term *shugen* covered the appropriate performance of a practice, that is, exo-esoteric Buddhist rituals, by practitioners (prevalently Buddhist monks), who were believed to develop extraordinary powers and may (or may not) have resided in mountains. A stable convergence between the word *shugen* and mountain practices performed by specialized ascetics (*yamabushi shugyō* 山伏修行) does not appear until the end of the twelfth century.[9] In a similar way, during the Heian period, the word *geza* denoted a group of religious professionals, mostly esoteric masters (*ajari* 阿闍梨), whose empowerment (*genriki*) was a consequence of mastering mantras (*shingon* 真言) and *dhāraṇī* (*darani* 陀羅尼), thanks to which they performed healing rituals (*kaji chiryō* 加持治療) as well as exorcisms (*yorigitō* 憑祈禱) against malevolent spirits (*mononoke* モノノケ) (Tokunaga 2001: 100–2).

Hasegawa Kenji 長谷川賢二 focuses his research on the associative and institutional forms among *shugenja* and, in particular, on the evolution of *shugen* ascetic groups (*shūdan* 集団) into sectarian organizations (*kyōdan* 教団), during the Muromachi period (1336–1573). Hasegawa noticed that the first phase of institutional organization among *shugenja* was not imposed from above by powerful temples run by aristocratic monks (*monzeki jiin* 門跡寺院) but originated spontaneously from below among the congregations of *shugenja* who needed to strengthen their authority over lay followers in local communities (*kasumi* 霞). Moreover, *shugenja* were gradually included within the heterogeneous group of the so-called "practitioners" (*gyōnin* 行人), a part of the institutional hierarchy of Buddhist temples. Besides *shugenja,* the category of *gyōnin*—also known as low-rank monks (*gesō* 下僧)—originally applied to other groups of religious specialists, such as "those of the halls" (*dōshu* 堂衆) who were affiliated with the East and West Golden Halls (Higashi Kondō 東金堂, Nishi Kondō 西金堂) of Kōfukuji 興福寺 in Nara. *Gyōnin* differed from the scholar-monks (*gakuryo* 学侶) who received a scholastic training and constituted the formal leadership of the temple. Although *gakuryo* were fully ordained while *gyōnin* were not, these two classes of religious professionals were indispensable to each other because they accomplished different institutional, liturgic, and manual tasks for the administration of the temple. In particular, *dōshu* did not limit their activities to mountain asceticism but also took care of maintenance works of temple buildings. Because those who belonged to the *gyōnin* group often came from rural classes, they constituted a sort of *trait d'union* between the *gakuryo* and the local population (Hasegawa 1990, 1994).

Hasegawa's most recent study sheds light on the institutional structure of the Kumano *sendatsu* groups in the Awa province (present-day Tokushima prefecture) in the fifteenth and sixteenth centuries. This research shows that very often the category of Kumano *sendatsu* embraced a variety of religious professionals with loose affiliations with local temples that freely fluctuated from Tendai to Shingon. During the Muromachi period, the authority of the Three Kumano Shrines (Kumano Sanzan 熊野三山), that is, the powerful guilds of *shugenja* in Hongū, Shingū, and Nachi, became increasingly weaker. Instead, the Kumano *sendatsu* started relying on the Shōgoin 聖護院 temple in Kyoto to settle their internal disputes and prevent the erosion of their parishes due to the increasing expansion of the new military aristocracy. Toward the end of the fifteenth century, Shōgoin consolidated its authority within the Jimon-ha 寺門派 (the Onjōji 園城寺 Tendai branch) and created the Honzan-ha to regulate the activities of the Kumano *sendatsu*. The actual power of the Shōgoin over Kumano *sendatsu* was probably extremely limited, but sharing its social capital with Kumano *sendatsu* groups through formal affiliations brought economic and organizational benefits to both parties. Kumano *sendatsu* frequently invoked their formal affiliation with Shōgoin as a legal means to reinforce their authority on local areas. At the same time, until the late medieval period, they seemed to act independently from Shōgoin's guidance even though this temple was the formal superintendent (*kengyō* 検校) of Kumano. It is only toward the end of the sixteenth and early seventeenth century that Shōgoin succeeded in establishing a real institutional control over various groups of local *shugenja* in eastern and western Japan, federating them under the Honzan-ha umbrella. For instance, Shōgoin documents compiled toward the end of the sixteenth century show that the local *shugenja* in the Tōhoku and Kinai areas stopped being generically referred to as "confraternities of ascetics" (*gyōja kō* 行者講) and were specifically described as *yamabushi*. Such a shift in Shōgoin legal terminology promoted a de facto institutional "shugendization" from above of the Kumano *sendatsu* groups (Hasegawa 2016).

Kondō Yūsuke 近藤祐介 follows up on Hasegawa's research on the formation processes that characterized Shugendō groups and focuses on the Honzan-ha institutional transformations in the Kansai and Kantō regions from the sixteenth century onward. For instance, Kondō observes that with the collapse of the manorial system (*shōen seido*) and the decline of the Ashikaga shogunate, Dōzō 道増 (1508–71), the Shōgoin head-monk, decided to bypass the two aristocratic temples (*inge* 院家)—Nyaku ōji 若王子 and Jōjōin 乗々院—that traditionally administered the Kumano *sendatsu* on behalf of Shōgoin. Dōzō's strategy consisted of expanding the right to request Shōgoin affiliation beyond the Kumano *sendatsu* groups, in order to also include the so-called un-affiliated *shugenja* (*mappa shugenja* 末派修験者), who were extremely numerous in every domain. In exchange, Dōzō requested *mappa shugenja* as well as Kumano *sendatsu* to pay an annual tribute (*yakusen* 役銭) directly to Shōgoin for being allowed to perform Shugendō practices such as the mountain-entry rituals or play the role of mountain guide (*yama sendatsu* 山先達) for pilgrims during the summer. This broader access to Shōgoin affiliation is also displayed in a terminological change. The nomenclature of Kumano *sendatsu shoku* 熊野先達職, which indicated the exclusive right of Kumano *sendatsu* to escort the pilgrims of their *kasumi* toward Kumano, became that of *nengyōji shoku* 年行事職, which referred to the extension of the same right to all *mappa shugenja* present on a specific territory independently from their institutional status. Kondō notices that in the second half of the Muromachi period, Kumano *sendatsu* became a powerful class of "administrative" *shugenja* (*yūryoku yamabushi* 有力山伏) who replaced the *inge* in governing *mappa shugenja*—now defined as "co-practitioners" (*dōgyō* 同行)—and reinforcing the parish networks on behalf of Shōgoin (Kondō 2010). Between the fifteenth and the sixteenth centuries, the leadership of Shōgoin also affirmed itself in the Kantō area after the decline of the Gachirin'in 月輪院, which administered the local groups of *shugenja* on behalf of the Ashikaga shogunate. Shōgoin federated the Kantō *shugenja*, expanding its authority through two new administrative centers—Gyokuryū-bō 玉龍坊 in Odawara and Fudōin 不動院 in Satte 幸手—and actively supported the political authority of the later Hōjō clan (*Go-Hōjō-shi* 後北条氏) in the Kantō domains (Kondō 2005). In the seventeenth century, when the Honzan-ha institutional organization was finally completed, the Tokugawa shogunate felt the necessity to directly intervene in order to limit Shōgoin initiatives aimed at monopolizing *shugenja* activities and ritual rights. Moreover, toward the end of the eighteenth century, *mappa shugenja* with Honzan-ha affiliation became less inclined to pay Shōgoin the onerous participation fees for the mountain-entry ritual, which did not grant them an actual hierarchical and economic advancement compared to the powerful and remunerative status of those *shugenja* who already had the title of *sendatsu* or *nengyōji shoku* (Kondō 2015: 129).

The formation processes and institutional history of the Tōzan-ha constitute the core of Sekiguchi Makiko's 関口眞規子 research, which follows and expands some of the analytical directions already explored by Suzuki Shōei in the 1960s. Sekiguchi begins by drawing a separation line between the Tōzan-kata 当山方 (self-administered groups of ascetics affiliated with Kōfukuji) and the Tōzan-ha (an early-seventeenth-century Shingon-style Shugendō institution administered by Daigoji Sanbōin 醍醐寺三宝院). The *dōshu* who resided at Kōfukuji can be considered an example of Tōzan-kata ascetics. From the Kamakura period to the end of the fourteenth century, *dōshu* specialized in two types of mountain practices: the *tōgyō* 当行 and the *nyūbu*. The first was a self-seclusion retreat, which took place in summer and winter on Mount Kasuga 春日山 every year. The second was an annual mountain-entry ritual performed on

Mount Ōmine 大峯山, the participation to which marked a hierarchical progression in the career of the *dōshu*. Toward the end of the fourteenth century, *shugenja*, who defined themselves as a "group of leaders" (*sendatsu shū*), separated from the *dōshu* and gathered together under the name of Tōzan-kata *sendatsu* 当山方先達, and by the end of the sixteenth century replaced the leadership of the *dōshu* in the organization of the mountain-entry ritual. In the sixteenth century, there were ascetics who had a double career as *dōshu* and, at the same time, as Tōzan-kata *sendatsu*, but it is clear that only the latter could aspire to the leadership of the organization (Sekiguchi 2015).

The main difference between Honzan-ha *sendatsu* and Tōzan-kata *sendatsu* resided in the nature of their respective lineages, which was territorial in the former and ritual-based in the latter. Honzan-ha *sendatsu* included their main disciples into the lineage by granting them legal and economic control over their parishes, which were spread over the whole territory of Japan. In contrast, Tōzan-kata *sendatsu* fostered their lineages by conducting secret transmissions about mountain rituals and specific religious practices. Their disciples could, in turn, use this esoteric initiation to legitimize their activities in ordinary society. It goes without saying that Honzan-ha *sendatsu* had very strong roots in the territory, while the Tōzan-kata *sendatsu* functioned on a more flexible basis, thanks to which multiple sectarian affiliations and local alliances could develop according to the circumstances.

At the beginning of the seventeenth century, Gien 義演 (1558–1626), the head-monk of Daigoji Sanbōin, defended Tōzan-kata *sendatsu* against Honzan-ha *sendatsu* in the context of acrimonious disputes over tributes, which all non-Honzan-ha *shugenja* were supposed to pay in order to be allowed to perform certain ceremonies for pilgrims, as well as the mountain-entry ritual. It is only at the beginning of the Edo period that Sanbōin actively began to gather Tōzan-kata *sendatsu* under the umbrella of the Shingon school, creating an institutional system that would later be defined as Tōzan-ha. Sekiguchi points out that before the Edo period, Tōzan-kata *sendatsu* were not necessarily affiliated with Shingon temples and their practices did not show specific Shingon features. For Gien, the principal problem in establishing Sanbōin's leadership over the Tōzan-kata *sendatsu* was that after Shōbō 聖宝 (833–909), none of the Sanbōin head-monks performed mountain ascetic practices. Sanbōin head-monks, therefore, lacked the ritual authority to be recognized as formal leaders of the Tōzan-ha *shugenja* who were affiliated with this temple. To overcome this obstacle, Gien strongly developed the cult of Shōbō through ad hoc ceremonies, and in 1668 Kōken 高賢 (1639–1707) became the first Sanbōin head-monk to revive and practice the mountain-entry ritual. It is likely that Kōken was also the creator of the transmission lineage called Ein-ryū 恵印流, whose purpose was to establish a blood lineage on behalf of the Tōzan-ha *shugenja* affiliated with the Sanbōin (Sekiguchi 2009). Like recent research by Hasegawa and Kondō, Sekiguchi's work is fundamental for understanding that both Honza-ha and Tōzan-ha were purely Edo period institutional forms of Shugendō that developed from a radical rearrangement of the medieval Shugendō organizations.

The second decade of the twenty-first century marked the beginning of what can perhaps be considered a "third wave" of Shugendō studies. The contributors to this book all belong to this new research trend. For example, Suzuki Masataka's most recent works focus on the intellectual history of Shugendō with special attention to the modern period, the relationships between Shugendō sites and world heritage politics, and Shugendō doctrines and practices related to the exclusion of women from ascetic sites (*nyonin kinsei* 女人禁制) (Suzuki 2002, 2018a, 2018b). The research of Hayashi Makoto concentrates on the transformations of Shugendō organizations from the end of the Edo period to the Meiji era. Hayashi focuses, in particular, on the institutional changes that affected Shugendō groups and their affiliations with Buddhist temples (see Chapter Five in this book, as well as Kawasaki 2006, 2015, 2017). The mutual fertilization between Shugendō and religious literature is another topic that is attracting the attention of numerous scholars. For instance, Kawasaki Tsuyoshi 川崎剛志 and Niki Natsumi 仁木夏実 take into account the interweaving of Shugendō discourses and *engi* narratives. Kawasaki's works explore the historical and religious background of important texts in Shugendō literature, such as the *Kongōsan engi* 金剛山縁起 and the *Shozan engi* 諸山縁起 (Kawasaki 2004, 2006). In a similar way, Niki sheds a new interpretative light on the *Minoodera engi* 箕面寺縁起, which is a hitherto understudied work for the understanding of medieval Shugendō (see Chapter Eight in this book). Art history also serves as a platform for observation and analysis from which Shugendō features can be reconstructed, as demonstrated by Fujioka Yutaka 藤岡穣, whose research is dedicated to the statuary of central Shugendō deities such as Zaō Gongen 蔵王権現 (see Chapter Ten in this book).

As is apparent from the examples mentioned above, the second wave of Shugendō studies concentrates heavily on the medieval and early modern history of the tradition, whereas the third wave takes into account the modern and contemporary period as well. The main reason for the emphasis on medieval and early modern periods may well have been a need to understand the formative process of Shugendō as an independent religious tradition. The focus on modern and contemporary Shugendō issues can be interpreted as an attempt to problematize Shugendō's relationship with its recent past and present. However, the achievements of recent research show that it is impossible to provide a static definition of Shugendō that would be valid for every historical period. Comparably to Shinto, Shugendō is made of a plurality of different institutional, doctrinal, and professional structures that are constantly shape-shifting to remain in tune with the specific socioreligious conditions of their historical milieus (see Carter, forthcoming).

Shugendō Studies Outside Japan

Shugendō, or more precisely Shugendō practitioners, have elicited interest outside Japan for several hundred years. The earliest Western accounts of *yamabushi* are those of Jesuit missionaries in the second half of the sixteenth century. These sources tend to present *Yammabos* or *Jamabuxi* under a harsh and critical light, as mountain practitioners are mostly perceived as praying to the devil and as demons themselves; and yet, those detailed descriptions provide the reader with a fascinating outsider's view of Shugendō and its organization. The Jesuit reports had a wide echo in Europe, where they made their way into various accounts of Japan, written by authors who did not actually travel to that country. Some of them picked up descriptions of *yamabushi* along the way. Renward Cysat (1545–1614), for example, a Swiss pharmacist, town clerk of Lucerne, and eclectic autodidact, issued a compilation of Jesuit accounts so successful that it was reedited twice in a row shortly after its first publication in 1586 (Rotermund 1965: 46). Drawing on the correspondence and yearly reports of Italian priests, he took over their associating the *Jamambux* with the devil (Wahrhafftiger Bericht von den neuerfundenen japponischen Inseln und Königreichen 1586).

One century later, the German physician Engelbert Kaempfer (1651–1716) rendered a more nuanced image of the *Jammabos*, with particular attention to their attire and rites. Kaempfer's account paved the way for a less stigmatized image of the *yamabushi*. In his *Heutiges Japan* (*Today's Japan*), mentions of *yamabushi* are frequent and common enough to indicate that Shugendō was part of the general religious landscape, even though its specificities in dress and practices set it apart from other traditions. Kaempfer sometimes assimilates *yamabushi* with "Shinto hermits," and draws a clear distinction between Shugendō and other Buddhist schools. In a survey of the religious population in Japan, he classifies *yamabushi* as an entirely independent current. Particularly remarkable is Kaempfer's detailed account of the various elements of the *yamabushi*'s attire, which evinces both the latter's consistency through time (as most accessories are still in use today) and Kaempfer's talents as a keen observer (Kaempfer 1999; Aceval 2011).

Closer to our times, nineteenth-century Western travelers to Japan, such as Basil Chamberlain (1850–1935), Émile Guimet (1836–1918), and Lafcadio Hearn (1850–1904), mention encounters with *yamabushi*, often reflecting the mix of scorn and caution consistently registered toward Shugendō practitioners in Japanese literature of the Edo period (see William Fleming's contribution to this book). In the classical and medieval periods, mountain practitioners tended to be depicted respectfully, if not with downright fear and awe. Although there are some critical assessments, overall, *yamabushi* were considered to have acquired special powers through the severity of their ascetic practices. With their gradual sedentarization in the Edo period, however, and a growing entanglement with "ordinary" society, Shugendō practitioners increasingly became subjects of derision, as their portrayal in *kyōgen* plays shows quite plainly (see Morley 1993).

Possibly the first (recorded) non-Japanese to be involved with Shugendō was Charles Pfoundes (1840–1907), an Irish self-made man, who joined the British colonial navy before settling down in Japan in 1863, where he played a significant role in the emerging Japanese merchant shipping industry (Bocking 2013: 19). While Pfoundes was in Japan, he became one of the founding members of the Folklore Society based in London, and contributed several Japanese tales to the first issue of the society's journal in 1878. Around the same time, Pfoundes went back to the UK, where he was actively, if controversially, engaged both with Theosophical circles and with the missionary branch of Jōdo shinshū 浄土真宗. He returned to Japan in 1893, and stayed there until his death in 1907. During that time, he was ordained in a variety of Buddhist schools, including Shugendō. In 1905, Pfoundes published an article on the Shugendō fire ritual for the *East Asia Magazine* under the title "The Fire Ordeal: An Esoteric Ceremony in Kobe. Described by C. Pfoundes, An Adept of the Order." To illustrate it, Pfoundes used a photograph of himself taking part in a Shugendō fire ritual held in support of the Japanese state during the war with Russia (Bocking 2013: 23). Another photograph of Pfoundes that circulated widely shows him dressed in Shugendō garb. Pfoundes was a colorful and divisive figure. He was also an enthusiastic and keen researcher who fits the description of a pioneer in "participant observation" (Bocking 2013: 28).[10]

In 1922, Rev. Georg Schurhammer (1882–1971), a German Jesuit priest, published what is most likely the first scholarly article on *yamabushi* written by a non-Japanese. Schurhammer, who dedicated many years to the study of Francis Xavier (1506–52), meticulously compiled and synthetized Jesuit sources on Japan that describe the *Yammabos* or *Jamanbuxi*, regularly comparing their comments with Kaempfer's descriptions (Schurhammer 1922). As invaluable as Schurhammer's study is, it remains a descriptive account. Analytical studies on Shugendō as a religious current by Western scholars do not appear before the mid-twentieth century. Between the 1960s and the 1970s, several general and introductory works were published on Shugendō and *yamabushi*. Gaston Renondeau (1879–1967) presented a historical overview of Shugendō, which he describes not as an independent tradition but merely as a "Shingon school for the lower classes" (Renondeau 1965: IX). Hartmut Rotermund, drawing on an extensive corpus of literary and religious sources, studied the image of *yamabushi* in medieval Japan (Rotermund 1968). While both Renondeau and Rotermund aimed at giving an overall picture of Shugendō, H. Byron Earhart was the first to introduce a regional aspect to Shugendō studies by focusing his research on one particular site, Haguro in northeastern Japan (Earhart 1970). In 1975, anthropologist Carmen Blacker (1924–2009) published *The Catalpa Bow: A Study on Shamanistic Practices in Japan*, which rapidly became a reference work both in the West and in Japan. While the first three studies mentioned are eminently historical in character, Blacker's work is anthropological in scope. Although the practices and traditions described by Blacker do not center on Shugendō as such, *The Catalpa Bow* has long been considered one of the works that best describe the religious world in which Shugendō practitioners are immersed. Both Earhart's and Blacker's studies were translated into Japanese (Earhart 1985; Blacker 1995). As a rule, all the above-mentioned books provide a valuable entry point into the subject to this day, even if the respective approaches of the authors may now appear dated.

A few years later, Anne Bouchy, who has long collaborated with Gorai Shigeru, began to publish her own anthropological research on Shugendō, both in French and in Japanese. Particularly remarkable is her discovery of manuscripts by Hayashi Jitsukaga 林実利 (1843–84), a Shugendō practitioner famous for being the last to "cast away his body" (*shashin* 捨身) by throwing himself off the Nachi waterfall (Bouchy 1977, 1978). From the 1980s onward, Allan G. Grapard, a specialist in Shinto studies, has published a number of articles and books on subjects pertaining to Shugendō. One of his earliest works, entitled "Flying Mountains and Walkers of Emptiness: Toward a Definition of Sacred Space in Japanese Religions" (Grapard 1982), became a key reading for the following generations of scholars. Much like Blacker's *Catalpa Bow*, this particular article figures in almost every bibliography on Shugendō-related topics in Western languages to this day. In it, Grapard exposes his concept of "mandalization" of the Japanese landscape, by which he means the specific apprehension and usage of space found on certain mountains linked to Shugendō. This neologism has long since made its way into the common vocabulary both of Shugendō studies and that of studies on sacred space in the field of cultural anthropology. It clearly constitutes the core of Grapard's thought, and it inspired many subsequent scholars in Japanese studies and beyond. In his most recent book, Grapard presents an in-depth exploration of "mandalization" through a vast study on aspects of Shugendō in Kyūshū, especially on Mount Hiko, a region that is lately attracting growing attention (Bouchy ed. 2013, Grapard 2016).

In 1989, the *Japanese Journal of Religious Studies* published a special issue on "Shugendō and Mountain Religion in Japan." Edited by Paul Swanson and Royall Tyler, this volume was a landmark in the international recognition of Shugendō as a legitimate research topic. In line with the tradition of the journal, the special issue presented both translations of articles by Japanese scholars and articles by Western scholars. It was also the first concerted effort to introduce Shugendō as the "central tradition of Japanese mountain religion" outside Japan (Tyler and Swanson, eds. 1989a: 94). Even in terms of scholarship in Japanese at that time, this special issue was groundbreaking as it provided a synthetic overview of Shugendō as a tradition both coherent and multifaceted. This carefully crafted special issue is a major stepping-stone for all subsequent studies on the subject in Western languages. In that, the stated aim of the editors, namely, "partly to acknowledge previous work on the subject and partly to help stimulate further inquiry," was certainly achieved (Tyler and Swanson, eds. 1989a: 95).

Since the turn of the millennium, a new generation of Western studies on Shugendō has emerged, several of which claim a more or less direct Grapardian influence. Max Moerman, for example, one of the contributors to this book, states that he followed Grapard's injunction to "study religious phenomena *in situ*" (Moerman 2005: 3). Moerman's goal was to analyze the relationship between society and cosmology in a premodern religious society and to examine the social construction of a religious landscape through research on the Kumano pilgrimage based on scenes of the Nachi mandala (Moerman 2005: 4–5). In a similar perspective centering on "space and place," Heather Blair worked on the political and historical role of aristocratic pilgrimages to Mount Kinpu 金峰山 in the Heian period. Her discussion of an unpublished manuscript, in particular, shows retired emperor Shirakawa's role in the precipitation of the conflict between Kōfukuji and Mount Kinpu (Blair 2015), thereby providing a sequel to Royall Tyler's two insightful articles on Kōfukuji and Shugendō (Tyler 1989, 1990). Carina Roth also places herself in Grapard's footsteps with an analysis of the symbolic topography of the Kii peninsula seen through the lens of *Shozan engi* 諸山縁起, a twelfth-century foundation narrative (Roth 2014). In a different perspective, although again with reference to Grapard, Tatsuma Padoan integrated a study of the mythological narratives associated with Mount Katsuragi 葛城山 in his semiotic analysis of "actors, networks and languages of the religious experience" (Padoan 2011). George Klonos worked on an Edo-period corpus of documents centering on Mount Ōmine; his main contribution is the deconstruction of the general assumption in Shugendō studies that the Edo period was a time of decline for this religious tradition (Klonos 2012). Lindsey DeWitt approached gender issues in her research on the ever-controversial issue of *nyonin kinsei* and *nyonin kekkai* 女人結界, the two core expressions denoting "female exclusion" from certain mountains, the paradigmatic example being that of Mount Ōmine (DeWitt 2015). Lastly, under the initiative and supervision of Thomas D. Conlan, Princeton University Library recently acquired (2015) a host of medieval and early modern documents related to Sakuramoto-bō 桜本坊, one of the oldest Shugendō temples in Yoshino. A rare find, the documents shed new light on contractual relations between professional Shugendō practitioners and their parishioners throughout the country. Once reconstituted and duly catalogued, the collection will be made available online, and will hopefully inaugurate a new avenue of collaboration between Japanese and international researchers on the model of a first workshop held in July 2019.

While the studies just mentioned address mostly central Japan, the traditional cradle of Shugendō, a vast corpus of studies focusing on Shugendō mountains all over Japan has developed over the past few decades, in the wake of the book series *Sangaku shūkyōshi kenkyū sōsho* 山岳宗教史研究叢書 (1975–84; [2000]), which brought academic attention to sites of mountain practice across the entire country. Beginning with Earhart's pioneering work, Dewa Sanzan 出羽三山 in the Tōhoku region has especially benefitted from solid scholarship for many years now. Gaynor Sekimori, who has firsthand knowledge of, and access to archival material in the Haguro region, works mainly on the modern period by analyzing the dynamics of the separation between *kami* and buddhas in the early Meiji era (Sekimori 1995, 2005). Andrea Castiglioni focuses on neighboring Mount Yudono 湯殿山 and its ascetic tradition, represented by the self-seclusion practices performed by a special class of professional ascetics known as "lifetime practitioners" (*issei gyōnin* 一世行人) (Castiglioni 2017a, 2017b, 2019). Both Sekimori and Castiglioni feature chapters in this book. Ōuchi Fumi specializes on the development of a vocalized liturgy in Tendai Buddhism, with particular expertise in the Haguro tradition (Ōuchi 2009, 2011, 2016). Frank Clements examined documents from the Sanada Gyokuzō-bō archive, an elite *yamabushi* family active during the Edo period (Clements 2019). The Buddhist hells of Tateyama 立山, too, have been the focus of sustained attention, both in past and present practice (Seidel 1996, 2003; Formanek 1998; Averbuch 2011; Hirasawa 2013). Mount Fuji has naturally also been under scrutiny, most recently by Byron Earhart, to whom that mountain has been a beacon of interest at regular intervals in his career (Earhart 1989, 2011, 2015). Close by on Mount Ōyama 大山, Barbara Ambros tackled the complex issue of the development of the parish system and the interactions between lay confraternities, religious specialists, and temple networks (Ambros 2001, 2008). Neither Mount Fuji nor Ōyama harbor uniquely Shugendō traditions. Moreover, both Earhart's and Ambros's research highlight how a variety of religious institutions and social infrastructures intersect on a same site. Carter's forthcoming book on Togakushi takes a similar approach (Carter, forthcoming). Janine Sawada's work examines similar crossroads between popular cults and established religions (Sawada 1993, 2014, forthcoming; see also her contribution on visual material related to Mount Fuji in this book). Farther down south and west, Shugendō history and practice in Kyushu, long neglected in Western languages, are the subject of two important recent studies. First, there is the above-mentioned monograph by Allan Grapard, centering on Mount Hiko, the Kunisaki peninsula, and the Usa Hachiman shrine complex (Grapard 2016; see also Grapard 1986, 1989). Second, *Cahiers d'Extrême-Asie* published a special issue edited by Anne Bouchy and dedicated to Sasaguri 篠栗, a municipality in northern Kyushu with strong historical links to a variety of *shugen* networks and routes (Bouchy ed. 2015). In addition, a number of studies focus on mountains throughout the country (for a comprehensive list until 2005, see Sekimori 2009). Among the more recent ones, Caleb Carter, one of the contributors to this book, is working on the invention of the *shugen* traditions on Mount Togakushi (Carter 2014, forthcoming).

Both because it is a living tradition (albeit at a severely reduced dimension in comparison to pre-Meiji times), and because it historically emphasizes practice, Shugendō also attracts researchers working on its "embodied" aspects. Pierre Simon, for example, carried out ethnographical research on the "ritual course" on Mt. Katsuragi by examining the historical evolution of the twenty-eight stages of the circuit as well as the motivations of contemporary participants (Simon 2008). Tullio Lobetti discusses the evolution and goals of ascetic activities in the context of contemporary Shugendō (Lobetti 2014). Mark McGuire reflected on Shugendō's place in the wider trend toward "eco-civism" and on the repercussions of the registration of the Kii peninsula on the UNESCO World Heritage list (McGuire 2013). It is significant to note here that most researchers on Shugendō "enter the mountain" at least at one point in their career. Not all report about their experience, but some do. Paul Swanson, for example, offered a pioneering description of a Shōgoin mountain entry he took part in 1977, which, like Grapard's article on flying mountains, has become a classic (Swanson 1981). Four decades later, Raji Steineck provided a detailed account based on his participation in a Daigoji Sanbōin mountain entry in 2009 (Steineck 2012).

Only on rare occasions is Shugendō material also examined through the lens of art history (e.g., Pfister 1988; Sawa 1989; ten Grotenhuis 1999; Zitterbart 2008)—which is surprising when one considers the richness of its heritage.[11] This tentative listing of studies is far from exhaustive; it is limited to works that center explicitly on Shugendō-related matters. Its principal objective is to show that Shugendō awakens interest in a wide variety of disciplines and, as a subject of study, may be tackled from equally varied perspectives. Moreover, many of the more recent works cited above are either dissertations or publications originating from dissertations, which is proof that the study of Shugendō is vital for many junior scholars. Finally, it may be interesting to note that Shugendō has also attracted a number of filmmakers. In 2011, the School of Oriental and African Studies in London organized a Shugendō film festival and workshop centering on three contemporary documentaries (Kitamura 2005; Abela and McGuire 2010; Roth and Roth 2010).

If the 1989 special issue of the *Japanese Journal of Religious Studies* was the first compilation of studies on Shugendō in English, a symposium held in 2008 at Columbia University was the first large-scale academic event devoted to this religious tradition outside Japan. Entitled "Shugendō: The History and Culture of a Japanese Religion" and dedicated to Carmen Blacker, the symposium gathered numerous Japanese and

Western scholars and its results were published the following year in a special issue of *Cahiers d'Extrême-Asie* (vol. 18). Comparing the introductions of these two volumes offers an insight into the growth of Shugendō studies and the development of Japanese and Western historiography of the discipline two decades apart.

In their 1989 introduction, Royall Tyler and Paul Swanson emphasize not only that "for many centuries, all mountain cults in Japan were dominated by Shugendō and, more concretely, by Shugendō adepts," but that the sum of these localized entities created an actual and distinct "Shugendō culture" (Tyler and Swanson, eds. 1989a: 94). The articles chosen for the special issue aimed at presenting the work of major scholars in the field (Gorai, Miyake, Wakamori) and at introducing to the public the great variety of angles and locations from which Shugendō and mountain religion can be approached (R. Tyler, S. Tyler, Earhart, Sawa). Tyler and Swanson situate the heyday of Shugendō between the Heian and the Kamakura periods, coinciding with the development and maturation of the "exo-esoteric system" (*kenmitsu taisei*), in Kuroda Toshio's definition, whose work was very influential at the time the special issue came out. The editors further stated that "even in the Edo period, Shugendō was an old tree, no longer growing" (Tyler and Swanson, eds. 1989a: 95), which is perhaps the one statement in their volume that was most positively challenged and defeated in the ensuing decades.

Bernard Faure, Max Moerman and Gaynor Sekimori's introduction to the 2009 special issue of *Cahiers d'Extrême-Asie* came out exactly twenty years after Tyler and Swanson's, at a time in which interest in and for Shugendō had gradually regained some momentum, both in Japan and abroad. The editors observe the reconstitution of Shugendō groups throughout Japan, the growing participation in Shugendō rituals by people with no particular connection to *shugen* organizations, as well as an increasing number of books and media reports on Shugendō aimed at a wider audience (Faure, Moerman and Sekimori 2009: 1). Tyler and Swanson underscored the need to recognize the existence and importance of a "Shugendō culture," to which Moerman and Sekimori added two more elements. First, Shugendō is to be seen as a religion in its own right, not simply as an accretion of elements extracted from different religious traditions. Second, as a religious tradition of its own, Shugendō has a distinct history, which must be recognized, against claims that it belongs to the "timeless realm of folk religion" (Faure, Moerman and Sekimori 2009: 2). Through the examination of religion, history, and culture, the authors of the special issue intended to garner a better grasp of Shugendō and develop a "working definition" for it, both past and present.

The editors identified two developments in Japanese scholarship that encouraged academic interest for Shugendō from the 1960s onward: on the one hand, studies in combinatory religion—what is known as "associations of *kami* and buddhas" (*shinbutsu shūgō* 神仏習合), and on the other, local and regional studies. In many ways, non-Japanese scholarship also follows these trends. The *Cahiers d'Extrême-Asie*'s special issue reflects the double evolution both of scholarship on Shugendō and of Shugendō as a contemporary living tradition. Taken together with two articles by Anne Bouchy (Bouchy 2000) and Gaynor Sekimori (Sekimori 2009) aiming specifically at presenting the state of the field in Shugendō studies, the introductions to both volumes give an in-depth view of the historiography of Shugendō from its beginnings to the present. Moreover, these synthetic presentations come probably closest to giving a general idea of Shugendō as a religious tradition, since there is a distinct lack of an updated general reference work in Western languages beyond two translated volumes synthesizing Miyake Hitoshi's encyclopedic body of research on Shugendō (Miyake 2000, 2005).[12]

Shugendō Romanticism and the Quest for the Original Japanese Spirit

Shugendō is not only the subject of academic discourses. For decades, it has also been the topic of popular, nonacademic accounts that see it as one of the sources (if not *the* source *par excellence*) of Japanese religion and spirituality, as directly related to some distant past—very often, the Jōmon prehistoric civilization. It goes without saying that the average Japanese understanding of Shugendō (it is surprising that many Japanese know nothing about it) is informed more by nonacademic accounts than by scholarly research. A typical example among many is religious scholar Kubota Nobuhiro 久保田 展弘 (1941–2016). As the subtitle of his book on the subject makes clear, Shugendō is a "universe of primordial life-force." According to Kubota, Shugendō is at the core of the totality of Japanese religion, as it has at its foundation the principle of "coexistence of life" (*seimei kyōson* 生命共存; Kubota 2005: 12), a vague formula that suggests a not-better defined harmony between humans and nature. This is possible because the core of Shugendō is an attitude of awe toward, and veneration of, nature—which is also at the very basis of Japanese religion as a whole (Kubota 2005: 11). In practice, this fundamental attitude results in the principle of *ikashiai* 生かしあい, a term that is difficult to render in English but which suggests promoting and sustain each other life's possibilities (Kubota 2005). And yet, despite its fundamental role in Japanese spirituality, Kubota says that Shugendō has always been considered heretical within Japanese Buddhism and religion in general (Kubota 2005: 10)—without giving any explanation as to why such a fundamental religious movement ended up being marginalized. In any case, because of its stance toward nature, Shugendō is a necessary force against the supremacy of science in today's society: "science sees nature as the Other," and as such, it also sees humanity as a relativized Other (Kubota 2005: 22). The prominence of science has resulted in a "crisis that now threatens life" on our planet (*ima, inochi no kiki ni sarasarete iru*: Kubota 2005: 9), the very first sentence in the book. There is, therefore, the need to retrieve human beings' primordial life force (*genshi no inochi* 原始の命: Kubota 2005: 9, 23), and this can be done by reestablishing an ancient connection with the sacred space of mountains (mountains are "pure life force," *junsui seimei* 純粋生命; Kubota 2005: 58). There are many ways to do this, including "forest bathing" (*shinrin'yoku* 森林浴; Kubota 2005: 21), but, of course, the path of Shugendō is the most comprehensive and successful one.

It is interesting to highlight the fundamental presuppositions of Kubota's treatment of Shugendō: the idea that Shugendō is both historically marginal (if not even heretical) but at the same time existentially fundamental to Japanese religiosity; its purported harmony with nature, which is inexplicably lost today to most people (one wonders, if harmony with nature is so central to and constitutive of the Japanese religious experience, why was it abandoned?); the idea of a core spirituality, dating back to the origin of Japanese civilization, which continues to exist in some form and can be retrieved; the opposition to contemporary, scientific, and technological society. These themes are part of a larger project about Japanese cultural identity, which, since the Kokugaku 国学 (Nativism) movement in the eighteenth century, is often seen as a form of anti-technological and anti-establishment primitivism; in the early twentieth century, this attitude intersected with a critique of modernity as a Western construct (and the critique of the negative consequences of science of technology as caused by a supposedly Western attitude toward nature is often present in contemporary Japanese *Nihonjinron* 日本人論).

The negative attitude against modern science, which supposedly establishes nature as a distinct Other, rather than as part of a harmonious whole, takes many shapes in Japan. For instance, and notably, Buddhist scholar Sueki Fumihiko 末木文美士 argued, in the wake of the Tohoku Triple Disaster of March 11, 2001, that Nature *is* indeed the Other, and a powerful one at that, and needs to be respected and feared; idealizations of harmony are not helpful in dealing with natural disasters. On the other hand, Sueki also wrote that natural disasters are never "natural" because they are consequences of human decisions and activities, which now involve science, technology, and economic practices, imported from the West, that have reduced the original Japanese sense of wonder and respect for nature (Sueki 2012).

A very influential voice in claims about the ancient origins of Japanese spirituality and Shugendō's role in it is Nakazawa Shin'ichi 中沢新一. One of the leading members of so-called Neo-Academism between the late 1980s and early 1990s, which promoted a different type of intellectual discourse that took seriously issues of religion and spirituality in a way that was informed by contemporary poststructuralism, Nakazawa later turned to Neo-Nativism and intellectualistic *Nihonjinron*. For more than two decades, Nakazawa has been arguing that the prehistoric Jōmon civilization still informs many aspects of Japanese life and culture today. Nakazawa, too, has written about Shugendō as a primordial religious tradition based on ancient mythical thinking. He sees Shugendō as a cult of the mountain as a mother deity, in which the goddess gives birth to a child in the forest and the child later becomes a *shugenja* in the mountain, in a somewhat circular fashion (Nakazawa 2006: 226). Nakazawa focuses, in particular, on Shugendō in Usa (Kyushu), the original center of Hachiman's cult, and claims that it is connected to ancient Korean shamanism on the one hand and to other shamanistic practices in Okinawa and northeastern Japan (Nakazawa 2006: 227–38). Nakazawa, then, proceeds to romanticize the mountains beyond their feminine divine nature. He writes that the mountain is the realm of the death and of freedom, deeply related to concepts of femininity and infancy (Nakazawa 2006: 238), and inhabited by special groups of people who chose to live outside of regular society (Nakazawa 2006: 238–9). For Nakazawa, then, Shugendō—elaborating on the standard idea of Shugendō as heretical and marginal—is not simply the negative of society, as it were an anti-state. Rather, it initially developed in parallel with the formation of the early

Japanese state; he argues that the idea that the cosmic force was not located in a nature that was completely separate from human society, but could be tapped into, controlled, and appropriated by humans, lies at the basis of both early Shugendō and ancient state (Nakazawa 2006: 244–5).

Nakazawa's deeply a-historical approach and sweeping generalizations, glossed over as instantiations of mythical thinking and structural analyses, are more obfuscating than clarifying. Similarities between ancient forms of shamanism in the Korean peninsula, which we know only through later textual descriptions and archeological findings, and rituals in present-day Okinawa and Tohoku, even if they existed and were not completely far-fetched, should not be necessarily explained by actual continuity through time and space. In addition, Nakazawa, like Gorai Shigeru and many other authors, hypothesizes the existence of an "early Shugendō" which predates any historical records—even the actual use of the very term "Shugendō" (which, as discussed in this book, only appears in the thirteenth century). What is also striking is the emphasis on a romanticized prehistory as the source of everything and the reliance on abstract speculations on primitive thought (of course based on very contemporary and local Japanese themes) as ways to understand the supposedly unchanging core of Japanese culture and spirituality.

Nakazawa's sophisticated treatment of these a-historical topoi, informed by cultural anthropology and contemporary philosophy, among other disciplines, has a noble precursor, namely, artist and criticist Okamoto Tarō 岡本太郎 (1911–96). After the Second World War, Okamoto left Paris, where he had received a PhD in ethnography (he studied with Marcel Mauss) and had begun a career as an artist (he knew Picasso and leading artists and intellectuals of the time) and went back to Japan. Influenced by his studies on primitive societies, Okamoto began to actively pursuing forms of primitivism in his artistic production. In parallel, he began to study Japanese culture also in order to retrieve elements of primitivism there that he could use in his art. One wonders if his approach to Japan was simultaneously a reaction against war-time propaganda focused on the emperor and the imperial divine genealogy—an attempt to identify a different spiritual foundation for Japan. Okamoto wrote several essays on Shugendō, following his visit to Dewa Sanzan in the late 1950s.

Okamoto's starting point is a form of romanticism, manifested in his positing a simple, pure, and primitive sense of the sacred typical of so-called undeveloped societies, which he also envisions as the core of Japanese religion and culture as a whole—what he called "the secret of the Japanese people (*Nihon minzoku no himitsu* 日本民族の秘密)" (Okamoto 2011a: 279). For Okamoto, this simple and pure spiritual core can still be found hidden under the thick layers of formalism and ritualism (*keishiki* 形式, *gishiki* 儀式) in present-day shrines and temples (Okamoto 2011a: 277–8). Okamoto was clearly striving for the alleged primitive, undeveloped elements he believed were still part of Japanese culture at his time. He specifically identifies that primordial sense of the sacred with *utaki* (Jp. *ontake*) beliefs in Okinawa (a place he had visited and impressed him very much) and with Shugendō, which he claimed is the "direct and positive experience of such primordial (*kongenteki* 根源的) atmosphere (*kehai* 気配)" (Okamoto 2011a: 279). More specifically, for Okamoto the essence of Shugendō is a spirit of "adventure for the unknown" (Okamoto 2011a: 289), an attraction toward the outside, the abnormal, the criminal, all manifestation of "human vitality" that manifests itself as "energy that resists the structures of society" (Okamoto 2011a: 290)—in other words, as a reaction against stable social communities and their rules. Interestingly, Okamoto considers Shugendō, in its reactions against stable norms, an "internationalism of the spirit," as opposed to the narrow nationalism of agricultural society (Okamoto 2011a: 353). This anti-societal force takes one to the outside of organized human spaces, that is, the mountains, which Okamoto envisioned "not necessarily as nature, but as inanimate places separate from human relations" (Okamoto 2011a: 291); there, in this separate place, humans were to subject themselves to "torture" in order to challenge their body and spirit. Okamoto calls this urge toward the outside and self-torturing "Romantic passion" (Okamoto 2011a: 293) and "Japanese Romanticism" (*Nihontekina romantizumu* 日本的なロマンティズム) (Okamoto 2011a: 297).

He continues his own peculiar reflections on Shugendō in another influential essay, entitled *Bi no juryoku* 美の呪力 (The magic of beauty) (Okamoto 2011b). Okamoto writes:

> The secrets of life are hidden in the depth of forests and at the top of mountains, remote from the everyday dimension. People want to reach the source of the "sacred," which both transcends and sustains humanity. However, those are forbidden sacred spaces. To reach them is a sin and is also dangerous.
>
> (Okamoto 2011b: 160)

This is when the shaman intervenes. In Japanese mountain religion, the *shugenja* plays the role of the shaman (as Okamoto explicitly states, "There is no doubt that, originally, the *shugenja* were shamans") (Okamoto 2011b), a mediator between humans steeped in the everyday, profane dimension of life, and the dangerous and uncontrollable sacred dimension of reality. *Shugenja* are people who are different from the others, with special features and powers; originally, they wanted to escape the narrow confines of their tribes and went to the mountains in search of the origin of fire and water, away from the everyday dimension of life (Okamoto 2011b).

As we can see, Okamoto was not interested in the historical study or sociological analysis of Shugendō groups. Rather, he was unabashedly and unapologetically using certain images about them—images he himself contributed to create—in order to give shape to his own primitivist poetics. What is new in Okamoto is the idea that *shugenja* were shamans and magicians, people who control and transform the natural elements, because of their direct connection with the life force and the essence of reality. In fact, Okamoto had predecessors: the Theosophists in the late nineteenth and early twentieth century were already imagining the *yamabushi* as magi, members of Adept societies, the Japanese equivalent of the superhuman beings, related to higher dimensions of reality, that Helena Blavatsky claimed to have found in the mountains of Tibet and elsewhere.[13]

This type of romantic idealization of the past is a typical aspect of Japanese ethnology (*minzokugaku*), which was explicitly conceived by Yanagita Kunio and other practitioners as Neo-Nativism (Shin-Kokugaku 新国学), with which it shares many elements, including the belief in the existence of an immutable core of Japanese sensibility and spirituality dating to the remotest past, remnants of which can allegedly be found in various aspects of Japanese culture even today. Of course, Gorai Shigeru and other earlier scholars might also have been an inspiration to Okamoto's quest for a primitive and original Japanese spirituality.

There is a thin line that separates neo-spiritual and neo-nativist claims from New Age spirituality, on the one hand, and the serious quest for a new way to interact with nature, also and especially through life styles and bodily activities (see Carter 2018; Roth 2019). We could apply to current interpretations of Shugendō the typology of animism introduced by Jolyon Thomas (2019). Thomas proposes to distinguish among three modalities of animism, each with different ethical and political vectors, which he describes as "pejorative," "recuperative," and "obscurantist." Typically, outside observers tend to consider animism a negative phenomenon, and thus are bearers of the pejorative position. For Japanese insiders, on the other hand, it is often difficult to distinguish between "recuperative" and "obscurantist" positions, because both are frequently intertwined with each other; as the previous discussion makes clear, a progressive approach at rediscovering positive values (peace, harmony, ecology, etc.) in more or less imaginary past worldviews ("recuperative" animism) often dovetails with nationalistic assertions of cultural superiority ("obscurantist" animism) (see Rambelli 2019, esp. 5–10).

A surprising feature of this type of romanticism is that Japanese authors (and, presumably, their readers as well) look at their own culture with both ignorance and amazement, with the perspective of hapless foreigners. And, in fact, in a sense they are. As L. P. Hartley famously wrote, "the past of a foreign country": the traditions that these authors idealize is no longer alive, and its texts are written in a language that is different and almost incomprehensible, expressing as it does concepts and worldviews long lost. However, on the other hand, William Faulkner famously wrote that "The Past is never dead. It's not even past": Shugendō is still alive today, and although some of its practices and beliefs may have changed, even dramatically, from past centuries, at least some of them have not, and in their permanence they show an important continuity with the past. Depending on whether we treat that past as a sort of unchanging archetype of Japanese spiritual authenticity or as just a relic of bygone eras, our approaches to and understanding of Shugendō will be radically different, and will have different political implications.

The Question of Gender and New Trends in Shugendō Studies

Like religious studies in general, Shugendō studies are an extremely fluid and constantly evolving field. In this section, we address some recent trends in Shugendō scholarship, which are merely sketched in some of the chapters of this book (see Chapters Four and Twelve in particular).

One of the main current orientations is without any doubt that of gender studies in the context of Shugendō: a volume with up-to-date research on this subject alone would be a very welcome endeavor. Seminal work on the obvious and controversial issue of female exclusion (*nyonin kinsei*) has been done most consistently by Suzuki

Masataka (Suzuki 2002, 2007, 2017). Suzuki, as well as several others scholars such as, for example, Kanda Yoriko 神田より子, have been studying the formative processes of Shugendō discourses about female exclusion from ascetic areas. One of their main contributions is the contextualization of these denial strategies in different historical and socio-local perspectives (Kanda 2011; Suzuki 2017).[14]

Because of its inherently problematic nature, this "ban" on women, who are to this day prohibited access to a small number of *shugen* sites, represents an immediate focus for all gender-related issues in Shugendō. While it is an important theme, which has yet to find a social resolution, it also monopolizes attention, thus obfuscating other developments and research on them. In the special issue on Shugendō issued by *Les Cahiers d'Extrême-Asie* in 2009, for example, Anne Bouchy presents recent shifts in numbers of Shugendō followers, all showing a strong increase in female attendance and engagement, which are bound to eventually create structural and hierarchical changes (Bouchy 2009). Bouchy's findings are corroborated by recent research by Kobayashi Naoko 小林奈央子 (Kobayashi 2017, 2019), and constitute one promising line for further study, all the more crucial since it is linked to the very future of Shugendō as a religious movement.

In their introduction to a special issue of the *Japanese Journal of Religious Studies* dedicated to questions of gender and religious practice in Japan, Kawahashi Noriko 川橋範子 and Kobayashi Naoko point out the importance of gendering religious practices in order to get a clear picture of the different relationships between female and male subjecthood within specific religious traditions. They emphasize that adopting a gender perspective does all but limit the analytical focus on female religious practitioners (Kawahashi and Kobayashi 2017: 2). A comprehensive approach including male religious practitioners is needed in order to shed light on the disparities and analogies of gender and sexual constructions among various types of social actors.[15] At the same time, disparities and power inequalities between genders should not be stigmatized only in relationship with members who belong to different gender groups, but must be examined also among members who share the same gender identity (for instance, gender discriminations perpetrated by women against other women).

Kobayashi makes a crucial observation about a sort of double threat in the analysis of women's agencies within the Shugendō context. On the one hand, if Shugendo structures are merely deconstructed as examples of patriarchal and androcentric discourses under which female *shugenja* are constantly and exclusively oppressed, the risk is to represent female Shugendō practitioners as powerless and passive agents. In this way, scholars may end up replicating the very discriminatory model they scrutinize. On the other hand, a "romanticization" of those cases in which female Shugendō practitioners have actually succeeded in affirming their active agencies by overcoming Shugendō androcentric blocks of powers and discriminatory structures may result in a dismissal of the necessity to problematize Shugendō discourses from a gender perspective (Kobayashi 2017, 2019).

In an important study examining the interrelations between gender an religion, Carolyn Bynum notes that every discourse and experience of gender and sexuality is always embedded in the private sphere of the individual: even within social actors belonging to the same gender, it is impossible to articulate an all-embracing gender critical theory that would speak uniformly for the plurality of voices composing gender narratives (Bynum, Harrell, and Richman 1986: 13). In that respect, Kobayashi describes, for example, the psychological distress felt by some female practitioners associated with the Shōgoin Monzeki Shugendō group during a 2006 gathering. The subject under discussion was the exclusion of women from Mt. Ōmine (specifically, Mt. Sanjōgatake in the Ōmine mountain range). The female *shugenja* attending the meeting were questioned by members of the Association for Lifting the Rule of Exclusion of Women from Mt. Ōmine ("Ōminesan nyonin kinsei" no kaihō wo motomeru kai 「大峰山女人禁制」の開放を求める会) about their reasons for not actively attempting to contest this ban. In contrast, male executives of the Shōgoin Monzeki, who supported lifting the ban for most ascetic spots (besides two) on Mt. Ōmine, became upset observing the difficulties experienced by the female *shugenja* in freely articulating their personal thoughts on Shugendō limitations for female practitioners to access specific ascetic sites on mountains (Kobayashi 2017: 117–18).

What about Shugendō discourses and gender articulations for male practitioners or the gendering processes dedicated to the material and visual representations of mountain deities (McCormick 2012)? For instance, during the Autumn Peak ritual (*aki no mine* 秋の峰) of Haguro Shugendō, the current male leader of the group (Daisendatsu) wears a ritual cap (*ayaigasa* or *hagai* 班蓋), representing a placenta (*ena* 胞衣), and carries on his back a portable altar (*oi* 笈) that symbolizes both the maternal womb and, at the same time, the various parts of the embryo's body (Sekimori 2015: 528–9). All these feminine and maternal elements ritually overlap with the male physicality, expanding the borders and blurring the divisions between gender and sexual polarities. An analogous mechanism can be detected in the secret vocabulary used by the male members of religious confraternities (*kō*) during ascetic retreats. Even in this case, most of the terms derived from the language of the female members of court aristocracy (*nyōbō kotoba* 女房言葉). They had the double function of engendering the communications between male *kō* practitioners according to feminine paradigms, as well as emphasizing the embryological meaning of their ritual actions.

Regarding premodern Shugendō structures, it is worth noticing that the social interactions between male Shugendō practitioners and female devotees who belonged to different age groups were extremely varied. For instance, after menopause, women gained access to ritual areas within the mountain, which were precluded to them before. Again, it would be a great advancement in Shugendō studies to take into account the socioreligious roles played by the *shugenja*'s wives, daughters, ritual partners such as the female mediums (*fu* 巫), and sexual partners such as the prostitutes who often worked in the villages nearby sacred mountains.

Still in the realm of gender or sexuality-related topics, another mostly overlooked issue is the gendering strategies used to visually represent the bodies of the mountain deities. For example, the Kamakura period wooden statues (*shinzō* 神像) of the three tutelary deities of Hongū, Shingū, and Nachi show a noticeable gender fluidity. The *kami* of Hongū and Shingū could manifest themselves alternatively as either female or male aristocratic members of the court. In contrast, the *kami* of Nachi is always embodied through the physicality of a female medium (Castiglioni 2015: 14–19).

The different hermeneutical discourses aimed at superimposing a female gender to the natural landscape of the mountain need to be historicized and probably detached from a bipolar (male/female) gender analysis in order to be embedded in multipolar or unipolar gender formative discourses (Laqueur 1990).

Although this short overview does not exhaust the possibilities for studying Shugendō from a gender perspective, this is certainly not the only avenue with unanswered questions. One recurrent topic, often illustrated and referred to in theater and literature, is the fact that premodern *shugenja* were frequently employed as spies during conflicts between local feudal lords, due to their advanced knowledge of the territory, in general, and mountains specifically.[16] It would be relevant for future Shugendō studies to take into account historical records dealing with such activities of Shugendō practitioners, to understand the impact of geopolitical conflicts on the expansions or contractions of *shugenja*'s ritual activities and institutional organizations.

Another mostly overlooked or neglected avenue of research is that of confluences and congruences between Shugendō and Shinto, on the one hand, and Shugendō and Onmyōdō, on the other. Because Shugendō borrows so heavily from (Esoteric) Buddhist texts and doctrines, most studies tend to underscore this proximity, while often just mentioning other influences on the side. Equally, since so much effort and energy have been put for so long in demarcating Shugendō as a quintessentially Japanese phenomenon (standing in for Shinto after the Second World War), it has been more important to look at differences rather than at similarities. Miyake Hitoshi did publish a study comparing Shugendō with other Japanese religions (Miyake 1996), and Murayama Shūichi wrote another seminal work on Shugendō and Onmyōdō in the context of temple-related materials (Murayama 1997). While these studies did not have an immediate echo, it seems that the current trend toward a more "holistic" approach to religious traditions should quite naturally lead to research looking at parallel or conflating evolutions, as exemplified by Sawada's chapter in this book.

Finally, one more area in Shugendō studies that would benefit from more sustained attention is text-centered research, which still lags behind other aspects of Japanese religious history, perhaps also because of the persistent heritage of Shugendō being described as a folk religion with little emphasis on written documents. Kawasaki Tsuyoshi has done remarkable work in this respect, but in-depth studies of single documents remain scarce, both in Japanese and in Western languages, with translations being even rarer.[17]

The Structure of This Book

Through a focus on thematic rather than disciplinary points of convergence, we aim at a critical reevaluation of the interpretative categories and research topics that have characterized Shugendō studies until recent times. Our goal is to disentangle such discourses from the yoke of folklore studies and relocate them within the broader track of religious and historical studies.

This book is organized into four parts. Part One, "Intellectual History of Shugendō Studies," examines the formative processes of Shugendō as an institutionalized religious tradition from a historiographical perspective. This section takes into account the intellectual agendas according to which, since the end of the nineteenth century, different generations of scholars have prioritized certain aspects of Shugendō while selectively dismissing others. In Chapter One, "A Critical History of the Study of Shugendō and Mountain Beliefs in Japan," Suzuki Masataka begins by presenting Shugendō as a zone of complexity where devotional practices dedicated to natural elements—mountains *in primis*—merged together with *kami* cults, Buddhist deities, and various conceptualizations of the ancestors' roles. In the second part of the chapter, Suzuki analyzes the influence of concepts such as "ethnic religion" and "ethnic culture" on the early Shugendō studies of the Meiji period, the subsequent reinterpretations of Shugendō infused with nationalistic overtones in the first half of the Shōwa period, and finally the definitive inclusion of Shugendō under the umbrella of folklore studies with the works of Hori Ichirō, Gorai Shigeru, and Miyake Hitoshi.

Part Two, "Constructed Topologies and Invented Chronologies," is dedicated to the study of premodern regional variations of Shugendō institutions and religious practices at four different cultic sites, namely, the Kumano Sanzan area in the Kii Peninsula, Mount Togakushi in Nagano prefecture, Mount Haguro in Yamagata prefecture, and Daigoji in Kyoto. All chapters of this section present ways in which Shugendō centers regulated complex networks based on symbiotic interactions between Shugendō professionals, Buddhist monks, lay members of religious confraternities, and lay devotees. In varied geographical and historical contexts, each of these social actors played a unique role in shaping the local identity of Shugendō. In Chapter Two, "Shugendō within Japanese Buddhism: Considerations on the Formation of Shugendō," Hasegawa Kenji clarifies the beginnings of Shugendō as an independent religious movement. He describes how Shugendō originates in Heian period mountain temples, before depicting the changes in its social composition in the early medieval period. Hasegawa is part of a group of scholars who challenge the received historiography of Shugendō, mainly by pulling it out of the quasi-hegemony of ethno-folklore studies and by redefining its place in Japanese religious history. In this chapter, Hasegawa stresses that Shugendō ought to be understood as an intrinsic part of the exo-esoteric Buddhist worldview and its institutions. Through careful analysis of the evolution of expressions such as *shugen* and *yamabushi*, Hasegawa gives a clear picture of the gradual emergence of Shugendō as a distinct— and thoroughly conceptualized—religious movement between the thirteenth and the fourteenth centuries. In Chapter Three, "Imagining an Ancient Tradition: Eighteenth-Century Narratives of Shugendō at Mount Togakushi," Caleb Carter examines the figure of Jōin, an influential Tendai monk and superintendent of Mount Togakushi in the first half of the eighteenth century. Carter gives special attention to Jōin's pivotal role in reinventing the history of the site to create a fictional Shugendō identity that responded to the social, economic, and religious needs of the mountain. An extremely interesting aspect in Jōin's narratives about an alleged Shugendō past for Mount Togakushi is the hybridization between Daoist and Shugendō elements. Thanks to such processes, Jōin produced new legitimizing discourses in order to boost the reputation of this particular mountain over other famous pilgrimage routes and Shugendō networks in the area. In Chapter Four, "Otake Dainichi Nyorai and Haguro Shugendō: Unearthing a Lost History," Gaynor Sekimori analyzes the cult of a female manifestation of the cosmic buddha, called Otake Dainichi Nyorai お竹大日如来, who is venerated in the village of Tōge at the foot of Mount Haguro. The management of devotional practices associated with Otake Dainichi Nyorai proceeded hand in hand with the socioeconomic growth of Genryō-bō 玄良坊, one of the most influential Haguro Shugendō families in Tōge, which directly organized most of the public displays of sacred icons and relics associated with Otake between 1740 and 1849. Sekimori's study demonstrates how skillful Shugendō practitioners were in their creation of ad hoc media and public events aiming at the circulation of devotional discourses in order to attract the interest of vast strata of the population in urban areas such as Edo. In Chapter Five, "Shugendō and Modernity Face to Face: The Daigoji Case," Hayashi Makoto focuses on the apparent death of Shugendō as a living religious tradition after 1872 and its rebirth as a research subject within academic and intellectual circles. Like Suzuki, Hayashi concentrates on Meiji period Shugendō, providing a close-up of the institutional vicissitudes that took place between Daigoji and its Shugendō branch (called Ein-ryū) in order to prevent the financial breakdown of the temple. In his analysis of this tormented period of Shugendō history, Hayashi underlines how the gradual inclusion of Shugendō texts within important editorial projects such as the *Japanese Buddhist Canon* (*Nihon daizōkyō*) helped preserve the Shugendō textual heritage but, at the same time, destroyed the aura of secrecy that had always typified the written productions of this tradition.

Part Three, "Imagining En no Gyōja and Fictionalizing Shugendō," sheds light on the narrative strategies set up to support Shugendō groups and identities in the premodern period. Starting off with the study of foundation narratives of temples and shrines (*jisha engi*) of the medieval period, this section ends with a study of the imagery of Shugendō practitioners as detected in Edo period literary sources such as vernacular fictions and dramas. In Chapter Six, "Between Companionship and Worship: A Reflection on En no Gyōja's Statuary Past and Present," Carina Roth elucidates various aspects of the contemporary cult of En no Gyōja. After giving an overview of the iconographical evolution of the founder figure of Shugendō, Roth analyzes the restoration process of a statue enshrined in a votive lodge at Gyōsen no shuku on the southern side of the Ōmine range. The study of this wooden icon reveals that even in contemporary Japan, an eighteenth-century statue of En no Gyōja can provide a dynamic space of interaction between Shugendō practitioners of different lineages, members of associations for the preservation of the territory, and lay devotees. In Chapter Seven, "En no Gyōja's Legitimization in the Context of Japanese Esoteric Buddhism," Kawasaki Tsuyoshi focuses on *Minoodera engi* emphasizing its role as one of the early matrixes for the hagiography of En no Gyōja as the founder of Shugendō. As a matter of fact, *Minoodera engi* appears to play an important role as the oldest document in which the figure of En no Gyōja is inserted into the Shingon lineage. By describing how En no Gyōja, in a dream, visits the Pure Land of Ryūju Bosatsu (Nāgārjuna) behind Minoo's waterfall and receives initiation to Esoteric Buddhism there, *Minoodera engi* subverts the traditional Shingon lineage by claiming that En no Gyōja's consecration preceded not only that of Kūkai, but even the transmission of Esoteric Buddhism to China itself. Kawasaki presents the influence of *Minoodera engi* in other documents, before showing how its daring proposition was received in the historical context of the time. Kawasaki's contribution is complemented by Niki Natsumi's. In Chapter Eight, "The Description of Mountains in *Minoodera engi*," Niki also takes into account the *Minoodera engi* but provides a special focus on the Chinese poetical tropes used to describe the waterfall that is the landmark of this *shugen* site, in order to show the literary interplay between aristocracy, priesthood, and *shugen* practitioners in the early medieval period. Through a detailed examination of expressions and metaphors depicting the site of the Minoo waterfalls, Niki analyzes the way in which twelfth-century *Minoodera engi* uses a literary genre (Chinese-style poetry) and, at the same time, coins a vocabulary of its own to promote the temple's agenda. Her close reading of the original text gives us rare insight into the very crafting of a *shugen* text. In Chapter Nine, "Images of the *Shugenja* in Edo Popular Fiction," William Fleming discusses representations of Shugendō practitioners in popular fiction and drama of the Edo period, uncovering motives drawn from Chinese tales. Fleming's contribution provides a fascinating foray on a double intertextual level. Not only does he look for literary renditions of *shugenja* in early Edo period *yomihon* (short-form historical narratives), but he also shows that the figure of the *shugen* practitioner is often used to translate shady religious characters in Japanese transpositions of Chinese literary works. More often than not, parodic Daoist priests in China become equally ridiculed *shugenja* in the Japanese version. True to the satirical vein of the genre, the portrayal of *shugenja* is rarely positive, but at the same time shows how familiar and deeply embedded in Edo society such figures were.

Part Four, "Materiality and Visual Culture," presents a panorama of non-written sources such as copper statues, devotional paintings, stelae, mounds, and paper talismans related to relevant figures and practices in Shugendō tradition. The aim of this section is to demonstrate how the study of material culture provides a fundamental help in filling the knowledge gaps about Shugendō pervasiveness in ordinary devotional practices among the elites as well as the subaltern classes. A look at Shugendō materiality also allows for the discovery of a network of religious interactions between humans (Shugendō practitioners, lay devotees, artisans) and nonhuman agencies (sacred objects) for the formation and diffusion of shared Shugendō discourses in society. In Chapter Ten, "The Cult and Statuary of Zaō Gongen," Fujioka Yutaka discusses the modalities according to which, since the late Heian period, the statues dedicated to Zaō Gongen, a local deity associated with Mount Kinpu in the Kii peninsula, reflect the changes in worship (doctrines and practices) to this deity. Fujioka points out that a peculiarity of the first copper statutes of Zaō Gongen is their light weight and unfinished external appearance. These elements show that these statues were probably thought of as temporary offerings to be deployed in private devotional rituals that preceded the actual pilgrimage toward the mountain. Because aristocratic pilgrims were also used to carrying such statues of Zaō Gongen with them during their ascent of the mountains, the portability of these figures played a pivotal role in their practical use and diffusion. In Chapter Eleven, "Religious Culture in Transition: Mt. Fuji," Janine Sawada embraces a variety of visual materials dedicated to Mount Fuji, ranging from pilgrimage mandalas (*sankei mandara* 参詣曼荼羅) to the ascetic drawings (*ominuki* 御身抜) of Kakugyō Tōbutsu 角行藤佛 (1541–1646?). Decoding the semantic aspects of these images, Sawada presents an interpretative shift in the religious meanings associated with Mount Fuji's landscape. The body of the mountain was originally envisioned as a real geophysical site toward which pilgrims were supposed to direct their devotional practices. Later on, in Kakugyō's ritual works, Mount Fuji became a totally transmogrified mountainous space characterized by strong talismanic value. In Chapter Twelve, "The Shape of Devotion: Mounds, Stelae, and Empowering Ritual Fasting in the Early-Modern Cult of Mount Yudono," Andrea Castiglioni gives another example of the expansion of regional *shugen* to the Kantō area through an analysis of devotional and ritual interactions surrounding votive mounds and stelae dedicated to Yudono Gongen as a highly localized manifestation of Dainichi Nyorai. In this chapter, Castiglioni concentrates on the regional propagation of the Yudono cult via a class of ascetics called "lifetime ascetics" (*issei gyōnin*), who constantly interacted with lay devotees and religious confraternities. Through several case studies set in the early Edo period, Castiglioni uncovers a plurality of rites surrounding these votive objects. Together with the variety of their inscriptions into local lore, they demonstrate the wide geographical diffusion of a cult that was initially strongly localized. In Chapter Thirteen, "Shugendō as Social Practice: Kumano Talismans and Inscribed Oaths in Premodern Japan," Max Moerman examines the role of printed *shugen* talismans (*goō hōin* 牛王宝印) produced at the Kumano shrines and used to warrant oaths in ritual, legal, political, or economic contexts from the medieval period onward. Whereas the use of talismans for protection is found in many religious traditions all over the world, their role in the performance of oaths is more distinct. Inscribed on the back of Kumano talismans that underscore the solemnity of the vow, "written solicitations" (*kishōmon* 起請文) represent a promise so binding that violating it can bring death upon the contractor of the vow. Moerman examines the evolution of this practice and its varied uses, an evolution that traverses the history of Japan, transcending all social classes, from the early medieval period to the end of the Tokugawa shogunate.

Part One

Intellectual History of Shugendō Studies

1

A Critical History of the Study of Shugendō and Mountain Beliefs in Japan

Suzuki Masataka
Translation by Gaynor Sekimori

In this chapter, I intend to discuss comprehensively, from the standpoint of a native anthropologist, issues concerning the present state of research into mountain beliefs (*sangaku shinkō* 山岳信仰) and Shugendō. A number of my topics have grown out of my own experience as an informant and interpreter for foreign scholars and from a sense of unease as an interested party regarding "cultural translation" in their studies of Japan. I present points for consideration rather than any conclusion.

The Multidimensional Relationship between Kami and Buddhas

Since its introduction to Japan in the middle of the sixth century, Buddhism developed a complicated fusion with indigenous beliefs, resulting in a combinatory system (*shinbutsu shūgō* 神仏習合) between the foreign buddhas and the native kami that grew out of their interactions and their mutual transformations, their conflicts and their frictions. Kami and buddhas came to be amalgamated, with the mountain, in particular, as a node, giving rise to beliefs and practices related to mountains that are peculiar to Japan, such as Shugendō. Intellectually, this amalgamation generated discourses such as the Original Enlightenment (*hongaku* 本覚) thought of the Tendai school (Stone 1999), *honji suijaku* (本地垂迹), or the idea that the kami are provisional manifestations of the buddhas (Teeuwen, Rambelli 2003), Ryōbu (Dual) Shinto (両部神道), textual interpretations known as "medieval *Nihongi*" (*chūsei Nihongi* 中世日本紀), and "inverted" *honji suijaku* (*han honji suijaku* 反本地垂迹), where it is Buddhist divinities that are considered manifestations of the kami. This kami–buddha combination was preserved in Japan over many centuries. Shrines of tutelary deities of the area stood in the grounds of temples; temples dedicated to the kami (Jingūji 神宮寺) were attached to shrines, and it was not uncommon for Buddhist statues to be *goshintai* (御神体), the physical objects embodying the kami. Fundamentally, this represents a multidimensional relationship between kami and buddhas, whose nature and character altered as times changed. This long intellectual and spiritual tradition that had existed from the sixth century was forcibly severed, and then reconstructed in a modern idiom, by the religious policy of the Meiji government, commonly known as separation of the kami from the buddhas (*shinbutsu bunri* 神仏分離). Let me begin by clarifying a few key terms and concerns:

(1) KAMI (神) refers to a named deity venerated in a shrine. Kami (カミ) as a folk concept are nameless natural spirits of things, like trees, rocks, and springs, which are not enshrined in a building or a built object. KAMI are controlled and institutionalized through ritual and doctrine, but kami are fluid and turbulent, and hard to control.

(2) Kami in their folk understanding are ambiguous; they blur and merge with, and are transformed by, concepts such as *mono* モノ and *tama* タマ (spirits) and *oni* オニ (malevolent entities). They develop through analogy and metaphor and are conceptually transformed. Two of a kind become linked together and go on to change from one to another.

(3) "Buddha," of course, is a Sanskrit term. The Chinese translation *fo* 仏 is pronounced both *butsu* and *hotoke* in Japanese; the former Sino-Japanese term *butsu* fused with the native concept of *hotoke* (ホトケ). "Buddha" metamorphosed in the course of its cultural translation from India to Japan via China and Korea, and its pronunciation changed as it became indigenized in each place.

(4) The folk term *hotoke* is polysemic in meaning; it can refer to Buddhist statues, the names of divinities, the Buddhist Dharma, a dead person, the spirit of the dead, "enlightened souls" (*kakurei* 覚霊), *mitama* (soul, spirit) or ancestors, according to context, time, place, and person. A different concept is formed through contact and develops through metonymy, and meaning is transformed as specific parts overlap.

(5) The metaphorical character of "kami" blurred with the metonymic character of "hotoke," overlapping the relationship between KAMI and buddhas and tinged with a duality, thus giving rise to a complex hybridity.

(6) Kami as a folk concept were essentially invisible, but they were given form as kami sculptures (*shinzō* 神像) under the influence of Buddhist statues, thereby becoming visible KAMI in the shrine. When Buddhism arrived in Japan, the Buddha was expressed in tangible form through statues, but "buddhas" also became "hotoke" as a greater invisibility gradually accrued. Meanwhile, the basic idea remained that buddhas are visible and kami are invisible, and resulted in the development, as a consequence of their mutual influence, of secret buddhas (*hibutsu* 秘仏) and secret kami (*hishin* 秘神).

(7) Kami and *hotoke* as folk concepts are found in written sources through expressions like *reikon* (霊魂 soul/spirit), *seirei/shōryō* and *shirei* (精霊/死霊 soul, spirit of the dead), *shinrei* (神霊 kami spirit), *goryō* (御霊 malevolent spirit), *ki* (気 spirit), and *chikara* (力 power). Their meanings developed to the second and third degree when the power of imagination was added to the understanding of intellectuals, based on the reading of the Chinese characters used to write them.

(8) The world "before the kami" was the natural universe. The power of the wild within all of heaven and earth (*ametsuchi* 天地)—mountains, rivers, seas, heavenly bodies, the cosmos—melded with KAMI, buddhas, kami, and *hotoke* to function as "life" or "life-force." This is an understanding of the world that is not found in the one-dimensional concept of Nature of the modern West.

The multidimensional relationship between KAMI, kami, buddhas, and *hotoke* has taken a number of different directions. In terms of how it is expressed, it combines oral traditions and written documents, giving rise to a discursive space that made full use of both the Chinese and Japanese readings of Chinese characters. The three features of this constantly changing multidimensional relationship are complexity, multi-functionality, and hybridity. At the basis of this model is the possibility of reestablishing a historical relationship among these three dimensions.

For example, ideas and practices surrounding the so-called "kami–buddha combination" in the late Heian period, such as *honji suijaku*, *gongen* (権現 avatar) and *wakō dōjin* (和光同塵 softening radiance, mingling with humans), go no further, in terms of the multidimensional relationship between kami and buddhas, than a view that emphasizes the KAMI and buddhas ([1] in Figure 1.1) and stop with a partial explanation of an enormous worldview. "Japanese Buddhism" developed independently, but in the course of its acceptance by the people at large, it faced demands to provide explanations and practices that contradicted its doctrine that denied the existence of souls and spirits. Today, Nichirenshū 日蓮宗 and Kōyasan Shingonshū 高野山真言宗 accept their existence, but other sects and schools have a more ambiguous approach to the question (Fujimura 2015). The kami–*hotoke* relationship ([4] in Figure 1.1) and the buddhas–*hotoke* relationship ([6] in Figure 1.1) are intimately related to this issue.

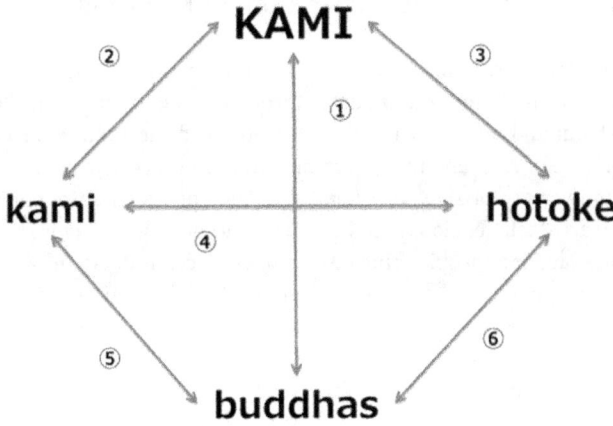

Figure 1.1 The multidimensional relationship between kami and buddhas.

Shugendō, the representative example of kami–buddha fusion before the *shinbutsu bunri* legislation of the late 1860s, developed systematically in a way peculiar to Japan, characterized by the fusion of KAMI, buddhas, kami, and *hotoke*. It intricately combined the six dimensions (Figure 1.1) described in points (1) to (6) above. In the course of its individual development in various localities, it gave meaning to the mountains and centered its practices there, as embodying the power of nature. Practitioners acquired special powers through mountain practice, and upon returning to their villages they provided magico-religious prayer rituals (*kaji kitō* 加持祈禱) for practical benefits on behalf of local people. These practitioners were generally called *yamabushi* 山伏 or *hōin* 法印. In terms of doctrine, the purpose of their practice was to attain buddhahood in this body (*sokushin jōbutsu* 即身成仏), an idea strongly influenced by Esoteric Buddhism, but ultimately it was to become one with nature—to become a "living kami" in order to bring people to salvation. Lying at the basis of this was the idea that mountains were mandalas and that the buddha-nature (*busshō* 仏性, Skt. *Buddha-dhātu*) was inherent within mountains, rivers, and seas. In the long run though, it went beyond Buddhist doctrine to say that all natural phenomena, whether sentient or not, were one. Shugendō exerted a great influence through mountain beliefs and practices all over Japan, but it disappeared after being banned in 1872; efforts to restore it have been ongoing since 1946. Recognizing the existence of spirits, it has overcome the doctrinal contradictions of Buddhism, and this was undoubtedly the reason it was accepted widely among ordinary people. In contrast to the Buddhist temples that dealt with funerals and memorial services for their parishioners during the Edo period, *shugenja* were active as lay *hōin* and practitioners providing practical benefits for local people. The two (temple priests and *shugenja*) thus formed a mutual and complementary relationship. The force that has sustained Shugendō throughout can be defined the "imagination of hybridity."

Shinbutsu bunri, the "Separation" of Kami and Buddhas

The multidimensional relationship between kami and buddhas, KAMI, and *hotoke*, was destroyed, transformed, and reconstructed through the policy of the Meiji government to separate kami and buddhas. The year 2018 marked the 150th anniversary of the Meiji Restoration of 1868 and many commemorative events were held. It also marked the 150th anniversary of *shinbutsu bunri* and thus provided an opportunity to re-examine the early Meiji religious policy that brought such a great change to the spiritual culture of the Japanese people. This also implies a reconsideration of the nature of Japan's "modern period." As far as mountain beliefs and practices are concerned, the past 150 years have been a time of dramatic change, beginning with the clarification (*hanzen* 判然), mandated by the Meiji government, of what is a buddha and what is a kami, and the lifting of the exclusion of women from sacred sites. This change is clearly exemplified by the eradication, revival, reconstruction, and recreation of Shugendō, and by the revival and decline of confraternities associated with pilgrimages to sacred mountains. This period of "modernization" saw government intervention in both mountain beliefs and Shugendō, as premodern mores and folkways were considered behind the times. The study of mountain beliefs and Shugendō brought to the surface behavior and ideas that seemed to reject the "modern," thereby making Japan's modern period a subject for reflection.

The series of legislation known as the "kami–buddha clarification edicts" (*shinbutsu hanzenrei* 神仏判然令) issued after April 1868 was a result of restorationist fundamentalism that aimed to "purify" Shinto by "clarifying" the kami–buddha amalgamation that then prevailed.[1] The purpose was to make Shinto the state religion, but an anti-Buddhist movement emerged that carried out the violent destruction of Buddhist statues and temples (Tamamuro 1977; Grapard 2011). This was probably an unintended outcome. The term *shinbutsu bunri* was not used in the early Meiji years. An order from the Jingi jimukyoku 神祇事務局 (provisional office dealing with kami affairs, February to June 1868) dated March 28, 1868, stated that "there are numbers of shrines which from ancient times have been known as such-and-such Gongen and as Gozu Tennō 牛頭天王, for example, and which use Buddhist designations for the titles of their kami" and "shrines whose anthropomorphic image is a buddha or bodhisattva." Such shrines were required to change. In addition, "shrines with Buddhist statues displayed as the original form (*honji*) of the kami, or having such Buddhist implements as gongs or bells, should remove them immediately." This was a sifting out of the amalgamation aimed at establishing what belonged to what group. People reacted to the violence that followed by quietly hiding away Buddhist statues and implements in a form of "soft resistance," and continued to make pilgrimages to mountains under the cloak of invisibility lent by groups affiliated with Shinto and by confraternities associated with the new Shinto sects (Kyōha Shinto 教派神道) that gradually came into being after 1875.

Pilgrimages to sacred mountains, shrines, and temples received a boost by the expansion of the railway network from the 1880s. Confraternities revived, proliferating and reaching new prosperity. In times of war, pilgrimage became a prop for people's faith and the matrix of Japan's spiritual culture (see also Chapter Five by Hayashi Makoto). The clarification edicts did not stretch to geographical renaming, so mountains with names associated with Buddhist thought and with buddhas and bodhisattvas remained. These included Jizō, Kannon, Amida, Yakushi, Fugen, Dainichi, Kokūzō, Gokuraku, Jigoku, Zaō, Fudō, Ontake, Myōkō, and Misen. Mountains called Gongen and Tengu 天狗 still dot the landscape. Based on combinatory thought, Gongen ("avatar") refers to the provisional form taken by kami as the "manifest traces" (*suijaku* 垂迹) of the "original forms" (*honji* 本地) of buddhas and bodhisattvas. Tengu are pre-Buddhist mountain deities sometimes considered enemies of Buddhism; however, from around the fifteenth century, *shugenja* came to be referred to as *tengu*. Place names that predate *shinbutsu bunri* act as a stimulus to memory.

Shugendō was banned in September 15, 1872, by order of the Dajōkan (Council of State). Considered the epitome of kami–buddha admixture, it was dismembered and eliminated as if a scapegoat. As many as 170,000 *shugen* were laicized; subsequently, they became Shinto priests, were ordained as Buddhist monks affiliated with one sect or another, or simply left the religious life entirely, many taking up farming (Nakayama 1984: 426).[2] Those responsible for the violence against Buddhism in the early years of the Meiji era were primarily nativist scholars (*kokugakusha* 国学者), former Buddhists who had laicized as Shinto priests, and lower-ranking Shinto priests. Though their ideas may have been subtly different, they were united in the noble cause of obeying the emperor's orders, which they adroitly reinterpreted, upsetting the traditional values system. Around the same time that Shugendō was banned, the government also set forth policies to stamp out "superstition" and "bad practices," and abolished popular religious practitioners such as female spirit mediums (*miko* 巫女), yin-yang masters (*onmyōji* 陰陽師), itinerant flute-playing monks (*komusō* 虚無僧), and pilgrimage guides (*oshi* 御師).

Meanwhile, the Shintoification of mountain beliefs and practices continued. The invention of the term *shintaizan* 神体山, referring to the mountain itself as the abode of the kami, was welcomed by shrines, which used it freely, and the expression *kamiyama* 神山 (kami mountain) was also increasingly used. We cannot but be aware that modern mountain beliefs have overcome the turbulence of *shinbutsu bunri*.

Can we reevaluate *shinbutsu bunri* socially? In the early years of the Meiji period, the provisional office dealing with kami affairs, the Office of Kami Affairs (Jingikan 神祇官, June 1868–August 1871), the Ministry of Kami Affairs (Jingishō 神祇省, August 1871–March 1872), the Ministry of Religion (Kyōbushō 教部省, March 1872–January 1877), and the Ministry of Home Affairs (Naimushō 内務省, 1877) promoted the institutionalization and modernization of shrines and temples, setting up a system of parishioners' representatives for them. At the economic and social level, in 1871 the government ordered that shrine and temple land be reverted to the state (*shajiryō agechirei* 社寺領上知令), thereby destroying the traditional economic basis of religious institutions. This massive redistribution of wealth was intended to lay the foundation for the rapid modernization of society. The destruction of vested interests represented a "world renewal" (*yonaoshi* 世直し), stimulating cultural, social, political, and economic reorganization. In cultural terms, the traditional system of hereditary shrine priests was abolished and a new hierarchy created, shrines were ranked and mythology was reinstated, setting in place a spiritual unity of the people and a system that could be skillfully used in war. The treasures of temples and shrines that had been damaged in the course of the anti-Buddhist movement were "rediscovered" through the eyes of foreigners such as Ernest Fenollosa (1853–1908).[3] In 1897, the Ancient Shrines and Temples Preservation Law was enacted for the preservation of cultural properties through the designation of "national treasures," based on Fenollosa's surveys. This set up an institutional framework for preserving and protecting cultural assets. Ironically, it was the attack on Buddhism in the early Meiji years that led to the administration of such assets and the registration of Japan's cultural heritage.

Reconsidering Combinatory Religion (*shinbutsu shūgō*)

A discussion of *shinbutsu bunri* inevitably involves a re-examination of the concept of *shinbutsu shūgō*, the combinatory association between kami and buddhas, and a reassessment of modern scholarship in this area. As far as may be determined from historical sources, the expression for this relationship in 1868 was *shinbutsu konkō*

神仏混淆, kami–buddha admixture, regarding which the kami–buddha "clarification" edicts had been published. These, in turn, led to the movement known as *haibutsu kishaku* 排仏毀釈 (literally, "exclude Buddhism and destroy Śākyamuni").[4] The term *shinbutsu bunri* was not used in this period. The edict employed the words "clarification" and "exclusion of Buddhism" not "destruction of Buddhism."[5] "Exclusion" developed into "abolition" and led to "destruction," with the unintended result that Buddhist temples and images were subject to mass destruction.

The concept of *shinbutsu bunri* does not extend back to the beginning of the Meiji period but emerged in the 1900s as a technical term in relation to *shinbutsu shūgō*. Its first occurrence is in an article by the Tendai monk Shutara Ryōen 修多羅亮延 (1842–1917) entitled "Shinbutsu bunri to shinkan sōryo" (Shrine priests, temple monks, and *shinbutsu bunri*), which appeared in the journal *Bukkyō shigaku* (Buddhist Historical Studies) in 1912 (Sakamoto 2005: 24; 2007: 162). It was reprinted in the first volume of the *Meiji Ishin shinbutsu bunri shiryō*, published by Tōhō shoin in Tokyo in 1926.

The term *shinbutsu shūgō* emerged as a retrospective concept at a stage when it had become possible to look back over the past, forty years after the events. It appeared for the first time in the title of a book by Adachi Ritsuen 足立栗園[6] published in 1901 called *Kinsei shinbutsu shūgō ben* (*Shinbutsu shūgō* in the early modern period).[7] Tsuji Zennosuke 辻善之助 (1877–1955) pioneered the use of the word as a technical term in 1907 in an article entitled "*Honji suijaku* setsu no kigen ni tsuite" (The origins of the theory of *honji suijaku*), which was published over six issues of the journal *Shigaku zasshi*.[8] Its central theme was expanded in his *Nihon bukkyōshi no kenkyū* (A Study of the History of Buddhism in Japan, 1919). Tsuji had studied under Murakami Senshō 村上専精 (1851–1929) at the Imperial University of Tokyo, and between 1920 and 1926 he gathered documents and oral accounts concerning *shinbutsu bunri* from all over Japan. These were published in five volumes, divided by region, between 1926 and 1929 as the aforementioned *Meiji Ishin shinbutsu bunri shiryō* (Murakami, Tsuji, Washio 1926–29).

Nationalist feelings grew as a result of the Sino-Japanese War (1894–95) and the Russo-Japanese War (1904–5), strengthening the unity of the Japanese people. Following the establishment of "modern Shinto," the term *shinbutsu shūgō* appeared as a dichotomous concept that "combined" Shinto and Buddhism on an equal basis.[9] It served to explain the legitimacy of the Meiji policy of *shinbutsu bunri* that had negated it. The actuality of the Meiji move from kami–buddha "admixture" to "clarification" was replaced by the concept of a move from *shinbutsu shūgō* to *shinbutsu bunri*. This implied a negative representation of the terms *konkō* 混淆 and *shūgō* 習合 and the supremacy of Shinto over Buddhism.

When Tsuji Zennosuke began collecting his records about *shinbutsu bunri* in 1920, the Shinto world was at an important turning point. Meiji Jingū was formally dedicated on November 1 that year, signaling the arrival of a "central" shrine for Tokyo. In 1921 it jumped to the top place as the premier destination for New Year visits.[10] The establishment of Meiji Jingū was an important cultural moment that changed people's behavior.[11] I employ the term "modern Shinto," my own coinage, to describe the direction Shinto took toward the development of Shrine Shinto for the masses, the type of Shinto popularized as a result of the development of the railways and the publishing media. "Modern Shinto" began in 1912 with the establishment of the Meiji Japan Society (Meiji Seitoku Kinen Gakkai 明治聖德記念學會, literally Society to Commemorate the Sacred Virtues of the Emperor Meiji); lectures on Shinto studies at the Imperial University of Tokyo by Katō Genchi 加藤玄智 (1873–1965), the main force behind the Society, promoted emperor veneration and a discourse of "Japan as the land of the kami." Emperor veneration also infiltrated the public opinion through the Japan Youth Hall (Nippon Seinenkan), established in 1921;[12] the opening of the Meiji Memorial Picture Gallery in 1926, honoring the Meiji emperor and his consort, Dowager Empress Shōken, lent strength to emperor veneration and the permeation of Shrine Shinto among the Japanese. Following the erection of Meiji Jingū, popular pilgrimage to "temples and shrines (*jisha* 寺社)" became pilgrimage to "shrines and temples" (*shaji* 社寺). The term *shinbutsu bunri* took root with the publication of the five volumes of the *Meiji Ishin shinbutsu bunri shiryō* between 1926 and 1929. The relationship between kami and buddhas became unified and the dichotomous concepts of *shinbutsu shūgō* and *shinbutsu bunri* cast their spell over people. Later, Tsuji Zennosuke made full use of historical sources to clarify empirically the corollary that Buddhism had become corrupted in the early modern period.[13]

The period between 1920 and 1929 when the *Shinbutsu bunri shiryō* was being compiled was also the time when Yanagita Kunio 柳田國男 (1875–1962) gave an academic framework to his interest in popular tradition (*minkan denshō* 民間伝承), later called "folklore studies" (*minzokugaku* 民俗学). It was also the time when Uno Enkū 宇野圓空 (1885–1949) and Oka Masao 岡正雄 (1898–1982) were expanding the concept of ethnology (*minzokugaku* 民族学). The journal *Minzoku* 民族, which owed its existence to Oka, was published between 1925 and 1929, and it was during those years that the word "ethnology" came into general use.[14] The role played here by Oka Shoin, the publishing company where Masao's brother Oka Shigeo 岡茂雄 (1894–1989) worked as an editor, was very great.[15] Through such publications, folklore and ethnography as academic fields may be said to have formed a counter-discourse to the growth of "modern Shinto." However, during the war, government pressure forced them to develop in a direction where they were utilized by the Movement to Promote the Japanese Spirit (Nihon seishin undō). One of this movement's proponents, Kihira Tadayoshi 紀平正美 (1874–1949), published *Nihon seishin* 日本精神 (The Spirit of Japan) in 1930 with Iwanami Shoten, a book that propounded the unity of the people through the Japanese spirit. Particularly after the Manchurian Incident of 1931, which gave Japan the excuse to invade northeastern China, the Movement to Promote the Japanese Spirit encouraged an "ethnic nationalism" that aroused pro-war sentiments.

Shinbutsu shūgō is a modern concept, and although as an unequal dichotomy it should have been termed *busshin shūgō* 仏神習合, coming into association with *shinbutsu bunri* it became estranged from the flexible, versatile pattern of traditional Japanese religion, morphing into a concept which was the unconscious recipient of fundamentalist ideas about Shinto supremacy.[16] As a result, this modern discourse of *shinbutsu shūgō* has been easily utilized in different periods and fields, such as medieval studies and Shugendō.[17]

The Idea of the "Founder" and the Present

Traditions associated with those who "opened" mountains all over Japan have come down to us through legendary history (*engi* 縁起) and oral lore. Since, however, the year of the foundation (the "opening of the mountain," *kaizan* 開山) is regarded as a later fabrication and even the very historicity of the founder is often open to question, the dates of the foundation and the identity of the founder have remained outside the concerns of historiography and have not been considered from the standpoint of intellectual history (see also Chapter Three by Caleb Carter and Chapter Eight by Niki Natsumi). From around the year 2000, sacred mountains and sacred sites all over Japan have been celebrating the 1250th or 1300th anniversary of their founding. Associated with this has been a remarkable reaffirmation of their origins and a reconstruction of orthodoxy (Tables 1.1 and 1.2).

Founder legends follow two patterns. In one, a Buddhist monk climbs and venerates a previously unclimbed mountain and makes it a sacred site by performing rituals and magico-religious prayers (*kitō* 祈禱); in the other, the founder is a hunter who encounters a deity on the mountain, becomes awakened into the sin of taking life, and takes refuge in Buddhism. Founders come from a broad spectrum of people—officially ordained Buddhist monks, *shidosō* 私度僧 (privately ordained monks), *ubasoku* 優婆塞 (unordained practitioners), *hijiri* 聖 (wandering ascetics), *zenji* 禅師 (shamanistic religious specialists), shamans,[18] hunters, mountain dwellers (*yamabito* 山人), *shukkesha* 出家者 (people who had taken Buddhist ordination), *hansō hanzoku* 半僧半俗 (ordained monks with wives and children), ascetics, and laymen. The beings that guided the founders on the mountain included indigenous people, hunters, and local tutelary kami, and among the creatures that guided them were crows, hawks, deer, bears, snakes, and dragons. Making their way into the fastness of the mountain they

Table 1.1 Founder Traditions And Modern Commemorative Events

Year	Sacred site	Anniversary	Year of foundation	Founder
2018	Hōki Daisen	1,300 years	718	Kinren
2018	Rokugō Manzan	1,300 years	718	Ninmon
2017	Saigoku 33 Kannon circuit	1,300 years	718	Tokudō
2017	Hakusan	1,300 years	717	Taichō
2016	Nikkōsan	1,250 years	766	Shōdō
2015	Kōyasan	1,200 years	816	Kūkai
2014	Shikoku 88 temple circuit	1,200 years	815	Kūkai
2007	Hakonesan	1,250 years	757	Mangan
2005	Sagami Ōyama	1,250 years	755	Rōben
2000	Ōminesan	1,300 years	701	En no Gyōja
1993	Hagurosan	1,400 years	593	Nōjo Taishi

Note: Places have variously calculated the years by actual (*man*) and counted (*kazoe*). The inauguration years of the Saigoku and Shikoku pilgrimage circuits have also been included.

Table 1.2 Founders And Foundation Years

Mountain	Founder and year
Mt. Hiko	Zenshō (531), Ninniku (538), Hōren (seventh to eighth centuries)
Various places	En no Gyōja (634–701)
Various places	Gyōki (668–749)
Tateyama	Jikō (701)
Mt. Ishizuchi	Jakusen (758)
Mt. Togakushi	Gakumon (849)
Osorezan	Ennin (862)
Mt. Fuji	Matsudai (1149). Some sources give En no Gyōja or Shōtoku Taishi

Note: Figures not listed in Table 1.1.

encountered buddhas, bodhisattvas, and kami who often appeared to them in caves. We also notice a deep connection with water as many numinous beings appeared out of ponds, in the form of, for example, crystals (Kumano, Mt. Hiko), nine-headed dragons (Hakusan, Hakone, Togakushi) and *oni* (ogres).

As these tales became "history," the founders were identified with personal names and the foundation was assigned a year from the official chronology. For instance, Mt. Haguro and Mt. Hiko dated their foundation to a year from the era of the ruler Kinmei (r. 539–71), whose reign is associated with the introduction of Buddhism to Japan (either in 538 or in 552).[19] This founder lore should be considered "pseudo-history" rather than simply "fake history." Much of it is situated in the Nara period (710–94).[20] It is a "retrospective history," superimposing the "opening" of the mountain on the formation of the Ritsuryō state that began with the promulgation of the Taihō Code in 701. The aim here was doubtless to strengthen legitimacy. With the Ritsuryō state came the compilation of official histories and gazetteers. Following the move of the capital to Heijōkyō (Nara), edicts were issued which resulted in the conversion of oral lore to writing; this is how *Kojiki* 古事記 (Record of Ancient Matters, completed 712), *Fudoki* 風土記 (gazetteers whose compilation was ordered in 713),[21] and *Nihon shoki* 日本書紀 (Chronicle of Japan, completed 720) came to be (Table 1.3). *Nihon shoki* was the template for a series of later official histories and a source for interpreting mythology.[22]

We must interrogate at what point the retrospective history of founder lore meets the chronology of the official histories. Founder lore aimed to construct another history from that of the official chronicles. Much of it was in the form of orally transmitted legendary history, whose conversion to writing has taken a long period from ancient times down to the present. What was the purpose of constructing history, in particular pseudo-history? This lore established the orthodoxy and authority of the new practice of climbing mountains in worship. By superimposing the date of a mountain's "opening" with the establishment of the Ritsuryō 律令 state and by designating a particular person as founder, mountain beliefs can be seen as creating a history that supported the secular administrative system based on the court and as ought to bring stability and spiritual unity to the state.

Table 1.3 Writings And Capital Transfer In The Nara Period

Year	Anniversary	Era
2020	*Nihon shoki* 1,300 years	Yōrō 4 (720)
2013	*Fudoki* 1,300 years (Hitachi, Harima 2015)	Wadō 6 (713)
2012	*Kojiki* 1,300 years	Wadō 5 (712)
2010	Move of the capital to Heijōkyō 1,300 years	Wadō 3 (710)
1994	Move of the capital to Heiankyō 1,200 years	Enryaku 13 (794)

By elucidating the discourse of founder lore, which confirms the "origin" of mountain pilgrimages based on retrospective history, we can recognize in it a reconstruction of popular beliefs and an indigenization of beliefs from abroad, thus giving Buddhist doctrines and practices a Japanese color. Founder lore is a type of discourse that indicates changes in the spirit of the age. Although rituals on mountain tops were taking place from before the eighth century,[23] the relationship between Buddhism and mountain beliefs and practices entered a new stage in the Nara period, almost 150 years after Buddhism's introduction to Japan. The consecration ceremony of the Great Buddha of Tōdaiji in 752 also celebrated two hundred years since the transmission of Buddhism to Japan (552). A new periodization is thus made possible based on lore: (a) 150 years from the transmission of Buddhism to the beginning of lore concerning mountain founders, (b) 1150 years during which a mixture of kami and buddha worship widely developed in the mountains, and (c) 150 years since the Meiji *shinbutsu bunri* policy. The interpretation and repositioning of founder lore opens up a broad understanding of Japanese history in which temples and shrines thrived on the admixture of Buddhism and mountain beliefs and practices. It also looks again at the 150 years of the modern era. Do events surrounding the 1300th anniversary of a mountain's foundation as a religious center act as a stimulus to reconsider its beliefs and practices introspectively? This is a question for future study.

Changes in Founder Myths

Recent archaeological investigations at Nara period sites on the summits of mountains may have encouraged the idea that lore concerning founders reflects some truth (Tokieda 2016). Excavations on the summit of Sanjōgatake in 1984 yielded two tenth-century golden Buddha images and also confirmed the existence of a platform for the fire-ritual dating from the eighth century. Items excavated from the summit of Mt. Misen 弥山, also in the Ōmine range, likewise date back to the eighth century. As mountain pilgrimage was given new meaning, founder lore could be regarded as a discourse asserting its orthopraxy. Local folk beliefs merged with Buddhism, with the mountain as a point of contact; this gave rise to a new discourse about origins. Orthodoxy was guaranteed by the authority of ideas from abroad. On the other hand, Buddhist practitioners localized practices from overseas and established praxis sites within the realm of nature.

Caves number greatly in places traditionally associated with founders. They were believed to be places where spirits (*tama*) dwelt, and became sacred sites associated with kami and buddhas. Many caves contain the element "tama" in their names, such as the Tamadono no iwaya 玉殿岩屋 at Tateyama[24] and the Tamayakutsu 玉屋窟 at Mt. Hiko; buddhas and bodhisattvas, dragons and crystals, and other numinous entities were believed to have manifested themselves there. Springs at river sources were also sites of spiritual connection with KAMI, kami, *hotoke*, and buddhas. Buddhist monks sought out sites in mountains for their ascetic training and encountered the spiritual entities of the place through the guidance of hunters or the original inhabitants. Sometimes it was the hunters themselves who encountered a buddha or bodhisattva and took refuge in Buddhism, vowing not to take life any more. In all events, caves were the sites of many of such encounters that demonstrate the adoption of Buddhism within founder lore. The historical chronicle *Shoku Nihongi* 続日本紀 describes the activities associated with Buddhist ascetic training in an entry dated tenth day of the tenth month of 718. An edict to the Office of Monastic Affairs (Sōgō) divided Buddhism according to two practices, namely, study and learning at monasteries and temples on the one hand, and ascetic training in hermitages and caves in the mountains on the other hand. This suggests that many Buddhist monks went into the mountains to practice. Minowa Kenryō 蓑輪顕量 writes: "It is thought that beliefs related to mountains predating the arrival of Buddhism in Japan, specifically that mystical powers could be attained there, were inherited by Buddhist monks" (Minowa 2015: 17). The division between monastery and forest/mountain dwelling that already existed in Indian Buddhism developed in the course of its transmission through China to Japan. Forest dwelling was linked to *shikan* 止観 (Skt. *vipaśyanā*) and *zenjō* 禅定 (Skt. *samādhi*) meditational practices; "caves" as sites of these practices represent the merger of Buddhism with popular beliefs. Springs also perform an important function in founder lore, but caves are definitely their core.

In the Nara period, agriculture became increasingly more important than hunting in terms of people's livelihoods, and burial mounds (*kofun*) gradually lost importance with the diffusion of Buddhism.[25] It was a time of great change, when imperial authority and a new political order were being established based on a novel worldview. Buddhism spread throughout the land, and a national policy envisioning Buddhism as state protector took shape around the *kokubunji* system of regional temples. Mountains became places of ascetic practice, where the forest tradition of Indian Buddhism and Chinese ideas about immortals (*shenxian* 神仙) merged. The practice began when Buddhist monks secluded themselves in the mountains to undertake ascetic training. The first instance of mountain/forest Buddhism supported by documentary evidence is the Jinenchi-shū 自然智宗, the school of Spontaneous Wisdom, based at Hisodera (also called "Genkōji") in Yoshino. The Chinese monk Daoxuan 道璿 (Dōsen, 702–20), who studied the Kegon school 華厳宗, and Shin'ei 神叡 (d. 737), who studied the Hossō school 法相宗 at Gangōji 元興寺, are recorded as having undertaken this practice. The school of Spontaneous Wisdom placed emphasis on the recitation of *dhāraṇī* and the *gumonjihō* 求聞求法, a ritual for attaining perfect memory, in order to become one with the unconditioned principle of the universe (Sonoda 1981). The early Hossō school had close links with mountain/forest asceticism, and it also included early esoteric elements of the type predating the transmission of the Shingon school by Kūkai 空海, known to scholarship as *zōmitsu* 雑密.[26] Kūkai as a young mountain practitioner encountered the *gumonjihō* in the Yoshino mountains,[27] and upon his return from China developed a mountain Buddhist practice that had Esoteric Buddhism at its core.

By contrast, the anti-authoritarian En no Ozunu 役小角 (later known as En no Gyōja, d. 701?) was a lay mountain practitioner based in the Katsuragi mountain range. He is mentioned in an entry in the *Shoku Nihongi* dated 699. Early on he is depicted as an adept of mountain practices with few Buddhist elements. However, from the mid-Kamakura period (1192–1333), his Buddhist identity was emphasized and he came to be venerated as the founder of Shugendō. Among monks, the role of Gyōki 行基 (668–749) of the Hossō school was significant in bridging the gap between authority (official state Buddhism) and anti-authority (heterodoxical practices) and overcoming state oppression of non-officially sanctioned practices (Augustine 2005).[28] He had also trained at Gangōji and undertaken practice in the mountains, and received popular support in his fundraising efforts for erecting the Great Buddha at Tōdaiji 東大寺 in 752. Many temples, both on mountains and plains, claim him as their founder,[29] and there is the possibility that lore concerning him as founder spread much earlier than that of En no Gyōja.[30] Lore concerning foundations by eminent monks developed widely following the establishment of temples on Mt. Hiei 比叡山 by Saichō 最澄 and on Mt. Kōya 高野山 by Kūkai early in the ninth century.

The next stage of the development of mountain religion saw the merging of founder lore with Shugendō. We should now discuss when En no Gyōja was mentioned in founder lore in general and when he specifically came to be considered the founder of Shugendō (see also Chapter Six by Carina Roth and Chapter Seven by Kawasaki Tsuyoshi). The progression by which he became firmly established as the founder of mountain practice, according to the historical record, was, in ritual terms in 1092,[31] in textual terms in 1257,[32] and iconographically in 1309.[33] According to Hasegawa Kenji, practices by *yamabushi* to attain noumenal powers (*genriki* 験力) were systematized sometime between the end of the thirteenth and the fourteenth centuries. The term *shugen*, which implied a positive value for *genriki*,[34] changed its meaning to refer to actions and process that led to its attainment. In *shugen* and *Shugendō* exo-esoteric Buddhism coexisted (Hasegawa 2016: 24–5, 258–9). Tokunaga Seiko argues that *shugen*, as the manifestation of noumenal power, came to refer to mountain practices in the twelfth century, and came to be seen as a "Way" (*dō* 道) after the mid-thirteenth century, as one component of exo-esoteric Buddhism (*kenmitsu Bukkyō* 顕密仏教) (Tokunaga 2003: 5). The transformation of En no Gyōja into the founder of Shugendō occurred in parallel with this process of change. The first document linking En no Gyōja and Zaō Gongen is the *Konjaku monogatarishū* (twelfth century), and the anecdote about the manifestation of Zaō Gongen to En no Gyōja appears in a number of works including the *Shasekishū* (1283),[35] the *Kinpusen himitsuden* (1337), and the *Kinpusen sōsōki* (fourteenth century). Thus, the lore about Zaō Gongen changed together with that about En no Gyōja between the thirteenth and fourteenth centuries (see also Chapter Ten by Fujioka Yutaka). We should also consider changes in terms such as *gagen* (臥験) and *yamabushi* (山伏, 山臥). The *Hikosan ruki* 彦山流記 (1213,

from Mt. Hiko) and the *Kenkōji ruki* 顕光寺流記 (1458, Mt. Togakushi) record the existence of ascetic practices in caves, even when both Mt. Hiko and Mt. Togakushi were controlled by Tendai and Shingon (see also Chapter Three by Caleb Carter). The relationship between the terms *gagen*, *yamabushi*, and *shugen* is not clear. *Tosō* (mountain asceticism) has a close connection with the monks Sōō 相応 (831–918) of Mt. Hiei and Shōbō 聖宝 (832–909) of Daigoji. During the Kamakura period founder cults spread, the exoteric-esoteric system became established, ascetic training in the mountains became organized, and Shugendō was systematized, leading in the fifteenth century to the development of Shugendō as a religious organization on its own with the formation of the Honzan-ha. The *En no Gyōja hongi* 役行者本記 (early sixteenth century?) is a voluminous work that commits much of the founder lore to writing.[36] As a result, legends spread all over the country linking En no Gyōja to the founding of local mountains. The unification of the legends about him from the fifteenth century on occurred on the background of the growth and expansion of the Honzan-ha.

Uno Enkū and Shugendō as an "Ethnic Religion"

It is often said that Shugendō is something unchanging and unique to Japan. Shugendō, banned in 1872, was looked upon with some nostalgia and its restoration, through historical reconstruction, only added to this tendency; there was a strong desire to save it so that it could survive. What is the basis for the discourse about Shugendō's unique Japaneseness? To answer this question we should look at why Shugendō came to be entangled with concepts such as "ethnic religion" (*minzoku shūkyō* 民族宗教), "ethnic culture" (*minzoku bunka* 民族文化), and "deep" or "fundamental culture" (*kisō bunka* 基層文化). Let us first consider the problems associated with the beginnings of academic research on Shugendō through an overview of the works of Uno Enkū 宇野圓空, Wakamori Tarō 和歌森太郎, Sakurai Tokutarō 櫻井徳太郎, Gorai Shigeru 五来重, and Murayama Shūichi 村山修一.

The first scholar in Japan to undertake an academic study of Shugendō was Uno Enkū (1885–1949). His graduation thesis at the Imperial University of Tokyo in 1910 was entitled "Shugendō in the Heian Period," which he published in expanded form in 1934 as *Shugendō*. His publisher, Tōhō shoin, had already put out the five-volume *Meiji Ishin shinbutsu bunri shiryōshū* (1926–9). Uno was a Jōdo Shinshū monk who had studied ethnology in Europe for three years. He returned to Japan in 1923, and in 1925 spent six months on a study trip to Southeast Asia. In the same year he published *Shūkyō jinruigaku no teishō* 宗教人類学の提唱 (A Proposal for the Anthropology of Religion), where he introduced Mgr. A. Bros and his "ethnologie religieuse" to a Japanese readership. He resigned his position as a professor at Ryūkoku University in 1926 to take up a lectureship at the Imperial University of Tokyo, where he became an associate professor the following year. He received his doctorate in 1934 and became a full professor in 1942, when he was also awarded the Imperial Prize of the Japan Academy. He was a professor in the Institute of Oriental Culture (Tōyō bunka kenkyūjo, now the Institute for Advanced Studies on Asia) at the Imperial

University of Tokyo and became its director in 1943. His most important publications were *Shūkyō minzokugaku* (Ethnology of Religion) in 1929[37] and *Maraisha ni okeru tōmai girei* (Rice-Planting Rituals in Malaysia) in 1941.[38] Uno developed the field of religious studies initially established by Anesaki Masaharu 姉崎正治 (1873–1949) by shifting from textual study to fieldwork and played an important role in repositioning it along a broad horizon that linked it with ethnology and comparative studies of foreign countries. He had assisted Anesaki when he set up the study of religion at the Imperial University of Tokyo in 1905 and was appointed the president of the Japanese Association for the Study of Religion (Nihon shūkyō gakkai) when it was founded in 1930. Like Akamatsu Chijō 赤松智城 (1886–1960), his scholarship was influenced by Bronislaw Malinowski and Émile Durkheim and was very interested in the cultural diffusion theory. He gradually moved from textual study to investigating actual conditions and from the 1930s moved toward the anthropology and sociology of religion (Chŏn 2008: 107–29). During the Second World War, he headed the Nanpō study group organized in 1942 at the Imperial University of Tokyo and published in the same year *Daitōa no minzoku to bunka* (Peoples and Culture of Great East Asia) through the Educational Department of the Ministry of Education. He was also involved in the translation and publication of ethnographies from the Solomon Islands, the Philippines, and other places, and collaborated in colonial policy, speaking, for example, of the guiding role of the "Japanese spirit" in the Great East Asia Co-prosperity Sphere. He highlighted the ethnic similarities between Japan and East and Southeast Asia, in their shared culture of rice cultivation and ancestor worship. His aim was to understand ethnic groups through religion. He regarded the "Japanese spirit" as a cultural principle different to the monotheism of Europe. During the war, he planned a spiritual uplift by promoting the "ethnic spirit" (*minzoku seishin* 民族精神) of all the peoples in Great East Asia. It underpinned the government-led "southern advance" in war (Ōsawa 2015) and aided the development of Japanese fascism by intellectuals.[39] In linking ethnology and religious studies, Uno was concerned with ethnic policy studies; with his student Sugiura Ken'ichi 杉浦健一 he helped providing an intellectual scaffolding for the emergence of the "Southern Co-prosperity Sphere" (*nanpō kyōeiken* 南方共栄圏). At the root of his thought was the idea of ethnicity (*minzoku* 民族). He used this term many times in his *Shugendō* (1934). Let us look at some examples (emphases by the author).

> Shugendō was formed as a group of practitioners of austerities (J. *zuda* 頭陀, Skt. *dhūta*) focused on concepts drawn from Buddhism, and Esoteric Buddhism in particular. These also included Chinese ideas which had become part of folk beliefs at the time. However, at the root were <u>ethnic beliefs and rituals (*minzokuteki no shinnen to girei*)</u> concerning mountains and forests. In this sense, while on the surface Shugendō was completely a stream of Buddhism, it was <u>a type of Buddhism that had become remarkably ethno-localized (*minzoku-ka sareta Bukkyō*)</u> and Shugendō was substantially accepted as a <u>Japanese type of religious ritual (*Nihonteki na shūkyōteki girei*)</u>. Its existence lay in its natural emergence as an ethnic religion (*minzokuteki na shūkyō* 民族的な宗教). (Uno 1934: 5)

Behind Shugendō's formation are many kami-buddha combinatory ideas. (Uno 1934: 6)

[Prior to the Kamakura Buddhism,] a large number [of its elements] had already been ethno-<u>localized (*minzoku-ka*)</u>, and did not derive from the new religious sects and schools [of the Kamakura period]. (Uno 1934: 6)

Being grounded in an ethnic religious consciousness (*minzokuteki shūkyō ishiki* 民族的の宗教意識) is the reason why Shugendō spread so ubiquitously as a religion for the common people. (Uno 1934: 6)

Shugendō was not simply a product of combinatory ideas, but was in fact permeated by them. Retroactively, it can be seen as the movement that gave rise to those ideas from the needs of actual practice. In this respect, it must be said that it played an important role in the development of the <u>national religious consciousness (*kokuminteki shūkyō ishiki*)</u>. (Uno 1934: 6)

Ethnic beliefs (*minzokuteki shinkō*) that are the source of faith are, more than anything else, the veneration of mountains and forests, and the original Shugen rituals are the products of that faith. (Uno 1934: 9–10)

The practice of various rituals concerning taboos and the removal of pollution, based on ideas of religious purity, is undoubtedly the most remarkable characteristic of our <u>ethnic religion (*minzokuteki shūkyō*)</u>. (Uno 1934: 9)

These examples may be summarized as follows. Shugendō is a set of Japanese religious rituals (*Nihonteki na shūkyōteki girei*) and a type of Buddhism that has become ethno-localized (*minzoku-ka sareta Bukkyō*), grounded in ethnic beliefs (*minzokuteki shinkō*), namely, veneration of mountains and forests. It is based on combinatory religious ideas (*shūgō shisō*) under the influence of Esoteric Buddhism. It is an ethnic religion (*minzokuteki shūkyō*) that places emphasis on ritual and practice. At its core is the ethnic spirit (*minzoku seishin*), through which it played an important role in the development of a national religious consciousness (*kokuminteki shūkyō ishiki*).

The word *minzoku* (民族) came to be used in Japan in the context of nationalism. The first example of its use in this way dates from 1878, in the *Tokumei zenken taishi Bei-ō kairan jikki* 特命全権大使米欧回覧実記 (A true account of the observations of the ambassadors plenipotentiary of America and Europe) edited by Kume Kunitake (1839–1931).[40] The term later appears in Tokutomi Sohō 徳富蘇峰's (1863–1957) news magazine *Kokumin no tomo* 国民の友 (The People's Friend, 1887) and in Miyake Setsurei's 三宅雪嶺 *Shinzenbi Nihonjin* 真善美日本人 (Truth, Goodness, and Beauty of the Japanese People, 1891). Its political implications were strengthened when it was used as a translation of the English "nation."[41] In the wake of its victory in the Sino-Japanese War (1884–85), Japan was drawn into the "Yellow Peril" discourse. The theory of the inequality of the races, propounded by Count Joseph Arthur de Gobineau (1816–82), gave rise to a lively debate about racial superiority or inferiority, and Mori Ōgai 森鷗外 (1862–1922) published a refutation of the idea of the Yellow Peril.⁴² After the Russo-Japanese War (1904–5), the term "Yamato minzoku" (大和民族) appeared in Tokutomi Sohō's *Kōjin no omoni* 黄人の重荷 (The yellow man's burden), contributing to the strengthening of nationalism. The concept of *minzoku* spread in the time between the Sino-Japanese and Russo-Japanese Wars, when awareness of the outside world grew stronger, and, through the activities of enlightened thinkers, it came to express a Japanese type of nationalism that was mixed with a reaction to the concept of race. This gave rise to a growth in Japanese national consciousness, which saw its foreign colonies as ethnically heterogenous and the Japanese mainland as ethnically homogenous.⁴³ The increase in the number of its subjects as the territory of the Empire of Japan grew bred the awareness of the existence of multiethnic groups.

The original of Uno's *minzoku* was the German word *Ethnos*. With a strong connotation of cultural bonding, it was influenced by the idea of Kulturkreis (culture field) as developed by Wilhelm Schmidt (1868–1954) and the Vienna school of ethnology.⁴⁴ The publication of a Japanese translation by Oka Masao of an article by Wilhelm Schmidt and Wilhelm Koppers entitled "The Purpose of Ethnology" in the first issue of the journal *Minzoku* (1925–9), edited by Oka and Yanagita Kunio, was very important for the establishment of ethnology (*Minzokugaku*) as an academic field in Japan. Here *minzoku* corresponded to the German *Ethnos*.⁴⁵ Contributors to the journal took an interdisciplinary stance, conflating *minzokugaku* 民族学 (ethnology), *minzokugaku* 民俗学 (folklore), and *jinruigaku* (anthropology, particularly natural anthropology).⁴⁶ Oka Masao had a deep interest in social movements and believed that ethnic groups were at their base, leading him to advocate the study of ethnology (*Minzokugaku*); later, he attempted to understand the basic structure of Japanese culture. Uno's *Shūkyō minzokugaku* (Yaesu Shobō, 1929), *Shugendō* (1934), and *Minzoku seishin no shūkyōmen* (1935)⁴⁷ were published amid these mutual exchanges among scholars.⁴⁸ *Shūkyō minzokugaku* is Uno's most important work, with its approach that compares agricultural and funerary rituals and concepts about the soul among so-called primitive ethnic groups, as well as a new way of looking at Japan from the outside. Uno's understanding of Shugendō as an "ethnic religion" (*minzoku shūkyō* 民族宗教) was in a sense his application of "ethnologie religieuse" to Japan. The 1920s and 1930s, when Uno published his works, was a time when various academic disciplines took form and developed through academic associations. *Nihon Shūkyō Gakkai* (Japanese Association for Religious Studies) was established in 1930, *Nihon Minzoku Gakkai* 日本民族学会 (Japanese Society of Ethnology)⁴⁹ in 1934, and *Minkan Denshō no kai* 民間伝承の会 (now *Nihon Minzoku Gakkai* 日本民俗学会, Folklore Society of Japan) in 1935. After this, ethnology and folklore gradually drew apart.⁵⁰ Uno Enkū was associated with these three academic associations and performed the role as a bridge among them.

Uno's study of Shugendō with *minzoku* (Ethnos) as its keyword remained a pioneering work and was in a sense the prehistory of the field; research began in earnest after this book was published. In this regard, Kihira Tadayoshi's *Nihon seishin* (The Japanese spirit), published at this time, also exerted a great influence on Shugendō studies.

Wakamori Tarō, "Japanese Fascism," and the Study of Shugendō

Until now there has been a lack of attention for the extent to which the concept of *minzoku* (Ethnos) has been used in Shugendō studies; in particular, there has been no consideration at all as to why such discipline emerged during the war period. The first proper study of Shugendō was Wakamori Tarō's *Shugendōshi kenkyū* 修験道史研究 (A study of the history of Shugendō, Kawade Shobō, 1943).[51] This work is highly regarded for placing Shugendō in an historical context;[52] however, Wakamori also makes an extensive use of *minzoku* 民族 as is clear from the following examples (emphases by the author).

> Cultural history, covering both the fundamental and superficial layers of culture (*kisō bunka* 基層文化, *hyōsō bunka* 表層文化), vividly expresses the specific characteristics of ethnic culture (*minzoku bunka* 民族文化). (Wakamori 1972: 296)

> [It] is a manifestation of the ethnic culture (*minzoku bunka*), shaped by Japanese culture as a whole. (Wakamori 1972: 299)

> [Its] uniqueness was most significantly manifested in medieval society. (Wakamori 1972: 299)

> What might be called an unheroic ethnic religion (*minzoku shūkyō* 民族宗教), such as Shugendō. (Wakamori 1972: 300)

> Shugendō is significant in that it is characterized by a mutual enforcing relationship with the features possessed by the Japanese ethnic group (*Nihon minzoku* 日本民族). (Wakamori 1972: 303)

> With the promotion of *Nihonshugi* (Japanism, Japanese nationalism) and the ethnic awareness movement (*minzoku jikaku undō* 民族自覚運動), heightened during a time of war, [people] are paying attention to the pilgrimages (*tosō*) and ascetic practices (*kugyō*) on the mountains characteristic of Shugendō, and there is an emphasis on its devout religiosity. (Wakamori 1972: 306)

Wakamori's work, published in 1943, reflects the situation under the wartime regime and recognizes the influence of "ethnic awakening" through emphasis on Japanism (*Nihonshugi*). The mental and physical discipline of Shugendō, like that of the military, was highly estimated, built as it was on the three pillars of pilgrimage, asceticism, and religiosity.[53] The influence here of *Nihon seishin* (The Japanese Spirit), a 1930 work of Kihira Tadayoshi, is very evident. Wakamori's division of ethnic culture into fundamental and surface layers is based on the theory of the German folklorist Hans Naumann (1886–1951);[54] and he understood Shugendō as an "ethnic religion" situated at the point of contact between fundamental and surface culture. As a whole, Wakamori followed in Uno Enkū's footsteps.

The influence of group mountain climbing as an educational activity introduced during Japan's modernization is also a factor for the attention paid to Shugendō during the war. The Movement for General Mobilization of National Spirit (*Kokumin seishin sōdōin undō* 国民精神総動員運動) was inaugurated in 1937 to cultivate the Japanese spirit and train the Japanese people in both mind and body, and the Railway, Education, and Health Ministries encouraged walking trips and mountain climbing.[55] The development of tourism was also linked to total war, and the attention paid to Shugendō in it was part of the same phenomenon. When the National Mobilization Law was enacted in 1938, mountain climbing came under the umbrella of the Marching and Alpine Division of the Great Japan Sports Association. It was considered part of combat training and was promoted for the purpose of marching practice and physical training. In terms of ideology, the influence of *Kokutai no hongi* 国体の本義 (Fundamentals of Our National Polity), published by the Department of Education in 1937, was great.

Published the same year as Wakamori's *Shugendōshi kenkyū* and of equal importance is Murakami Toshio's *Shugendō no hattatsu* 修験道の発達 (1943). It was a pioneering work that placed Shugendō within the framework of Shingon Esoteric Buddhism. Murakami had studied with Uno Enkū, and in his preface he wrote, placing himself firmly in Uno's line of thought, "The ethnic spirit of the Japanese people works richly in Shugendō, an ethnic religion made in Japan (*kokusan no shūkyō*)" (Murakami 1978: 4–5). Murakami had graduated from the Imperial University of Tokyo in 1930 and then worked as an official in the Religious Affairs Bureau of the Department of Education, where he was assigned work concerning the administration of religious and educational policy. During the war he was sent to China and Southeast Asia, where he performed similar tasks. In this sense, Murakami can be seen as putting Uno's theories into practice in the field.[56]

What is noticeable here is the correlation with the times. Why was it was possible to publish in 1943, under wartime conditions, two academic works about Shugendō?[57] The print run for Wakamori's book was 1,500 copies, and for Murakami's 2,000. Murayama Shūichi, who was to study the history of Shugendō in the postwar period, also published his first work, *Shinbutsu shūgō to Nihon bunka* (Kōbundō Shobō—Kōryō bunko, 1942) at this time.[58] The reason that paper was made available to publish works about Shugendō is probably because Shugendō was thought to be highly appropriate for inspiring the "Japanese spirit."

Publications relevant to our discussion here were not just limited to Shugendō. Around the same time, Yanagita Kunio's *Nihon no matsuri* (Kōbundō 1942) had a print run of 5,000 copies[59] and Matsudaira Narimitsu's *Matsuri* (Nikkō Shoin 1943) had one of 2,000 copies.[60] In the number of copies printed, we can detect an intention to educate the masses. *Matsuri*, the journal of the Sairei kenkyūkai (part of the research center of the Tokyo University Library) which Matsudaira directed, continued to be published between 1941 and 1944 (Nos. 1–21). Uno, who continued compiling ethnographies and making translations in those areas of Southeast Asia occupied by the Japanese army, had two books republished in 1944, namely, *Shūkyō minzokugaku* (Yaesu Shobō) and *Maraisha ni okeru tōmai girei* (Nikkō Shoin).[61] Studies of Shugendō and folk beliefs were considered to fortify the Japanese spirit and promote the awakening of national unity and ethnic consciousness. The understanding of Ethnos (*minzoku* 民族) through religion in Uno's *Shūkyō minzokugaku* was used during the war to awaken the "ethnic" (民族) or "national" (国民) spirit of the "Japanese Ethnos."[62] Such studies were considered to conform to the regime of total war.

The discourse that supported total war was "Japanism" (*Nihonshugi* 日本主義). The Japanese spiritualism at its core can also be termed "Japanese fascism." It appeared in the late 1920s and early 1930s as a discourse of patriotism and civic nationalism (*kokuminshugi* 国民主義) in an attempt to forcibly construct the identity of Japanese society (Hayashi 2010: 34). In a condition of total war from the 1930s, all possible resources were used to mobilize the Japanese for the war effort. In *Nihon ideorogīron* (*Japanese Ideology*; Hakuyōsha 1935), the Marxist philosopher Tosaka Jun (1900–45) wrote that the term "Japanese spirit," widely circulating since the Manchurian (Mukden) incident of 1931, was an element of Japanese fascism, emotional, lacking any consistent logic, and difficult to define.[63] Fascism came rapidly to the forefront after the Manchurian Incident, and Japanism was part of it. Authors who discussed Japanism included the Hegelian philosopher Kihira Tadayoshi, the right-wing literary critic and journalist Takasu Yoshijirō (1880–1948), the founder of the Buddhist commune Mugaen, Itō Shōshin (1876–1963), the scholar of classical Chinese Yasuoka Masahiro (1898–1983), and the philosopher of pan-Asianism Kanokogi Kazunobu (1884–1949). Kihira, a central figure in this group, presented his argument in *Nihon seishin* and *Chi to gyō* 知と行 ("Knowledge and Action," Kōbundō Shobō, 1936), arguing that "at the basis of both Japanese mythology and the various religions imported into Japan there is the true essence of the soul of the Japanese people, the 'Japanese spirit'" (Gorai 1977: 589).[64] Gorai Shigeru, who was later involved in Shugendō research, was fascinated by Kihira's lectures on Hegelian philosophy, which had a great influence on his subsequent studies. Another author, who was a student at that time and later developed the study of popular beliefs (*minkan shinkō* 民間信仰), and also married the daughter of Yanagita Kunio, was Hori Ichirō 堀一郎 (1910–74). The Institute for National Spiritual Culture (Kokumin seishin bunka kenkyūjo 国民精神文化研究所, 1932–45),[65] established by the Japanese government under the direct control of the Ministry of Education, became the center of the discourse on "Japanese spirit" and the "national spirit" of Japan. Kihira was a member of the institute and continued his research there. The institute played a core role in the publication of *Kokutai no hongi* (Fundamentals of our National Polity) by the Ministry of Education in 1937, which commissioned its scholars for the compilation.[66] Hori Ichirō joined the Institute in 1939 and worked under Kihira;[67] he wrote works extolling the Japanese spirit[68] and ethnographies about foreign cultures.[69] Following the outbreak of the Second Sino-Japanese War in 1937, the National Spiritual Mobilization Movement (*Kokumin seishin sōdōin undō*) was announced in August of that year. The role of the Institute for National Spiritual Culture was very important in producing a discourse that became pervasive among the people. Its influence extended to shrine festivals and to memorial services for temple founders.

If we consider as the starting point of Japanese fascism the annexation of Korea by Japan in 1910, we can see, from the viewpoint of intellectual history, each following decade to be a step in a series of changes: the annexation in 1910, the erection of Meiji Shrine in 1920, the publication of *Nihon seishin* in 1930, and the celebrations marking

2,600 years of imperial rule in 1940. Japanese nationalism strengthened in stages and became more radical. The political use of Shugendō occurred in the last stage, the high point of Japanese fascism, when attempts were made to employ it to unify the spirit of the masses. At its basis was state control and discipline of body and mind.

Establishing Shugendō Studies: Hori Ichirō, Gorai Shigeru, Miyake Hitoshi

The Institute for National Spiritual Culture was disbanded after the end of the war, but it was from among people connected with it that research into mountain beliefs and practices subsequently began. The Sangaku shinkō kenkyūkai was formed and published a number of monographs through the publisher Jinja shinpōsha, including *Nihon ni okeru sangaku shinkō no kōkogaku kōsatsu* (Archaeological study of Japanese mountain cults) by Ōba Iwao in 1958, *Nihon ni okeru sangaku shinkō no genshō keitai* (Primordial forms of mountain cults in Japan) by Hori Ichirō, *Sangaku shinkō to jinja* (Mountain cults and shrines) by Miyaji Naokazu, and *Nihon ni okeru sangaku shinkō no rekishi* (History of mountain cults in Japan) by Higo Kazuo, all in 1959. Hori Ichirō had become a central figure in the group and published two compilations of his work, *Minkan shinkō* (Popular beliefs) in 1951 and *Waga kuni minkan shinkō rekishi no kenkyū* (Studies in the history of popular beliefs in Japan) in 1953. He preferred the term *minkan shinkō* 民間信仰 (popular beliefs) to *minzoku shūkyō* 民俗宗教 (folk religion); still, he veered towards religious studies, incorporating ideas of Mircea Eliade and Robert N. Bellah (1927–2013) (the English translation of his work used the term "folk religion").[70]

Research on mountain beliefs and practices had begun before the war with the theory of ascetic training by Kishimoto Hideo (1903–64), then based in the Religious Studies Research Centre at the Imperial University of Tokyo, and was further enriched by the studies of, among others, Hori Ichirō on folk beliefs, Yanagawa Keiichi (1926–90) on religious confraternities (*kō*), Miyake Hitoshi 宮家準 (1933–) on Shugendō rituals and the theory of folk religion, Sakurai Tokutarō (1917–2007) on *kō* groups and female shamans, and Miyata Noboru 宮田登 (1936–2000) on spheres of belief. Miyake Hitoshi published *Shugendō girei no kenkyū* (Studies in Shugendō ritual) in 1971, followed by comprehensive studies of Shugendō ritual, thought, organization and regional development. Shugendō by then had become an academic field of its own. The formation of an academic network with the establishment of the Sangaku Shugen Gakkai 山岳修験学会 in 1980 (it became a nationwide association in 1984) and the collection of documentary sources through the publication of the eighteen-volume *Sangaku shūkyōshi kenkyū sōsho* 山岳宗教研究叢書 (Meichō shuppan, 1975–84) resulted in a thriving research environment that cast the legacy of Japanese fascism into oblivion.

Gorai Shigeru had been interested in the combinatory relations between Buddhism and folklore since before the war, and transitioned from Buddhist folklore studies to research on Shugendō. Gorai had been a student at the Imperial University of Tokyo at the same time as Hori Ichirō. He studied Indian philosophy and Buddhist Studies. His antipathy toward doctrinal Buddhism brought him to formulate his own theory of Buddhist folklore and the Buddhism of the common people out of his interest for folk Buddhism that had developed independently of sects. His study of Shugendō was an extension of this interest.[71] Buddhism, Gorai said, was a tolerant religion, with its own individual beliefs and culture. He wrote: "Only the outer garments of folk customs were changed by Buddhism; they were able to survive unchanged down to the present. [...] Buddhist folk customs are a valuable folkloric patrimony once the outer garment of Buddhism is removed" (Gorai 2007: 12). Gorai argued that the study of folk Buddhism facilitated the understanding of Japan's "ethnic culture." As Buddhism was accepted by people in the provinces, an "indigenization" had to occur together with its combination with the "ethnic religion" (*minzoku shūkyō*) of Japan (Gorai 2007: 126). Gorai was an essentialist, strongly influenced by Yanagita Kunio. However, he said that it was impossible to construct a theory of a "unique religiosity" that excluded Buddhism, as Yanagita had done, and placed great importance on actual, lived Buddhism in his attempt to separate out the "native religion" at its root. Kihira's influence persisted in Gorai's sympathy for the common people's way of life.

We should note here that the use of terms such as "ethnic culture" (*minzoku bunka*) and "ethnic religion" (*minzoku shūkyō*) continued into the postwar period. After the war, Wakamori Tarō switched his interest from history to folklore studies, from Shugendō to folklore in general, and from "ethnic culture" to "fundamental culture" (Ōtsuka minzoku gakkai 1972), seeing folk studies as "the academic field that investigates the character and essence of the fundamental culture of an ethnic group."[72] His student Sakurai Tokutarō also made "the spiritual and religious history of the Japanese ethnic group" the subject of his research in a work from 1962, "Kō shūdan seiritsu katei no kenkyū" (A study of the process of formation of *kō* associations) (Sakurai 1998: 10). At first, he used the term *minkan shinkō* (popular beliefs) extensively to refer to "people's everyday beliefs that grew up among indigenous populations living in local communities," but later he dedicated himself to the study of shamanism. Sakurai did not question what such "unique religiosity" was, but rather sought to define "ethnic religion" as the arena where the "combination" (*shūgō*) between the fundamental and surface layers of Japanese culture took place. As we can see, Ethnos was always at the core of his interests.

"Folk religion" is a central theme for Miyake Hitoshi, which he understands within the framework of the opposite concepts of "founder religion" and "natural religion." The former tends toward world religions, while the latter toward ethnic religion. "Ethnic religion" and "world religion"[73] are used here as contrasting concepts from the field of religious studies (Miyake 1994: 28–9). Here, "folk religion" is that domain where folk beliefs and combinatory religion mix in complex ways. Of central importance is who is involved with them: common people (*jōmin* 常民) in the case of folk beliefs and popular religious figures in the case of combinatory religion. Miyake's main focus is folk religion as the site of a complex interplay between these two types of religiosity, and his Shugendō studies are an extension of this. This approach represents a change from the "ethnic religion" of Uno and his successors. Miyake went beyond any vestige of prewar "Japanese fascism" and established Shugendō studies based on objectivity as an academic field.

The Creation of a Different History

The study of Shugendō and mountain beliefs and practices is now at an important turning point in Japan. Scholars address many topics related to them in fields such as history, archaeology, literature, performing arts, and religious history, but, in fact, the general study of mountain beliefs per se is in rapid decline and is becoming a thing of the past. People are even forgetting that many mountains all over Japan were the focus of belief. Many mountain confraternity (*kō*) members are aging and they are not being replaced by a new generation due to falling birth numbers. Confraternities without a leader or a *sendatsu* are in danger of extinction. Shugendō and mountain cults have changed radically in the modern period, due first of all to the collapse of a broad spectrum of political, economic, social, and cultural connections as a consequence of *shinbutsu bunri*. A second factor was the introduction of modern values, and particularly changes in people's religious consciousness that resulted from an emphasis on economic growth. Maintaining ritual purity as a prerequisite for climbing a sacred mountain and observance of taboos associated with sacred places have rapidly declined. A third element is the rise of alpinism and mountain climbing for sport, with a consequent loss of interest in the history of mountain cults. Finally, the development of motorization brought about a decline in pilgrimage to sacred mountains. This is, in fact, a crucial development. Railways contributed to the reinvigoration of mountain-based cults by connecting populated areas with the base of mountains, but the construction of motor roads, ropeways, and cable cars in the mountains[74] led to the destruction of the old pilgrim paths, and villages that provided lodgings and guides (*oshi*) fell into decay. Customs related to mountain pilgrimage, such as staying in lodgings (*shukubō*) run by religious specialists associated with the mountain, undertaking purification, wearing special attire, participating in rituals, chanting sacred texts, and ascending the mountain under the guidance of the *sendatsu*, have steadily fallen into abeyance, and the networks and infrastructure associated with them have broken down. Climbing sacred mountains as a religious practice continued until around the mid-1960s, but the rapid economic growth after that time altered people's thinking and behavior; their values changed completely.

The tragic eruption of Mt. Ontake on September 27, 2014, was a crucial event. Kiso Ontake was, with Mt. Ishizuchi in Shikoku, a center of living mountain beliefs, but it is possible that the eruption will cause its rapid decline. Even now, restrictions remain in place that forbid people access to the summit.

Mountain climbing for pleasure began in Japan in 1874 when the Englishmen William Gowland (1842–1922),[75] R. W. Atkinson (1850–1929), and Ernest Satow (1843–1929) climbed Mt. Rokkō in Kobe. The Japanese Alpine Club was founded in 1905, but mountain climbing tended to be the preserve of the wealthy and of intellectuals. The first mountain climbing "boom" in Japan was triggered by the ascent in 1956 of the Nepalese mountain Manaslu by an expedition led by Maki Yūkō (1894–1989). Mountain climbing became popular among people in the 1960s, at the height of the period of high economic growth, and continued into the mid-1970s, spurred by the participation of university climbing clubs and regular people. In this connection, the publication of *Nihon hyaku meisan* (One hundred famous mountains of Japan) by Fukuda Kyūya (Shinchōsha 1964) was also very influential. The second boom came around 1990, when the people who had enjoyed climbing during the first boom, now in their middle age, returned to the mountains with their friends and took new pleasure in this activity (Koizumi 2001). A third boom began in 2007, when mountain climbing became fashionable among the young, in addition to its continuing popularity among the middle-aged and senior people.[76] Motorization had, however, turned mountains into tourist and leisure spots, causing mountain pilgrimages to decline and the old beliefs and practices to be forgotten.

However, what triggered a resurgence in interest in mountain beliefs was the UNESCO World Heritage program, which began in 1972 with the World Heritage Convention. Japan was the last of the developed countries to join it in 1992, and then began to inscribe properties on the World Heritage List. In the post–Cold War world, Japan switched its international relations stance toward "cultural diplomacy" and considered UNESCO World Heritage as a means to do so. The Japanese politics of culture began in earnest. As the World Heritage List grew, it also included mountains, roads, and sites associated with Shugendō and mountain cults. The inclusion of the temples and shrines in Nikkō in 1999 was not particularly remarkable, but interest in sacred mountains increased with the UNESCO Thematic Expert Meeting on Asia-Pacific Sacred Mountains held in Wakayama in 2001 (Yamamoto 2010: 96). In 2004, with the listing of the "Sacred sites and pilgrimage routes in the Kii mountain range" (including Mt. Ōmine Okugake and Kumano Kodō routes), Mt. Kōyasan, Kumano, and Mt. Ōmine, all associated with mountain beliefs, became World Heritage sites. Dispute, however, arose about the listing as a World Heritage site of an area still enforcing women exclusion (Suzuki 2002).

The World Heritage program has three components, namely, cultural, natural, and mixed (both cultural and natural), and listing is dependent on "outstanding universal value," predicated on the idea of "cultural value." What is considered "world heritage" is, however, gradually changing. Since a large number of items on the original list were properties associated with Christianity, there was a certain bias toward the northern hemisphere. In an effort to overcome this north–south cultural divide, the idea of "cultural landscape" was introduced in 1992 (Suzuki 2015a). As a result, the number of Japanese sites on the UNESCO list increased rapidly. In 2013, "Mt. Fuji, sacred place and source of artistic inspiration" was listed as cultural heritage. This new value given to beliefs and traditions drew attention to mountain pilgrimage customs and practices (see Chapter Eleven by Janine Sawada), shrines and temples at the foot of the mountain, and villages of *oshi* (pilgrim guides). Okinoshima island, which bans women and subjects men to various taboos, was listed in 2017, bringing to the fore a growing concern about the relation of religious beliefs and cultural heritage.[77] Promotion of world heritage registration continues in Japan, supported by both public and private sectors, as a matter of national prestige, in a marked trend toward cultural nationalism. However, the idea of the "cultural" has changed, and we may ask whom does "culture" belong to.

Separate from its World Heritage program, UNESCO began registering intangible cultural properties in 2001. Designation criteria changed in 2009,[78] after which performing arts associated with Shugendō and mountain beliefs have been listed

(Hayachine kagura in 2009, Nachi dengaku in 2012). Shugendō and mountain cults are being re-evaluated as cultural resources, and since 2000 they have rapidly become objectified as such, with the consequence that initiatives to turn them into heritage sites and tourist spots have increased. UNESCO's concept of heritage has been used to maximum effect in rural revitalization schemes for local communities (*chiiki okoshi* and *chiiki kasseika*).

In Japan, a number of sacred mountains and sites associated with Shugendō and other practices have been made objects of protection and conservation as cultural assets. Among them are nationally designated sites deemed of high value either historically or academically and identified by the government as requiring protection. Places associated with mountain beliefs so designated include Mt. Hōman, Mt. Hiko, Mt. Shura, Mt. Isurogi, Kumano sanzan, Mt. Kongō, Mt. Mitoku, Mt. Chōkai, and the Awa pilgrimage trail. The category of "important cultural landscape" was added to the law protecting cultural properties in 2005 and designation of sites began the following year. The purpose is to identify the cultural value of landscapes, protect and preserve them, so as to ensure their future survival. Mt. Kubote and Mt. Kosuge are also included in the list. Additionally, the *shukubō machi* (pilgrim lodging districts) and *monzenmachi* (urban settlements at the gates of the temple/shrine) of Mt. Togakushi, Sakamoto at the foot of Mt. Hiei, and Shiramine below Mt. Hakusan have been recognized as important conservation districts for their traditional buildings. Important intangible folk cultural properties include the Yamakita Mineiri, the Oku Misawa Hana Matsuri, the Shōreisai of Mt. Haguro, and the Ogatsu Hōin Kagura (Ishinomaki). Thus, Shugendō and mountain beliefs and practices have come to be valued as part of "traditional culture." In 2015 the Agency for Cultural Affairs began the "Japan Heritage" program, giving recognition to "stories based on unique regional histories and traditions" with the aim of "revitalizing local communities through comprehensive maintenance and utilization of tangible and intangible cultural properties and their strategic promotion in Japan and overseas." The plan is to designate one hundred such sites by the time of the Tokyo Olympics in 2020. The program brings together tangible and intangible cultural properties and combines the transmission of knowledge with the promotion of tourism. Localities must create a story when applying for recognition. A "story" associated with mountain beliefs and practices selected in 2015 combines Mt. Mitoku in Tottori, famous for its Heian-period Nageiri-dō enshrining a statue of Zaō Gongen, and Misasa Onsen under the title "A site for the purification and healing of the six senses of perception: Japan's most dangerous national treasure and a world-famous radon hot spring." Also selected were Dewa Sanzan (its story is "A journey to rebirth amid the sacred nature of Dewa Sanzan") and the Shikoku pilgrimage ("Shikoku pilgrimage: Circular pilgrimage route and unique pilgrimage culture"). Sites added in 2016 include Ōyama in Sagami ("Isehara city and the Mt. Ōyama pilgrimage: A destination for worship and leisure of Edo commoners") and Hōki Daisen ("Daisen Gyūba Ichi: Japan's largest livestock market born from the worship of Bodhisattva Jizō"). Each locality is creating a modern-sounding catchphrase with a new story—a different history. Many such histories are being born.

Toward the Future

A big development occurred in 2016, when the government of Japan designated August 11 as a national holiday under the name of "Mountain Day." The legislation stated that the holiday was to provide "opportunities to become familiar with mountains and appreciate the benefits we receive from them." Then-Crown Prince Naruhito (now reigning emperor) contributed an article to *Sangaku*, the journal of the Japanese Alpine Club, entitled "Rekishi to shinkō no yama wo tazunete" (Visiting mountains that are sites of history and worship) in 2016 (Naruhito 2016: 7–36). Mountain beliefs were familiar to the prince, who had studied the history of medieval Japanese transportation, and he wrote of his memories of more than twenty-five years' experience climbing over 170 mountains. Boards commemorating his visits have been erected by local enthusiasts and many of these mountains are now becoming new sacred sites. The first national Mountain Day ceremony was held at Kamikōchi in 2016 and the second at Nasu in 2017; the third took place at Hōki Daisen in 2018. Naruhito and his family attended the first. The 2018 meeting of the Nihon Sangaku Shugen Gakkai was held at Hōki Daisen and there is a strong possibility that the mountains chosen in the future for the national Mountain Day ceremonies will be sites associated with mountain beliefs. This will perhaps result in the association of sacred mountains with national discourse. Hōki Daisen celebrated its 1300th anniversary in 2018 and held large-scale events, including the Mountain Day ceremony and the Nihon Sangaku Shugen Gakkai meeting.[79] The mountain website states: "In 2018 Daisen, the acclaimed peak of Tottori prefecture, commemorates the 1300th anniversary of the founding of the temple Daisenji. Communities at its base, tourist and economic groups will join forces to launch the 'Daisen 1300' festivities."[80] Its advertising uses the catchphrase "Japan's oldest sacred mountain, mentioned in the *Izumo fudoki*" and states that "Daisenji was founded in the eighth century and its history is older than the *Izumo fudoki* and the *Nihon shoki*." The website indeed contains a chronology of this history.[81] Daisen represents a typical case of the production of alternative history. The legend about the mountain's opening has been turned into a factual event. We live at a time when mountain beliefs and practices have been appropriated by local governments and the media, utilized as resources, objectified and broadly appropriated.

In 2017, the 1300th anniversary of the founding of Hakusan was celebrated in various locations. Special events were held at the mountain trails leading to the summit from the ancient provinces of Echizen, Kaga, and Mino, and at Shirahamahime Shrine (in Kaga Banba), Eisenji Hakusan Shrine (in Echizen Banba), Nagataki Hakusan Shrine (at Mino Banba), and the nearby Natadera, among others.[82] According to the Hakusan city website, the events aimed at

> look[ing] again at the long 1300-year history [of the mountain] in order to pass on to future generations the important historical, cultural, and environmental legacy bequeathed by our ancestors. We are engaged in deepening the understanding and appreciation of Hakusan through interaction and cooperation among citizens.[83]

As we can see, the main purpose of these events was community revitalization. The main activities included climbing the mountain while wearing a *tasuki* (July 1), having climbers return water to the mountain (July to mid-October), exhibitions of national treasures and important cultural properties, and commemorative trips. Among the souvenirs we find bike stickers and magnet sheets with the Hakusan logo. Shirahamahime Shrine began its preparations in 2015, running events almost every month, with the main ones centering on the 1300th anniversary of Hakusan.[84] Activities included publications, commemorative climbing of Hakusan, special exhibitions of sacred images, folk performing arts, and lectures. Of special interest was the completion in May 2017 of an animated film commemorating the anniversary based on the founding legend. *The Story of Taichō* can be viewed in three parts on the shrine's website. No kami names appear, other than *megami* (goddess). The entire tale is based faithfully on Buddhist *engi* literature: the tale of Fuseri no Gyōja and Kiyosada Gyōja, the story of a bowl made to fly by mystical power, and the appearance of a nine-headed dragon. In its atmosphere, it closely resembles the program *Manga Nihon mukashi banashi* (Japanese Tales of Long Ago, Animated), made for television in 1975. In the film we also find a modern introduction to the Hakusan Shrine and a "hymn to Hakusan." In addition, Hoshi Yoshiki of the group Himegami composed a musical suite entitled "Hakusan" to commemorate the anniversary, consisting of three movements: "Hakurei tenshō" (The White Mountain Shines), "Miare" (The Deity Appears), and "Shingen no mori" (The Awe-inspiring Forest-Shrine). Shinto influence is clear in these titles. It is significant to note in this respect that buddhas and kami are differentiated even in media usage. Animation is well suited to represent the founding legend, and this overlaps with the popularity of anime pilgrimage guides to sacred places. We live in an age when people will perhaps climb Hakusan attracted by the anime version of Taichō's founding legend, with which they feel a deep familiarity. The active promotion of events connected to the founding of mountains in recent years may herald the advent of a "post-modern Shugendō" that exploits virtual reality and the media.

Mountain beliefs are increasingly used as cultural and tourist resources. The proclamation of "Mountain Day" as a national holiday may signal the arrival of a time when these old beliefs and practices come to be considered the root of Japanese culture, a time when modern people living in an advanced economy think again about their lifestyle and their relationship with nature. A common characteristic of modern life is that terms related to sacred sites have become fashionable words and are compounded with expressions about cultural heritage. They include a spate of katakana words derived from English, such as "spiritual landscape," "power spot," "ecopark," and "geopark."[85] Modern representations are hybrids: what looks at first glance like something ancient is expressed in terms of a foreign culture and terminology. The continuity of Japanese culture is being supported by skillfully changing its outer cover to adapt it to new circumstances. The imaginative power of hybridity is at the root of Japanese culture and is the potential for its continuity.[86]

Part Two

Constructed Topologies and Invented Chronologies

2

Shugendō within Japanese Buddhism: Considerations on the Formation of Shugendō

Hasegawa Kenji
Translation by Carina Roth

My intention in this chapter is to reflect upon the formation of Shugendō from a historical point of view and method. Based on the analysis of concrete historical materials, I argue first that Shugendō needs to be positioned within the development of Japanese Buddhism (exo-esoteric Buddhism) and its temples. Second, I argue that the Japanese medieval period, especially the end of the thirteenth and the fourteenth centuries, should be understood as a transitional period for the formation of Shugendō. A discussion of this religious movement's formation process is necessary because of the nature of the historiography surrounding the understanding of what Shugendō is. The academic understanding of Shugendō to this day can be broadly divided into two types of discourse.

The first type of discourse is the theory of historical formation. Nowadays widely accepted, it started long ago with Wakamori Tarō's classical studies (Wakamori 1972 [1943]). Today, this stance is represented by the foremost scholar in Shugendō studies, Miyake Hitoshi (Miyake 1996, 1999a, 1999b). It sees Shugendō as a religion based on ancient Japanese mountain cults, which took shape at the end of the Heian period under the influence of shamanism, Buddhism, Daoism, and Shinto. Its specificities include the pragmatic character of mountain practice, the emphasis on worldly benefits acquired through incantations, the absence of a clearly defined founder, and the fact that Shugendō is managed by *yamabushi* 山伏/山臥. Chronologically, this phenomenon began as a primitive mountain cult, evolved as mountain practice embedded in early Japanese Buddhism, and molded itself into Shugendō during the Heian period. This tradition became established in the medieval period, then evolved into sectarian Shugendō during the early modern period. In recent years, however, Miyake has amended his interpretation based on the results of recent historical research (Miyake 2012a, 2012b).

The second type of discourse on the formation of Shugendō centers on its putative native or primordial character. Gorai Shigeru, known as the founder of Buddhist folk studies (*bukkyō minzokugaku* 仏教民俗学), was its main advocate. This position understands Shugendō as a religious phenomenon representing the oldest cultural layer of the Japanese archipelago as a "wild," "primordial" tradition going very far back in time. Shugendō is taken to represent simultaneously the bone and marrow of Japanese Buddhism and an ethnic religion (*minzoku shūkyō* 民族宗教) that developed exclusively in Japan. Additionally, because it attributes a common essence to *yamabushi* and common people, this interpretation also sees Shugendō as being subsumed in folk beliefs and culture (Gorai 1970, 1975, 1980).

Several problems arise from these two interpretations. Even the discourse emphasizing historical formation, while claiming to take into account historical steps and transition points, mostly emphasizes Shugendō's distinctiveness and continuity as a religion centering on mountains. The historicity of Shugendō, however, is not clearly defined. On the other hand, the discourse on Shugendō as a native or primordial religion clearly lacks a historical perspective and thus favors subjective interpretations. As a result, a supra-historical approach to Shugendō has become the norm and constitutes the dominant understanding so far.

Mountain cults or religious elements associated with mountains are often equated with Shugendō, and the assumption that Shugendō existed in every region or mountain has led to the fact that expressions like "Shugendō of such and such mountain" are used as a matter of course. As a result, the actual state and evolution of Shugendō are often not investigated (Wakamori ed. 1975–84). In such a context as well, it is safe to assume that Shugendō is seen as a fundamentally supra-historical religious tradition. Given this background, it is only natural that methods used in Ethnology and Religious Studies became dominant in Shugendō studies, especially in the postwar years. Moreover, hardly anybody envisioned Shugendō as a worthy research subject in the context of historical studies, for instance, by relying on written documents (Hasegawa 2016). The very nature of Ethnology and Religious Studies as academic disciplines entailed that the study of strictly historical processes was not a priority. The fault also lay on the side of the historians, even though Murayama Shūichi's general outline of Shugendō history, and Suzuki Shōei and Shinjō Mieko's empirical research constitute exceptions to the rule (Murayama 1970; Shinjō 1999 [1980]; Suzuki 2003 [1964, 1965]).

Eventually, it was in the field of medieval Japanese religions that a big shift occurred toward an interest for historical studies on Shugendō. The trigger to this shift was the questions raised by Kuroda Toshio on the exo-esoteric system (*kenmitsu taisei* 顕密体制) and the distribution of power among medieval temples and shrines (Kuroda 1980, 1995). In turn, Kuroda's propositions led to a deep reinvigoration of historical studies in medieval religions and religious institutions. On the one hand, Kuroda focused on redefining exo-esoteric Buddhism, which had been considered a remnant of classical Japanese Buddhism as the dominant ideology running through the medieval state and society. On the other hand, he saw the power residing in exo-esoteric temples and shrines as constituting a tremendous political and social source of influence that had spread its roots widely in Japanese society. Kuroda led the way by emphasizing the need to take up these themes concretely through the study of the history of temples and shrines. His initiative was immediately followed by a large number of studies on exo-esoteric Buddhism and religious institutions by a wide group of scholars.

It is in this context that, from the end of the 1980s onward, a new perspective on Shugendō emerged. Studies considering Shugendō as one of the religious forms that evolved out of exo-esoteric Buddhism and temples during the medieval period began to flourish. Thanks to this repositioning of the historical discourse on its formation, Shugendō acquired a historical presence. I am part of this current, as are Tokunaga Seiko and Sekiguchi Makiko (Tokunaga 1998, 2001, 2002b, 2003, 2014, 2015; Sekiguchi 2009, 2015). Recently, Kondō Yūsuke 近藤祐介 has joined our ranks and is actively involved in related research (Kondō 2015, 2017a, 2017b). Over the next pages, I will present research results coming mainly from Tokunaga, Sekiguchi, and my own work (Tokunaga 2001, 2003; Sekiguchi 2009; Hasegawa 2016). After looking at the relationship between classical Buddhism and mountains, I will clarify the formation process of Shugendō as it occurred between the classical and the medieval period. In order to do so, I will examine the evolution of the meaning of the expression *shugen* and juxtapose it with what we know about contemporary mountain practice and *yamabushi*.

Mountain Practice in Classical Japanese Buddhism Prior to the Formation of Shugendō

Already before the formation of Shugendō, Buddhism and mountains were closely interrelated: mountain practice was an integral part of Buddhism in the classical period and temples were built in that environment. Let me briefly sketch out the situation.

In the Nara period, there was a type of mountain practice in which privately ordained monks engaged. However, official monks also entered the mountains, where they practiced esoteric rites and learned the Kokuzō Gumonji ritual (*Kokuzō Gumonji hō* 虚空蔵求聞持法; Sonoda 1981). At that time, mountain practice may actually be considered as an integral part of the basic monastic curriculum. The creation of the system of Ten Court Meditation Masters (*Naigubu Jūzenji* 内供奉十禅師), whose task was to protect the emperor by way of incantatory powers (*juryoku* 呪力) acquired in the depths of the mountains, is another proof of the important role granted to mountain practice. There are numerous examples of temples built on mountains, such as Mt. Kōya and Mt. Hiei, founded by Kūkai and Saichō, respectively, to cite only the most famous examples from the early Heian period. Before long, these institutions would yield enormous power of influence and promote the diffusion of Esoteric Buddhism while using mountains as their basis.

Beginning from the tenth century, records of rebirth in Amida's Pure Land (*ōjōden* 往生伝) and Buddhist didactic tales (*setsuwa* 説話) report the activities of numerous "holy men" (*hijiri* 聖) (Inoue 1971; Kikuchi 2011). *Hijiri* performed religious practices in the harsh natural environment of mountains, plains, rivers, and seas, while simultaneously creating links between towns and the countryside by going back and forth between them. Around the same period, literary works such as *Utsubo monogatari* うつほ物語 (tenth century) and *Genji monogatari* 源氏物語 (eleventh century) reveal the presence of practitioners called *yamabushi* 山伏/山臥. In the *Genji monogatari*'s

"Spring Shoots" chapter (no. 34), *hijiri* are described as secluding themselves in the depth of the mountains: "holy men climbed high onto mountains, deep into caves." Also, judging from expressions such as a "*yamabushi*'s *hijiri*-like heart" (*yamabushi no hijirigokoro* 山伏の聖心), which uses the character for *hijiri*, it is clear that *yamabushi* were considered to have withdrawn themselves from the secular world in the same way as "holy men" did. *Hijiri* and *yamabushi* expressed related concepts, the borders of which remained undefined. Later on, in *Shinsarugakuki* 新猿楽記 (eleventh century), esoteric monks performing prayers as "persons of power" (*genja/genza* 験者) and "masters in incantations" (*shingonshi* 真言師) are called "*yamabushi* practitioners" (*yamabushi shugyōja* 山臥修行者). *Ryōjin hishō* 梁塵秘抄 (twelfth century) uses the expression "*yamabushi shugyō* 山臥修行" to describe practices performed by *hijiri*. In this case, *yamabushi* designated the activity of "lying down in the mountains" (*yama ni fusu* 山に伏[臥]す), to be understood as originating in a form of practice involving mountain retreats (Okano 2017). I argue that this evolution indicates the emergence of the expression "*yamabushi*" as designating *hijiri* who specialized in mountain practice and while entertaining contacts with the aristocratic society.

According to *Shinsarugakuki* and *Ryōjin hishō*, the first sites of practice were Kumano and Ōmine, before extending to sacred mountains in every province, including the coast of Shikoku and the Noto peninsula. Mountain practice had also acquired more defined features by the Insei 院政 and Kamakura periods. This may be inferred from the contents of *Shozan engi* 諸山縁起 (twelfth century), illustrating the fusion with the Esoteric Buddhist worldview, according to which the Diamond and the Womb realm mandalas, as well as their Buddhas and other deities, were envisioned as residing on the mountain ranges of Ōmine and Katsuragi.[1] Simultaneously, "lodges" or "stations" (*shuku* 宿) were built following the consolidation of practice and itineraries. This evolution could also be understood as the point in time in which "austerities" (*tosō* 抖擻; Skr. *dhūta*), to which I will come back later, and *yamabushi* practice started being considered as a systematized "way." Buddhism's relation with mountains thus continued from ancient Japan. Especially Esoteric Buddhism, as well as holy men (*hijiri*) and *yamabushi* alike, was deeply connected to Shugendō. As we will see later on, the word *shugen*, for example, is closely related to Esoteric Buddhism. In this sense, it is not exaggerated to say that ancient Japanese Buddhism included the premises of Shugendō. However, in ancient Japan there was no awareness of an immediate permutation between mountain Buddhism or temples, *hijiri*, and *yamabushi* on the one hand, and Shugendō and *shugenja* on the other. The problem lies in the space between "being related to" or "resembling" Shugendō, and "being Shugendō."

Meaning and Evolution of the Term *Shugen*

As stated above, Shugendō and Esoteric Buddhism are inseparable. However, Shugendō came to be seen as distinct from Esoteric Buddhism. What transformations could have led to that? I intend to investigate this evolution by examining the meaning of the term *shugen* and the circumstances of its use.

Originally, *shugen* was a word used to designate outstanding incantatory or thaumaturgic skills, often used to praise Esoteric Buddhist monks who performed prayers as "persons of power" (*genza/genja* 験者) in aristocratic circles. The first occurrence of *shugen* is in *Nihon sandai jitsuroku* 日本三代実録, in an entry for 868 (ninth day of the seventh month), according to which "In the deep mountains of the district of Yoshino, in the Yamato province, there lived a novice. His name was Dōju 道珠. He entered the mountains as a youth, and has yet to step out of them. The emperor heard that he possessed *shugen*." The expression "to possess *shugen*" indicates that what is understood under *shugen* here is the fact that Dōju had acquired outstanding powers, and that the fame they gave him had come to the ears of Emperor Seiwa (850–881; r. 858–76). Although Dōju was a mountain recluse at Yoshino, it is clear that, in this case, *shugen* did not refer to mountain practice.

Another example of a similar use of the word *shugen* as a skill is to be found in a 980 (second day of second month) entry in *Bōji shizaichō* 某寺資財帳 (*Heian ibun* nr. 315), where Nin'en dai wajō 仁延大和尚 is described as "trained in virtues and powers" (*shutoku shugen* 修徳修験). Elsewhere, *Heihanki* (also *Hyōhanki*) 兵範記 states in an 1152 entry (21st day of the fifth month) that "today, as a result of the prayers of Gyōbu ajari Ninken 刑部阿闍梨仁顕, [the regent's illness receded], his hand and feet cooled off, and his face recovered some coloring. [...] There was no relapse after that. [Ninken's powers] should be called *shugen*." Moreover, a similar example of skill assessment can be found in a passage of the eleventh-century *Dai Nihonkoku Hokekyō genki* 大日本国法華経験記, describing Mudōji no Sōō kashō 無動寺の相応和尚[2] as a monk who "excels in austerities, and whose *shugen* is unimaginable."

As previously mentioned, Esoteric Buddhist monks who specialized in ritual prayers were usually called *genza* or *shingonshi*, and they appear in *Shinsarugakuki* as *yamabushi shugyōsha* 山臥修行者, "*yamabushi* practitioners." This shows not only that mountain practice had come to be seen as a necessary means in order to acquire thaumaturgic powers, but also that the stabilization of the connection between mountains and powers brought about a transformation in the meaning of the expression *shugen*. In the twelfth and thirteenth centuries, *shugen* designated not only special skills but also the actions and the process, that is, the training (*shugyō*, "practice") leading up to them. Alternatively, *shugen* came to refer to actions (*kitō*, "ritual prayers") related to thaumaturgic powers, both usages showing that the expression took on a broader meaning. *Konjaku monogatarishū* (twelfth century; vol. 17–18) states that a monk from Bitchū province named Ashō 阿清 "enjoying *shugen* as a natural disposition, toured mountains and crossed seas, all the while performing severe ascetic practices." In this instance, *shugen* may be understood as referring to a training aimed at acquiring powers enough to be praised. Moreover, *Kawachi no kuni Kongōji sō Akan okibumi* 河内国金剛寺僧阿観置文 (1191.6.1; *Kamakura ibun* nr. 536) mentions mountain entry practice being forbidden for "*shugen* practitioners" (*shugen gyōja* 修験行者). While in this case *shugen* may be understood as describing activities occurring in the mountains with the purpose of attaining powers, the authenticity of the document in itself is not entirely guaranteed, and some caution is necessary. *Azuma kagami* 吾妻鏡, in an entry for 25.8.1217, uses the expression *shugen* in a different meaning: "Concerning the retired sovereign's disease: there is an ongoing epidemic that began on the tenth day of the seventh month. Although every single knowledgeable high-ranking monk was zealous in *shugen*, there is no improvement." The expression to be "zealous in *shugen*" clearly designates an activity. In this case, it is appropriate to see it as indicating the incantations (prayers) or demonstrations of the power to heal.

Mountain Practice and *Yamabushi/Shugen*

If mountains and *shugen* are in intimate relation with each other, the relationship should be all the more inseparable in the case of *yamabushi*. We are now going to look at the process through which *shugen* and *yamabushi* came to be seen as identical. Originally, *yamabushi* practice meant retreats in the mountains. However, the practice model used in Shugendō designates austerities (in mountains and forests) that accompany peregrinations through mountains and countryside. What I would like to address first is the shift from mountain retreat to austerities. As shown in *Shinsarugakuki*, holy mountains were to be found in all provinces: "Kumano, Kinpu, Tateyama in Etchū, Hashiriyu in Izu, Konpon chūdō, Daisen in Hōki, venerable Mt. Fuji, Shirayama (Hakusan) in Echizen, Kōya, Kokawa, Minoo, Katsuragawa, etc." 熊野、金峰、越中立山、伊豆走湯、根本中堂、伯耆大山、富士御山、越前白山、高野、粉河、箕面、葛川等. However, since the same text specifies that "while traversing Ōmine and Katsuragi, one treads the secluded paths (*hechi* 辺道)," it is plausible that in the eleventh century there was already a pioneering model of austerities.

In the twelfth century, *Ryōjin hishō* states that "*hijiri* carry out *yamabushi* practice in winter, when they make tree leaves their huts and the autumn foliage has finished scattering, when the sky is lonely, the first frost and snow falls, piling up on moss as if it were a cushion, and the water that flows between the rocks turns into ice." Such passages show that the modelization of practice continued. At the same time, it is likely that the gradual change toward ascetic practice began at this time. Among the signs of this evolution, I would count the fact, mentioned earlier, that practice routes or "stations" (*shuku*) on the Katsuragi range are described in *Shozan engi*. At the latest in the thirteenth century, practice models similar to that of the Katsuragi range spread widely, as "austerities" (*tosō*) took place and stations were defined in the provinces as well, possibly set up by *yamabushi*. Let us consider Mt. Iō (Iōzen 医王山) in Etchū province. In *Kantō gechijō* 関東下知状, an entry for Kakitanji 柿谷寺 [*sic*] dated to the third month of 1262 (*Kamakura ibun* nr. 8775) states: "This [temple] was built as a private [institution], but, according to the customs of Hokurikudō, there are earlier examples of determining stations along the way to accommodate *yamabushi* when they cross the mountains. Therefore, this temple is the first station on Mt. Iō." Along with the fact that *yamabushi* were "crossing mountains," it is clear that stops were established on their way, both as waypoints and as sites of mountain practice.

From all this, it results that between the eleventh and the thirteenth centuries, mountain practice slowly evolved toward the practice of austerities. At the same time, from the thirteenth century on, we observe an increased degree of awareness regarding *yamabushi* in contemporary society, with their presence at temples becoming more evident and their activities within local society more prominent, following the increasing success encountered by the Kumano pilgrimage (Kumano sankei 熊野参詣) as well as the horizontal relational model used by *yamabushi* with their practices and incantations (Tokunaga 1998, 2003; Sekiguchi 2009; Hasegawa 2015, 2016). It is probably correct to consider the circulation of activities and austerities performed by *yamabushi* both inside and outside temples as occurring in parallel with the setting up of places of practice.

In the context of the spreading of asceticism and the fact that *yamabushi* activities were taking on an organized shape, it is likely that *yamabushi* practice was recognized as a system bringing together various components with austerities as a common denominator. Examples of the usage of *dō* 道 ("way") to express systematization gradually appear. *Shijū hyaku innenshū* 私聚百因縁集 (1257) bears the first mention of the expression "*yamabushi* way of practice" (*yamabushi no gyōdō* 山臥の行道). Later, in *Daigoji sōgō daihōsshira mōshijōan* 醍醐寺僧綱大法師等申状案 (entry for December 1273; *Kamakura ibun* nr. 11509), the clergy (*shuto* 衆徒) are shown to be critical of Dōchō 道朝, in favor of whom Daigoji abbot Sanbōin Jōsai 醍醐寺座主三宝院定済 (1220–82) had abdicated from his title. Dōchō was a *yamabushi*, and the clergy complained that "so far, there is no example of ascetic practitioner who took office as a chief abbot. Dōchō has a taste for the Single Way of *Yamabushi* (*yamabushi no ichidō* 山伏の一道), but he has not learned the depths of Esoteric Buddhism yet."

As for the actual content of mountain practice, one particular document probably dating back to the second half of the thirteenth century or the first half of the fourteenth, *Butsumyōin shoshi meyasu-an* 仏名院所司目安案 (*Kamakura ibun* nr. 14032), stands out. This document about the head monk of a temple called Butsumyōin describes "*shugen* practice" (*shugen no narai* 修験の習い) at the hands of *yamabushi* as comprising "austerities on the Two mountains, One Thousand days on Rōzan, winter retreat at the Cave of the Shō, the Shikoku pilgrimage and that of the Thirty-three holy places of Kannon in the Western provinces." It is likely that various elements such as austerities on Ōmine and Katsuragi and pilgrimages were known as *yamabushi* practice and considered equivalent to the "Way of *yamabushi*" mentioned earlier. As evidenced in documents such as the 1291 *Shoō no hide* 正応の碑伝 of Hasuge jinja 八菅神社 (Kanagawa) or the colophon of a 1388 *Mahāprajñāpāramitā sūtra* copy held by Kanzenji 勧善寺 (Tokushima), such activities were widely performed between the thirteenth and the fourteenth centuries. I would argue that *shugen* and *yamabushi* began to be seen as a set at that time.

Around the mid-thirteenth century, En no Ozunu 役小角 (En no Gyōja 役行者) began to be venerated as the ancestor of *yamabushi*, which corroborates the previously mentioned tendency. The earliest example indicating this evolution is provided by *Shijū hyaku innenshū*, which states that "if we enquire about the origins of the way of *yamabushi* practice, all will say it started with En no Gyōja's activities" (Miyake 1985, 2000a). Even earlier on, En no Ozunu had been known as a legendary mountain practitioner, but it is likely that with the manifestation of *yamabushi* as an independent movement such as the Single Way of *Yamabushi* or *Shugen* practice, the veneration of En no Gyōja took on new aspects.

I would like to draw attention to the evolution in meaning of the term *shugen* and the gradual delimitation of its object, as indicated in *Jien kishōmon* 慈円起請文

(*Daisenpōin jōjō kishō no koto* 大懺法院条々起請事, 1206). This document, included in *Mon'yōki* 門葉記, describes different categories of monks: "There are four types of monks. First, the exoteric school, second the esoteric school, third the *genza* 験者, and fourth the preachers [...] The *genza* are affiliated to the esoteric, the preachers to the exoteric." Even though *genza* were still part of Esoteric Buddhism, yet by the beginning of the thirteenth century they were envisioned as a distinct category. It is difficult to determine whether this was related to the perceived intrinsic connection between powers and mountain practice, as seen in *Shinsarugakuki*, or whether *genza* simply refers to *yamabushi*. It is equally possible that the ambiguity of the category of esoteric monks had an influence on the expression *shugen*, as on the contents of its object.

Status of *Yamabushi* and *Shugen* in Temple Society

Even though the existence of *yamabushi* as a distinct group of Buddhist specialists was now recognized, what was their position in the social structure of temples? We have seen in the *Daigoji sōgō daihōsshira mōshijō'an*, that the Daigoji clerics refused the nomination of a *yamabushi* as abbot for the following reason: "Dōchō has a taste for the Single Way of *Yamabushi*, but he has not learned the depth of Esoteric Buddhism yet." This statement shows that, from the perspective of Shingon monks, the "Single Way of *Yamabushi*" was not considered as orthodox Esoteric Buddhism. Similarly, *Butsumyōin shoshi meyasu'an* includes the sentence "this head priest, from the onset, has nothing to do with *yamabushi*, and does not perform *shugen*," which shows that, indeed, *yambushi* and *shugen* were valued negatively. Even though the presence of *yamabushi* or their practice was not negated within temples, it is clear that they were not given access to high positions. This amounts to saying that *yamabushi* were not recognized as legitimate monks, but such was the general perception in the thirteenth and fourteenth centuries.

In *Futsū shōdōshū* 普通唱導集 (1297), a distinction is made between "two kinds of arts, within and outside society." In a list of various crafts and professions, in which "within society" refers to the secular world, and "outside" to the realm of Buddhism, *yamabushi* are placed in the latter category. However, in *Shasekishū* 沙石集 (1283; vol. 6–9), a preaching monk is described in the following way:

> He looked like a man, and indeed was wearing something like a stole (*kesa* 袈裟). But he didn't have a high hat (*eboshi* 烏帽子), he was not a child, nor a monk, nor a commoner, nor was he a 'heap of shit' (*kuso* 屎): he looked rather to be a 'little shit' (*birikuso* びり屎), a *yamabushi*.

In the fourteenth century, *Keiran shūyōshū* 渓嵐拾葉集 states that "Mii gyōbu sōjō 三井刑部僧正 was a poor and most illiterate person. Hence, he became a *yamabushi*." Although *yamabushi* were members of the clergy, they were of a low status, and it is clear that they were considered inferior persons on the social ladder. Moreover, in *Sō Kakuken denchi kishinjō* 僧覚賢田地寄進状 (*Katsuoji monjo* 勝尾寺文書, no. 799), a document included in the second volume of the history of Minoo city (*Minoo-shi shi* 箕面市史; 1312.18.06), there is the passage: "he did not have the capacity to become a learned monk, but anyhow he entered the Way of *shugen*." This simply meant that *shugen* practitioners were considered people who lacked the skills for studying. Thus, it is likely that the previous examples from Daigoji or Butsumyōin were not exceptions but ordinary cases. As a matter of fact, every temple organization of a certain scale presented some degree of class hierarchy, and *yamabushi* were often seen as members of inferior classes. To sum up, both *yamabushi* and the *shugen* that is expected from them were situated on the fringes of exo-esoteric Buddhism and their temples (Hasegawa 2015, 2016).

Development of Shugendō as a Concept

Between the end of the twelfth and the fourteenth centuries, when *yamabushi* and *shugen* became inseparable and their practice came to be called "Single Way of *yamabushi*" or "*shugen* practice," Shugendō began to be considered one branch of Buddhism. Documents often refer to it as simply *shugen* or "the Way of *shugen*," and acknowledge it to be a religious system that is different from exoteric and Esoteric Buddhism (Tokunaga 2002b, 2003, 2015; Hasegawa 2016).

On this background, because *yamabushi* were gradually appointed to important offices, their existence could no longer be overlooked. It became then necessary for exo-esoteric temples to give Shugendō a status, also in order to integrate it. That is how Shugendō, while being considered neither exoteric nor esoteric, became the third element of exo-esoteric Buddhism.

Among the earliest documents that present this viewpoint, *Tengu zōshi* 天狗草子 (Onjōji version; 1296) explains that Onjōji 園城寺 (also Miidera 三井寺) promotes training in exoteric Buddhism, Esoteric Buddhism, and the "Single way of *shugen*":

> As far as the teachings of this temple are concerned, there are Shingon 真言, Tendai 天台, Hossō 法相, and Kusha 倶舎. Should you go to other temples, either there is Exoteric Buddhism, but no Esoteric Buddhism, or vice versa. Even if you were to find both exoteric and esoteric [traditions], there would be no Single way of *shugen*. It is only in our temple that you can study all three in order to serve our sovereign and the country.

Furthermore, the 1299 copy of *Daigoji engi* states: "After the passing of En no Gyōja, there were great snakes on Ōmine, and practice was interrupted. The venerable master [Shōbō 聖宝 (832–909)] dispelled them and subsequently restored the Way of *shugen* back to its former days." The expression "Way of *shugen*" is used to describe Shōbō's restoration of practice on Ōmine.

In the fourteenth century, examples become numerous. Similarly to the previously mentioned *Sō Kakuken denchi kishinjō*, the "Way of *shugen*" is often set in opposition to doctrinal study. However, what stands out is the juxtaposition of "exotericism, esotericism, and *shugen*." What comes to mind first is the context of dominant temples vying for influence (*kenmon jiin* 権門寺院). In *Ōmi Onjōji gakutō shukurōtō mōshijō* 近江園城寺学頭宿老等申状 (*Kamakura ibun* no. 27012), estimated to date back to 1319, the cumulation of the "Three ways of exotericism, esotericism and *shugen*" is emphasized as Onjōji's point of excellence. Similarly, *Ōmi Binmanji sō dōjishō jitōdai shinshiki* 近江敏満寺僧・同寺荘地頭代申詞記 (*Kamakura ibun*, no. 31259; 1330.10.27) describes the position of Supervisor of the Three Shrines of Kumano (*Kumano Sanzan Kengyō* 熊野三山検校), which was mainly transmitted within Onjōji, as representing "generations of virtuous *shugen* patriarchs" and as a *de facto* self-appointed manager of Shugendō. As a matter of fact, Kumano supervisors were employed as "Kumano guides" and *genza* for retired sovereigns, emperors, and the aristocracy; they also promoted the unification of the Three Shrines of Kumano and their *sendachi*,[3] a process that eventually led to the formation of the Honzan branch (*Honzan-ha* 本山派) of Shugendō (Tokunaga 2002b; Hasegawa 2016). That is the reason why Shugendō is valued so highly at Onjōji. An entry in *Go-gumaiki* 後愚昧記 (1367.14.05) describes one Onjōji monk named Ninshō 任承 as someone "cumulating both the esoteric school and Shugendō," which shows that the study of Shugendō in parallel with other schools was more than just an ideal.

Furthermore, on the side of Enryakuji, too, the fourteenth-century *Shokoku ikken hijiri monogatari* 諸国一見聖物語 (also *Sanmon hijiri no ki* 山門聖之記) speaks of the "three ways of exotericism, esotericism, and *shugen*." However, in that particular instance "Shugendō" refers to a practice specific to one temple, namely, Katsuragawa Myōōin 葛川明王院. In opposition to the "Way of *yamabushi*," which designates austerities on Ōmine, Katsuragi, and Kumano, "Shugendō" here points to "practitioners of the Northern Peak." The practice at Katsuragawa was actually not performed by *yamabushi*, but by scholar-monks. It seems quite clear that there was a wide range of interpretations for the expression "*shugen* practitioners" (*shugen gyōja* 修験行者), as well as for that of "Shugendō" itself (see, for example, *Dainihon shiryō* 7, volume 1, for the year 1393.12.9).

Similar examples dating from the same period can also be found at provincial temples. This suggests that the general features of Shugendō and of the parallel between "exotericism, esotericism, and *shugen*" were by then widely accepted. It also shows to which degree *yamabushi* activities and practices had spread throughout society. *Shinkei yuzurijō* 心慶譲状 (*Kamakura ibun* no. 30872; 1330.18.01) is a document related to the head priest of Kongōfukuji 金剛福寺 at Ashizurimisaki 足摺岬 in Tosa province. It praises Sonkei 村慶, Shinkei's successor, with these words: "[he] cumulated achievements in both the exoteric and the esoteric schools, and excelled in the way of *shugen*," an indication that training in these three areas was highly valued. In Wakasa province too, *Myōtsūji shuto sōjōan* 明通寺衆徒奏状案 (1334) extols the virtues of cumulated learning in "the three matters of exotericism, esotericism and *shugen*."

In other words, *shugen*, originally connected to Esoteric Buddhism, had by then become a system that was separate not only from exotericism but also from esotericism, and had taken a front-stage position in history. However, this evolution should not be understood in terms of religious organization, but in terms of integration as a concept.

Shinkei yuzurijō saw the "way of *shugen*" as separate from the exo-esoteric system; one step further and Shugendō had become its additional component.

It is not easy to explain the purport of Shugendō. At Onjōji, for example, *Jitokushū* 寺徳集 (1345) describes Miidera (i.e., Onjōji) and its schools as "being the sole entity that serves the country" by cumulating the "three matters" of "exotericism, esotericism, and *shugen*." The same argument is used at Myōtsūji: "[we, the clergy at Myōtsūji] pray for peace upon the country by way of the three matters of exotericism, esotericism, and *shugen*." Prayers for the "protection of the country" served as a unifying factor. In that sense too, Shugendō must be considered as being part of the framework of exo-esoteric Buddhism and its institutions.

Conclusion

In this chapter, I began by examining the meaning and evolution of the expression *shugen*, of mountain practice, and of *yamabushi* and ended with a discussion of the formation of Shugendō as a concept. Many obscure points remain as Shugendō is not a clear-cut phenomenon, but I think that we have at least ascertained the historical process through which it came into being.

Even after Shugendō was established as one of the constitutive elements of exo-esoteric Buddhism and its institutions, it took a long time until a concrete organization emerged. It is a well-known fact that the system centering on the Honzan branch (linked to Tendai Buddhism) and on the Tōzan branch (linked to Shingon Buddhism) took shape in the early modern period. Moreover, the formation processes of these two branches were not parallel (Sekiguchi 2009, 2015; Kondō 2015, 2017b). The end of the thirteenth and the fourteenth centuries indeed represented a transitional period for the history of Shugendō.

Further research on the development of the organization of Shugendō is needed. It is important to note that the study of Shugendō history, including my own work, has been overly restricted to the Honzan and Tōzan branches. As a result, a variety of issues have been overlooked (Hasegawa 2015, 2016). It would for example be worthwhile to look at the type of Shugendō that developed at the Katsuragawa Myōōin in relation with the Sanmon branch of Tendai Buddhism, or at the connection between practice on Ōmine and *yamabushi* at Tōji. With regard to Tōji in particular, *Tōji jisō shūgaku kotogaki tsuikaʾan* 東寺寺僧修学事書追加案 (*Kamakura ibun* no. 27728; 1321.2) includes a regulation according to which both scholar-monks and *yamabushi* had to perform similar practices at Ōmine and Kumano. Thus, it is now necessary to look at Shugendō and *yamabushi* from a different perspective. Similarly, it would be important to investigate thoroughly the relation between Tōji and Kumano's *nagatoko-shū* 長床衆, who were affiliated to both Tendai and Shingon schools. Furthermore, when reflecting on the organizational development of Shugendō, it is equally necessary to consider its relationship with the organization of sacred mountains and religious institutions throughout the country.

3

Imagining an Ancient Tradition: Eighteenth-Century Narratives of Shugendō at Mount Togakushi

Caleb Carter

The common narrative of Shugendō is one of ancient origins, romanticized as a tradition born in the distant recesses of Japanese civilization and mountain culture. Vague measures of its past ride on modern myths of Japan—homogeneity, a country of antiquity, and a people of exceptional spirit—have flourished since the early twentieth century.[1] Yet these ideas should not be simply equated with modernity (see also Chapter One by Suzuki Masataka and Chapter Five by Hayashi Makoto). As scholars of early modern intellectual history have observed, a number of movements in the eighteenth century turned to the past for legitimacy as well: Confucian philologists sought models of ideal governance from the Chinese classics, Shinto and Buddhist clerics alike conceived of new "divine ways" (*shintō* 神道) rooted in their country, and scholars of National Learning (*Kokugaku*) discovered the true Japanese spirit (*magokoro* 真心 as penned by Motoori Norinaga) in Japan's earliest texts.[2]

Among these wayfarers of the ancient period, practitioners of Shugendō had their own motivations to connect with the past. Shugendō was still novel, if not unheard of, in many parts of the country at the start of the Edo period. The *sendatsu* of the Honzan branch had only been expanding into new territories beyond the Kii peninsula (under Shōgoin) for roughly a century, and the Tōzan branch had just recently received national recognition under Tokugawa Ieyasu's Shugendō regulations (*Shugendō hatto* 修験道法度) of 1613 (Sekiguchi 2009). To give the school sound footing, its advocates needed to construct narratives of ancient origins that would elevate Shugendō's standing in society and increase patronage to its affiliated mountains.

The following pages take Mount Togakushi (in present-day Nagano prefecture) as an example of this process (Figure 3.1), paying special attention to the contributions of the Tendai cleric Jōin 乗因 (1682–1739).[3] Jōin served as the mountain's chief administrator (*bettō*) from 1727 to 1738. During this time, he constructed a long, uninterrupted history of Shugendō at Togakushi that aimed to elevate the cultural prestige and appeal of the site, drawing visitors from far and wide. To accomplish this task, he took up an old genre of temple-shrine narratives: *engi*, or "origin accounts." This chapter explores how Jōin used these stories—not only to position Shugendō at

Figure 3.1 The mountains of Togakushi (right) and Nishidake (left) above the pond of Kagami. Photograph by Caleb Carter.

the very center of Togakushi's past but to imagine Shugendō as one of the world's great traditions (see also Chapter Seven by Kawasaki Tsuyoshi and Chapter Eight by Niki Natsumi).

Early Modern Vernacular Religion and the Spread of Shugendō

Jōin's writing reflects both the growing popularity of Shugendō and the use of storytelling in the early modern vernacular diffusion of religious systems. The seventh-century semilegendary founder of Shugendō, En no Gyōja, often lay at the center of this project. The profusion of printing and bookmaking, production of *jōruri* theatre, and dissemination of Shugendō in the first half of the Edo period brought his near-mythic character to villages, mountains, and cities across the country. Works like *En no Kimi keiseiki* 役君形生記 (1684) provided extended commentary on En no Gyōja's legendary life while genres of vernacular and illustrated publications (e.g., *Nara-ehon* and *kanazōshi*) suited a wider, nonspecialist audience (Miyake 2000a: 152–76, 192–5). The *Wakan sansai zue* (c. 1712) dedicated three pages to the legendary feats of the mountain ascetic (vol. 3, no. 73: 242–245). His image appeared in the *ukiyo-e* prints of Katsushika Hokusai (1760–1849) and others. At the local level, legendary visits by En no Gyōja were penned into the newly embellished *engi* and wooden icons of him were carved and displayed outside of mountain temples.[4]

This activity was not unique to Shugendō but also widespread across Buddhist sects, as clerics devised stories connecting figures such as Hōnen, Shinran, Rennyo, Nichiren, and Dōgen to their local temples (Tsutsumi 2008). Such legends were often written into temple *engi* that were expanded from medieval versions, though the objectives and writing styles of the two eras differed significantly. Medieval *engi*, many of which were produced in the twelfth and thirteenth centuries, were intended to cement the authority of patrilineal lineages with particular temples, territory, and ritual programs. The growing political and economic instability of the Kamakura period rippled outward into the provinces, prompting shrine-temple complexes to shore up their own claims over landholdings as land stewards (*jitō*) and military governors (*shugo*) staked out their own.

In contrast, the political circumstances of the Edo period were far more stable. While Buddhist temples received a fixed income through the enforced patronage system (*danka seido*) or revenue from government-allotted agricultural estates (as was the case for Togakushi), this revenue could be supplemented by a range of activities: public displays ("curtain unveilings," *kaichō*) of deities, the distribution of talismans, private rituals, popular festivals, mountain guiding, and so forth. These endeavors naturally relied on broad interest among the populace, and it was often local legends that aided this effort. By describing the miracles of a site's deity, inventing connections to famous founders, and fabling historical ties with a school like Shugendō, religious specialists boosted enthusiasm for their services and sites of affiliation. Unlike the medieval precedents, these *engi* were composed in cursive vernacular style and often transferred to woodblock print, ensuring diffusion to an expanded readership.

Beyond shrine and temple narratives, a search for origins captured the interests of intellectuals of all stripes. Confucian scholars like Itō Jinsai (1627–1705) and Ogyū Sorai (1666–1728) investigated Confucian classics for guidance on ethical behavior and proper governance. Turning inward to the search for national origins, scholars of National Learning located the primordial spirit of the Japanese through mytho-political texts like the *Kojiki* (712). Buddhist and Shinto clerics alike formulated new "divine ways" (*shintō*) that expanded from late medieval articulations. While the objects of investigation varied considerably, these efforts sought answers from the past that reimagined the country at large.

Shrine and temple *engi* also looked to the past but, in contrast, were rooted in the interests of local communities. Cognizant of an emergent national community, their authors attempted to connect their own sites to the broader landscape. This opportunity was not lost to the clerics and *yamabushi* of Togakushi. While travelers from far and wide increasingly ventured into Shinano province's northern plains to reach the famous temple complex of Zenkōji, a full-day ascent into the mountains of Togakushi required a bit of additional coaxing. In order to entice visitors to go the extra distance (about six *ri*, or twenty-five kilometers), the community at Togakushi needed to secure its own position as a place of unparalleled numinous efficacy and national renown. The growing popularity of Shugendō made it an obvious choice in fulfilling this agenda. To do so effectively though would require a rewriting of the past, given its relatively recent encounter with the school.

The Arrival of Shugendō to Togakushi

The introduction of Shugendō at Togakushi happened relatively late when compared with its emergence on the Kii peninsula. While material evidence of ascetic practices on the slopes of Togakushi date back to the late Heian period, a self-conscious school of Shugendō only emerged in the sixteenth century, thanks to a pivotal transmission from Mount Hiko. In the mid-1520s, the Hiko ascetic Akyūbō Sokuden 阿吸房即傳 (fl. 1509–58) purportedly initiated Togakushi's chief administrator and his successor into the Hiko-style Peak Entry (*mineiri* or *nyūbu*) and shared two collections of *kirigami* of Shugendō ritual protocols.[5]

The first evidence that the nascent lineage of Shugendō had taken root at Togakushi appears in a text known as the *Shugen mondō* (Inquiries into Shugen[-dō]).[6] According to its colophon, it was composed in 1561 and belonged to Togakushi's central temple of Chūin. Its tone and vocabulary reflect the school's emergence at Togakushi as a self-conscious system at this time. For example, the authors took pains to distinguish Shugendō from the traditional schools of Buddhism while simultaneously placing it on par with them. In another sign of the school's recent appearance, the text is abundant in Shugendō lexicon (*yamabushi*, *sendatsu* 先達, *nyūbu*, and *shugen*) that was absent from Togakushi in the fifteenth century and earlier.

Much of the content in the *Shugen mondō* recalls its origins in northern Kyushu. This includes a lineage of Shugendō passed down from En no Gyōja to a Hiko practitioner named Chikō no Gyōja 智光行者 before its eventual transmission to Togakushi (*Shugen mondō*: 391). It also provides detailed explanations of peak entry rituals based on the three seasonal entries in the Hiko region. Advancing the logic, calendar, and institutional parameters of the Hiko peak entries, the *Shugen mondō* reveals the extent to which Togakushi had incorporated the Shugendō of northern Kyushu:

> To begin with, the spring entry is referred to as the Spring Peak. It signifies the progression from seed to fruit and constitutes the practice of the Womb Realm. It is called the peak of forward movement, because one moves upward in pursuit of awakening. Furthermore, the autumn entry is referred to as the Autumn Peak. It signifies a turning from fruit back toward the seed and constitutes the practice of the Diamond Realm. It is called the peak of reverse movement, because one moves downward in order to transform living beings. Together they make up the two practices of the twofold [mandalas]. The beginning and end of the flower offering ritual concerns neither seed nor fruit but rather the practice of seed and fruit as one form as well as the nonduality of the Womb and Diamond. One fully obtains the realization of one's own body as a buddha (*sokushin sokubutsu*) in this way. Upon the fourth completion of the Three Peaks Practice (*sanbu shugyō*), one achieves the rank of *sendatsu*. He is then able to guide novices (*shinkyaku*), enabling them to attain perfect and complete buddhahood.
>
> (*Shugen mondō*, 388)

Given the parallels in the ritual calendar and symbolism in this passage with the writings of Akyūbō, the link between the two sites is unmistakable.[7]

As Shugendō continued to develop at the site, its adherents also worked to construct a historical narrative for its legacy at Togakushi that superseded the Hiko transmission. This effort began with En no Gyōja. The lineage in the *Shugen mondō* had mentioned En but made no concrete connection of him to the site. Suggestions of his historical presence, however, were put forth in the early Edo period when wooden images of him were placed alongside Gakumon Gyōja 學門行者 (traditional founder of the mountain) at each of the three temples.[8] The icons of either were carved from Japanese cypress (*hinoki*). Two are extant: one of En no Gyōja (125.5 cm in height) and one of Gakumon Gyōja (78.5 cm in height). According to one estimation, they were produced in the Keichō era (1596–1615) (Kobayashi 1993: 59). Dual placement of En and Gakumon icons at the temples hinted that both played a role in Togakushi's origins.

Shugendō took on institutional form at Togakushi in 1707 when the mountain's chief administrator, Shigi 子義 (appointed in 1702), was granted permission from Kan'eiji to establish an official branch for the mountain's *yamabushi*. Known as the *Togakushi-ha yamabushi*, the branch gave the site's practitioners legal and institutional backing. This structure was necessary given the encroaching presence of Honzan *yamabushi*, who competed for the patronage of the regional population. Shōgoin (headquarters of the Honzan branch) had been establishing a presence in Shinano since the end of the sixteenth century, dispatching its *sendatsu* into the region. Beginning with the temples of Hokkedō 法華堂 (present-day Saku City in central Nagano prefecture) and Wagōin 和合院 (present-day Matsushiro in Nagano City), the Honzan branch gradually extended its reach across the province over the course of the seventeenth century. By 1686 Wagōin administered 163 Honzan temples across northern Shinano, including Togakushi's own district of Minochi. By the 1720s the Honzan branch claimed the greatest number of temples in central and southern Shinano, followed by the Tōzan branch (Nagano Kenshi Kankōkai 1987: 611–14). The Togakushi branch provided an institutional counterweight to this rising influence. With the official backing of the Togakushi temples, Togakushi's *yamabushi* now received formalized training, initiation, and rank, all to be approved under the authority of the chief administrator (Wakamori 1980: 428). Similar to the case of Haguro (where a branch of Shugendō was established in 1641), the branch was ultimately overseen by the Tendai head temple of Rinnōji 輪王寺 at Nikkō (Miyake 1996: 455–9).

Jōin and His Creation of a Mythic Past

Jōin arrived at Togakushi two decades later. While he came to fully espouse Shugendō during his tenure there, there is no evidence that he was interested in it before arriving at the mountain. Instead, his career took shape in the elite circles of the Tendai institution. Preceding his appointment at Togakushi, he had tutored the royal prelate (*hōshinnō*), Dōnin 道仁 (1676–1733; subsequently appointed *zasu* of the Tendai sect), served as abbot to sub-temples at Mount Hiei (historical center of Tendai) and Kan'eiji (Tendai's early modern administrative center), and received initiation (perhaps solely) into the lineage of Sannō Ichijitsu Shintō 山王一実神道, which provided the doctrinal foundation for the deification of Tokugawa Ieyasu as a divine avatar (*gongen*) (Sonehara 2001: 8–10; Bodiford 2007: 242–3).

Jōin's tenure at Togakushi, dating from 1727 to 1738, marked the apex of his career. While the site's Tendai affiliations stretched back to at least the late thirteenth century, the Togakushi shrine-temple complex was formally brought into the Tendai institution in 1633 by the powerful prelate Tenkai 天海 (1536?–1643). Its new status as a direct branch (*jikimatsu*) of Kan'eiji gave it hierarchical oversight of all Tendai temples in Shinano and neighboring Echigo. Coupled with his appointment to manage the site, Jōin ascended to the high ecclesiastical rank of *daisōzu* and received the distinction of a purple robe from the emperor. As administrator to the sprawling complex at Togakushi, he now held sweeping authority over its three main temples, fifty-three sub-temples, and two adjoining shrines in addition to all non-Tendai temples, businesses, and estates (totaling one thousand *koku* in measure) located within its territory, and finally, the mountain's branch of Shugendō. It was in this last element that Jōin concentrated his efforts.

The growing presence of Shugendō at Togakushi apparently impressed Jōin enough that he decided to expend significant energy and personal capital on further adjoining it to the site. One of the ways in which he took on this effort was by tying Shugendō to the mountain's history through embellishments in its origin accounts. Jōin most likely drew from stories circulating at the time, adding new points of contact and committing them to written form. Despite his own position within the Tendai institution, these narratives placed Shugendō—not Tendai, interestingly—at the center of Togakushi's religious culture and identity.

Like others before him, Jōin used the figure of En no Gyōja as a starting point for the origin narrative of Togakushi Shugendō. In various accounts, he described En no Gyōja as the mountain's earliest visitor. In the *Togakushisan daigongen engi* ("Origins of the Great Avatars of Mount Togakushi": 197–8), Jōin writes of En no Gyōja's alleged ascent of Togakushi and worship of the mountain's principal deity, the nine-headed dragon Kuzuryū 九頭龍 (Figure 3.2). He needed, however, to tread lightly in this point of revision. Such a move placed En no Gyōja's visit before the legendary entrance of Gakumon Gyōja, the mountain's long-esteemed founder. So as not to disturb this hallowed timeline, Jōin gave the two men distinct roles: while En no Gyōja took on a lay form (*zokugyō*), Gakumon came to the site as a priest (*sōgyō*). In different circumstances, this comparison might suggest the classical structure of reciprocity in the Buddhist Sangha—in other words, En no Gyōja acting as lay patron and Gakumon as a priest who produced merit and provided the teachings of the Buddha. In this case, however, Jōin relied on the long-standing depiction of En no Gyōja as a layman (*ubasoku*). For him, the respective designations of layman and priest were not one of hierarchical differentiation but rather complementary fashion. Both, as he wrote, constituted "the founding masters who transmitted the initiation of Kenkōji," a collective reference to the mountain's temples (*Togakushisan daigongen engi*: 225).

With the placement of En no Gyōja and Gakumon as dual founders of the mountain, Jōin recast Gakumon as a devout practitioner of Shugendō. In one passage from the *Togakushisan daigongen engi*, Gakumon blows a *horagai* (conch shell horn) and wears

Imagining an Ancient Tradition

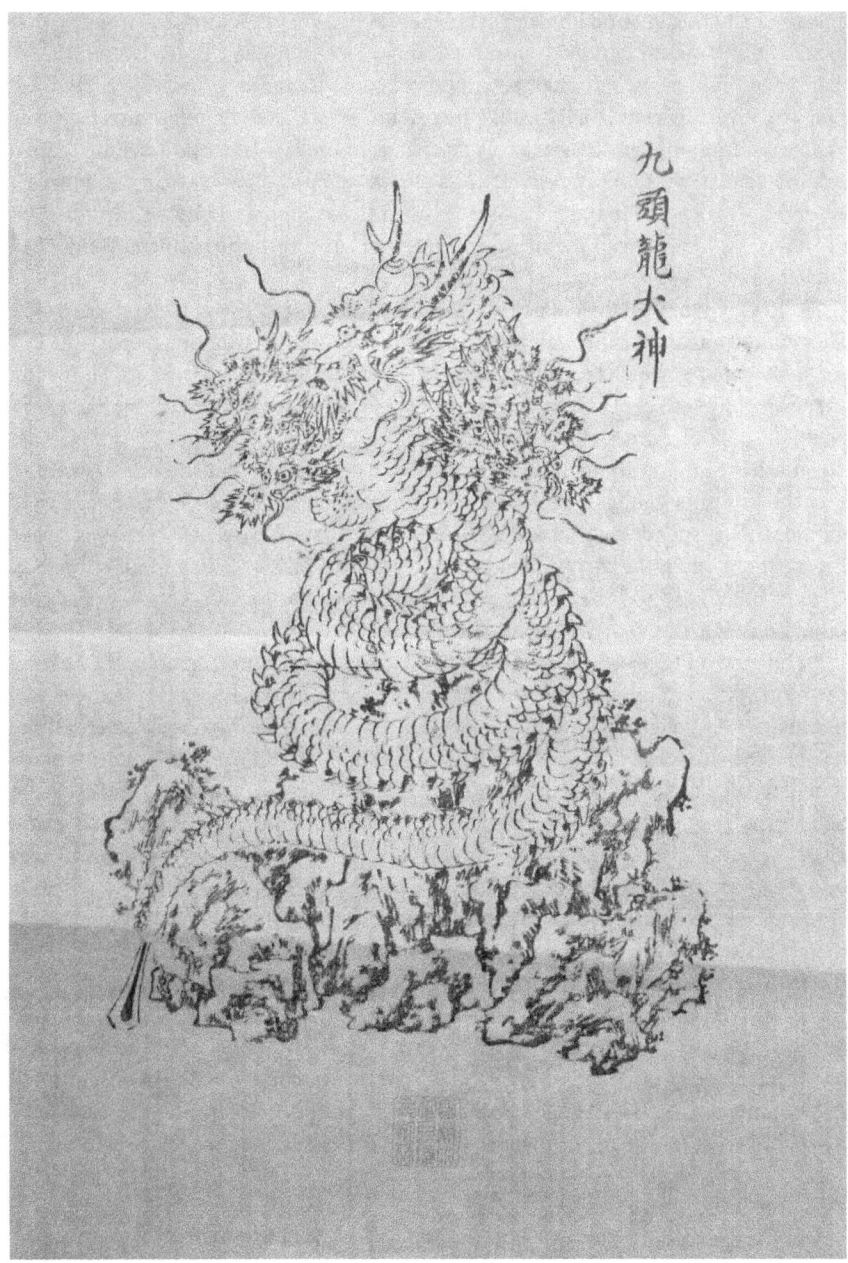

Figure 3.2 Kuzuryū no Ōkami, Meiji-period *ofuda*. Courtesy of Futazawa Hisaaki (private collection).

a *tokin* cap, both signature implements of the *yamabushi*. Cementing the transmission of Shugendō, Gakumon now "transmitted Noble En no Gyōja's efficacious techniques, maintained longevity, and attained supernormal cognition and marvelous abilities" (*Togakushisan daigongen engi*: 212). This figure was a notable departure from the Tendai-leaning itinerant he was first depicted as in the late-thirteenth-century *Asaba shō*. In that text, he is simply described as a scholar and practitioner (*gakumon shugyōja* 學問修行者) devoted to the *Lotus Sūtra*.[9] By firmly situating Gakumon as an adherent of Shugendō, Jōin merged the site's traditional narrative with the nationally renowned Shugendō.

Following from this early point of origin, Jōin imagined a sustained lineage of Shugendō transmitted through the generations. Reinterpreting Togakushi's history from this perspective, he located a demise and subsequent restoration of Shugendō in the late fifteenth century. In an annals of the site, Jōin recounted the assassination of the Tendai cleric and forty-first administrator Tōkōbō Senchō 東光房宣澄 by Togakushi's Shingon monks amidst a dispute between the two sides. He lamented that the "Taimitsu Shugen profound and innermost secrets" of the mountain were temporarily suspended with the death of Senchō. Auspiciously, however, the lineage was restored when the forty-second administrator, Senshū 宣秀, and his successor, Gizōbō Eikai 義藏房榮快, received Akyūbō's transmission in 1524 (*Togakushisan shinryōki*: 462).

While the murder of Senchō is corroborated by textual and epigraphical evidence, the way in which Jōin described the episode is informative on his views on Shugendō. Because he had envisioned a lineage of Shugendō that traced back to En no Gyōja, he regarded the lineage lost with Senchō as belonging to Shugendō. From this basis, Jōin interpreted Akyūbō's transmission as the recovery—not origin—of Togakushi Shugendō. Through this subtle manipulation of the plotline, Jōin interlaced place, narrative, and tradition into a dramatic episode of Shugendō's supposed near disappearance from Togakushi.

Alongside this imagined ancient lineage, Jōin portrayed Togakushi as a flourishing medieval site of Shugendō. In doing so, he relied on a work known as the *Shugen shūyō hiketsu shū* (Essential secret teachings of Shugen[-dō]). The collection of fifty ritual transmissions (*kirigami*) was compiled by Akyūbō and his predecessors at Mount Hiko between the late fifteenth and early sixteenth centuries. Its inclusion in the *Shugen gosho* (Five books of Shugen-[dō])—published in woodblock in 1691—made it one of the most well-known Shugendō texts of the Edo period. Drawing directly from Akyūbō's prose, Jōin steeped Togakushi in an illustrious heritage of Shugendō:

> Our lofty founder, Noble En [no Gyōja], internally resided in the inner realization of the original awakening of Vairocana. From far away he walked to this mountain range and practiced the secret method of sudden awakening in this very body (*sokushin tongo* 即身頓悟). En externally relied on the sovereign seal of the bodhisattva Nāgārjuna in order to divine its trace from afar to this mountain. Through this effort, he magnificently expanded the recondite teachings of the "opened *stūpa*" of the southern region of India (*Nanten*). How virtuous was his unification of the exoteric and esoteric practices and the mysterious concordance

between the two laws of phenomena and principle! How valuable are the most secret of methods and the innermost of profound secrets [of Shugendō]!

(*Togakushisan daigongen engi*: 195)

These words are taken from *Shugen shūyō hiketsu shū*, but Jōin masks this origin, titling the section, "An Announcement on Initiation of the Inner Mountain Transmission of the Togakushi Double Realm Peaks" (*Togakushi ryōkaizan buchū denjū kanjō keibyaku*). Through this redesignation of place, Jōin applied Akyūbō's description of a medieval Shugendō center (possibly Hiko) onto his own mountain.

Projecting Shugendō Back to Ancient China

Beyond retelling Togakushi's history, Jōin imagined Shugendō as one of the great traditions of East Asia, on par, if not synonymous, with Daoism. The connection may have not been too far-fetched, given the appearance of Daoist imagery and practices in earlier sources in Japan.[10] Poems in the *Kaifūsō* (751), for example, portray Yoshino as a Daoist paradise inhabited by flying immortals (Ooms 2009: 147–8). En no Gyōja is described in the *Nihon ryōiki* (early ninth century) and subsequent temple origin accounts (e.g., *Shozan engi*) as manipulating spirits, flying atop a five-colored cloud, and conducting longevity practices. In Togakushi's own mid-fifteenth-century origin account, Gakumon Gyōja is likened to an immortal, "his rank among the worthies (*son'i* 尊位) difficult to estimate," and "his virtue and efficacy (*tokugen* 德驗) superior in the world." At the end of his life, he allegedly "ascended into the sky without a burial" (*Togakushisan Kenkōji ruki*: 377).

Building from these Daoist allusions, Jōin explicitly merged Shugendō and Daoist lineages through an assemblage of historical figures and places. His main point of entry on the Daoist side was the Way of Celestial Masters (Tianshi dao), a choice based on references he seems to have culled from Chinese Buddhist sources.[11] He began with the great temple of Shangqing gong 上清宮, located on Mount Longhu 龍虎 (Jiangxi province). As the seat of the Celestial Masters' Zhengyi 正一 lineage, Shangqing gong emerged as a hub of Daoist activity from at least the northern Song dynasty (Goossaert 2011: 867–8). Recognizing its importance in the tradition, Jōin wrote of a shrine by the same name (J. Jōshōgū) in the village below the Togakushi temples. There it housed a golden icon of Laozi.

> Since ancient times, the area of Togakushi known as Okami 御上 has been known as a forest for concentrating the mind (*jōshin rin* 定心林). In this vicinity exists a reflection of the Nachi three-tiered waterfall; as such, the Kumano *gongen* visits it in the utmost sincerity. Jōshōgū 上清宮 now stands there and is called the premier Daoist abbey of this divine country (*shinkoku dai ichi dōkan* 神國第一道觀). Inside is enshrined a golden statue of the Supreme Lord Lao (*daijō rōkun* 太上老君) that was transmitted from the other country [China]. En no Gyōja treaded on this ground, undoubtedly visiting from Kumano.
>
> (*Togakushisan daigongen engi*, 213)

There is no evidence to confirm the shrine's historical existence outside of Jōin's claim, leaving one to wonder if it existed at all. Indeed, such a claim would have been strange to residents who would have clearly known otherwise, but Jōin's target audience was most likely people who had never set foot on the mountain. Perhaps such a description might have enticed them to visit someday.

In another allusion to Daoist connections, Jōin ties Shugendō back to Celestial Masters founder Zhang Daoling 張道陵 (second century) as well as the military strategist Zhang Liang 張良 (d. 187 BCE), later claimed in Daoist circles to be an ancestor to Daoling (Penny 2011: 1230–1).

> Zhang Liang was a minister to the founder of the Han and eventually became the Marquis of Liu. As a feudal lord, he studied the way of the immortals and prayed for the eternal stability between heaven and earth. Liang's eighth-generation descendant, Zhang Daoling, recited the *Daode jing* from the age of seven. He became a *shugen* practitioner, propitiated a golden image and recited the Buddhist scriptures. For these reasons, he received the rank of Celestial Master from the eastern *tathāgata* [Laozi] and Supreme Celestial Worthy, as explained in the *Shengxuan jing* of the Daoist Canon. Later he secluded himself at Mount Longhu of Xinzhou and transmitted his teachings to his descendants. The position of celestial master has been passed down through unending succession and is revered by the emperors in generation after generation.
>
> (*Togakushisan daigongen engi*, 228)

Through a hybrid discourse drawing upon Shugendō, Daoism, and Buddhism, Jōin elevates the site of Mount Togakushi and the pedigree of Shugendō. The school, he claims, was practiced by none other than the founder of the earliest Daoist movement (Zhang Daoling of the Celestial Masters). By his account, Togakushi served as the locus where Shugendō and Daoism intertwined. The resulting narrative placed Shugendō in the distant recesses of Togakushi's history and shoulder to shoulder with one of China's great traditions.

Contested Visions

Jōin's portrayal of Shugendō as ancient school at Togakushi with close ties to Daoism demonstrates a concerted effort by him to raise the reputation of the site and the status of Shugendō—most likely uncontroversial issues among the clerics. Nonetheless, textual and epigraphical evidence suggest that he eventually took this vision too far. On 9/19 of 1738, the mountain's clerics issued a formal letter of complaint that describes Jōin as breaking radically with the mountain's established customs and regulations in order to reshape its institutions around Shugendō. Signed by representative clerics writing on behalf of the majority of the mountain's clergy, it was sent to Kan'eiji's administrative temples of Gannōin 願王院 and Kakuōin 覺王院 (Sonehara 2010: 31-6).

Details from the letter indicate that Jōin was attempting to reorient the established Tendai codes of the mountain toward Shugendō. To this effect, it charged that he had issued a set of regulations on 8/28 of 1738, calling for an overall institutionalization of Shugendō at the mountain that would have supplanted the current administrative order. Changes he sought included an overhaul of the mountain's training curriculum toward one emphasizing Shugendō doctrine, the wearing of white robes (the color of *yamabushi* garb) by all clergy, and several Daoist insertions (which he understood as synonymous with Shugendō) like chanting the *Daode jing* (*San'in shuto shingi*).

The revisions imposed by Jōin may have fallen in line with his vision of Togakushi as a premier site of Shugendō, but they did so at a cost in the eyes of his defectors. A sweeping shift away from Tendai Buddhism toward Shugendō at Togakushi would have represented no less than a demotion for the Tendai clerics of the site, given the higher institutional status of Tendai. In the first month of the new year, he was found guilty by the commissioner of temples and shrines (*jisha bugyō*) and sentenced to exile on an island south of Edo (Futazawa 1997: 99). Although clerics and *yamabushi* at Togakushi continued their involvement with Shugendō for the remainder of the Edo period, Jōin's policies were reversed under the direction of Kan'eiji and his textual legacy was forced underground.

Conclusion

Ultimately, Jōin's policy ambitions for Togakushi Shugendō proved to be out of line with the institutional interests of the majority of the community, but his narratives linking place and tradition exemplify the ways in which mountain temples and shrines sought to deepen their ties with Shugendō in the Edo period. This layering of Shugendō into the histories of sites across the country had two effects. First, Shugendō became incorporated into the identity and ritual culture of many previously unconnected places. Second, it contributed to the conceptual transformation of Shugendō into a national tradition of ancient origins.

This second implication is not too distant from the efforts of Japan's modern intellectuals, who have likewise imagined Shugendō as an ancient tradition of the folk. An association of age with prestige has, moreover, tended to privilege medieval Shugendō (even in places where its existence is historically questionable) over early modern developments. Twentieth-century scholarship on Jōin offers a case in point. Yoneyama Kazumasa (1971: 44–7) portrayed him as attempting a restoration (*fukkō*) of medieval Shugendō to the mountain. That conclusion, however, adopts Jōin's own romanticized vision of a site with ancient Shugendō roots. Wakamori Tarō (1980), in turn, cast Jōin as an outsider who imposed a blend of Daoist worship and orthodox Shugendō onto the mountain that varied substantially from a medieval culture of strict asceticism. This conclusion also locates an idealized form of Shugendō in the medieval period only to be followed by spiritual decline in the Edo period.

In this light, Jōin's project offers an early modern precedent to modern historiography on Shugendō in its romanticization of the past. Yet in the eighteenth century, such a narrative was critical for the mountain's community. Since its emergence on the Kii peninsula, Shugendō, like other religious traditions, was legitimized by its relationship to the past, real and imagined. Jōin's writing reflects this ongoing process in the eighteenth century. Alongside temporal elasticity, the spatial dimension of Shugendō also had to be extended for mountains like Togakushi where the roots of Shugendō did not penetrate as deeply. If a lineage of Shugendō had only arrived on Togakushi's soil in the last two centuries, then surely it amounted to nothing more than a recent sedimentary layer atop the mountain's cultural landscape. Yet to imagine a long illustrious legacy of Shugendō at Togakushi was to place the site at the center of the tradition and on par with the great peaks of the world. The narrative of Togakushi Shugendō, naturally, could be written in no other way.

4

Otake Dainichi Nyorai and Haguro Shugendō: Unearthing a Lost History

Gaynor Sekimori

This chapter focuses as much on the process of "unearthing" as on the product of what has been "unearthed," in order to demonstrate the variety of sources and materials that may be utilized to study issues related to Shugendō. In particular, it draws attention to the breadth of documentation available for the study of Haguro Shugendō. The topic chosen is Otake Dainichi Nyorai お竹大日如来, a deity enshrined in the grounds of the Koganedō 黄金堂, at the entrance to Tōge 手向 at the foot of Hagurosan 羽黒山 (Yamagata prefecture). Otake, a servant woman from Edo, has been revered by generations of Haguro *yamabushi* as a manifestation of the cosmic Buddha Dainichi (Figure 4.1). Since legend gives her only a tenuous connection with Dewa Sanzan (the Three Mountains of Dewa: Hagurosan, Gassan, Yudonosan), the question arises as to how she came to be revered at this place, particularly considering Shugendō's ambivalent attitude toward the female presence. However, since Hagurosan itself had always been open to female access, there may have been good reason to enshrine a deity who was clearly a woman, since by the middle of the eighteenth century, women's pilgrimage was expanding all over the country.

More broadly, though, her enshrinement should be understood as relating to political and social changes taking place in the seventeenth century, when the hierarchical and affiliation structure of religious centers was being restructured in response to Tokugawa religious policy, and specifically to the power struggle that was taking place between Haguro Shugendō and the other Shugendō lineages and between Hagurosan and Yudonosan. In particular, the Otake Dainichi cult seems to have been very closely related to the fortunes of a Haguro *yamabushi* family with the house name of Genryōbō 玄良坊, and the central concern of this chapter is the "appropriation" of the cult by this family.

I will not address directly the issue of why a low-ranking servant woman should have become the subject of a popular cult, nor indeed am I concerned with trying to prove her historicity. We can find certain topoi within *setsuwa*, Noh plays, and folktales from northern Japan that resonate with the Otake legend, and while I think there is sufficient evidence to suggest that Otake was a historical figure, whether or not she actually existed is not crucial to the development of her cult, or to how she was represented within it.

Figure 4.1 *Shugenja* revering the Otake Dainichidō. August 2008. Photo by Gaynor Sekimori.

The Legend of Otake: *Engi*, *Etoki*, and *Setsuwa*

Otake's legend is woven from a number of strands, embracing both Yudonosan and Hagurosan, and also two Edo temples, Shinkōin and Zentokuji. The earliest known reference to the legend, contained in the seventeenth-century chronicle *Gyokuteki inke*, in fact, links her cult with Yudonosan, not Hagurosan. An entry recording the death "on the 21st day of the third month last year [i.e. 1638]" of Otake "the servant of Sakuma Zenpachi, town head of Ōdenmachō," praised her for not wasting food and for feeding beggars, outcastes, and animals. It says that, according to "a shrine priest at Yudonosan called Satō Miyauchi," she appeared after her death in the foothills of Yudonosan bathed in a golden light, as the central figure in a triad, flanked by the

Sakuma husband and wife.[1] This Yudonosan connection is significant and perhaps represents the earliest layer of the legend. It is repeated in, for example, the *Shinkōin engi* (see below) and in some nineteenth-century popular woodblock prints, to the exclusion of any mention of Hagurosan.[2] We will return to the implications of the Yudonosan connection below.

A second version, composed by Genryōbō Chūshin in 1740 as a simple text written on the occasion of the first Otake *degaichō* 出開帳 (public display of her sacred icon) in Edo, unsurprisingly turns the focus on Hagurosan. Here the story revolves around a holy man (*hijiri*) from the Hiki district (present Kumagaya) of Musashi province, who deeply desired to venerate the living embodiment of Dainichi. He had been in the habit of visiting Hagurosan and staying at the Genryōbō lodging. One night he had a dream that told him, if he wanted to revere Dainichi's countenance, to go to Edo and "revere Takejo, the maidservant of the Sakuma family." The lodging's master, Genryōbō Sen'an, had also had the same dream, so they set off for Edo together. Upon inquiry they found that the Sakuma husband and wife were waiting for them to come, having had the same dream. When they peeped into Takejo's room to revere her, they saw that she also emitted a radiance from her body that lit the room. She died a few days later, on the 21st of the third month of 1638, ascending to paradise on a purple cloud. She was renowned for never wasting even a grain of rice and for giving most of her own food to beggars and hungry animals. To convey Takejo's honest poverty and compassion, the Sakuma had a life-size statue of Dainichi made and installed it on an altar in their home. Later, during the Kanbun era (1661–73), it was taken to Hagurosan.

This is a very obvious attempt to appropriate the legend of Otake by inserting the presence of the Haguro *yamabushi* Genryōbō Chūshin, claiming that it was his ancestor who had gone to Edo with the unnamed ascetic. There is no mention here of any connection with Yudonosan. Further, the connection of the Sakuma with the installation of the statue at Hagurosan, and by extension with Genryōbō, is implied, though not stated explicitly.

In his "Edojin no hassōhō ni tsuite" (On the thought patterns of the people of Edo), Ishikawa Jun wondered whether the "novel idea" of transforming a lowly Sakuma housemaid into Dainichi Nyorai would ever have occurred to anyone if the Noh play *Eguchi* had not preceded it (Ishikawa 1990: 328). Underlying this play is the tale of the ascetic Shōkū Shōnin that appeared in a number of medieval *setsuwa* collections. According to Story 95 in the *Kojidan*, for example, he was told in a dream oracle to visit an *asobi* (prostitute) in Kanzaki. There she appeared to him as the bodhisattva Fugen, riding a white elephant and shining forth light from her forehead. He worshiped her and left for home in tears. She then died and the sky was filled with fragrance, signifying her rebirth in the Pure Land.[3] The skeleton of this tale resembles Genryōbō's *Otake Dainichi ryaku engi* too closely for there not to have been some crossover. Perhaps it is Genryōbō that Ishikawa should acknowledge as the author of the "novel idea" of superimposing the old legend onto contemporary reality (Ishikawa 1990: 330).

A new text was written by the current Genryōbō for the *degaichō* held in 1777 at Atagosan Zenpukuji in Edo[4] and is made up of three sections: the humility and frugality of Otake, the visit of the ascetic to Edo, and the benefits accruing, especially to woman, through a devotion to Otake Dainichi. It praised Otake as an exemplar of

Buddhist virtues, "always abstemious, restraining her own appetite and giving her food three times a day to the poor and hungry," and emphasized that she protected women, freeing them from the suffering of eternal transmigration and from the shackles of the five obstacles and the three dependencies. Interestingly, Sen'an's role is omitted in favor of the presence of the Sakuma ancestor, Kageyu, and emphasis is placed on the centrality of the image, the main icon of the *degaichō*, and on the patronage of the Sakuma family.[5]

It mentions Yudonosan more specifically than previously: the ascetic had practiced there, and the Yudonosan Dainichi is identified as the *honjibutsu* of Otake ("Venerating this Tathāgata is the same as venerating the true countenance of the *honji*[*butsu*] of the [Yu]dono peak"). There is nothing strange here. Whatever the political difficulties Hagurosan had with the four Yudonosan temples (discussed below), the Yudonosan Dainichi was the central figure in the triad of Dewa Sanzan deities and Yudonosan itself was the most sacred Inner Precinct (Figure 4.2).

Figure 4.2 The *honjibutsu* of Dewa Sanzan. Center: Dainichi (Yudonosan); left Kannon (Hagurosan); right Amida (Gassan). Photo by Sekimori collection.

Haguro would not exclude it and, in fact, given the political situation, it made all the more sense to claim it exclusively. This text seems to reflect to some extent the tale of Otake contained in the 1749 *setsuwa* collection *Shin Chomonjū*, and there may also be a reverse influence, in that, describing Otake's vision of her postmortem wanderings, it says that she found a seat reserved for her by Amida in the "Golden Palace" (Ōgonkyū).[6] This closely resembles the name of the Koganedō (Golden Hall) at Haguro. The text also mentions that people had seen her at Yudonosan, reciting the *nenbutsu*.

The composition of the 1777 text may also reflect the account of Otake Dainichi Nyorai contained in the *San'yama annai shūhyō*, a guide to sacred sites (*haisho* 拝所) in the Three Mountains published in 1755.[7] Here a priest from the Zen temple of Chōjōji in Hitachi province vowed to visit the Three Mountains forty-eight times in order to see a living embodiment of the Tathāgata. On completion of the practice, he spent the night at a lodging on the summit of Gassan, where he had an oracular dream in which a white-haired old man told him to revere Take, the maidservant of Sakuma Kageyu in Edo. He went to Edo and when he prostrated himself before her, "she ascended into the void manifesting the form of the venerable Dainichi." An ascetic (*gyōnin*) from the Hiki district of Musashi province also had the same dream and visited Otake at the same time. The Sakuma enshrined the statue of Dainichi at Hagurosan, while the drainboard that she used is even now at Zōjōji in Shiba.[8] There seems to be an attempt here to remove attention from the Genryōbō narrative. Also of interest is the mention of the drainboard in the possession of Zōjōji (of which the above-mentioned Shinkōin was a subtemple) whose importance will become apparent below.

A new *etoki* text was prepared for the *degaichō* at Ekōin in Edo in 1849. Known as the *Otake Dainichi Nyorai engi emaki*, it consists of three handscrolls containing nine polychrome illustrations by reputable artists and an accompanying text placed before the illustrations.[9] Its colophon, written by Yamazaki Tomoo (1798–1861), states that the work was based on an *engi*, then in poor condition, that belonged to a *shugen* family with the house name Genryōbō, and that at the request of Kōdō *ajari* (the current Genryōbō), its text had been newly written by Kurokawa Harumura and the illustrations redrawn by nine artists based on the originals. What these originals were and when they were made is, however, unknown. These set out the structure of the *engi* narrative, which is, in parts, virtually identical with the 1740 one, with certain pious elaborations. However, there is an emphasis here on the transfer of the statue, the building of the Dainichidō, and the role of Genryōbō that is not found in either the 1740 or 1777 *engi*.

(1) Jōren, an ascetic (*gyōja*) from Hiki district in Musashi province, receives an oracular dream while staying at the lodging of Genryōbō Sen'an at Hagurosan.
(2) Jōren and Genryōbō Sen'an travel to Edo to pay homage to Takejo (Otake) at the Sakuma residence at Ōdenmachō icchōme.
(3) Jōren and Sen'an revere a radiant Takejo at the Sakuma residence.
(4) Takejo shares her own food with beggars.
(5) Takejo attains buddhahood at daybreak on the twenty-first of the third month.
(6) Crowds venerate Takejo at the Sakuma residence through a statue of Dainichi Nyorai.

(7) This statue of Dainichi Nyorai is taken from Edo to Hagurosan.
(8) A new hall is built to house the statue in the grounds of the Koganedō.
(9) Crowds flock to the new Dainichidō.

A third strand of the legend represents a more shadowy connection, as well as evidence of a further appropriation, to an Edo temple called "Shinkōin," the Nenbutsudō of Zōjōji, said to have been the funerary temple of the Sakuma family and where Otake was buried. This version, which appears in the *Edo meisho zue* quoting from the *Shin Chomonjū*, omits all mention of Hagurosan, and rather stresses the virtues of Otake's drainboard, which hung from the ceiling of the temple's gateway, symbolizing those of Otake herself (*Edo meisho zue* vol. 1: 277). There are two woodcut illustrations in the text: one of Shinkōin showing the gate where the drainboard was hanging, with stalls and crowds outside it, and the other of Otake standing at the entrance to the kitchen, giving food to a priest seeking alms (*Edo meisho zue* vol. 1: 272–5). Shinkōin also published its own *engi*, *Otake Dainichi Nyorai engi narabini mizu-nagashi-ita no yuraiki* (date unknown). It omits any mention of Haguro and the Dainichidō there, and is closely related to the version from the *Shin Chomonjū* quoted in *Edo meisho zue*, making much of Otake's drainboard "now" treasured at Shinkōin, which was also mentioned in the *San'yama annai shūhyō*. Two strands of the Shinkōin narration are of particular interest: a connection with Yudonosan and the centrality of the drainboard. Here, it was an ascetic priest practicing at Yudonosan who prayed that he might see the living embodiment of Dainichi. He dreamt of a golden pagoda in which there was an illuminated seat, but no figure. Beside it was a priest who said, "This used to be the seat of Dainichi, but that form now has manifested among human beings, as Take, a servant of the Sakuma." He went to Edo where he heard of Otake's praiseworthy conduct, and was told her drainboard often emitted a radiance. Sakuma himself had a dream of Dainichi, who said he bequeathed the drainboard to living beings for their benefit and to establish a divine connection. Sakuma donated it to Shinkōin. Later, Lady Keishōin saw it and developed a strong devotion to Otake, and donated a wrapping cloth and box for it. The text concludes by saying that "those who reverently view this sacred object will without any doubt be relieved of illness and catastrophes and be wealthy and long-lived, with all their wishes granted."[10]

While this text shows parallels with the Hagurosan *engi* regarding a dream revelation, the center stage is taken by the drainboard, reputed to have been bequeathed by Dainichi to benefit living beings. Its purpose is clearly to extol its merits, further enhanced through a connection with Lady Keishōin, the very influential mother of the Shogun Tsunayoshi. It was certainly the object of popular devotion, and perhaps also of periodic displays (*kaichō*) at Shinkōin. But this did not prevent Genryōbō from exhibiting the "true" drainboard, among other artifacts, to an avid public during the 1849 *degaichō*, as an illustration in the novel *Ogen Otake monogatari* shows (Figure 4.3).[11]

To recapitulate, it seems likely that Otake was a minor cult figure in Edo, revered for her "wifely" virtues as a paradigm for virtuous women. Somewhat later she became also identified as a protector of women. A Yudono ascetic may have initially been involved in popularizing the cult, but his role was later appropriated by Genryōbō

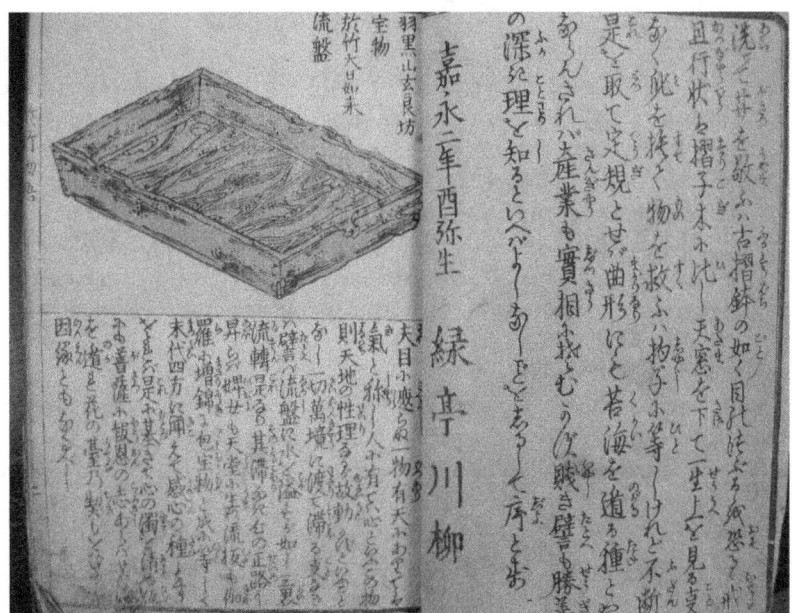

Figure 4.3 Illustration of drainboard, *Ogen Otake monogatari*. Courtesy of the Ideha Cultural Museum. Photo by Gaynor Sekimori.

of Haguro. How this came about is open to conjecture, but there is no doubt that Genryōbō was behind the *degaichō* that were held four times in Edo between 1740 and 1849, which, in turn, spawned a vast quantity of artistic and literary material in the nineteenth century. It is tempting to see Shinkōin's entry on the scene as an attempt to take advantage of Otake's popularity by offering Edo devotees a permanent focus of attention in the form of a sacred object authenticated by no less a person than a Shogun's mother.[12]

Genryōbō and the Dainichidō

Genryōbō is the house name of Haga Shichiemon, a Tōge family prominent during the Edo period as the supervisor (*dōmori* 堂守, *bettō* 別当) of the Otake Dainichidō. Like most households of similar high status (ranked *onbun*), it laicized in 1874 under pressure from Nishikawa Sugao (1838–1906), the newly appointed shrine head whose remit was to impose the requirements of the legislation to "clarify" buddha and *kami* worship.[13] The management of the Dainichidō then reverted to Shōzen'in, the supervisory temple of the Koganedō, in whose grounds the Dainichidō stands, and it also took charge at that time of various items related to Otake in the possession of Genryōbō.[14] The Haga Shichiemon house subsequently remained a wealthy and influential landowner in Tōge.

According to the *etoki*, Genryōbō's connection with the Otake cult was based on his control of the Otake Dainichidō at Hagurosan. The *Otake Dainichi Nyorai engi emaki* (1849) affirms that "a hall 3.5 *ken* square was newly constructed and Genryōbō was appointed *bettō*."[15] This accords with Shōzen'in records that say the Dainichidō was built in 1666 through the efforts of Genryōbō, Haga Sen'an (d. 1679), who became its *dōmori*, and that a statue of Dainichi in veneration of Otake was sent from Edo at the same time. Though this dating cannot be independently confirmed, the architecture reveals a sophistication that points to Edo craftsmen, not local carpenters, and this supports the claim that the building was commissioned externally.[16] More substantial evidence for a dating from around this time comes from dedicatory texts found inside the Otake Dainichi statue, dating from the Kanbun era (Saitō 1965: 29).

There seems to be no reason not to accept the temple dating. The hall's existence can be confirmed by the end of the seventeenth century, when it appears as Sakuma Dainichi in the *Haguro mōde sode kagami*, published around 1702.[17] Its presence can be attested also in the *Sanzan gashū* of 1710, where it is called "Sakuma no Dainichi" in the text, and though it is not named in the illustration, it can be identified through its distinctive roof structure. It is mentioned, as we have seen, in the *San'yama annai shūhyō* of 1755 and appears in the official map of 1791.[18] Notably, the illustrations all show the same architecture. It is illustrated in later official and pilgrim maps, and is part of the liturgy extolling the deities of the various halls in the mountains recited during services conducted during the annual Akinomine fall mountain-entry retreat.

Genryōbō's name first appears in the public record in an affidavit (*kishōmon* 起請文) dated Kanbun 7.12.23 (January 1668), a year after the Dainichidō is said to have been constructed.[19] Significantly there had been no mention of "Genryōbō" in the parish confirmation documents issued by Ten'yū Bettō in the mid-1630s.[20] The wealth of other *onbun* houses was based on the possession of "parishes" (*kasumiba* 霞場, *dannaba* 旦那場) scattered around northern and eastern Japan, but with no income from parishes, and, therefore, from pilgrims, what was the source of Genryōbō's status and wealth? Genryōbō was granted the status of *onbun*, the upper tier of Tōge *yamabushi*, in 1778, thus making the house direct retainers of the Bettō, and by the early nineteenth century it was one of highest ranking of such retainers.[21] It was a discovery of a map dating from around 1820 in the archive of Dewa Sanzan Jinja that provided the first documentary proof of the family's wealth.[22] It shows the comparatively large size of their landholding, and by 1854 Genryōbō had bought three additional plots, making the family one of the largest landholders in Tōge.[23] Their high status is demonstrated by the fact that they were one of the four *onbun* houses on Matoba kōji, just west of the Dainichidō, which provided official lodgings (*shukuya* 宿屋) below the mountain for the *daisendatsu* during the Akinomine.[24]

Could it have been the Otake cult, developed by the Genryōbō ancestor Sen'an, that provided the means by which this status and wealth had been achieved? Had Sen'an been working in Edo some time prior to 1638 (when Otake is said to have died) to foster personal relationships, with an eye to developing a parish there, and in the process made contact with the wealthy Sakuma family? We have seen already through the *engi* literature how Sen'an gained control of the Otake narrative, completely overshadowing the role of the Yudonosan ascetic. The establishment of the hall at Hagurosan can be said to have represented the culmination of his endeavors. The question remains though, did Sen'an happen across the cult and decide to appropriate it? Did he have a prior personal relationship with the Sakuma family? If he died in 1679, it was possible he could have travelled to Edo in the Kan'ei era and met Otake. However, the exact circumstances surrounding the appropriation of Otake probably will have to remain within the realm of conjecture unless further documentation is located.

Yudonosan and the Otake Narrative

The various *etoki* and *engi* suggest a contestation of ownership and throw light on geographical, political, economic, and religious relationships between center and periphery during the Edo period. There are two aspects to this: the relationship between Hagurosan and Yudonosan, and the relationship of the religious institutions of the Three Mountains to the central government.

Hagurosan and Yudonosan belonged to two different religious and institutional traditions. The shrine-temple complex of Jakkōji dominated Hagurosan. Essentially a medieval entity, it was a loose network of various lineages and sects with its own Shugendō tradition. At the end of the civil war period in the late sixteenth century, however, it was in disarray because of internal conflicts, when different factions supported different regional power holders, and these laid waste the mountain physically and administratively and loosened traditional alliances. Yudonosan, by contrast, was centered on four temples, established relatively later in comparison with Jakkōji, which were affiliated with various Shingon schools (see Chapter Eleven by Andrea Castiglioni). Like Jakkōji they had rights of entry to the Yudonosan shrine, where they were allowed to bring pilgrims and perform rituals. These temples were associated not so much with Shugendō per se as with ascetic practitioners called *gyōnin*, who committed themselves to lifelong service to the *kami* and buddhas of Yudonosan.

To keep the danger of uncontrolled religion in check, the newly emergent Tokugawa shogunate issued a series of sect-specific regulations called *hatto*, delineating a clear hierarchical structure. The 1613 *Shugendō hatto* placed all Shugendō groups under the authority of either the Tōzan or the Honzan lineage. This meant that nominally Haguro Shugendō had to exist under the umbrella of one or the other, with which it had no traditional links but rather a great deal of antipathy. After much maneuvering, in 1641 Jakkōji, in the person of its Bettō, Ten'yū (*c*.1594–1674), placed itself under the protection of the Tendai temple Kan'eiji in Edo, the dominant religious power of the time, thereby removing it from either Tōzan or Honzan authority. All temples in the Hagurosan complex, whatever their previous affiliation, were then required to become Tendai, losing their former autonomy. The Yudonosan temples, however, refused to change affiliation, despite Jakkōji's attempts to make them direct branch temples. In the ensuing process of both legitimization and resistance, a new polarized discourse emerged. *Engi* were revised or rewritten. Ten'yū inserted a Tendai past for Hagurosan that had never existed, while Yudonosan temples emphasized a unitary Shingon tradition associated with Yudonosan. This was "a spectacular fictionalization of [their] respective religious traditions and sectarian origins" (Castiglioni 2015: 67).

Relations between the Yudonosan temples and Jakkōji remained tense throughout the course of the Tokugawa period. Their uneasy relationship was marked by a number of lawsuits taken to the Bakufu in the mid-seventeenth century and continuing with disputes over border, entry, and ritual rights which had begun to simmer from around 1730 and boiled over in 1786, closely related to who was entitled to the fees paid by pilgrims. An inconclusive decision by the Bakufu in 1799 engendered great resentment among the Yudonosan temples and led to the mutual harassment of *sendatsu* and pilgrims. This was the atmosphere within which the metaphorical relationship between Hagurosan and Yudonosan was being negotiated in the Otake cult as it was pursued by Genryōbō in the eighteenth and nineteenth centuries.

We have already observed that Yudonosan appears to be associated with the earliest layer of the Otake narrative in the *Gyokuteki inken*; the very centrality of Dainichi, the *honjibutsu* of Yudonosan points to this. The *Shinkōin engi* continues this strand, adding the presence of the Yudonosan ascetic who received an oracular dream. Genryōbō appropriates this by having the ascetic go to Hagurosan and stay at the lodging of Sen'an, and then involving Sen'an in the discovery of Otake. All the same, there is no evidence that any of the Yudonosan temples attempted to cash in on the popularity of the Otake cult through the Yudonosan connection. It is interesting, however, to note that some painted images (*osugata*) issued by the Yudonosan temple Dainichibō in the Edo period, featuring Kūkai meeting Yudonosan Gongen, depict the Gongen in the white robes of a Yudonosan ascetic with notably feminine facial features. Hondōji, one of the Yudonosan temples, is known to have held a 60-day *degaichō* at Ekōin in 1759 of its statue of Dainichi, and another, Chūrenji, exhibited its Taizōkai Dainichi there in 1821. But with Dainichi appropriated by Hagurosan, it is tempting to surmise that the Yudonosan temples sought an alternative, rival *misemono* 見世物 (shows or exhibits). Whereas Otake was the "living" embodiment of Dainichi, after the middle of the eighteenth century, the Yudonosan temples had a potential answer: the Yudonosan *sokushinbutsu* ("self-mummified" priests) were the eternal manifestation. This, however, is a question for another occasion.

Genryōbō and Edo

The expanding city of Edo was a magnet for *yamabushi* wanting to found or increase parishes in the same way Tōge *yamabushi* had done earlier in Tsugaru and Nanbu, for example. However, scope for individual enterprise was restricted by the activities of a number of high-ranking Jakkōji sub-temples (known collectively as the "Honbō"[25]), which were staking a claim to the burgeoning population and riches of Edo by employing lower-ranking Haguro *yamabushi* to develop parishes, known as *dannaba*, in the eight Kantō provinces on their behalf. These temples possessed rights of access to the parishes (*zaichō-ken*), pilgrimage rights, and the right to issue amulets (*ofuda*).

Since it was too late in the day for an individual *yamabushi* of minor importance like Genryōbō to create parishes in the traditional sense, as to do so would have brought him into conflict with the interests of the Honbō, he may have been spurred to develop his influence in another way.

There is little information about Haguro activity in Edo itself. In 1653, Ten'yū set up six supervisors (*gyōnin-gashira*) and four consultants (*sōdan rōbun*) to oversee Haguro *shugen* resident in Edo and the eight Kantō provinces.[26] These ten senior priests were known collectively as the Edo *jūrō* and also acted as liaison between the local Haguro *yamabushi*, the other sects, and the authorities.[27] This system was probably a defensive measure as much as anything else, protecting Haguro interests against those of other *shugen* groups. According to Gyōchi (1778–1841), it was triggered by a dispute between Honzan-ha and Haguro over supervisory rights, which led to the exclusion of each from the other's mountain-entry practices (*Konohagoromo, Suzukakegoromo, Tōun rokuji*: 301–2). In 1746, there were 361 Haguro *shugen* living in Edo and Musashi province, plus eight fully ordained priests with temples and two *miko*.[28] What proportion of these were in the city itself is unknown; it is likely that most were living in rural villages surrounding Edo, providing the same kind of services as village *shugen* elsewhere: rites of passage, divination, exorcism, various rites, and prayer rituals (*gokitō*). As *zaichō*, the Honbō sent subordinates annually to the villages in the parish and managed village confraternities formed to make pilgrimage to the Three Mountains. There do not seem to have been organized parishes in Edo itself, however, and Haguro *shugen* there would have constantly vied with other purveyors of popular religious rites for clients. In 1641, Ten'yū had asked Tenkai to expedite with the Bakufu the selection of a suitable site in Edo to enshrine the "divided spirit" (*bunrei*) of Haguro Daigongen, but there is no evidence that this ever happened. That Haguro-affiliated temples existed in Edo from 1617 is evident from the list appearing in a document recording the establishment of the Edo *jurō*, but there is no information about their activities (*Fujiokaya nikki* vol. 1: 176). In all likelihood, it was Genryōbō and his application of the Otake legend that had the greatest effect in drawing public attention to Hagurosan and the cult of the Three Mountains of Dewa.

Simply being the supervisor of the newly built Dainichidō could not have brought in the wealth to establish Genryōbō as one of the most prominent families in Tōge. Though the supervisor had complete control of the income generated through the hall (donations, sales of amulets, etc.), he also had the responsibility to maintain the building, which could be a burden in the rigorous northern climate. Where then did his wealth come from? I suggest it was based on the income generated from the four *degaichō* held in Edo between 1740 and 1849. There are only indirect references from later sources to financial outcomes, but it is tempting to surmise that Genryōbō's surprising prominence in Tōge society was largely due to such income.

The Otake *Degaichō*

The public display of icons that were either semi-secret or from remote places was a feature of the social and religious life of Edo from the middle of the seventeenth century. Called *kaichō* (literally, "opening the curtain"), they might be held either in the home temple or more commonly in a temple space, such as at Sensōji or Ekōin, rented by a religious institution located outside Edo. These latter were known as *degaichō* and tended to be large-scale events that incorporated mass entertainment—both carnival attractions (*misemono*) like acrobatics, fine crafts, exotic animals and people, novelties and doll tableaux, but also performing arts like Kabuki, *bunraku*, *kagura*, and Noh. The more famous—and well advertised—the statue or relic on display, the greater the crowds expected to visit during the course of the event, which usually lasted sixty days.

In theory, *kaichō* were strictly regulated by the Bakufu. Application was made to the superintendent of temples and shrines (*jisha bugyō*) and permits were granted on the basis of the need for the temple to raise funds for repairs and such. Initially only five permits were issued per season. Much documentation was involved as permissions had to be received from domain authorities and head temples, and the exhibiting temple had to make detailed reports to the *jisha bugyō* both before and after the event. A thirty-three-year interval was set between regular *kaichō* by any one institution, though special *kaichō* were permitted, when, for instance, a temple needed to raise money to reconstruct a hall that had burned down.

Successful *degaichō* were very lucrative, despite the massive expenses involved, as venues had to be rented from host temples (*yadodera*), and special halls (*kaichō koya*) built on these plots.[29] With success so very important, extensive advertising was essential to attract the populace. *Engi* were widely publicized before the event and preparations included building offices, erecting additional offertory boxes, listing up potential donors, organizing volunteer helpers, arranging special performances on a stage in front of the Hondō, and encouraging *misemono* purveyors to take part (Nam-lin Hur 2000: 81). The participation of important people, such as the Shogun and his household, could make or break a *kaichō*, and weather was also a decisive factor. Drawing crowds was crucial: not just the image itself, but objects related to the figure and related attractions and events, were very important. Because attracting an audience was vital, about 70 percent of *degaichō* were held at three temples with easy access to the Sumida river, namely, Ekōin (Honjo), Eitaiji (Tomioka Hachimangū in Fukagawa), and Sensōji (Asakusa). The first Naritasan *degaichō* held at Eitaiji in 1703 earned over 2,000 *ryō* over sixty days (Bond 2009: 97) and the Zenkōji *degaichō* at Ekōin in 1778 drew 270,000 people per day (over 1.5 million over the sixty-day period?). While a successful *degaichō* generated substantial profits for the exhibiting temple and the entrepreneurs who provided the ancillary attractions and goods, there are instances recorded where the expected crowds and profits did not materialize and the temple was forced to sell off some of its exhibits.

Genryōbō took the statue of Otake Dainichi to Edo for public display four times: 1740 (site unknown), 1777 (Atagosan Enpukuji) (Hiruma 1980: 142), 1815 (Sensōji), and 1849 (Ekōin). Little is known about the first two *degaichō*, other than the *engi* composed for narration. A novel, *Otake Dainichi rishōki*, was published the same year as the second.[30] According to the *Fujiokaya nikki*, the 1777 *kaichō* was a failure and to get the money needed to return, Genryōbō deposited (pawned!) the drainboard which was one of his treasures at Shinkōin and acquired the money to depart. On the occasion of the 1815 *kaichō*, negotiations for its return failed when thirty *ryō* were demanded. It then served as an attraction for a secondhand dealer

(*Fujiokaya nikki* vol. 1: 158). This is a curious episode, given that the existence of the Shinkōin drainboard was well known by 1749 (*Shin Chomonjū*). Were there perhaps two "genuine" drainboards? Or were there two pieces of the same drainboard? The conundrum will remain unless new evidence is found. Also, if the event was a failure, how was it that Genryōbō was awarded *onbun* status the following year? Surely only success could have been rewarded in this way.

The 1815 and 1849 *degaichō* are recorded in contemporary diaries, notably the *Fujiokaya nikki* and the *Saitō Gesshin nikki*, as well as in Gesshin's *Bukō nenpyō*. They describe the flamboyant entry processions of the image that were an important part of the buildup, and focus particularly on the sacred treasures on show and other spectacles. The 1815 event was held in the Nenbutsudō, in the grounds of Sensōji, for sixty days from the 21st of the seventh month (*Fujiokaya nikki* vol. 1: 158. *Bukō nenpyō* vol. 1: 52). The statue traveled from Senju to Imagawabashi in procession. Paying tribute to Otake's domicile, it passed through Ōdenmachō, and then arrived at Sensōji via Asakusabashi and Kuramae dōri. According to the *Bukō nenpyō*, various items associated with Otake were also displayed, including a tea kettle, an apron, and a cord to tie back the sleeves of a kimono: Saitō commented that the purple crepe apron sash was unusual (*Bukō nenpyō*: 52). The *Fujiokaya nikki* describes some of the items presented: a *saiku* gold cuckoo from Ōdenmachō, a *saiku* glass squirrel on a vine trellis from two Yoshiwara courtesans, and a garden scene from the main backer (Tentokuin Kingyū) (*Fujiokaya nikki* vol. 1: 158). According to the *Fujiokaya nikki*, men and woman, young and old, thronged to the *kaichō* and there was a great number of donations (*Fujiokaya nikki* vol. 1: 176). Its popularity was aided by a visit by the kabuki actor Bandō Mitsugoro III and other celebrities. Unsurprisingly, it made a great deal of money.

There does not seem to have been a new *etoki* written for the *kaichō* but woodblock print, *Otake Dainichi Nyorai osanai etoki*, a story by Jippensha Ikku and illustrated by a young Kuniyoshi, was published to coincide with the *kaichō*.[31] Ikku stated he had heard the story from "a person in the village (Tōge)," but it is clearly a fictional narrative of a different complexion to the *etoki* produced by Genryōbō. In brief, it tells how Otake was the gift of Dainichi to a childless couple living at the foot of Mt. Yudono. She venerated her parents, and after her mother's death she and her father embarked on the Saigoku pilgrimage to pray for her salvation. They were saved from various perils by the radiance of Dainichi emitted from their bodies. Later they went to live in Edo where Otake worked for a family called Sakuma, and she came to be thought of as a manifestation of Dainichi. Such illustrated abbreviated *engi* were sold together with *ofuda* to visitors and contributed to the profits of the *kaichō*.

One of the only references to the financial backing of an Otake *kaichō* can be found in the *Fujiokaya nikki*, concerning the 1815 *kaichō*. The event was held under the name of Hagaya Zenbei of Nakahashi in Edo as *hotsugansha*. A man called Kōsuke living in Kanda and wanting to profit from the *kaichō*, borrowed thirty *ryō* from the priest Kingyū of Tentokuin in Akasaka to bring the statue to Edo. However, travel expenses ate up all the money and since rent on the Nenbutsudō would be at least thirty *ryō*, he asked Kingyū for a further fifty *ryō*. Kingyū refused and decided to take over the *kaichō* himself as promoter, together with a man called Tomiyasu with whom he had previous dealings, and sponsored the entry of the procession from Senjū to Sensōji. The success of the *kaichō* gave the promoters great profits. Kōsuke, the original promoter, asked Kingyū for a share, and being refused, appealed to the *jisha bugyō*. This led to the conviction of the promoters, and Kingyū was exiled to Miyakejima in the eighth month (*Fujiokaya nikki* vol. 1: 174–8). Whatever the accuracy of this incident, it raises questions about how *kaichō* were financed and the intricate dealings, both monetary and personal, that went into organizing and running a *kaichō*. How this affected Genryōbō is unknown, but he must have profited considerably.

The 1849 *degaichō* at Ekōin is the best documented and attests to the amount of preparation and display that went into staging it. Three documents submitted by Genryōbō remain, his application to the Jakkōji office to hold the *kaichō*, in which he cites funds needed for repairs to the hall (1848), a memorandum dated Kaei 2 [1849] 4.12 concerning the first day of the *kaichō*, and a notice dated Kaei 2 [1849] 10.9 concerning the end of the *kaichō*.[32] According to the *Fujiokaya nikki*, the image, inside a *zushi* wrapped in red brocade, arrived at Senjū on the 28th of the third month, where it was met by fifty-three groups of the Mokugyō confraternity (which regularly welcomed and farewelled *kaichō* deities) carrying cotton banners inscribed with their name and chanting the *nenbutsu*, members of the Haguro *goma* confraternity, an escort of around 200 people provided by the Magome family, a number of *yamabushi* dressed as if for mountain-entry, carrying axes and swords, and a large group of *tobi* (scaffolding tradesmen). Genryōbō's party was preceded by men carrying a *hasamibako* and consisted of three men wearing black silk *haori*, two samurai and a *yamabushi* holding a sword.[33] They escorted the statue to Ekōin, by way of places associated with Otake. However, opening of the *kaichō* was postponed until the 5th of the following month owing to a rain-delayed sumo tournament at Ekōin, and this is borne out by the memorandum of 4.12 noted above. The diary also notes a further delay caused by the death of Tokugawa Narikatsu, lord of the Kii domain, which meant the *kaichō* did not actually open until 4.11 (*Fujiokaya nikki* vol. 3: 473).

The importance of "treasures" to enhance the religious experience is clear from a further text produced by Genryōbō, *Otake Dainichi reihō no katari*, describing items that were on display at the *degaichō*. These included an *osugata* image of Otake in secular form, the cloth strainer, the drainboard, her apron and sleeve sash, her teapot, as well as things associated personally with Genryōbō Sen'an: a crystal Jizō, a statue of Arasawa Daishō Fudō Myōō, and Benkei's portable altar (Togawa 2005: 266–9). The narrative associated with the crystal Jizō and Benkei's *oi* served to further Genryōbō's agency. The crystal Jizō had called to Sen'an when he was returning from a 100-day retreat. He took it back to his residence. As news of its potency spread, people came from near and far. All who venerated the statue would escape illness and catastrophe, and, in particular, young children would be protected from illness. Concerning Benkei's *oi*, Genryōbō says it is the very portable altar Benkei was carrying on the flight north. All who venerated it would escape the sword, illness, and catastrophe and be protected on land and sea (Togawa 2005: 267–9).

The *Fujiokaya nikki* reported in detail about what was on display and the entertainments offered. In the main section were the *honzon*, a wooden seated statue of Otake Dainichi Nyorai, flanked by a wooden statue of Fudō Myōō, which, according to the *Reihō no katari* had been carved by the Tendai master Enchin and used by Sen'an for his private devotions (*nenjibutsu* 念持仏) (Togawa 2005: 268). An inscribed tablet (*gaku*) above the altar pictured Otake with a poem said to have been written by Keishōin. Also displayed here were two *gaku*, both depicting Otake ascending to heaven on a cloud; one was made of copper, donated by the Mokugyō confraternity, and the other was a painting on wood, said to be by Kuniyoshi, donated by Chojiya Hanbei of Ōdenmachō.[34] Five long lanterns (*nagachōchin*) were set before the altar.

As noted above, Genryōbō had prepared a new *etoki*, the lavishly illustrated *Otake Dainichi Nyorai engi emaki*, but the *etoki* based on it apparently took more than ninety minutes to perform, which had an adverse effect on the turnover rate. Therefore, a thirty-minute *etoki* was substituted and the *emaki* was placed with the other treasures on display (Togawa 2005: 260). This abbreviated version may be that recorded in the *Fukiokaya nikki*, as related to Fujioka Yoshizō by the retired priest of Tokuganji in Gyōtoku (Ichikawa, Chiba prefecture). Though signed by Genryōbō, it makes no mention of Sen'an, and simply says that the "sacred statue" of the *kaichō* had "flown off back to Yudonosan in Dewa Province and was placed in the Koganedō in the upper course of the Bonji river" (*Fujiokaya nikki* vol. 3: 473). It is surprisingly devoid of the Haguro connection, and remains an enigma.

Fujioka then proceeded to the treasure hall and listed what he saw. Besides the items listed in the *Reihō no katari*, he mentions seeing a statue of Hachiman Tarō from Arasawa, a tablet inscribed with the words "Otake Dainichi Nyorai," a painting of a priest kneeling before Otake aged forty-two,[35] and a statue of the *gyōja* from Hiki district. Saitō Gesshin, who visited Ekōin on 4.25, also lists a number of the above and adds "Otake's front tooth" (*Saitō Gesshin nikki* vol. 4: 248). Money was not only made from selling *ofuda* and such like but also from donations: Fujioka mentions one of forty-five *ryō* (*Fujiokaya nikki* vol. 3: 474).

The popularity of a *kaichō* was not determined simply by its deity but also by the secular *misemono* (shows or exhibits) on offer. These had become a *sine qua non* for attracting large crowds to an event, especially in the course of the nineteenth century.[36] There were a large number of entertainments in the grounds of Ekōin. Fujiokaya lists, among other *misemono*, a comparatively expensive automaton (*ayatsuri ningyō*) show, with performances of *Igagoe dōchū suguroku* and *Wada gassen* (this was very popular and had large attendances), an illustration of the rebuilding of the Ise Shrines, blow guns (*fukiya*), female sumo, a human-faced puppy, the strong man Ōikari Umekichi, and Sakakiyama top-spinning tricks (*Fujiokaya nikki* vol. 3: 474).

The *degaicho* of 1849 promoted a large volume of secular art and literature using Otake Dainichi Nyorai as the topos. Saitō Gesshin mentions that "Kuniyoshi has made a large number of *nishiki-e* ... and many of them are of Otake Dainichi, whose *kaichō* is this year" (*Saitō Gesshin nikki* vol. 4: 242). Around fifty different prints are known to exist, and these almost invariably transform her from a servant-saint into a beauty. They were created as souvenirs of the *degaichō* and also in response to its popularity. They can be divided broadly into *engi* prints, with at least a semireligious flavor (Otake as a servant, Otake as a teacher, Otake ascending to heaven), prints exhibiting female virtues (Otake as a model servant), and caricature *ken* prints featuring Otake with two other popular deities of the time, Okina Inari and Datsueba. Kuniyoshi was the most prolific artist, but there are prints also by Kunimaro, Kuniteru, Kunichika, and Toyokuni. In literature, too, fictionalized biographies such as the *Otake Dainichi Nyorai osanai etoki* (1815) developed into illustrated novels where only the bones of the Otake legend remained, for example, *Ogen Otake monogatari*, by Ryokutei Senryū and illustrated by Kuniyoshi, and *Takejo Ichidaiki, Kogane no hana sakuragi sōshi*, by Gyokuransai Sadahide, 1845–6. Otake is also found in Kabuki; for example, *Futatsu cho oiro no dekiaki* (1864) by Kawatake Mokuami (Shinshichi), combines, with little mutual relevance, the Otake *setsuwa* with a revenge episode. In 1900 she even appeared in the *shushin* textbook as Takejo, a model woman.

Probably the last Otake *degaichō* was that held in Sakata in 1876 by Shimizu Kōden of Kongōjuin, a former Jakkōji priest determined to preserve the Shugendō heritage. Attendances were poor and Shimizu was forced to pawn the *maetate* statue to repay the money lent by backers. It was bought by a *tatami* maker from Hirose (Haguro machi) and donated to a temple in Tsuruoka, Zengenji, which erected an Otakedō for it and began issuing its own *osugata*, which was exactly the same as that which Genryōbō had produced, but with the legend "This sacred buddha, formerly at Hagurosan, is now enshrined at Zengenji in Tsuruoka."[37] Today Shōzen'in continues to print *osugata* from its own woodblock based on the Kuniyoshi *gaku*, and they are sold mounted on scrolls at the Koganedō, but the statue of Otake is relegated to the back of the Dainichidō, its prime of place taken by the three *honjibutsu* statues transferred from the Main Hall in the early Meiji period. Otake has become a figure of curiosity rather than an object of devotion.

This study of the relationship between the Otake cult, Genryōbō, and the pre-Meiji Shugendō world has attempted to demonstrate not just the story of the rise of one *shugen* house, but how a broad variety of sources can be used to further the study of topics related to Shugendō as a whole (see also Chapter Thirteen by D. Max Moerman). It has presented the theory that Genryōbō's rise was related to Otake *degaichō* in Edo, but unless specific financial records associated with them appear it must remain informed conjecture. Nevertheless, the exercise has elucidated a number of themes that contribute to a broader contextualization of Haguro Shugendō—the appropriation of *engi*, the mechanics of *kaichō* and, by extension, the effects of Meiji religious legislation on its traditional organization and culture.

5

Shugendō and Modernity Face to Face: The Daigoji Case

Hayashi Makoto
Translation by Andrea Castiglioni

On September 15, 1872, the Council of State transmitted to the local authorities a decree for the abolition of Shugendō (Shugenshū 修験宗). The government ordered local officials to communicate to the *shugenja* under their administration to affiliate with the Tendai or Shingon schools. In practice, those *shugenja* who belonged to the Honzan-ha and Haguro-ha branches were requested to move their affiliation to the Tendai school and those of the Tōzan-ha to the Shingon school. As a consequence of this law, *shugenja* faced the risk of disappearing forever, and the term *shugenja* itself of becoming a dead word. However, this did not happen and even today people called *shugenja* still perform their religious practices. Moreover, the term "Shugendō" is still in use in the academia as well as in the ordinary society. From this point of view, it is possible to conclude that the law for the abolition of Shugendō not only failed to reach the deepest strata of society but also had a limited social impact. One who firmly believed in the inefficacy of the law against Shugendō was Yanagita Kunio (1865–1972).

> In every region there are many independent *shugenja* who discontinued their affiliations with temples while maintaining the suffix *in* 院 after their names without residing in temples and keep performing propitiatory rituals (*kitō gyō* 祈禱業) living as lay men in society. In this way female mediums (*azusa miko* 梓巫女) and *shugenja* received a public recognition for almost forty years until now without any real interruption.
>
> (Yanagita 1990: 627–8)

Yanagita underlines the fact that the laws of the government did not really affect the religious activities of female mediums and *shugenja*, who survived at the bottom of society living as lay persons. In the interpretation of a rigorous folklorist such as Yanagita, it was impossible for a mere state law to change the path of deeply rooted

---

The Japanese version of this chapter is published in Tokieda Tsutomu, Hasegawa Kenji, Hayashi Makoto, eds. *Shugendō shi nyūmon*, 11–31 (Tokyo: Iwata shoin 2015).

phenomena. However, was this really the case? It is impossible to ignore that the law for the abolition of Shugendō actually shattered the lives of *shugenja*, confusing and humiliating them. Yanagita developed an interest in Shugendō in the first years of the Taishō period (1912–26), when *shugenja* were reorganizing themselves here and there. Therefore, the historical phenomenon attested by Yanagita was the renaissance of Shugendō from the end of the Meiji (1868–1911) to the Taishō period. In this chapter, I will take into account the twists and turns of Shugendō from the emanation of the law for its abolition in the early Meiji period to its reconstruction during the Taishō period. I shall start presenting the so-called incident of the "separation from the main temple" (*rikamatsu jiken* 離加末事件), which involved the subsidiary temples (*matsuji* 末寺) affiliated with Daigoji from 1888 to 1894. In the second part of the chapter, I shall analyze the birth of Shugendō studies in connection with the hitherto understudied problem of the self-nominated *shugenja* (*isseisō* 一世僧) and the institutional readjustment of Buddhist temples.[1]

The Relationships between Main and Subsidiary Temples in the Shingon School

As is well known, the Shingon sect is divided into two distinct organizations: the Kogi branch (Kogi Shingonshū 古義真言宗) and the Shingi branch (Shingi Shingonshū 新義真言宗). In the early modern period (1600–1868), their relationships were complicated.

> From the middle ages to the first part of the early modern period, the usual criterion for the designation of the relationships between main and subsidiary temples in the Shingon school was the presence or not of transmission lineages (*hōryū* 法流) (the imperial mandate to carry out esoteric rituals for the protection of the state such as the *mishiho* 御修法 was limited to the twelve lineages known as Yataku jūniryū 野沢十二流), which were exclusive monopolies of temples such as Ninnaji or Daigoji.
>
> (Sakamoto 1982: 124)

The term *jisō* 事相 indicates the procedures of esoteric rituals the transmission of which was limited to the temples of the Kogi branch such as the Daigoji, Ninnaji, and Daikakuji but was also extremely important for the monks who belonged to the Shingi branch. In fact, a major requirement for the Shingi branch monks was to receive training in the "main [Shingi] temples for the transmission of the teachings" (*kyōsō honji* 教相本寺) such as Hasedera and Chishakuin, in order to define their own temples as subsidiaries of a Kogi main temple in terms of ritual matters. Moreover, the so-called Four Temples of Edo (Edo shikaji 江戸四箇寺) were Shingi temples with a great administrative authority and could issue orders to all the other subsidiary Shingi temples in the provinces. With the fall of the Tokugawa regime, the power of the Four Temples of Edo (based on the administration of the ritual rights in temple-shrine complexes) declined, and the conflicts between Shingi subsidiary temples and Kogi main temples slowly came to the surface.

Among the Kogi branch temples, which held the monopoly for the transmission of the esoteric ritual procedures, Daigoji had an overwhelming number of subsidiary temples. The Shingi subsidiary temples nominated by the Kogi main temples were defined "officially designated temples" (*kōshō jiin* 公称寺院). It can be argued that the term *kōshō* was specifically used to emphasize the fact that a certain temple belonged to the Shingi branch. Between these "officially designated temples," subsidiaries of the Shingi branch, and the main temples of the Kogi branch, there were continuous tensions about various issues, which caused a situation of great instability. These "officially designated temples," which already had conflicting relationships with their main Shingi temples since the Edo period, began to experience unexpected requests and interference from the Kogi temples. The mediation power of the Four Temples of Edo between the Kogi main temples and the Shingi subsidiary temples was terminated, and this facilitated the explosion of conflicts that had simmered for a long time. The abrogation of the doctrinal instructors (*kyōdōshoku* 教導職) produced a bursting effect on all these disputes.

The Shingon School Incident of the Separation from the Main Temple

Before describing this incident, it is necessary to say something about the chief administrators of Buddhist temples (*kanchō* 管長) in the modern period. On April 30, 1872, the Council of State nominated a chief administrator for each Buddhist sect. A few days before, on April 25, the Council also selected a group of doctrinal instructors, and on April 28 it issued three laws about doctrinal regulations. It appears that the nomination of chief administrators was conceived as constituting a sort of set together with that of doctrinal instructors. At the same time, the Ministry of Doctrine (Kyōbushō) was expected to act as intermediary for disentangling the religious ties between Shinto priests and Buddhist monks. On June 9, the officers of the Ministry ordered the chief administrators to begin to manage their sect's subsidiary temples, thus placing them in the position of de facto administrators of those temples. Because of these circumstances, and with the subsequent cancellation of the doctrinal instructors, it was obvious that the role played by the chief administrators had drastically changed.

On August 11, 1884, the Council of State decided to abolish the doctrinal instructors and entrusted the chief administrators with the task of appointing chief monks of subsidiary temples and promoting or demoting Buddhist religious personnel. According to the third article of the doctrinal regulations, each Buddhist sect had to create its own doctrinal rules and sectarian system *as if* it was following the instructions of the chief administrators. Then, on the same day, the Council of State gave the chief administrators the status of officials appointed by the Emperor (*chokuninkan* 勅任官). In this way, chief administrators were granted government authority and could be placed at the top of each Buddhist sect with unlimited administrative powers. The transition from the early modern system based on main temples to the modern system based on chief administrators brought substantial changes in every Buddhist sect. The government created, at the same time, a system of chief administrators and a sectarian system by appointing chief administrators at the top of each Buddhist sect. The government got rid of the contradictory figure of the doctrinal instructors and adopted a laissez-faire strategy demanding a sort of self-regulation from each Buddhist sect. Nevertheless, this laissez-faire policy triggered internal turmoil and contrapositions in every Buddhist sect, which eventually became quite serious. The problem of the separation of subsidiary temples from the main temple, which affected the Daigoji, derived from these measures taken by the government.

In 1887, Daigoji established its internal temple legislation. In December 1888, Daigoji dispatched agents to the Shingi branch temples in Tokyo to collect a tax of twenty *yen* from each to implement the new temple legislation. This action sparked the rebellion of the Shingi branch temples. Painfully realizing that the new Daigoji legislation granted rights only to the Kogi temples and reserved all the duties to the Shingi temples, the chief monks of the latter refused to pay the tax. The Shingi monks complained that the new legislation was approved without consulting the subsidiary temples and that all important administrative positions had already been occupied by Kogi monks, "reducing the monks of the Shingi subsidiary temples to mere executors without any administrative power" (Murayama 1934: 179). The subsidiary temples of Daigoji gathered in a league asking for a revision of the temple legislation, but the chief monk of Daigoji replied by handing in his resignation and forcing the general election of his successor. Because this election would have been based on the temple legislation, the chief monk was aiming to obtain a de facto recognition of this statute. The election saw a contraposition between Daigoji and its Shingi subsidiary temples, which presented a request to the Ministry of Internal Affairs to postpone the vote. In so doing, the problem changed from a private matter within Daigoji to a broader one that involved the entire Shingon sect.

In October 1892, there was the Shingon sect Assembly for Legislative Consultations, during which a first meeting between the Shingon branches took place. The Shingi subsidiary temples of Daigoji put on the agenda the revision of the temple legislation, which triggered discussions, disorders, and eventually the breakup of the assembly. Acting as a confederation, the Shingi temples presented a formal petition to the administrative office of the Shingon sect to revise Daigoji's new legislation, but the main temples of the Kogi branch rejected it. The administrative office attempted to find a compromise between the parties, but declared "an agreement could only be based on the ancient custom of the Tokugawa period, which delegated the authority to the chief monks of the two main temples of the Chizan 智山 branch and Buzan 豊山 branch" (Murayama 1934: 196).[2] In other words, the administrative power of the Shingi branch had to return to Chishakuin and Hasedera, as in the Edo period.

In 1894, the chief monk of Daigoji received a notice of separation from the main temple from his counterpart of Chishakuin, which was followed by a monetary compensation on April 15. At that time, 1,009 subsidiary temples changed their affiliation, leaving Daigoji to join the Shingi Chizan branch. The Shingi Buzan branch, in contrast, had extremely negative opinions about this matter and some Buzan monks addressed formal petitions against this change of affiliation to the Ministry of Internal Affairs and the Chizan branch. These frictions between the Chizan and Buzan branches were overcome in 1895, when 1,455 subsidiary temples of Daigoji joined the Buzan branch, thus marking the conclusion of the separation incident.

What made this incident a scandal was the revelation that Chizan and Buzan branches had paid a monetary compensation to Daigoji for the transfer of its subsidiary temples (the "officially designated temples") under their authority. This transaction provoked harsh critiques at Daigoji circles as well as in the Chizan and Buzan organizations. The magazine *Meikyō shinshi* wrote about this "trading of temples":

> What was the need for Daigoji to sell its subsidiary temples? What was the need for Chishakuin to buy them? It is now time to be wary of this issue. Independently from the reasons, the trade of temples is really something that should be avoided as it is absolutely revolting. It is like an unfilial son who sells his house to repay the debts with gamblers and prostitutes and becomes like a predator who deserves nothing but contempt.
>
> (*Meikyō shinshi* 3452, 1894: 10)

After this incident almost all the Shingi "officially designated temples" of Daigoji joined the Chizan and Buzan branches; only 160 subsidiary temples remained affiliated with Daigoji. This situation drastically changed the destiny of the *shugenja* who were members of the Daigoji branch of Shugendō (Daigoji-ha *shugenja* 醍醐寺派修験者). These *shugenja* represented the most important source of income for Daigoji, whose financial bases were greatly compromised after the separation of the "officially designated" temples. In 1901 the institutional organ that gathered the Daigoji *shugenja* was called "Shugen division" (Shugen bu 修験部). The following year the name was transformed into "Ein division" (Ein bu 恵印部), which perpetuated the legitimate transmission of the esoteric rituals of the Ein lineage (Ein hōryū 恵印法流) based on the initiation that Shōbō 聖宝 (832–909) had received from Nāgārjuna (*c*.150–250) on Mt. Ōmine.

In this way, former Tōzan-ha *shugenja* who had been under the control of Shingon monks for a long time raised their rank within the Daigoji hierarchy and gained access to the status of perpetuators of legitimate esoteric transmissions. The following quotation shows how this fact boosted the pride of the Daigoji *shugenja* and allowed them to oppose criticism coming from other sectors of society.

> Our Ein division constitutes the center of the famous esoteric transmissions of the Daigoji branch of the magnificent Shingon school. The development of this division contributes to the maximum expansion and improvement of the principles that characterize the Daigoji branch. When someone mentions the Daigoji branch, the Ein division immediately comes to mind. When the Ein division is mentioned, everybody believes in its distinctive prominence and shining perfection. In accordance with this reality, [the Ein division] incredibly helps improving the

spiritual nobility of its followers. Those arrogant monks who keep saying that [the Ein division] is superfluous and detestable merely cast doubts on the honesty of our followers and raise critical voices similar to injuring arrows.

(*Jinben* 15: 2)

The initial sentence, which locates the *shugenja* at the center of the Daigoji branch, serves to stress their consciousness of being members of a famous and ancient temple. Indeed, the fact that the Daigoji elevated the rank of *shugenja* within its hierarchic system might have contributed to increase their awareness about their new preeminent position. For instance, the following passage shows how Daigoji *shugenja* were actively aiming at a restoration of Shugendō: "We created [publishing house] Seiyaku kyōkai 聖役協会, we print a journal called *Jinben*, and we are also planning to establish a temple hall for our practitioners and to publish the treasured scriptures of Shungendō (Shugen *hōten* 修験宝典)" (*Jinben* 15: 1). Table 5.1 shows the timeline of the relevant facts, which had an impact on the Daigoji branch *shugenja*.

Table 5.1 Timeline Of The Main Events Of Modern Shugendō

1872	Abolition of Shugendō
1873	*Shugenja* begins to be incorporated in the Tendai and Shingon schools
1876	The *shugenja* incorporated in the Shingon school are called "spurious school" (*zōshū* 雑宗)
1879	The *shugenja* controlled by the Sanbōin 三宝院 are defined as "servants" (*chikashi* 近士)
1881	Daigoji builds the Ein education facility
1887	Daigoji establishes a new internal temple legislation
1895	Conclusion of the incident about the separation of the subsidiary temples from Daigoji
1898	*Shugenja* made a formal petition to the Ministry of Internal Affairs to restore their religious status
1900	Independence of the Shingon school Daigoji branch
1901	The "Shugen division" (Shugen bu) is established within the temple system and the term "servants" is cancelled
1903	The term "Shugen division" in changed to "Ein division" (Ein bu)
1909	The publishing house Seiyaku kyōkai starts printing the magazine *Jinben*
1910	Sanbōin revives the Ein consecration ritual
1914	The first volume of the *Nihon daizōkyō* 日本大蔵経 edited by Nakano Tatsue is printed. The project is completed in 1921
1916	The Ein temple for the transmission of the Dharma (Ein denbōin 恵印伝法院) is established
1919	768 temples affiliated with the Ein denbōin are incorporated within the Shingon school. The Ein division is abolished
1920	The "Shugendō office" (Shugendō shūmuchō 修験道宗務庁) is founded in the Daigoji branch
1921	The first issue of the journal *Shugen kenkyū* is published

The Formation of Shugendō Doctrinal Teachings

After the subsidiary temples' separation incident, *shugenja* considerably increased their power within Daigoji. A reason for this was the canonization of the Shugendō doctrinal teachings (Shugendō *kyōgaku* 修験道教学). The person who made the greatest efforts for the realization of this project was Umiura Gikan (1855–1921), the chief monk of Engakuji, a Shugen temple of the Daigoji branch at Fukaura in the village of Nishi Tsugaru in Aomori prefecture (*Jinben* 125, 1919: 3–5; *Shugen kenkyū* 2, 1922: 12–30). Umiura was born in 1855 and witnessed the effects of the "destroy the buddhas, annihilate Śākyamuni" movement (*haibutsu kishaku*) as well as the abolition of Shugendō. Lamenting the decline of Shugendō lineages, Umiura went to Daigoji and volunteered to do research on Shugendō. At Daigoji, Umiura received the transmission of Shugendō lineages and could access the old doctrinal commentaries. He copied the Shugendō texts that were transmitted at Daigoji, and in 1881 presented almost fifty volumes of his research results to Daigoji Sanbōin. However, the restoration of Shugendō teachings did not happen despite Umiura's expectations. In 1888, the president of the Tokyo Imperial University asked the chief administrators of every Buddhist sect to donate their commentaries as historical documents for research on Eastern philosophy. As soon as Umiura heard of this, he rushed to make a donation of the Shugendō commentaries, which were facing the risk of disappearing forever, but the chief administrator of the Shingon sect did not give his approval. Running out of patience, Umiura wrote a direct petition to the president of the university to make a donation of personal documents, to which the president happily consented. In 1891, a collection of fifty volumes titled *Shugenshū sōsho* 修験宗叢書 was deposited in the library of the Tokyo Imperial University. In 1908, Umiura, together with Ōmiwa Shin'ya 大三輪信哉 and others, founded the publishing house Seiyaku kyōkai at Daigoji, and the following year they began publishing the journal *Jinben*. This was a gazette, which hosted essays on doctrinal matters, news from the Buddhist world, records about the activities of the Ein division, and also advertisements for drugs and Buddhist implements. Thanks to *Jinben*, the Shugen temples of the Daigoji branch could share various information. The other journal, *Shugen kenkyū*, published from 1921, was targeted to reach an audience beyond the Daigoji branch, thus envisioning a sort of trans-sectarian Shugendō. Umiura was also the central figure of this other editorial project.

Let us now focus on the three main aspects that characterize the activities undertaken by the group of scholars of Shugendō doctrines centered around Umiura, Ōmiwa, and Ushikubo Kōzen 牛窪弘善 (1880–1942).

First, they gathered written sources on Shugendō teachings and commentaries, and made available these materials to the public. The donations of documents to Daigoji and the Tokyo Imperial University library show the intention to obtain a public recognition of the value of Shugendō sources. Umiura was aware of the risk of extinction for Shugendō and expressed his feeling of urgency in these words: "Nowadays, the meaning of the doctrine is disappearing, as if razed to the ground. Thinking of this, it is impossible to be at peace with myself during day and night" (*Shugen kenkyū* 2-1, 1922: 15). The task of collecting even the most marginal documents on Shugendō bore fruit and Nakano Tatsue (1871–1934), the chief editor of the *Japanese Buddhist Canon* (*Nihon daizōkyō* 日本大蔵経), included in the collection a section titled *Shugendō Commentaries* (*Shugendō shōso* 修験道章疏). Although Nakano was a scholar monk of Nishi-honganji, he studied Kakuban (1095–1143), the patriarch of the Shingi branch of the Shingon school, and had great consideration for Shugendō. In a letter that Nakano addressed to Umiura we find the following passage:

> During the compilation of the *Nihon daizōkyō* I received a lot of encouragement from Shugendō members beginning from you. In order not to lose our karmic ties for the sake of the Buddhist path, I intend to do whatever I can for the restoration of the Vehicle of Supernatural Powers (Genjō 験乗).
> (*Shugen kenkyū* 1–1, 1921: 8)

Nakano gratefully received the donation of documents, which had been collected by the scholars under Umiura's guidance, and assured his support for the restoration of Shugendō, which he defined as the "Vehicle of Supernatural Powers." According to Nakano's view of religion, Shugendō represented a perfect example of universal religion (*fuhen shūkyō* 普遍宗教), even more than standard Buddhism. The *Shugendō shōso* in the *Nihon daizōkyō* did not simply provide scholars with fundamental documents, but also served to forcefully assert the academic value of Shugendō.

Second, texts like *Shugendō hōgu yōge* 修験道法具要解 and *Shugen anjin gishō* 修験安心義鈔 contain written interpretations on Shugendō ritual protocols and ritual implements. Although Shugendō written materials were considered to be secret texts, which could be transmitted only to initiated practitioners, Umiura and his group opened this secrecy to the public. With the collapse of the two old Shugendō branches, Honzan and Tōzan, the system of methods that could be used to transmit ritual procedures and implements also disappeared. Journals like *Jinben*, *Shugen kenkyū*, and the articles written by Umiura's group of scholars can be seen as editorial replacements of the old methods to circulate Shugendō knowledge. *Shugen kenkyū* even published an article that explored the possibility of organizing correspondence courses to actively support *shugenja* training. In 1932, the Denpō gakuin 伝法学院 was established at Daigoji with the specific intent to provide learning activities for young *shugenja* (Kinenshi shuppan iinkai, ed. 1995). The activities of Umiura and his group aimed to shed light on Shugendō doctrines and rituals, and the establishment of the Denpō gakuin represented the concrete realization of their efforts.

Third, Umiura and the other Shugendō scholars desired to place Shugendō within Japanese Buddhism and Mahayna Buddhism more in general. Because of this, they turned their attention to Shōtoku Taishi (574–622). They saw Shōtoku Taishi not simply as a Mahayana devotee and the founder of the Japanese civilization but also as the figure who built the foundations of Shugendō. Umiura's interpretation was as follows:

> Shōtoku Taishi is the principal initiator of the culture in our country. He centered the roots of Japanese civilization on Buddhism, formulated the Seventeen-article legal code, and set the foundations for the government. The thirty years of his regency represent the origin of the practices and supernatural obtainments

(*shuren gentoku* 修練験得) of Japanese Buddhism; they disregard the divisions between laymen and monks in accordance with the guiding principles of Mahayana Buddhism. [...] Our E no Kimi Jinben Daibosatsu 役君神変大菩薩 [En no Gyōja] admired the spirit of Shōtoku Taishi and widely diffused Japanese Mahayana Buddhism by performing Shugendō as a commoner (*heiminteki* 平民的) in mountains, forests (*sanrinteki* 山林的), and households (*kateiteki* 家庭的).

(*Shugen kenkyū* 1-1, 1922: 9)

En no Gyōja inherited the spirit of Shōtoku Taishi and accomplished the ascetic practices of a sort of domestic Shugendō while maintaining his status of layman (see Chapters Six and Seven). The Daigoji branch of Shugendō emphasized the existence of a secret lineage that started with Shōtoku Taishi, continued with En no Gyōja, and was transmitted to Shōbō. The Shugendō of En no Gyōja was in line with the spirit of Shōtoku Taishi. The Buddhist scholars of this period were accustomed to prizing Mahayana Buddhism independently from sectarian divisions and exalted the virtues of Shōtoku Taishi. The first article of the manifesto printed on the inside cover of *Jinben* states: "The present association supports the teachings and instructions of three holy men: Shōtoku, Jinben, and Shōbō, which meet the standards of an international religion." Since Shōtoku Taishi was considered to be the cultural hero of Japanese Buddhism, the inclusion of Shugendō within this picture allowed this religious tradition to be publicly recognized as a central component of Japanese Buddhism without relying on Saichō (767-822) or Kūkai (774-835). Ōmiwa actively described Shugendō as Japanese Buddhism.

All the successive generations of the founders of Buddhist schools dedicated themselves to the teachings of E no Kimi Ozunu 役君小角 [En no Gyōja] achieving great benefits. Without following the precepts of E no Kimi it was impossible to promote the development of Japanese Buddhism.

(*Jinben* 2, 1909: 24)

Ōmiwa is saying that patriarchs such as Saichō, Kūkai, Hōnen (1133-1212), Shinran (1173-1262), Nichiren 日蓮 (1222-82), and Dōgen (1200-53) were able to establish their sects within Japanese Buddhism precisely because they followed the footprints of their forerunner En no Gyōja. In this way, Shugendō was not presented as a tributary river of Japanese Buddhism but as the very center of the mainstream. In the next pages we will see that this interpretation was not limited to Ōmiwa. The common understanding was that the sects of Japanese Buddhism were initially introduced from China but undertook a process of Japanization, thanks to the fact that En no Gyōja built the bases of Japanese Buddhism.

The Emergence of the Self-nominated *Shugenja*

There were two types of *shugenja*: those who administered temples and centered their activities around them, and others who did not administer temples and worked as guides (*sendatsu*) for lay members of religious confraternities (*kōsha* 講社) or performed exorcisms and propitiatory rituals (*kaji kitō* 加持祈禱). Both types were considered *shugenja*, but the Daigoji branch specifically defined the second group with the term *isseisō*, which refers to a self-nominated *shugenja* who did not belong to any specific Shugendō lineage. Around 1909, when *Jinben* began to be published, the majority of the people who applied for the license of religious master at Daigoji were self-nominated *shugenja*.[3]

For those *shugenja* who were born in Shugendō families with temples and inherited their religious status, these self-nominated *shugenja* constituted a serious problem.

> If we look at the propagation of the other Buddhist schools such as the Nichiren school, it is clear that it became the important school of these days not simply by spreading the practice of reciting the title of the *Lotus Sutra* but also by performing healing rituals for lay people in order to convert them and finally bring them to join their school. In a similar way, all the Shinto congregations and Tenrikyō practice healing rituals, convert people, and invite them to become members of their congregations to perform rites of passage, marriages, and funerals. Even though the Shugen school (Shugenshū) performs exorcisms and propitiatory rituals, there are not conversion activities and nobody is invited to join the Shugen school. Although the Shugen school is centered on the principle of providing worldly benefits (*genzeshugi* 現世主義), this is also the principal cause of its unsuccessful development. Another fundamental reason is the fact that the self-nominated *shugenja* ignore the correct procedures for funerals and ancestors worship rituals. I strongly hope that precise and clear instructions about ritual protocols for the rites of passage, marriages, and funerals, as well as the best ways to exhort people to join the Shugen school, will soon be fixed on paper on behalf of the self-nominated *shugenja*.
>
> (*Jinben* 14, 1910: 25)

Even though *shugenja* performed exorcisms and propitiatory rituals, they did not include in their repertoire rites of passage, marriages, and funerals. Therefore, even the persons who requested exorcisms did not become Shugendō devotees and this contributed to the underdevelopment of Shugendō organizations. In contrast, the Nichiren school, Shinto groups, and Tenrikyō converted those people for whom they practiced healing rituals in order to transform them into parishioners and provide them with rites of passage, marriages, and funerals. To eliminate these differences, the author of the article hopes for the creation of ad hoc instructions about Shugendō-style rites of passage, marriages, and funerals. The following document expresses the opinion that it was necessary to have instruction sessions specifically designed for the self-nominated *shugenja*:

> If we look at the life-stories of the self-nominated *shugenja* who are members of the Ein division, we understand that their backgrounds are very different. Some of them joined the [Ein] division after receiving a Shinto training, some look like itinerant ascetics who recites Amida's name (*nenbutsu gyōja* 念仏行者), and others have personal spiritual inclinations. The reasons for taking refuge in this

division are almost infinite. Many of them joined our division to obtain the license of religious master and put in practice their abilities to be in contact with spirits on the behalf of society. [...] Even though these persons respect the guidance of our Shingon Ein division it is rare that they convince their households to join us. One person becomes a devotee of our patriarch Jinben Bosatsu, but his relatives may be followers of another sect or may not care about religious matters. The problem is that even though a person becomes a religious master of the Daigoji branch Ein division, he does not change the religious affiliation of his family members and thus entrusts the performance of fundamental rituals such as funerals to other sects. Despite the fact that he became a religious master of the magnificent Daigoji branch of the Shingon school and provides his services of exorcism and propitiatory rituals on behalf of ordinary people, he stays away from the critical moments of life, which are marked by ritual activities such as funerary ceremonies, offerings to ancestors, preaching, and the transmission of teachings. Therefore, the value as a religious master of the Daigoji branch and the glory of this school cannot be duly promoted. [...] I strongly auspicate the organization of a system of instructional meetings on behalf of the religious masters of the Ein division.

(*Jinben* 16: 3–4)

Even though *shugenja* obtained the license of religious masters from the Daigoji branch and performed exorcisms and propitiatory rituals, in many cases their families cultivated a different faith. Religious activities should not be limited to exorcisms and propitiatory rituals but also had to include funerary rituals, preaching, and assemblies for the transmission of the teachings. The passage ends by pointing out the necessity to build facilities to hold instructional meetings specifically designed for the self-nominated *shugenja*.

This problem began with the skeptical comments and criticism of fully ordained monks and lay followers against self-nominated *shugenja*. This type of *shugenja* attracted a considerably increasing number of laymen who worked as guides for the pilgrims on Mount Ōmine, or performed ascetic practices on mountains to develop spiritual powers, or again practiced exorcisms and propitiatory rituals. All these persons could easily receive a license of religious master at Daigoji and act like a *shugenja*. Daigoji was not in a position to contrast or marginalize these self-nominated *shugenja* because it was economically dependent on them. In the following section, I focus on the issue of the reorganization of temples, which happened in this period.

The Reorganization of Temples

On August 10, 1906, the reorganization of shrines and temples began following an imperial decree ordering the confiscation of unused religious sites and the reassembling of temples and shrines. According to this decree, the Minister of Internal Affairs gave its approval to expropriate unused lands located within the precincts of shrines and temples, after reassembling their buildings in one location. On the 14th day of the same month, the administrative directors of the divisions of Shinto shrines and of religion, respectively, which operated under the control of the Ministry of Internal Affairs, issued a circular to promote the territorial reorganization of temples and shrines. It is well known that a consequence of this decision was a remarkable concentration of multiple *kami* into single shrines all over Japan. The text of the circular states: "There are approximately 870,000 temples with about 837,000 main halls, many of which are in decline with no Buddhist service being performed. It is clear that [these buildings] are temples by name but not in reality" (Umeda 1971: 108). The administrative office of the Ein division at Daigoji followed this imperial decree and nominated a committee for the promulgation of rules on the reorganization of its temples, with the aim to abolish all non-operative temples (*Jinben* 116, 1918: 19). The temple reorganization, which was supported by the Ein division, started in 1914 and ended in 1917, with the approval of the temple chief administrator about the cancellation of the Ein division and the decision to reserve a different treatment for the self-nominated *shugenja*. Even the plenary assembly of the Shingon school discussed and approved this resolution. Within the Ein division there were antagonistic approaches to this decision. Some members underlined the fact that it was not necessary for the Ein division to give up its history and lineage transmission and be absorbed within the Shingon school. Another critical opinion stressed that it was unfair to compare the Ein division with the Shingon school; the former should wait to merge with the latter until an improvement of its temples and members occurs.

The next citation describes the temple reorganization from the *shugenja*'s perspective. If the decree was thoroughly enforced, the majority of the almost five hundred Ein division Shugen temples would most likely collapse. To avoid such a scenario, a reorganization of temples had to be quickly put in place beginning with a redefinition of main halls, lodges for monks, and side buildings from private properties of the chief monk and his familiars to temple properties.

> Due to the present legislation and the intentions of the legal administrators, temples can be easily abolished. If there is an official injunction, a temple can be eliminated. After receiving a notice of public sale of the confiscated property, the reconstruction works must be completed within one hundred days or the temple can be expropriated. Of course, the temples without a resident monk are included [in this decree] [...]. Approximately, there are more than five hundred temples affiliated with the Ein division. If the present legislation is strictly applied, it is possible that almost all of them will be regretfully subjected to an abolition ordinance. It goes without saying that some of these temples possess marvelous properties. Because most of these properties are registered as private properties of the chief monk, in the case of an abolition ordinance issued by a reckless legal administrator, it will not be possible to avoid facing an adverse fate.
>
> (*Jinben* 82, 1916: 2–3)

It was essential to redefine the buildings, statues, and ritual implements of temples not as private belongings but as temple properties. Many of the Shugen temples were based on a hereditary system, which completely disregarded the idea of temple property and considered all the objects in the temples as belonging to the family of the chief monk. In the same period, other sects also made investigations about their temple properties (*Jinben* 119, 1919: 19).

In May 1919, Daigoji promulgated new canonical texts and doctrinal regulations and in July announced that 768 temples of the Ein division were absorbed within the Shingon school (*Jinben* 124, 1919: 9). In December of the same year, the Ein division was abolished and merged with the Shingon school, which had been separate until then. In January 1920, Daigoji established the administrative office of the Shugendō school and issued a set of rules for Shugendō. These regulations did not affect those *shugenja* who administered temples belonging to the former Ein division, but the self-nominated *shugenja* who did not possess their own temple: the latter had to inherit the Shugendō ranks directly from Daigoji.

These drastic changes that affected the *shugenja* of the Daigoji branch seemed to throw Shugendō into a critical and chaotic situation; however, on the contrary, they caused a sympathetic interest toward Shugendō from various sectors of society. From the institutional point of view the Shugen temples were absorbed within the Shingon school; this operation left out the self-nominated *shugenja*. What revitalized Shugendō were exactly the religious activities of these self-nominated *shugenja*.

The Birth of Shugendō Studies

An issue of *Jinben* published in 1919 contains this sentence: "The number of lay members of religious confraternities who participated in the mountain rituals organized by Daigoji this year in spring was incredibly high compared to last year. This is something without precedent" (*Jinben* 121, 1919: 8). After the reorganization of temples, the self-nominated *shugenja* were excluded from the Daigoji institutional system and were progressively marginalized. In contrast, lay guides and ascetics who were attracted by the mountain-entry rituals and sacred spots in the mountains kept performing ascetic practices and exorcisms, maintaining close ties with their followers. From the end of the Meiji period and throughout the Taishō period, there was a Shugendō boom. This was not limited to Shugendō because in the same period Tenrikyō, religious confraternities associated with the Nichiren school, and those dedicated to the cult of Mount Ontake 御嶽山 also experienced fast growth, which was probably due to underlying social reasons.

What revivified Shugendō from within was the group of scholars of doctrinal matters who gathered around Umiura. On the outside there were figures such as Nakano Tatsue, Yanagita Kunio, and Uno Enkū (1885–1949). First of all, I want to focus on the strategies of the doctrinal studies scholars and analyze the journal *Shugen kenkyū*, which was edited by Umiura's group, as examples of Shugendō renascence (Ishiguro 2009). The pivotal element of this journal was the publisher, Shugen kenkyūsha 修験研究社, based in a group of Daigoji branch *shugenja* in Shizuoka prefecture but also included other *shugenja* from all over Japan. Among them there were also Tendai *shugenja* and Haguro-branch *shugenja*, and they all referred to their group as "New Shugendō" (Shin Shugendō 新修験道) (*Shugen kenkyū* 2-6, 1922: inside cover).

This group was critical of the absorption of the Daigoji-branch Shugen temples within the Shingon school. At the beginning, Umiura also belonged to this critical faction, which, however, always kept good relations with the pro-absorption reformist faction in spite of the different views on this matter. The critical faction was contrary to the separation between *shugenja* who administered temples and self-nominated *shugenja* without temples because both groups had to be treated equally as Shugendō supporters. As Takai Issai 高井一斎 (1897–1951), the chief editor of *Shugen kenkyū*, explained:

> More than seven hundred Shugen temples moved backward on the path of history and were included within the Shingon [school]. In this bad moment [Shugendō], which had always disregarded the doctrinal disputes typical of the Shingon school, cut a ludicrous figure. Nevertheless, the present historical moment clearly indicates the victory of Shugendō, which is standing in the middle of a forked road like a roaring lion. Studies on national thought (*kokumin shisō* 国民思想) [show that] it is constituted by the amalgamation of theories and beliefs such as devotion for the *kami*, Buddhist compassion, and the Confucian ideal of proper behavior. It is impossible to remove any of these ideas and beliefs from the interiority of the Japanese. If even one of them were to be eliminated, the spiritual world of our country (*wagakuni seishinkai* 我国精神界) would be destroyed and the spirit of Great Japan (*Dainippon-damashii* 大日本魂) would fall apart. Ideas and beliefs of the people of this country are ideas and beliefs of Shugendō. Since the first issue of this journal our editorial group has described [Shugendō] as a religion of "true practice and true results" (*jisshu jitsugen* 実修実験). Among all religions the one, which better focuses on the notion of true practice and true results is our Shugendō.
>
> (*Shugen kenkyū* 2–1, 1922: 9–10)

Takai points out that Shugendō is a religion of true practice and true results, which transcends esoteric rituals and transmissions, includes Shinto, and represents the peculiarity of the Japanese mindscape as embracing a multiplicity of ideas and religious beliefs. The fact that Shugendō is defined as indifferent to the esoteric rituals and transmissions serves to place it in a neutral position with regard to Tendai and Shingon sectarian positions. There was a shared understanding that Shugendō could stand above all the other Buddhist sects if its council was not held at a specific temple but on Mount Ōmine, which represents the original place of mountain asceticism and where all *shugenja* should gather independently of their sectarian affiliation.

> The Shōgoin of the Tendai sect is a marvelous Shugen main temple, such as those at Yoshino, Haguro, and Daigoji of the Shingon sect. However, none of them has a universal value for Shugen because they are great temples associated with specific sects and branches. So, what can be the universal main temple of Shugen? It is Mount Ōmine in Japan. This mountain is the universal main temple for ordinary Shugen and is also the original place of ascetic practices. Shōgoin or Daigoji

cannot encompass all of Shugen, but Mount Ōmine can. Since last year I have been strongly advocating for a coalition to form in order to spread Shugen.

(*Shugen kenkyū* 3–8, 1923: 1)

Takai was trying to create a new confederation of *shugenja* who were now divided among sectarian branches and main temples. Those *shugenja* who were affiliated with the Tendai or Shingon schools should consider that performing ascetic practices on Mount Ōmine was the strongest bond for all *shugenja* beyond sectarian temple affiliations, doctrinal teachings, and ritual procedures. According to a revolutionary Shugendō scholar such as Takai, once Shugendō is liberated from the yoke of the sectarian main temples it could be reinvented as a general entity that transcends all the divisions separating Buddhist sects.

As a response to these tendencies, other scholars tried to demonstrate the value of Shugendō in different disciplines. Here I take into account three figures: the previously mentioned Nakano Tatsue; the founder of folk studies Yanagita Kunio, who studied ethnology with Marcel Mauss (1872–1950); and the pioneer of religious ethnology Uno Enkū. Folklore studies (*minzokugaku* 民俗学) and ethnology (*minzokugaku* 民族学) were new scientific fields and until the emergence of these modern disciplines Shugendō could not receive attention. As long as the mainstream of religious studies in academia focused on the philosophy of religions, Shugendō was disregarded as an evil heresy, a superstition, or in any case something vulgar and debased, which did not deserve to be studied (see also Chapter One by Suzuki Masataka). When the humanities in Japan changed their structure, new concepts such as folk customs, ethnic groups, practices, and rituals came to be taken into consideration, and Shugendō became a legitimate subject of research. Nakano was a scholar monk of the Nishi Honganji; he was not particularly interested in Shingon or Zen in general, but had great appreciation for Tenrikyō and Shugendō. Without this shift in value, it would have been impossible to even conceive of including the *Shugendō shōso* in the *Nihon daizōkyō*. As Nakano wrote:

> The Japanese religions most scrupulously and widely preached abroad, in Europe and the United States, are not the ones that consider themselves as the greatest Buddhist schools such as Shingon, the Pure Land, or Zen, but rather this school [Shugendō] and Tenrikyō. By practicing exorcisms and propitiatory rituals [Shugendō and Tenrikyō] can immediately help those people who suffer because of diseases. Because of this, it is easy to take refuge in Buddhism even for those foreign peoples who speak bestial idioms. Therefore, these are not "tribal religions" (*toraibaru rerijon* トライバル レリジョン), limited to a single ethnic group, but are "universal religions" (*yunibāsaru rerijon* ユニバーサル レリジョン) because they are endowed with the most essential elements to become global religions for all people (*banmin fusaiteki shūkyō* 万民普済的宗教). The doctrines of the established Japanese Buddhist sects are not particularly interesting because they follow with difficulty the footsteps already traced by Chinese Buddhism. Only Shugendō developed in Japan independently when in China Esoteric Buddhism was still waiting to be transmitted. Our patriarch Gyōja Jinben Daibosatsu created

in advance a karmic relation with the manifestation body of Ryūju Bosatsu [Nāgārjuna] and received the transmission of texts and rituals. [...] The best quality [of Shugendō] is that it opposes the decline of the unity between *kami* and buddhas (*shinbutsu icchi* 神仏一致), which is particularly suitable for the people of this country who has grasped the essence of Shinto since the ancient past.

(*Shugen kenkyū* 1-2, 1921: 13-14)

For Nakano, Shugendō has two relevant characteristics. First, together with Tenrikyō it is the only religion that can offer immediate help to people who suffer from illnesses; thus, these two religions can spread anywhere in the world and possess all the elements to become global religions. Second, Shugendō is connected with Shinto and perfectly matches the national character of the Japanese. As we can see, Nakano was not simply a philologist but also a new type of Buddhist scholar who freely used concepts such as global religions and ethnic religions.

While working on his essay on holy men (*hijiri ron* ヒジリ論), Yanagita Kunio thought that the diffusion of popular beliefs (*minkan shinkō* 民間信仰) was supported by three types of holy men: long-hair monks (*kebōzu* 毛坊主), low ranking yin-yang masters (*kakyū onmyōji* 下級陰陽師), and mountain ascetics (*yamabushi*). These figures were half-monk half-laymen specialists who were expert in exorcisms and propitiatory prayers. Yanagita thought that *yamabushi*, that is, *shugenja*, were not originally related to Buddhism. The following quotation is from "The lay *yamabushi*" (*Zoku yamabushi* 俗山伏), an article written by Yanagita in 1916:

In a certain sense, Japanese Shugendō has returned to a pre-1613 condition. What has been destroyed is not the hierarchic system of the *yamabushi* but, on the contrary, the right of the Shingon school to transform the *yamabushi* into regular monks (*maru bōzu* 円坊主).

(Yanagita 1990: 628)

Yanagita wrote this at the time in which Daigoji was in the midst of the temple reorganization process. It is impossible to think that a regular reader of *Shugen kenkyū* like Yanagita was not interested in the decisions taken by the Daigoji branch *shugenja*. In the article mentioned above, Yanagita seems to suggest that *shugenja* without temples who perform exorcisms and propitiatory rituals traveling all around the country are the closest figures to the original *shugenja* who lived before the emanation of the Shugendō edict in 1613. Yanagita is saying that the "right of the Shingon school" to absorb *shugenja* finally came to an end and those *shugenja* who remained autonomous could finally flourish again. It appears that Yanagita recognized the old vestiges of holy men of the past more in the self-nominated *shugenja*, whose number was increasing in that period, rather than in the *shugenja* who administered temples.

Another protagonist in the establishment of Shugendō studies was Uno. He learned religious studies at Tokyo Imperial University and graduated with a dissertation on "Shugendō in the Heian Period" (*Heian jidai no Shugendō*). After knowing about Uno's dissertation topic, Ushikubo Kōzen proposed to publish his work in *Jinben*. After this publication, Uno became the most influential scholar of religious ethnology working on Shugendō. Uno defined the value of Shugendō in the following terms:

According to the present legislation of Japan, Shugendō cannot be considered as an independent sect. In the past, the Shugendō temples, which were transformed into sects, were affiliated with what are now known as Daigoji branch of the Kogi Shingon sect and Jimon branch of the Tendai [sect] (Tendai Jimon-ha). The former group [of Shugendō temples] created a distinctive institutional system called Ein division to mark their difference for the Shingon school. The latter group was considered as regular subsidiary temples of the main temple Shōgoin. The original religious structure of Shugendō was not based on temples, but emphasized the practices of individuals rather than the monks, and regarded lay ascetics (*zaike no gyōja* 在家の行者) as fundamental figures. In recent years this path has been remarkably revived thanks to devotees (*shinto*) who spontaneously organized movements of support [on behalf of *shugenja*] rather than temples and their networks of parishioners (*danto* 檀徒). (Uno 1934: 1)[4]

In this passage, Uno states that the most important elements in Shugendō are not the temples but the practices of individuals such as the devotees who organize spontaneous movements. Uno seems to directly link the resurgence of Shugendō to the increase of lay ascetics and lay members of religious confraternities. From the point of view of the Shingon monks, the self-nominated *shugenja* were nothing other than ignorant and negligent figures; but for Yanagita and Uno, these lay *shugenja* represented the archetypal *shugenja* of the past. Uno adopted the concept of "ethnic group" and described Shugendō as a "national Buddhism" (*kokuminteki bukkyō* 国民的仏教).

Superficially, Shugendō is just one among the various Buddhist sects, but its vitality derives from the fact that it came to existence spontaneously as an ethnic form of Buddhism (*minzokuka sareta bukkyō* 民族化された仏教), the essence of which was accepted as a Japanese type of religious ritual. In other words, although Shugendō is still Buddhism it differs from imported Buddhism, imbued with Indian and Chinese theories, and became national Buddhism thanks to the adaptation of these [foreign] theories to the lifestyle of this [Japanese] ethnic group. [Shugendō] was the forerunner of all the new Buddhist sects of the Kamakura period because it preceded them by hundreds of years and stayed more in tune with the Japanese people than any other of these schools.

(Uno 1934: 5–6)

The expressions "ethnic form of Buddhism" and "ethnic religion" proved particularly helpful to reinvent the value and meaning of Shugendō. The interpretation of Shugendō as the forerunner of the new Buddhist sect of the Kamakura period was anything but eccentric, and also the group of scholars around Umiura was convinced of the same. Skillfully using keywords such as "ethnic group" and "national Buddhism," Uno succeeded in expressing in academic terminology what Umiura and his group had not been able to make clear enough.

Together with Nakano and Yanagita, Uno also prized the religious activities of the *shugenja* without temples against *shugenja* with temples because these scholars saw in the former the semblance of the primordial *shugenja*. Nakano turned to a new concept in religious studies such as the idea of universal religion to emphasize the salvific power of Shugendō. At that time, concepts such as folk customs and ethnicity (groups, practices, and rituals) were much appreciated in the humanities. Umiura and his group, moving away from the perspective of Buddhist practitioners, developed the idea that Shugendō transcended temple and sectarian divisions. Yanagita and Uno distanced themselves from the old mainstream represented by the philosophy of religion and, also under the influence of cutting-edge trends in European academia, became pioneers of folklore studies and the ethnology of religion in the Japanese academic world. The doctrinal study of Shugendō initiated by Umiura and his group, Nakano's compilation of the *Nihon daizōkyō*, Yanagita's folklore studies, and Uno's religious ethnography constituted the four essential conditions without which Shugendō studies could not be as they are today.

Part Three

Imagining En no Gyōja and Fictionalizing Shugendō

6

Between Companionship and Worship: A Reflection on En no Gyōja Statuary Past and Present

Carina Roth

Elusive Existence

In the "World of Shugendō" (*Shugendō no sekai* 修験道の世界),[1] En no Gyōja 役行者 is presented, in one breath, as the founder of Shugendō and the ancestor of all *yamabushi*. "En the Ascetic" or "En the Practitioner" is a charismatic religious figure known for his special powers acquired through ascetic practice in the mountains. Said to have lived in central Japan around the seventh century AD, he gradually came to be seen as the head of *yamabushi*. Early accounts use his personal name, E(n) no Kimi Ozunu 役ノ君小角 ("En Little Horn") or En no Ubasoku 役優婆塞 ("En the Lay Practitioner"; Skt. *upāsaka*).[2] "En no Gyōja" became his trademark appellation once he started being seen distinctively as the founder, the ancestor, or the leader of all *yamabushi* 山伏.[3] Even if factual evidence of his life is scant at best, he is almost unanimously treated as a historical person. Although nobody will dispute his legendary aura, episodes of his hagiography appear in much more recent accounts as if the events described had indeed happened.

En no Gyōja belongs to a small number of religious figures that have entered the Japanese collective imagination. Although he has left no teachings, writings, or disciples, he ranks close to Shōtoku Taishi 聖徳太子 (524–672), Gyōki 行基 (668–749), and Kōbō Daishi 弘法大師 (Kūkai 空海; 774–835) in terms of popularity. The sole account on En no Gyōja that may claim some historicity is a brief passage in *Shoku Nihongi* (797), dated to the summer of 699:

> E no Kimi Ozunu was exiled to the island at Izu. Ozunu first lived on Mount Katsuragi and was known for his magic. The Outside Junior Fifth Rank Lower Grade Chieftain of Korea Hirotari apprenticed himself to him. Later he came to envy his master's powers and slandered him, saying that Ozunu was leading people astray. As a result, Ozunu was exiled to a distant place. People say that

Ozunu enslaved the gods and demons and forced them to draw his water and gather his firewood. If they did not follow his orders, he bound them with spells.

(Transl. Keenan 1999: 343–4)

As sketchy as it is, this brief passage lays the ground for two of the most prevalent characteristics of En no Gyōja's aura through time: a possible inspiration for insurrection (accusation of "leading people astray") and the use of his powers to punish any hint at insubordination (binding unruly spirits with spells). Not long after *Shoku Nihongi*, one of the didactic tales in *Nihon ryōiki* (822) expands on the same few elements, without shedding any more concrete light on En no Gyōja's life (or existence). Moreover, no other source corroborates his alleged banishment and exile to an island off Izu upon imperial order. All subsequent hagiographies of En no Gyōja stem from those two early accounts, adding episodes over the years. They accompany the evolution and development of Shugendō to this day.

On the one hand, the textual tradition of En no Gyōja's hagiographies is well known. It has been widely followed and discussed over time, both in and outside *shugen* circles. In either case, his role as ideal founder and ancestor is heavily emphasized, even though some Shugendō sites make exception by venerating another founding figure. Dewa sanzan 出羽三山 in northern Japan is one such example, where Nōjo Taishi 能除太子 (562?–641?), son of Emperor Sushun 崇峻天皇 (553–92; r. 587–92), is considered as initiator of the mountain cult. In fact, many *shugen* mountains are linked to different "mountain openers" (*kaisan* 開山), often regional ones. En no Gyōja's uniqueness lies in his emerging as an overarching and federalizing persona, credited with the founding of a great number of *shugen* temples in all Japan (see Kawasaki Tsuyoshi's contribution to this book). Down to the contemporary period, a vast number of works are dedicated to that figure, originating from a great variety of sources (primarily temple publications, but also essays, novels, plays, *manga*, children books, etc.). From an academic point of view, beyond a range of articles by Japanese and non-Japanese scholars, only one comprehensive and critical study on En no Gyōja has been published so far, by Miyake Hitoshi, the foremost authority in Shugendō studies. In this work, he presents a synthetic overview of the evolution of En no Gyōja from the earliest texts to the Edo period (Miyake 2000a). Despite the marginal position of the religious current he is heralding, En no Gyōja clearly represents an inspirational figure for many different audiences.

While there is ample material to investigate En no Gyōja's textual "legacy," the iconographic tradition of this figure has been neglected so far. Given the marginal position Shugendō occupies nowadays in the Japanese religious landscape, this absence of interest would not be surprising were it not for the sheer number of En no Gyōja images preserved throughout the country. According to Ishikawa Tomohiko 石川智彦, one of the rare scholars to have worked more than cursorily on En no Gyōja iconography, they rank third after those of Shōtoku Taishi and Kōbō Daishi (Ishikawa 1999: 188; 2015; Ishikawa and Ozawa 2000). Miyagi Tainen 宮城泰年, patriarch of the Honzan school of Shugendō (Honzan Shugenshū 本山修験宗) and head of Shōgoin in Kyoto, the oldest temple dedicated only to that tradition, observed that "during the Edo period, there most likely was no village in Japan that did not have a chapel dedicated to En no Gyōja" (Miyagi 2017, my interview).

This chapter represents the first step of an ongoing enquiry into the reasons for En no Gyōja's appeal over the centuries. The overarching intent is to understand why this obscure and in many ways ambiguous figure has become a thoroughly recognizable icon that to this day triggers respect and worship, while at the same time being considered eminently approachable. Despite his gradual transformation into a divinized figure, perhaps best illustrated by his 1799 canonization as Jinben Daibosatsu 神変大菩薩 (Great Bodhisattva Jinben) by Emperor Kōkaku 光格天皇 (1771–1840; r. 1780–1817), En no Gyōja's most enduring feature seems to reside in his status as a human being who managed to enhance his own powers through ascetic practice. Although a wide array of sources transform him into an esoteric practitioner *avant la lettre* in order to fit him into medieval lineages (see Kawasaki's contribution to this book), En no Gyōja never loses his aura as a lay practitioner who cannot be fully molded into one of the existing schools of thought. In this chapter, I will show some of the ways in which this spectrum of veneration takes shape by focusing on a series of events surrounding the recent restoration of one particular statue of En no Gyōja. My objective is especially to look at the relationship that establishes itself between statues and people who worship them, what they represent for them, and what kind of different interactions these statues bring about over time.

Elements of Iconography

The overwhelming majority of En no Gyōja statues date from the Edo period. However, many of these statues were placed in mountain temples or chapels, hence exposed to the rigors of the Japanese climate. Because of strong differences in temperature and degrees of humidity, older statues may, therefore, have been lost due to natural decay. With less adverse conditions of conservation, the actual number of extant earlier statues could have been much higher (Ishikawa 2017, my interview). The end of the medieval period and the Edo period represent the moment of maximal expansion for Shugendō, by way of a system of parishes and confraternities. *En no Gyōja hongi* 役行者本紀 (sixteenth century), for example, one of the most extensive hagiographies of En no Gyōja links him to more than one hundred mountains (on this document, see Bouchy 1993; Miyake 2000a: 103ff.). They are remarkably well distributed all over Japan, reflecting both the spread of Shugendō in all provinces at the time and the centrality of En no Gyōja as a founding figure.

In the Edo period, Shugendō represented an established presence in the religious and social life of the country, in rural as well as in urban environments (see the contributions of Andrea Castiglioni, Janine Sawada, and Gaynor Sekimori in this book). In that context, the figure of En no Gyōja, envisioned as an ancestral founder, constituted a major vector of unification for the movement. His symbolic importance is all the more reinforced by the fact that *shugen* practice is so heavily localized and marked by regional practices. En no Gyōja, therefore, truly functions as a rallying force for Shugendō, even though his role varies slightly depending on specific *shugen* branches or sites. The production of images reflects this evolution, with peaks in the realization of statues or paintings centering on the centennials of En no Gyōja's death, especially in 1799, which coincides with Emperor Kōkaku's bestowing upon En no

Gyōja of the title of "Great bodhisattva" (Ishikawa 2017, my interview). Another significant element to take into account is the rise and decline of the worship of Zaō Gongen 蔵王権現 in relation to that of En no Gyōja. Zaō, a composite figure unique to the Japanese pantheon, is the main deity of Kinpusen and Ōmine, the most important sites of *shugen* practice in central Japan. The cult of Zaō can be traced back to the beginning of the eleventh century.[4] Some scholars suggest that veneration of En no Gyōja gradually came in competition with that cult, and that the exponential increase of En no Gyōja statues from the Muromachi period onward reflects his being considered more and more as a divinized figure (see Fujioka's contribution to this book). The striking decrease in statues of Zaō Gongen around the same time corroborates this analysis (Sawa 1989: 198; Miyake 2000a: 191).

Kinpusen sōsōki 金峰山創草記 (Record of the Founding of Mount Kinpu), a fourteenth-century compilation of *shugen* rites and traditions linked to Mount Kinpu, mentions a ritual dedicated to the image of En no Gyōja. Simply called *mieku* 御影供, "Offering to the August Image," it was first held on top of Mount Ōmine in 1103 (*Kinpusen sōsōki*: 122).[5] In a section devoted to the most important places of practice on Mount Ōmine, another early *shugen* compendium, *Shozan engi* 諸山縁起 (Origins of the Mountains; end of twelfth century), describes an image of En no Gyōja, greater than life and engraved on the wall of a cave at Jinzen 神仙, situated in the middle of the Ōmine range (*Shozan engi*, section 16: 132). These two examples appear to be the earliest written references to images. As far as extant statues are concerned, the oldest known and identified example is that of a statue dated to the twelfth century and held by Enrakuji 円楽寺, a Shingon temple purportedly founded by En no Gyōja on the northern foot of Mount Fuji.[6] Given that the earliest textual evidence for worship of En no Gyōja images also dates to the twelfth century, this demonstrates not only that En no Gyōja was venerated outside the Kinai region already in the early Kamakura period but also that the cult surrounding his image spread very quickly. The earliest known painted image of En no Gyōja is held by Matsuoji 松尾寺 (Osaka Prefecture), deemed to be approximately contemporary with Enrakuji's statue (Ishikawa 2015: 161). In both cases, En no Gyōja is flanked by two demons (*kijin* 鬼神), representing at first the mountain deities he is known to subdue, and later on his retinue. *Shoku Nihongi* states that *kijin* fetch water and carry wood for him, and this is how the two demons in the En no Gyōja triad are represented in both paintings and statuary: one of them carries a water gourd, the other an ax and a portable altar (*oi* 笈). They are a near constant element in En no Gyōja's iconography already since the first preserved images, even though they do not appear in textual sources before the end of the fourteenth century. That is also when they acquire their names, as well as various accompanying legends. The two demons are identified as Zenki 前鬼 and Goki 後鬼, most commonly translated as "Front demon" and the "Back demon," although other *kanji* appear too.[7] Medieval images and statues of En no Gyōja are rare, although he is frequently represented in Kumano and Yoshino mandalas. After the mid-Muromachi period, however, the number of extant images begins to increase and to spread, leading to the staggering number that are preserved today (Ishikawa 2015: 161).

In both paintings and statuary, En no Gyōja's archetypical appearance is that of an emaciated old man of fierce appearance, his mouth often open, as if he were chanting *dhāraṇī*. Wearing high *geta* 下駄 (wooden clogs), Buddhist robes, and a long hood (*nagatokin* 長頭襟) under a straw coat (*mino* 蓑).⁸ Overall, despite softer variations, in which En no Gyōja appears in a stately demeanor, in the prime of his life, and with rather appeased features, En no Gyōja is overwhelmingly characterized by a dynamic and concentrated stance, whether his facial expression is actively fierce or inwardly intent. As such, his depiction as a fearsome mountain practitioner is clearly perceived as reflecting the distinctiveness of Shugendō teachings and practice. This is the common denominator of all representations of En no Gyōja from the earliest images to the most recent ones, including contemporary children books and *manga*.

En no Gyōja Chapel at Gyōsen no shuku

This stern demeanor is also that of En no Gyōja's statue at Gyōsen no shuku 行仙の宿 (Gyōsen Lodge) on the southern half of the Okugake path (*Okugake no michi* 奥駈けの道), the most celebrated of *shugen* routes (Figure 6.1). Gyōsen no shuku is one of the numerous ritual stops that punctuate the Okugake path. From the Muromachi

Figure 6.1 En no Gyōja statue at the oratory of Gyōsen no shuku, Wakayama prefecture. Statue of Jitsukaga on the right. May 2017. Photo by Carina Roth.

period onward, when the route became standardized, these stops are called *nabiki* 靡.⁹ Gyōsen no shuku, the nineteenth *nabiki*, is situated between Kasasuteyama and Nuta no shuku (Figure 6.2).¹⁰ Hayashi Jitsukaga 林実利 (1843–84) was active in this area in the last years of his life. Jitsukaga was a *shugen* practitioner famous for having thrown himself off the Nachi waterfall at the end of the nineteenth century. His death constituted one of the last cases of "discarding the body" (*shashin* 捨身) or self-immolation in Shugendō (see Bouchy 1978, 1993 for a detailed account of Jitsukaga's life and writings). As a result of the prohibition of Shugendō in 1872 under the religious reforms of the Meiji government, the Okugake path fell into disuse, especially the less accessible and less frequented southern part. After the restoration of religious freedom with the establishment of the new Constitution in 1946, almost all mountain entries by the reinstated *shugen* organizations were concentrated, and still are, on the northern half of the trail, leading to further deterioration and decay of the southern

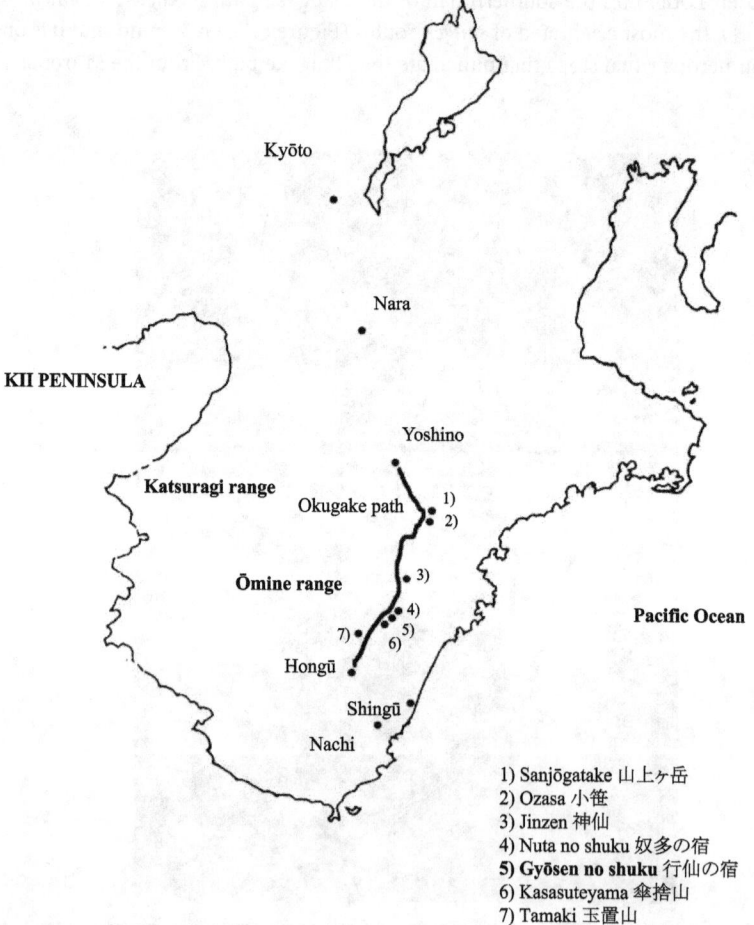

Figure 6.2 Map of the Kii Peninsula, with relevant topographical markings along the Ōmine Okugake route.

half (from Jinzen to Hongū, Figure 6.2). Apart from the different *shugen* organizations that enter the mountains ritually, several groups of lay volunteers function as de facto caretakers of the Okugake trail. Because places to stay the night are far and in-between on the southern part of the route, one of these associations, the Shingū Yamabiko Goup 新宮山彦グループ, decided to build a lodge between the halts of Jikyō no shuku and Tamaki. Founded in 1974 with the candid aim of "becoming familiar with nature through walking the mountains, and reflecting upon various things thanks to this experience," the Shingū Yamabiko Group is an association of volunteers, with no income nor fees, that raises money only for specific projects.[11] They are in charge of three mountain huts in the southern Ōmine range (Gyōsen no shuku, Jikyō no shuku, and Heichi no shuku).[12] Under the leadership of Tamaoka Toshiaki 玉岡憲明, the founder of the group, the whole area was investigated for a suitable place to build a hut as well as a chapel dedicated to En no Gyōja—even though, as Tamaoka points out, "Shingū Yamabiko Group is not a *shugen* association" (http://syamabiko.web.fc2.com/karimine_1000.html). They chose the narrow mountain saddle of Gyōsen no shuku, as it is relatively easily accessible from a national road passing a few hundred meters below on the eastern side. The most crucial problem was finding water, which is scarce along the ridges of the Ōmine range. After a day of intensive and unfruitful search, the party decided to pray to Jitsukaga, the nineteenth-century ascetic who had made this region the center of his practice. They promised to worship him along with En no Gyōja in the chapel to be built should he accede to their wish. At the end of the second day, a spring was indeed found, and the Yamabiko group held true to their promise. In 1990, they inaugurated a lodge and a chapel dedicated to En no Gyōja as its central figure with Jitsukaga at his side (Figure 6.1).

Despite being a lay group with no specific links to any *shugen* organization in particular, nor ritual practices per se, it appears clearly from the above that the *shugen* mindscape or worldview plays an important part in their perception of the region. As a further indication of this, building the hut was also a way to commemorate the life and work of Maeda Yūichi 前田勇一 (1913–81), who pioneered the revival of Minami Okugake.[13] Maeda was a well-known *shugenja* with strong links to Shōgoin, the head temple of Honzan Shugenshū. Because of Maeda's relationship to Shōgoin, Tamaoka asked the temple whether they could give them a statue of En no Gyōja to enshrine at Gyōsen no shuku. Miyagi Tainen, who was head administrator of the temple at the time, warmly consented to the request. Tamaoka was given two statues to choose from, taken from Shōgoin's large stock of images. Beyond the pieces commissioned by or granted to the temple itself over the centuries, a great number of items were brought to Shōgoin during the early years of the Meiji Restoration. By donating their images to the temple, smaller temples as well as private people managed to salvage their property during the anti-Buddhism campaign (*haibutsu kishaku* 廃仏毀釈) and the "separation of *kami* and buddhas" (*shinbutsu bunri* 神仏分離) (see Suzuki's contribution to this book). The history of many such pieces remains largely unknown. That is how, after only a slight restoration,[14] the present wooden statue, one of the anonymous contingent of Shōgoin's collection, was carried up to the mountain ridge. There, it was enshrined in its new chapel and animated through an eye-opening ceremony (*kaigan shiki* 開眼式) by Shōgoin monks in 1990.[15]

Over the course of their spring mountain entry in 2016, members of the Kumano Shugen organization, which is based at Nachi 那智 (one of the Three Mountains of Kumano at the southern tip of the Kii peninsula), signaled to the Yamabiko group that En no Gyōja's statue was in urgent need of repair: the varying temperatures and degrees of humidity up on the mountain (at an altitude of around 1000 meters) were taking a heavy toll on the statue. The Yamabiko group was already aware of the problem, and this remark sped up the process. Asamura Tomonobu 浅村朋伸, a Buddhist sculptor schooled at Onjōji, a temple deeply involved with *shugen* practice since the end of the eleventh century,[16] was asked to have a look at the statue, and it was decided to take it down for thorough repair. In order to do that, a "de-animation ceremony" (*oshōne nuki kuyō* お性根抜き供養) was required first.[17] It was performed by the head of Kumano Shugen, Takagi Ryōei 高木亮英, on July 4, 2016. Starting off at the sound of *horagai* 法螺貝 (ritual conches), the ceremony consisted in the recitation of various sutras and was concluded by three repetitions of the *Heart sutra*. After the Kumano Shugen members left, Asamura began to dismount the statue. Although it had been brought up in one piece, he disassembled it and wrapped all parts individually, about ten altogether. They were then placed onto a little monorail that functions as a lift for carrying goods to or from the mountain hut, and brought down to the road, a few hundred meters below, some thirty to forty minutes walking distance (Asamura 2017, my interview). Again, this shows how interactions unfold between a *shugen* group considered in a way as the "spiritual caretaker" of the mountain, and a lay group seen as a "secular caretaker" of the mountain.

When Asamura started working on the statue, checking out its different pieces, he discovered that a votive text (*ganmon* 願文) had been inserted in its body. The statue, which had so far been one anonymous member of the refugee household of Shōgoin statues, was now endowed with a definite identity. According to the votive text, the statue was commissioned by Buddhist priest Ganshin Hōin from Rishōin 理正院法印元信, born in 1672, a *sendatsu* 先達 (ritual guide) of the Ukai 鵜飼 family, described as devoted to the "Gyōja cult" (*Gyōja shinkō* 行者信仰). The *ganmon* is dated to the ninth month of 1702, and dedicated to peace and prosperity upon the land, as well as more specific wishes for health and well-being for a member of the Shōgoin administration, heard to be ill, for parishioners in general and for members of the Ukai family. The sculptor is named, as well as the leader of the eye-opening ceremony, the Imperial Prince Dōson 道尊親王, thirty-seventh patriarch of Shōgoin and Supervisor of the Three Mountains of Kumano. This is further indication that the Ukai family had strong links to Shōgoin.

The discovery of this *ganmon* was unusual. Secret caches in Buddhist statues are a well-known phenomenon in many Buddhist countries, and the subject of detailed research (see, for example, Brinker 2011; Robson 2014; Sharf and Sharf 2001). But, although En no Gyōja statues are often hollowed out, for reasons both of convenience (lighter to transport) and of conservation (less likely to splinter or fracture), there has been no record so far of an En no Gyōja statue holding any kind of document or object (Miyagi 2017, my interview; Ishikawa 2017, my interview). The *ganmon* was handed back to Shōgoin, where it is now securely kept with the other treasures of the temple. In exchange, Miyagi Tainen wrote a new document, explaining the story behind the gift of the statue to this oratory, as well as the discovery of the original *ganmon*, which he copied at the end of his own text (Figure 6.3).[18] Restoration of the statue was completed in spring 2017, and the eye-re-opening ceremony (*sai kaiganshiki* 再開眼式), which I had the opportunity to attend, scheduled for May 17. The eye-closing ceremony had been held by the Kumano Shugen organization, since they had noticed the statue's state

Figure 6.3 Restored statue of En no Gyōja with votive text by Miyagi Tainen. Courtesy of Shōgoin.

of decay and induced its being taken down for restoration. For the re-opening service, the Yamabiko group turned to Shōgoin, in light of both the discovery of the *ganmon* and the initial gift of the statue. The ceremony took place in front of the small oratory dedicated to En no Gyōja, at Gyōsen no shuku. Miyagi Tainen (eigty-six), two senior *shugenja*, and three monks of lesser rank, nimbly climbed up the steep mountain path leading to the small mountain saddle where the hut is situated. As soon as they arrived, they started preparing the altar for the service, as well as the wood and branches for a small ritual fire (*saitō goma* 柴燈護摩). Then, after a short and animated consultation on the sequence of the various ritual elements, the ceremony opened to the sound of *horagai*, followed by sutra chanting. Miyagi performed the actual eye-opening ritual, read the *ganmon* that was to be inserted into the statue, and the service closed with the recitation of several successive fast-paced *Heart sutras*. Asamura was present, as was Tamaoka (ninety-three), and some sixty onlookers, mainly Yamabiko members, as shown by the logo emblazoned on their jackets. Most of them were in their fifties or sixties, which reflects the reality of the dwindling membership of the group.[19] After a lively lunch of lovingly prepared *bentō* (packed lunch), the Shōgoin party set off down the mountain.[20]

My intention in giving a detailed account of this ceremony is to show how deeply veneration for En no Gyōja is embedded at different levels of society, and how familiar his presence, much rather than that of a simple statue, is felt to be, both by *shugen* practitioners and by people less directly involved with Shugendō as an organized tradition. In this context, I would like to draw attention to the role of the Shingū Yamabiko Group and other similar groups. They are lay groups of caretakers, whose connection to specific *shugen* organizations is kept intentionally low key, explicitly "so that they can serve everybody," as Kawashima stated (Kawashima 2017, my interview). While they have no official links to institutionalized Shugendō, at least not a as a group, they show a deep respect for *shugen* practices and practitioners. The same goes for mountains, considered to be sacred entities and residences for *kami* and buddhas alike, as appears clearly from numerous statements and blog archives on their website. The website of the Yamabiko Group is regularly updated and very rich in information. The group also developed a widely used application for mobile phones with information on the weather, trail conditions, etc. In this sense, their role is akin to a secular version of that held symbolically by Zenki and Goki for En no Gyōja, and concretely by their "descendants," who live(d) at the foot of Jinzen on Ōmine, of Nakatsugawa on Katsuragi, and who assist(ed) practitioners both logistically and ritually.[21]

As stated above, it was a member of Kumano Shugen who notified the Yamabiko Group of the dire state of En no Gyōja's statue. The head of Kumano Shugen, Tanaka Riten, celebrated the de-animation ceremony. The first eye-opening, or animation, ritual held in 1990 was performed by Miyagi Tainen, who officiated again in 2017, both because the statue was originally the property of Shōgoin and because the *ganmon* found inside it was closely connected with that temple. Moreover, the ceremony was also held in memory and honor of the late Maeda Yūichi, the instigator of the renewal of the Southern Okugake path, who was affiliated with Shōgoin. A variety of *shugen* organizations use the Okugake path. They are linked to different temples of the region that share the Ōmine range with its religious and symbolic aura as a common place of practice. On the one hand, *shugen* groups distinguish themselves by variations in ritual and attire, by different tunes of the *horagai*, and other elements. On the other hand, they are united by the fact that they "enter the mountain" (*mineiri* 峰入り) both reverently and ritually, albeit with great ease and familiarity. *Shugen* organizations engage the mountains on a spiritual and religious level, and they have the authority of their tradition to do so. Associations such as the Yamabiko Group see their role as custodians, which places them at a different level of interaction with the mountains, even if these levels are not exclusive of one another.

The building of a chapel for En no Gyōja was part of the original plan when the decision to set up a lodge at Gyōsen no shuku was taken toward the end of the 1980s. This was "entirely natural (*tōzen* 当然)," since En no Gyōja is the founder of mountain practice on Ōmine (Kawashima 2017, my interview). The Jitsukaga statue was an equally natural addition, both because of the ascetic's renown as an accomplished practitioner in that very region, and because prayers to him had helped find the water source. I would like to emphasize here the sense of proximity that characterizes the way in which *shugenja*, but also inhabitants of the region, as well as people who form associations like the Yamabiko Group, deal with figures of veneration, and even more so with En no Gyōja. In the case of *shugenja*, this proximity extends even to kinship, since they perceive En no Gyōja as their ancestor, who is forever present on the mountain range and its surroundings, both in spirit and in representation. *Shugen* practitioners often claim, quite literally, to walk in En no Gyōja's footsteps, or, alternatively, they feel his presence walking alongside with them. In the words of Tateishi Kōshō 立石光正, who runs Sangakurin 山岳林, a *shugen* temple in the Kumano mountains, this companionship is represented by the Buddhist staff (*shakujō* 錫杖), or by a simple walking stick, that becomes En no Gyōja as "another self" (*mō hitori no watashi* もう一人の私) or somebody with whom one "walks together" (*dōgyō* 同行). This recalls the expression *dōgyō ninin* 同行二人 ("two persons walking together"), used mainly by Shikoku pilgrims and symbolizing their walking alongside Kōbō Daishi. In that case, it is often the straw hat rather than the pilgrim's staff that represents Kūkai. There is a fluid continuity between En no Gyōja as a human being, ancestor and founder, and En no Gyōja as a figure of veneration. While the former status is emphasized by his name, the latter is perhaps best exemplified by his title of Jinben Daibosatsu.

The same continuity, albeit on a more modest scale, works also for Jitsukaga, whose statue is enshrined alongside that of En no Gyōja at Gyōsen no shuku. Statues are living beings, as shown by the twin ceremonies of eye-opening and eye-closing, that endow them with living spirit or in turn withdraw it from them. The perception of statues or images being alive is not so much a belief or an active act of veneration, as a simple acknowledgment of an animated, but not necessarily precisely identified, presence.[22] Even in the case of En no Gyōja at Gyōsen, on the very day of the eye-opening ceremony of the restored statue, people entered the chapel and cast a brief look at the "main deity" (*honzon* 本尊), but their attention was focused on the activity surrounding the chapel, not on the statue as such, despite the ceremony being held in its honor. Knowing that the statue is there, in its place, is fulfilling as such.

According to Ōkōchi Tomoaki 大河内智之, curator at the Wakayama Prefectural Museum, this sense of belonging and familiarity similarly accounts for the fact that when Buddhist statues or artifacts are stolen from a remote mountain chapel or temple, followers often cannot remember exactly what objects have disappeared (Ōkōchi 2016). Ōkōchi was referring to increasing thefts of Buddhist artifacts that affects the entire country but has been particularly severe in the Wakayama region between 2010 and 2011.[23] He sees this trend as accompanying a recent boom in commercial and private interest for Buddhist images and implements on the one hand, and the fact that, due to the aging population and the ever-expanding rural exodus, people who tend to temples and chapels in remote areas are old and few, on the other hand. The rise in thefts of religious artifacts represents another aspect of the growing problems of temples (and shrines) left without a resident priest. Unsurprisingly, most of the incidents occur in mountain villages and temples left unattended. One important *shugen* temple in the Katsuragi range, at Nakatsugawa 中津川, was also the object of such a robbery in 2010, when an En no Gyōja triad was stolen along with other objects.[24]

In that particular case as well as in several others in the Wakayama region, Ōkōchi underlines the fact that they occurred in temples and chapels so deeply embedded in the life of the village that nobody even knows what they held exactly. Even when artifacts were recovered, the actual owners were not always capable of identifying them, not out of indifference, but out of too much familiarity. At the same time, these images belong to the history and memory of a community, and Ōkōchi notes that when told of the robbery, the overall reaction of people was one of shocked incredulity. Even when a statue is valuable as an artifact, it is the affective relationship that counts, not its intrinsic artistic value.[25] This sense of familiarity (*shitashimi no kankaku* 親しみの感覚) is of course not limited to statues of En no Gyōja. However, because of his being considered first and foremost as a human being, albeit a very special one, and because of his strong link to this particular region, there is an added element of proximity and companionship. This familiarity may equally stem from the term *gyōja* 行者, literally "walking person," a generic term for a practitioner, underlining quite literally the concrete aspects of following a spiritual path.

As accomplished as En no Gyōja may be, he is still "on his way." In medieval texts, he is described as an embodiment of different Buddhist entities such as Fudō 不動, Benzaiten 弁財天, Hōki Bosatsu 法基菩薩, and others (*Minoodera engi* 箕面寺縁起, *Sangoku dentōki* 三国伝灯記, *Shozan engi* 諸山縁起).[26] Elsewhere he is put in relation with Emperor Kinmei 欽明 (509–71; r. 539–71) or placed into the Indian genealogy of Kumano Gongen (*Ōmine engi* 大峯縁起, *Shugen shinanshō* 修験指南抄).[27] Then in the Edo period, he becomes Jinben Daibosatsu. Although the title is honorific, it still reflects an evolution toward greater emphasis on the divinized aspects of the founder figure. Nevertheless, however fanciful and embellished the episodes of En no Gyōja's hagiography have become over the centuries, the ground note that resonates most durably is that of him being a "practitioner." Throughout Japanese religious history, there is a distinct current of belief and faith that circulates around the notion of *gyōja*: *gyōja shinkō* 行者信仰 (Gyōja cult), *gyōjadō* 行者堂 (Gyōja chapel), *gyōjakō* 行者講 (Gyōja confraternities). *Gyōja* very often stands for En no Gyōja, but not necessarily or essentially so, and not in all regions of Japan. During the twentieth century, both inside and outside of scholarly circles, Shugendō has long been described as the epitome of "Japanese Folk Religion" or "Japanese Mountain Religion." The contributions to this book show that this stance can be easily questioned when Shugendō is considered from a historical point of view as an organized body of religious practice, rites, and traditions—as is proven by the deep and recurrent links its main branches entertained right from the onset with imperial (Shōgoin or Ninnaji are *monzeki* temples) or shōgunal lineages (e.g., Daigoji and Hideyoshi's cherry-tree parties).

The worship of En no Gyōja, and that of his image, were created entirely within this frame, and much of the statuary and imagery reflect and recall his position at the head and center of a religious tradition. Simultaneously, the figure of En no Gyōja as a practitioner clearly steps beyond this fixed role and speaks to a much wider audience. This echo is mirrored not only in the impressive number of statues of En no Gyōja that are still extant, but in their manufacture. Often it is of rudimentary workmanship and the work of more or less skilled amateurs. The Muromachi statue stolen and then recovered at Nakatsugawa is one example of such artisanship, which some scholars name *gyōjakei no chōkoku* 行者系の彫刻, "practitioners' type of sculpture" (Kuno 1962). This trend seems to have been prominent enough as far back as the Muromachi period to have triggered a professional style imitating the amateur style (Ōkōchi 2012), as another Muromachi statue formerly enshrined at the Nakatsugawa Gyōjadō suggests. According to Ōkōchi, that sculpture is more refined than it appears at first glance, so that its simplicity could well be an artifice (Ōkōchi 2012: 15). This means that even in medieval Japan, En no Gyōja must have appealed to a diverse public. The objective of this chapter was to grasp part of what makes out En no Gyōja's allure, and why he appeals to an audience much wider than that of the Shugendō universe. Even if we take into account that this universe has shrunk to but a fraction of what it once was, it still does not explain the success of En no Gyōja as an inspirational figure. Beyond the emphasis on En no Gyōja's powers and accomplishments, which define him as the founder of Shugendō and make up the structure of his hagiography, he clearly taps into a source as fecund as dynamic, that lasts throughout all ages.

Appendix

Votive text (*ganmon* 願文) found inside En no Gyōja's statue

On the sculpting of En no Gyōja.
Time: 1702, in September.

For peace upon the land and the security of Japan, as well as in the hope that the venerable patriarch of Shōgoin [Imperial Prince Dōson 道尊親王] may go on living a long life.

Also for the sake of Imaōji Genmyō Hōgan 今大路源明法眼, whom I have heard is ill, from the family of the general administrators of the temple (*bōkan zōmu* 坊官雑務).

It is also the occasion to pray for the security and prosperity of the families of the many parishioners who offered their contribution; of those who practice with them, as well as of temple petitioners who intend to make donations; of all people offering their prayers and of Gyōja confraternities.

In the hope that Ukai Jirō, Hyōei, and Shinchi 鵜飼次郎兵衛信治, born sixty-three long years ago [in 1640] may live long and healthily without hindrance, together with wishes for the health and longevity of the whole Ukai family.

Leader of the eye-opening service: The venerable Supervisor of the Three Mountains of Kumano, Second-in-rank Imperial Prince Dōson.

Sculptor: Hiromichi no Sansaemon 広道の三左衛門 from the village of Okazaki 岡崎.

[Petitioner:] a *sendatsu* from the Ukai family, devoted to the Gyōja cult,
Seal-of-the-Law Ganshin Hōin from Rishōin 理正院法印元信, born in 1672.

He had this statue of [En no Gyōja] erected at the age of thirty-one, in the year of the Rat.

Sitography

https://www.citizen.co.jp/coy/archive/2004_01.html
http://syamabiko.web.fc2.com/introduction.html
http://syamabiko.web.fc2.com/karimine_1000.html

Interviews

Asamura Tomonobu	浅村朋伸. 2017, May 17	(Shimokitayamamura, Nara Prefecture). Personal interview.
Ishikawa Tomohiko	石川智彦. 2017, May 13	(Kyoto). Personal interview.
Kawashima Isao	川島功. 2017, May 17	(Shimokitayamamura, Nara Prefecture). Personal interview.
Miyagi Tainen	宮城泰年. 2017, May 16	(Kyoto). Personal interview.
Tateishi Kōshō	立石光正. 2017, May 22	(Koguchi, Wakayama Prefecture). Personal interview.

7

En no Gyōja's Legitimization in the Context of Japanese Esoteric Buddhism

Kawasaki Tsuyoshi
Translation by Carina Roth

My intention in this chapter is to examine and evaluate the role played by *Minoodera engi* 箕面寺縁起 in the formation process of Shugendō. There are several different perspectives on this process, understood as one of the paths taken by Buddhism in Japan during the late Kamakura period. Currently, the prevalent viewpoint stems from the field of historical studies, and sees the end of the Kamakura period as the period in which Shugendō both asserted itself by adding *shugen* to the existing exoesoteric teachings and appeared as a movement unified by prayers for protection of the state. This movement is generally considered to have been led by temples of the Jimon branch of the Tendai school, although similar trends existed also within temples of the Sanmon branch of Tendai Buddhism as well as in the Shingon school (see Tokunaga 2001, 2015; Hasegawa 2016).

From mid-Heian onward, *yamabushi* practice compared favorably with esoteric rituals as far as "efficacy" (*genriki* 験力) was concerned. However, from the perspective of orthodox Buddhism and its credo of a "Transmission through the Three Countries" (*Sangoku denrai* 三国伝来), *yamabushi* practice was considered vastly inferior (see *Shinsarugakuki* 新猿楽記, *Imakagami* 今鏡, etc.). Therefore, in order for Shugendō to establish itself as one of the official strands of Buddhism, *yamabushi* needed theories, discourses, and scriptures that integrated them into Buddhist orthodoxy. This was required even within esoteric temples that did accept *yamabushi* powers. What functioned as a scriptural basis for this were foundation narratives of temples and shrines (*jisha engi* 寺社縁起) that recorded the achievements of En no Gyōja, the ancestor of all *yamabushi* who was later revered as the founding figure of Shugendō (Takahashi 1990; Miyake 2000a). Emblematic of such texts are *Minoodera engi*, *Ōmine engi* 大峰縁起, and *Kongōsan engi* 金剛山縁起 (Kawasaki 2006, 2010).

Minoodera engi is a foundation narrative compiled in Sino-Japanese (*kanbun* 漢文) before 1173, at the end of the Heian period. It describes how En no Gyōja visited in a dream the Pure Land of Ryūju bosatsu 龍樹菩薩 (Nāgārjuna), situated in the Dragon Cave of the Metaki 雌瀧 waterfall at Minoo. There, in the presence of Ryūju bosatsu and Benzaiten 弁財天, through the intercession of Great King Tokuzen 徳善大王, En no Gyōja was the recipient of a ritual akin to the Esoteric Buddhist consecration (*kanjō* 灌頂, Skr. *abhiṣeka*). Upon completion of this rite, he founded Minoodera. Ryūju bosatsu was considered at that time to be the same person as Ryūmyō 龍猛, the first patriarch in the Shingon Denji 真言伝持 tradition.[1] Therefore, if En no Gyōja's "dream-consecration" is recognized as legitimate, En no Gyōja becomes an orthodox practitioner of Shingon Esotericism more than a hundred years before Kūkai 空海 (774–835) transmitted that tradition to Japan. In this sense, *Minoodera engi* includes elements susceptible to overturn the history of the Japanese Shingon school, known to have been founded by Kūkai. For a general introduction on *Minoodera engi*, I refer to my earlier research on this document (Kawasaki 2015, 2017). In this chapter, I shall clarify the process through which, despite being a lay Buddhist practitioner (*ubasoku* 優婆塞, Skr. *upāsaka*), En no Gyōja came to be accepted as a legitimate and orthodox figure by esoteric temples, by focusing on the discourses and reception surrounding *Minoodera engi* in the late Kamakura period.

Reception in the Kamakura Period

In the late Heian period, the influence of *Minoodera engi* extended well beyond Minoo, as demonstrated by the repeated use that Kōfukuji monks Kakuken 覚憲 (1131–1213), his disciple Jōkei 貞慶 (1155–1213), and their entourage made of it in other documents (e.g., *Sangoku dentō-ki* 三国伝灯記, *San butsujōshō* 讃仏乗抄, and *Ichidainomine engi* 一代峯縁起). As we shall see later, *Minoodera engi* was also one of the main sources on which entries on En no Gyōja were based in collections of biographies of eminent monks (*kōsōden* 高僧伝) compiled by monks from all Buddhist schools from the mid-Kamakura period onward. *Minoodera engi* relates the esoteric transmission bestowed upon En no Gyōja by Ryūju bosatsu through the intervention of King Tokuzen as follows:

> In the center of a palace, Ryūju bosatsu and Benzaiten were solemnly seated on top of a magnificent seat (*shōza* 床座). Shortly thereupon, the Great King [Tokuzen] arrived. After having examined the ten directions, he took perfumed water (*kōzui* 香水) from the Buddhist altar, poured some on the top of [En no Gyōja's] head, stroked it and said: "You will now go back to where you came from and, trusting in the unfolding of your strength, you will contribute to the spreading of Buddhism with all your faith and might." After that, although it felt wholly real, he awakened from his dream.
>
> (*Shoji engishū*: 125)

This passage constitutes the climactic scene of *Minoodera engi*. However, it seems to have been left out in anthologies of monk biographies compiled outside esoteric ranks, in which the episode is abridged and rendered innocuous. For example, the entry on En no Gyōja in the eighth fascicle of *Shijū hyaku innenshū* 私聚百因縁集, compiled in 1257 by Pure Land monk Jūshin 住信 (1226–1312), describes in detail how En no

Gyōja entered the dragon cave from the top of the Minoo waterfall, and how, after a dialogue with king Tokuzen, he stepped into Ryūju's Pure Land. The episode then continues in the following way:

> Even upon seeing this place, he could hardly fathom it nor express it in words. While still in his human body, he set foot in the Pure Land and became pure in body and mind. After having met the great saint Ryūju, he brought back to the world the expedient means of salvation (*saido* 済度), thereby upholding and expanding the Buddhist way. This is a most thankful matter.
> (*Shijū hyaku innenshū*: 6–7)

Elsewhere, in *Genkō shakusho* 元亨釈書 (fasc. 15, "En no Gyōja"), compiled in 1322 by Rinzai monk Kokan Shiren 虎関師錬 (1278–1347), the Minoo episode is summarized as follows:

> In times of old, [En no] Ozunu [役]小角 spent time on Mount Minoo in Settsu province. On the mountain there was a waterfall. In a dream, Ozunu entered the mouth of the waterfall, and met with the great master Ryūju. After he woke up, he built a temple, called it Minoodera, and made it the Pure Land of Ryūju.
> (*Genkō shakusho*: 220)

To the extent of my knowledge, the oldest document in which the bestowal of the esoteric consecration described in *Minoodera engi* is acknowledged as such, and, therefore, recognized as an esoteric ritual of transmission, is *Shichi tengu'e* 七天狗絵 (compiled in 1296; author unknown).[2] The Shōmyōji 称名寺 copy, one of the extant manuscripts of *Shichi tengu'e*, was transmitted within Shingon temples (Abe 2003; Takahashi 2003; Tsuchiya 2005; Yamaguchi 2015). It consists of ten volumes, of which the ninth is missing. The first five volumes describe the origins of seven types of *tengu* 天狗,[3] seen as monks of, respectively, Kōfukuji, Tōdaiji, Enryakuji, Onjōji, Tōji, as well as *yamabushi* and recluse monks. The fifth volume is devoted to the two latter categories. It begins by stating that Ōmine is "the mountain of the Two World mandala" (*ryōbu mandara no yama* 両部曼荼羅の山) and Katsuragi "the mountain of the Single Vehicle of the Flower of the Law" (*ichijō hokke no yama* 一乗法花の峯). A similar discourse, interpreting the two most representative mountain sites of *yamabushi* practice in Japan as the various peaks of Esoteric Buddhism, on the one hand, and as the peaks of an exoteric sutra on the other, is also manifest in the early Kamakura *Shozan engi* (compilator unknown). After that passage, *Shichi tengu'e* describes En no Gyōja's practice as centering on both mountain ranges, before claiming that "thereafter, both Kōbō Daishi 弘法大師 [Kūkai] and Chishō Daishi 智証大師 [Enchin 円珍 (814–91)] entered Ōmine and followed the ancient traces of [En no] Gyōja." This particular sentence is of the highest importance: through the mention that the two founders of Esoteric Buddhism in Japan walked in the footsteps of En no Gyōja on Ōmine, practice on Ōmine as the equivalent of the Two World mandala, was "returned" to Japanese esoteric temples. Here is how *Shichi tengu'e* presents En no Gyōja's practice:

En no Ubasoku first entered Mount Katsuragi when he was seven years old, and practiced there over the course of many years. Once he was a grown man, he visited Ōmine and practiced there thirty-three times. [...] Further, the waterfall at Minoo is the Pure Land of Ryūju and the sacred land of Benzaiten. In that high waterfall basin, there is a ninety-centimeter dragon that continuously spews black smoke. Having seen a five-colored ray of light, En no Gyōja entered Mount Minoo to look for its source. He dove into a deep pool atop the waterfall, opened a stone gate, and after having encountered Ryūju bosatsu, he received the Five Wisdoms and the Three mysteries of Dainichi Nyorai.

In comparison with the *Minoodera engi* passage, the setting of the scene as a dream and the existence of Tokuzen have been erased. The relationship between Ryūju bosatsu and En no Gyōja is also simplified. Moreover, the described consecration clearly stems from Shingon Esoteric Buddhism. While this indicates that Shingon consecrations were considered a historical fact and given due importance, it simultaneously leaves unexplained its relationship with practice on Ōmine as the equivalent of the Two World mandala.

The Debate on Main and Subsidiary Temples in the Shingon School

Toward the end of the Kamakura period, En no Gyōja's alleged Shingon consecration at Minoo, and, further, the place it should be ascribed in the history of Japanese Shingon Esotericism, became a subject of heated discussion within Shingon temples. In 1313, a debate on the relationship between main and subsidiary temples sparked up between Tōdaiji and Daigoji (Nagamura 1988; Inaba 2008; Kojima 2013), and lasted for several years. In this dispute, Tōdaiji sued Daigoji on the ground that the latter refused its status as a subsidiary temple of Tōdaiji. It is surmised that Shōchū 聖忠 (1268–1319), both the head of Tōji (Tōji ichi no chōja 東寺一長者) and that of Tōdaiji Tōnan'in (Tōdaiji Tōnan'inshu 東大寺東南院主), was deeply involved in this matter. When the legal dispute was in its second stage, as is evident in *Daigoji jūsojō* 醍醐寺重訴状, Daigoji contested the allegation that Tōdaiji's foundation preceded the introduction of the Shingon school to Japan. Through its *Tōdaiji sanjūsojō* 東大寺三重訴状, Tōdaiji intended to counter this refutation by using the argument of En no Gyōja's achievements, but the dispute seems to have subsided at this point, and it is highly likely that *Tōdaiji sanjūsojō* was never actually used.

In the extant draft to that document (*Tōdaiji sanjūsojō an* 東大寺三重訴状案), the dispute is referred to in two segments:

(1) In Emperor Shōmu's time (701–56; r. 724–49), before Emperor Kanmu's reign (737–806; r. 781–806), the teachings of the Three Mysteries [Shingon Esotericism] had not yet been transmitted, and because nobody was studying them, the ways of thinking were terribly shallow and careless. As a rule, the world stays the same and never changes, but things and situations arise according to opportunities. For instance, En no Ubasoku's Mount of Awakening [Bodai no mine 菩堤の

to have been chief administrator of Tōji (*Tōji bettō* 東寺別当) under Kyōkan 教寛 (1281–1337), who was head priest of both Tōji and Kajūji (Satō 2015: 117–83).

Shingonden is a compilation of hagiographies in seven volumes, "depicting how Esoteric Buddhism was transmitted from Ryūmyō in India to China by the 'Seven Shingon Patriarchs' (*Shingon shichi so* 真言七祖),[4] then brought to Japan thanks to the 'Eight Monks who Traveled to Tang China' (*Nittō hakke* 入唐八家),[5] where it expanded while displaying efficacy in a variety of manners" (Satō 2015: 368–70). The first volume is dedicated to the hagiographies of the Seven Shingon Patriarchs, the second to the miraculous effects of *dhāranī*, the third to the lives of the "Eight Monks who Traveled to Tang China." The four last volumes contain the biographies of Japanese esoteric monks (Satō 2015: 368–70). Ryūmyō's hagiography is included at the beginning of the first volume, and En no Ubasoku's at the beginning of the fourth. The latter entry was written based on several different accounts, with *Minoodera engi* playing a central role. The passage describing the consecration-like ritual, albeit brief, quotes the text of *Minoodera engi* almost word for word:

> In the central palace, there was a magnificent stage, on top of which Ryūju bosatsu and Benzaiten were solemnly seated. At this moment, Great King Tokuzen took perfumed water from the Buddhist altar, poured some on the top of En no Gyōja's head, stroked it, and said: "You will go back to where you came from, and with as much strength and will as you can muster, you will contribute to the spreading of Buddhism." After that, having seen himself coming up to the water surface, [En no Gyōja] woke up from his dream.
>
> (*Shingonden*: 228)

The only moment that does not appear in *Minoodera engi* is when En no Gyōja wakes up from his dream after having seen himself coming up to the surface of the water. There must have been a specific reason for this addition. Alternatively, it could also have meant that En no Gyōja woke up from his dream after entering the dragon cave from the top of the waterfall and having been granted consecration in Ryūju bosatsu's Pure Land. This interpretation coincides with the expressions "at the bottom of the waterfall" (*taki no moto* 瀧の下) and "at the bottom of the flying spring" (*hisen no moto* 飛泉の下) used in *Tōdaiji sanjū sojō*, although it is unclear what relationship the two documents entertained with each other.

The "En no Ubasoku" section in *Shingonden* is based on En no Gyōja hagiographies as well as on accounts of the entry of Reverend Ganjin 鑑真 (688–763) into the mountains. At the end of each segment, Yōkai adds a comment in which he specifies that he speaks in his own name, using the expression "in my opinion" (*shi ni iwaku* 私に云はく). In the following passage, he reflects upon the relationship between the transmission of Shingon Esoteric Buddhism to China/Japan and the esoteric transmission to En no Gyōja:

> In my opinion, En no Gyōja traveled to China in the year Taihō 大宝 1 (701; *kanoto ushi* 辛丑), which corresponds to the year Daitei 大定 1[6] under the reign

峰, i.e., Ōmine] is a secret place for the bestowal of consecration rites. Moreover, on Mount One Vehicle [Ichijō no mine 一乗の峰, i.e., Katsuragi], one of the halls of Narutaki temple 鳴瀧寺 displays its deities exactly as they appear in the Two World mandala. There is no one who would not recognize it as a holy place where ritual prayers are performed while worshiping representations of the five Luminous Kings. [En no Gyōja] received this esoteric teaching from Dainichi Nyorai at the bottom of the flying spring (*hisen no moto* 飛泉の下), at the temple of Minoo in Settsu province, while seeing the physical body of Great master Ryūmyō [Nāgārjuna] (*Tōdaiji sanjūsojō an*: 659).

(2) Under the reigns of Emperor Shōmu and Empress Kōken (718–70; r. 749–58 and 764–70), it was narrow-mindedly considered that Shingon had not yet been transmitted [to Japan]. This En no Ubasoku received the Two World consecration at the bottom of the waterfall at Minoo, and he demonstrated the Southern Peak [Nanzan 南山, i.e., Kumano] and Kinpu to be the Two World mandala (*Tōdaiji sanjūsojō an*: 671).

In comparison with *Minoodera engi*, and similarly to the previously mentioned example of *Shichi tengu'e*, the episodes of the dream and of king Daitoku are left out, whereas the consecration is explicitly described. The location of the consecration is also changed to below the waterfall and furthermore, while stating that they are one and the same, Ryūju is renamed Ryūmyō, that is, the name of the first patriarch in the Shingon Denji tradition. Another important point to take into account is the fact that the consecration at Minoo is coupled with the demonstration of Ōmine as being the Two World mandala. The first passage especially, stating that Ōmine "is a secret place for the bestowal of consecration rites," also includes the meaning that the Shingon Esotericism received by En no Gyōja from Ryūmyō has been transmitted to later generations of practitioners via mountain practice on Ōmine as "opened" (started) by En no Gyōja. Then, using En no Gyōja's achievements as evidence, the assertion emerged that Shingon esotericism existed in Japan long before Kōbō Daishi introduced it.

It may be premature to consider, on the basis of this debate alone, this discourse as the main position at Tōdaiji on the matter. However, in the context of the rivalry between Shingon main and subsidiary temples, it is significant that Tōdaiji promoted the argument that En no Gyōja received orthodox esoteric consecration before Kōbō Daishi.

Reconstructing the History of Japanese Shingon Buddhism

Roughly ten years after the debate discussed in the previous section, in 1325, the monk Yōkai 栄海 (1278–1347), from the Jison'in hall at Kajūji temple 勧修寺慈尊院, compiled *Shingonden* 真言伝. Yōkai was a high-ranking monk, who acceded to the rank of superintendent (*sōjō* 僧正). He was famous for having bestowed the vows upon Emperor Go-Daigo (1288–1339; r. 1318–39) and, later, upon Northern Court emperors. At the time of his compiling *Shingonden*, between 1323 and 1325, he seems of Chinese Empress Wu Zetian (624–705; r. 690–705). At that time Shingon's teachings had not yet been transmitted either to China or to Japan. In Kaigen 開元 4 (716), under Emperor Xuanzong's reign (685–762; r. 713–56), [Zen]mu'i [善]無畏 (Skr. Śubhakarasiṃha, 637–735) traveled to China for the first time, followed by Kongōchi 金剛智 (Skr. Vajrabodhi, 671–741) in the eighth year of the same era (720). Sixteen years had passed from the first year of the Daitei 大定 era (701) until the fourth year of the Kaigen era (716). Then, in the year Daidō 大同 1 (806), Kōbō Daishi brought the great teachings of the Twofold Mandalas back to Japan for the first time. Between the years Taihō 1 and Daidō 1, one hundred and four years had passed when Shingon was first introduced to Japan. Therefore, nobody knows the identity of the teacher who initiated En no Gyōja to Shingon. Nevertheless, En is the one who revealed the connection between Ōmine and the Twofold mandala. The singular character of our country is apparent once more in this matter. It is possible that these particular powers were bestowed upon En no Gyōja during his visit to Ryūmyō's Pure Land at Minoo, when he received the transmission of Shingon Esoteric Buddhism and was granted consecration.

(*Shingonden*: 228)

In this way, Yōkai verifies and validates, on the one hand, the fact that even at the time in which En no Gyōja traveled to the continent, Shingon Buddhism had not yet been transmitted to China, let alone Japan. On the other hand, Yōkai praises En no Gyōja's revelation of Ōmine as the Two World mandala as a proof of Japan's singular spiritual quality and surmises that the source of the "divine powers" that allowed En to achieve this had its origin in the transmission of Shingon Buddhism that occurred at Minoo. Hence, En no Gyōja's practice on the Ōmine mountains, and the fact that he demonstrated them to be the Twofold Mandalas, was of utmost importance for Japanese Buddhism.

Conclusion

The preceding pages showed that *Minoodera engi*, a document compiled at the end of the Heian period, did more than simply present a rewriting of the historical evolution within the spatial sphere of Minoodera. It was also considered a legitimate biography of En no Gyōja, not only beyond the precincts of the temple but also in other Buddhist sects. Toward the end of the Kamakura period, some institutions asserted the merit of practicing all three disciplines, namely, Exoteric Buddhism, Esoteric Buddhism, and *shugen*. In that context, it seems likely that among *kenmitsu* 顕密 temples, the fact that En no Gyōja had been initiated into Shingon Buddhism by Ryūmyō, the first Shingon Denji patriarch, in the cave at Minoo, was considered historical reality (*Shichi tengu'e*). This movement did indeed take place in the context of the dispute between main and subsidiary temples within the Shingon school, which started in 1313. Broadly speaking, Tōdaiji declared that the beginnings of the Shingon school in Japan must be told starting off with En no Gyōja's achievements. Moreover, when Yōkai, a

Kajūji priest, compiled *Shingonden* in 1325, he placed Ryūmyō at the very beginning of the first volume, followed by En no Gyōja at the head of the volume on Japanese Shingon, thereby demonstrating his personal conviction of the historicity of Ryūmyō's transmission of Shingon Buddhism to En no Gyōja.

In this way, at the end of the Kamakura period, *Minoo dera engi*'s discourse asserting the existence of Shingon Esotericism in Japan before Kōbō Daishi introduced it was very influential as a way to define Japanese Shingon. In turn, it can be surmised that this discourse also played an extremely important role in the formation process of Shugendō, which sees En no Gyōja as its founder.

8

The Description of Mountains in *Minoodera engi*

Niki Natsumi
Translation by Lindsey DeWitt and Carina Roth

Minoodera engi 箕面寺縁起 is a foundation narrative (*jisha engi* 寺社縁起) conveying the origins of Minoodera 箕面寺, a temple situated in the present-day Minoo City, Osaka prefecture. The site is well known even today for its waterfall. A Kamakura-period copy of the *engi* is held by the Archives and Mausolea Department of the Imperial Household Agency (formerly in the possession of the Kujō 九条 family); despite its publication in 1970 (*Shoji engishū* 諸寺縁起集), it was never subject to in-depth research. In recent years, however, Kawasaki Tsuyoshi 川崎剛志 (one of the contributors to this book) published a report on its formation and reception that clarified the following three points: first, the copy was preserved in the collection of Keisei 慶政 (1189–1268), a monk of the Kujō family; second, from the late Heian period to the early Kamakura period, the *engi* was included in several works and dictionaries thought to be penned by intellectuals of the day; and third; the *engi* played a major role in the history of Shugendō at that time (Kawasaki 2017). Now that its significance in Buddhist history—including Shugendō—has been confirmed, a more detailed textual analysis is called for.

Based on such considerations, this chapter aims at clarifying characteristics of certain textual expressions in the *engi*, with special attention to the way in which mountains are described, and centering on the waterfall that constitutes the symbol of Minoo. Why pay attention to textual representations of waterfalls and mountains, which form but a small part of the first half of the *engi*? The motif of mountains was by no means a minor theme in Chinese-style poetry and prose (*kanshibun* 漢詩文) of the Insei 院政 period (end of the eleventh to beginning of the thirteenth centuries), when the work is thought to have been completed. At a time when the range of activities open to government officials were restricted by family lineage, bureaucrats-cum-poets visited mountain temples and there entrusted their melancholy sentiments to the sights and wrote about them in poetry. *Honchō mudaishi* 本朝無題詩 (Japanese Poetry without a Subject; author unknown), a representative anthology of poetry in Chinese style from that era, contains numerous Chinese poems with such mountain temples as a theme. In this context, what are the characteristics of mountain descriptions in the *engi*?

Questions Raised by the Text

In the 1970 *Shoji engishū* edition of the text, the passage of *Minoodera engi* on which my analysis rests counts thirty-six lines. It goes from the second sheet, fourteenth line, to the third sheet, twelfth line. The translation is as follows (see appendix at the end of the chapter for its *kanbun* original):

> Thus, [En no Gyōja], at the age of twenty-five, on the 17th day of the 3rd month of the year Hakuhō 20 [680], in which Jupiter resided in *kanoe uma* [metal-horse], climbed the mountain following a stream. While he was ascending step by step, passing mountains and crossing rivers, there were three waterfalls on the way. (lines 1–7)
>
> Otaki [the male waterfall] is the uppermost of the falls. Its depth exceeds six meters, and the intense sounds of water falling and waves smashing resembles that of great thunder. There, [En no Gyōja] climbed up the rock in the east, raised up his staff, and placed it upright at his side. He was filled with joy, and his delight was second to none. A trace of his staff [from that time] still exists today, so behold it. A black snake lives at the bottom of the water. It lies down, coiled, with a body more than nine meters in length. Some people have on occasion seen its abdomen rising to the surface. (lines 8–13)
>
> Second is the waterfall Yūraku [jeweled necklace]. Drops of water fall incessantly from the cliff's stones and tributaries of the fall flow down ruggedly, as if piercing through beads of verdant moss. Apart from this nothing else is noteworthy [i.e., the appearance is the most intriguing aspect], so the name was taken from its appearance. (lines 14–20)
>
> The third fall is Metaki [the female waterfall]. At a height of 45 meters, its flow is extremely intense. The gushing downflow of water is just like bleached cloth, and the rippled appearance on the edges akin to embroidered silk. There is a dragon cave at its summit, inside which resides a ninety-centimeter dragon. When the dragon moves, it breathes out black clouds that darken the area, and it causes rain to fall regardless of the season. (lines 21–27)
>
> On top of this, overlapping peaks project upwards, striking the clouds that block the sun east and west; the deep flow of the valley that bores through rock carries fog north and south, hiding the moon. Waterside trees are exposed to storms, and vine-like grasses cling to flowers. White clouds billow in the wind, drifting around the mountainsides and making the scenery hazy. Creeper vines hang from the rocks and green boughs rise high. The vigor of water's edge vegetation, of flowing waters, enthrallingly beautiful in their appearance […] The silhouette of the forests, overflowing in elegance and beauty, unparalleled under the heavens, their origins ancient. (lines 28–36)

In my quotes from the text, I made revisions as appropriate, dividing the text into semantic blocks and adding punctuation marks to underline the fact that sentences were consciously structured in stanzas. Similarly, I added marks to the original text in order to indicate junctures in passages I deemed difficult to follow (e.g., in places with no formed stanzas or where the meaning is obscure). For us today, this style of composition is far from easy to read, but it is likely to have been difficult for Kamakura-period copyists too. Of course, guessing the contents in advance and then modifying and reading the original text so that it matches is not permissible in a textual analysis. However, judging from certain misprints (see notes in appendix) or from the examples taken up below, when reading this type of documents, one must take into account that some characters were potentially omitted.

For instance, if we look at lines 34–35 of our text:

渚卉木碧流之勢、太於幽奇、其粧
森風流美冠之姿、絶于天下、其来尚矣

The vigor of water's edge vegetation, of flowing waters, enthrallingly beautiful in their appearance [...]
The silhouette of the forests, overflowing in elegance and beauty, unparalleled under the heavens, their origins ancient.

While it is clear that the passage describes the mysterious environment of the water edge at Minoo and the rarely seen beauty of the forests, the meaning of *kishō* 其粧 is hard to grasp. As seen when the stanzas are lined up as above, there originally must have had two more characters after 其粧. The complete stanza ought, therefore, to be read as:

渚卉木碧流之勢、太於幽奇、其粧〇〇
森風流美冠之姿、絶于天下、其来尚矣

This kind of problem arises because, quite exceptionally, attention is paid to the stanza as structure, as it is the case in *Minoodera engi*. Despite such problems, lines 7–27 of our text are quoted almost word for word in the "Minoodera" section of *Iroha jiruishō* 伊呂波字類抄 (*Iroha Encyclopedia*; fascicle 9 [ten-fascicle version]), one of the oldest Japanese encyclopedias purported to date back to the early Kamakura period. Lines 2–27 are also excerpted in En no Gyōja's hagiography in *Shingonden* 真言伝 (fascicle four)[1]. It is, therefore, obvious that this passage has long been considered an important depiction of the waterfalls at Minoo.

Depictions of Mountains

What, then, do the quoted passages communicate in terms of content? In the following pages, I will take up one group of lines at a time, and attempt to interpret the meaning they convey.

【Lines 1–7】
Thus, [En no Gyōja], at the age of twenty-five, on the 17th day of the 3rd month of the year Hakuhō 20 [680], in which Jupiter resided in *kanoe uma* 庚馬 [metal-horse], climbed the mountain (*hansei* 攀隮), following a stream (*zuijū* 随従). While he was ascending step by step, passing mountains and crossing rivers, there were three waterfalls on the way.

First, the text begins with a description of the three waterfalls. The expression *hansei* 攀隮, "to scramble up," appears frequently in the mountain-temple poetry of *Honchō mudaishi*. *Suijū* 随従 originally means to follow a person but is used quite differently here to mean following the flow of a river. Also difficult to interpret is the expression *ōō* 往々, which literally means "sometimes" or "here and there," but in this case is closer to "going forward," translated here by "ascending." It would be more fitting without the repetition indicated by the sign 々. The same can be said for *yūyū* 有々, which seems appropriate to render, as does the *Iroha jiruishō*, by *yūryū sansho/takiga sansho ni ari* 有瀧三所 ("there were three waterfalls").

【Lines 8–14】
Otaki 雄滝 [the male waterfall] is the uppermost of the falls. Its depth exceeds six meters, and the intense sounds of water falling and waves smashing (*sairō* 砕浪) resemble that of great thunder (*dairai* 大雷). There, [En no Gyōja] climbs up the rock in the east, raises up his staff, and places it upright at his side. He is filled with joy, and his delight is second to none. A trace of his staff [from that time] still exists today, so behold it. A black snake lives at the bottom of the water. It lies down, coiled, with a body more than nine meters in length. Some people have on occasion seen its belly rising to the surface.

While it is common enough to compare the sound of a waterfall to that of thunder, the strength of words like "smashing waves" (*sairō* 砕浪), "spreading intensely" (*kōretsu* 拡烈), and "great thunder" (*dairai* 大雷) is impressive. However, I would like to underline that the expressions *sairō* 砕浪 and *kōretsu* 拡烈, as well as "rejoice" (*gaki* 賀喜) are peculiar and hardly used elsewhere.

【Lines 15–20】
Second is the waterfall Yūraku 瓔珞 [jeweled necklace]. Drops of water fall incessantly (*benra* 駢羅) from the cliff's stones and tributaries of the fall flow down ruggedly (*kōkaku* 礭确), as if piercing through beads of verdant moss. Apart from this, nothing else is noteworthy [because this sight is most enchanting], so the name was drawn from its appearance.

In the wake of the second excerpt 【Lines 8–14】, which depicts the majestic appearance of the waterfalls, the expression that stands out here is *kōkaku* 礭确, translated here as "ruggedly." Originally, it was used to describe fallow land. However, beyond rare occurrences, the term is hardly used in Heian-period Chinese-style poetry (*kanshibun* 漢詩文).[2] Moreover, the meaning of the word—that the soil surrounding waterfalls is barren—does not fit either. The expression is paired with *benra* 駢羅, a phrase expressing a state of "stretching out," so that I read it as showing a state of "being rough/rugged." Yet this seems contradictory to the original meaning, as the land is, in fact, lush and covered in moss. It seems the author selected an expression [and used it in a way] that departed from the original meaning to emphasize the steepness of the mountainous area where the waterfalls are located.

【Lines 21–27】
The third fall is Metaki 雌滝 [the female waterfall]. Tumbling from a height of more than forty-five meters, its flow is extremely intense. The gushing downflow of water is just like (*tei'i* 為体) bleached cloth, and the rippled appearance on the edges akin to embroidered silk (*inrin* 爾倫). There is a dragon cave at its summit, in which resides a ninety-centimeter dragon. When the dragon moves, it breathes out black clouds that darken the area, and it causes rain to fall regardless of the season.

The expression *tei'i* 為体 (just like) is paired with that of *inrin* 爾倫 (embroidered silk). *Inrin* is a Chinese word used, for example, by the poet Bai Juyi 白居易 (772–846), but *tei'i* is the noun form of *tei taru* 体為る (such a state), and is difficult to express in Chinese. The phrase *shōkoku* 衝黒 appears several times in *Honchō mudaishi*. However, in those instances, *shōkoku* remarks upon a state of darkness falling because the sun has set, whereas here the area is cast into darkness because a dragon spewed black clouds. The meaning is not completely different; perhaps it is an example of invoking the original meaning.

I interpreted the phrase *kōsui shishō* 降水之粧 ("gushing downflow") as the state of the waterfall's runoff. Expressing such beautiful appearances with *shishō* 之粧 ("this adornment"; *shō* 粧 means adornment) seems to be quite frequent in *kanbun* from the Insei period onward. Also note that the expression *kishō* 其粧 ("that adornment") appears again in line 34 of the *engi*, translated here as "their appearance."

【Lines 28–36】
On top of this, overlapping peaks project upwards, striking the clouds that block the sun east and west; the deep flow of the valley that bores through rock carries fog north and south, hiding the moon. Waterside trees are exposed to storms, and vine-like grasses cling to flowers. **White clouds billow in the wind, drifting around the mountainsides and making the scenery hazy. Creeper vines hang from the rocks and green boughs rise high.** The vigor of water's edge vegetation, of flowing waters, enthrallingly beautiful in their appearance […] The silhouette of the forests, overflowing in elegance and beauty, unparalleled under the heavens, their origins ancient.

Contrasting the peculiar vocabulary or the usage of words in a way that departs from the usual that we have examined in the strophes leading up to now, the depictions of mountains following thereafter are relatively easy to read. One question, however, needs to be treated separately from the issue of meaning. It concerns the two sentences marked in bold above, and will be discussed in the next section.

The Reception of *Chūbunshō*

A clearly identifiable source exists for the excerpt marked in bold above. As a matter of fact, lines 32 and 33 of our *engi* are nearly identical to the following passage in

Chūbunshō 仲文章, an eleventh-century instruction manual for Chinese-style poetry. The parts that differ are marked in bold.

【*Minoodera engi*, lines 32–33】
白雲靡風、不離山腰**依々也**。
薛蘿懸巌、不絶翠枝**聳々也**。
【*Chūbunshō*】
白雲**帯**風、不離山腰。
薛蘿懸巌、不絶**於松**枝。
孔子不忘本学友、
賢者重一室之朋。

Chūbunshō cites quotes and proverbs from various other works and explains them as lessons, formulating them by way of couplets. Previous studies have confirmed that it was completed by at least 1088 (*Shin shūsei* Chūmonjō *kaidai* 1993). Authorship and formation of *Chūbunshō* are unclear, but it seems to have been a quite well-known document in the Kamakura period. A variety of works reference it, including collected tales like *Hōbutsushū* 宝物集 (c.1180), *Sangō shiiki chūshū* 三教指帰注集 (1088),[3] as well as dictionaries like *Onkochi shinsho* 温故知新書 (1484).

Comparing the two excerpts above, apart from character differences marked in bold, we find that the author of the *engi* added the phrases *yoyo tari* 依々也 and *shōshō tari* 聳々也 to the passage taken from *Chūbunshō*. Moreover, there is a verse by Miyako no Arinaka 都在中 (fl. Mid-Heian) which recalls the first phrase of this couplet in Ōe no Masafusa's 大江匡房 *Gōdanshō* 江談抄 (fasc. 4–7).

【*Gōdanshō*】
白雲似帯囲山腰、青苔如衣負巌背
White clouds surround the space between the mountain's foot and middle like an *obi*, and green moss drapes over the backs of the rocks like a robe.

Arinaka, whose birth and death dates are unknown, was the son of Miyako no Yoshika 都良香 (834–79). Chronologically, he, therefore, clearly precedes both *Minoodera engi* and *Chūbunshō*. Yet the excerpts from these two documents share, on the one hand, the sequence of characters 風、不離, and, on the other hand, the expression 薛蘿懸巌. None of these expressions appear in Arinaka's verse, which renders the assumption of a direct reference to *Gōdanshō* difficult to defend. It is more likely that the author of *Chūbunshō* composed the couplet with reference to Arinaka's phrase, and that it was then used in the *engi*.

As shown in the *Gōdanshō* excerpt, the couplets 孔子不忘本学友、賢者重一室之朋 in *Chūbunshō* ("Confucius does not forget his former study friends, wise people value friends with whom they used to share space") follow the ones that overlap with the *Minoodera engi* segment. These passages carry the meaning of a wise person like Confucius valuing a friend who shares in his studies. The description noted above of creeper vines coiling about on the cliffs even if the wind blows and white clouds hanging in the mountains and pine boughs try to obstruct them is a metaphor for the profundity of such companions; our *engi* transposes the original meaning onto the scenery of the Minoo waterfalls.

All known quotes from *Chūbunshō* are formulated in the style "In *Chūbunshō*, it is written that …" ("*Chūbunshō ni ha, X to kakarete iru*" 『仲文章』には〜と書かれている). *Minoodera engi*, however, used *Chūbunshō* for the actual composition of the text. Our document thus presents an example of how to convert a source to fit one's own writing, while acknowledging the meaning of the original metaphor. At the same time, this gives us clues not only to determine on the basis of what sources *Minoodera engi* was written, or what kind of person its author was; our text also helps us understand in what manner *Chūbunshō* was utilized (Miki 2017).

Conclusion

Let us briefly review and sum up what we have found out so far about mountain depictions in *Minoodera engi*:

Usage of a vocabulary that does not occur in other Japanese or Chinese *kanshibun* (e.g., *kōretsu* 拡烈, *sairō* 砕浪, *shinteki* 津滴).

Usage of Japanized expressions, in which the original Chinese meaning of the words is not used (e.g., *zuijū* 随従, *kōkaku* 磽确, *tei'i* 体為).

Usage of phrases characteristic of the late Heian period (e.g., *hansei* 攀躋, [*kōsui* 降水] *shishō* 之粧, *shōkoku* 衝黒).

Elements 1 and 2 are indications of the isolated nature of the expressions found in *Minoodera engi*. In fact, with the single exception of *Chūbunshō*, the document taken up in the previous section, I have not yet been able to find a *kanshibun* work susceptible to have influenced our text. On the other hand, element 3 shows that in terms of vocabulary, *Minoodera engi* shares common traits with *kanshibun* works from the Insei period, such as *Honchō zoku monzui* 本朝続文粋 and *Honchō mudaishi*. These indications allow us to surmise that the work was written not long after 1173 (Kawasaki 2017).

The Insei period is often regarded as an era in which modelization, or typification, of literary expressions became prominent in the sphere of *kanshibun*. One end of the spectrum was represented by books like *Tekikinshō* 擲金抄 and *Bunpōshō* 文鳳抄, which collected examples of expressions according to themes such as natural features of the four seasons (e.g., "spring" 春, "rain" 雨, or "mountain" 山). Metaphors such as those describing the waterfalls in *Minoodera engi*, such as likeness to the sound of thunder or to water-bleached cloth appear in this kind of books as well. The author of the *engi* was not satisfied to merely adopt such expressions, however. Although some passages are borrowed from *Chūbunshō*, the author tried to relate the grandeur of the three waterfalls of Minoo as well as the steepness of the surrounding mountains. Such impressions are conveyed through words that may have been original coinages (e.g., *kōretsu* 拡烈, "spreading intensely," and *shinteki* 津滴, "incessant drops") or through peculiar usages that diverged from the original meaning of the expressions (e.g., zuijū 随従, "following," and *kōkaku* 磽确, "ruggedly"). In this sense, the depiction of mountains in the *engi* seems to combine both Insei-period *kanshibun*-esque elements and trends that were contrary to those elements.

What kind of person(s) stands behind our text, this *Minoodera engi* that influenced a whole variety of subsequent writings? The analysis of literary expressions as attempted here should be helpful in drawing us closer to them.

Appendix: *Minoodera engi*

Shoji engishū 1970: second sheet, fourteenth line, to the third sheet, twelfth line.

```
 1 然間、至于廿五時白鳳廿年歳次庚午春三月十七日
   攀躋于当山、
   随従于澗流。
   踰山済川、
 5 漸図上時、
   往々所見致、
   有々滝三所也。
   最上者雄滝也。
   深消長二丈余、落水砕浪⁴之響拡烈、如大雷発音。
10 則騰⁵于東楞之巌上、立於杖、懸於脇。
   賀嬉当頭、
   興意无二。
   其杖之跡在于今、可見。
   基渕之底、有黒蛇、蟠臥長三丈余、時浮出腹行見人者。
15 第二者瓔珞滝也。
   崖石津滴駢⁶羅、
   磜径余流磽确。
   只貫青苔之珠、
   无殊異之興。
20 且随于様体得於名称也。
   第三雌滝也。
   転躁烈峻、危高十五丈余。
   降水之粧、泊憑⁷涌流、為体似于瀑布。
   基渕之澱、抓沖浸影、齋倫染于錦繡。
25 頂上之壺者竜穴也。其竜色錦斑、長三尺余者、
   動吹於黒雲衝黒、
   白雨四季不定矣。
   加之
   巍複畳嶺者、高崛東也西憂於雲、礙於⁸日、
30 穿岩澗流者⁹、深崎北与南帯於霧、隠於月乎。
   泉木抵于嵐、蔓草嫺于花。
   白雲靡風、不離山腰依々也。
   薜蘿懸巌、不絶翠枝聳々也。
```

9

Images of the *Shugenja* in Edo Popular Fiction

William D. Fleming

This chapter examines Shugendō not through the lens of history or religious practice, but as seen in the popular literature of the Edo period. The focus is on Shugendō practitioners, known as *shugenja* or *yamabushi*. Like the historical *shugenja*, the fictional *shugenja* is a figure on the margins of early modern Japanese society, particularly from the perspective of popular authors and writers ensconced in the urban centers of Edo, Kyoto, and Osaka. Nevertheless, *shugenja* make regular cameos across wide swaths of early modern Japanese literature. In historical fiction and fantastic tales, they are found leaping through mountains, emerging from rocky shadows, dispelling demons and performing exorcisms, and coming to the aid of those in need with powerful magic. Reflecting the prevalence of the satirical strain in Edo fiction, there is also a significant body of jokes and comic anecdotes in which *shugenja* are held up as objects of ridicule, whether hapless charlatans who overestimate their own abilities or lustful hypocrites satisfying their carnal desires at brothels.[1]

Literary depictions of the *shugenja* are diverse, and vary widely according to the context in which they are found. Individual depictions are themselves often layered, multivalent constructions. This chapter devotes much of its attention to one specific context, collections of short-form historical narratives known as the early *yomihon* 読本. The stories in these collections typically feature an element of the supernatural or "strange," thereby opening the door for a range of mysterious figures, including the *shugenja*. Many *yomihon* tales were also cross-cultural adaptations that drew on Chinese source texts. This chapter examines the sorts of characters in Chinese fiction that were mapped onto the *shugenja*, and how the process of adaptation, which was by its very nature seldom an act of straightforward conversion, transformed the image of the *shugenja*. Certain aspects of historical Shugendō were emphasized and brought to the fore, often idiosyncratically, while at the same time a layer of residue remained from the source texts, reflecting the distinct historical, religious, and literary contexts in which they were produced. The result is something new, a hybrid fantasy combining elements of the historical *shugenja* and earlier Japanese imaginings thereof with new elements of continental origin.

Fools and Frauds

We begin, however, with comic depictions, where the *shugenja* is seen primarily through the lens of satire. Whether in picaresque fiction, satirical tracts, comic verse, or jokes, Edo comic literature presents a rich vein to mine for depictions of the *shugenja*. One of the most fertile sources is the genre known as the *hanashibon* 噺本, collections of humorous anecdotes and jokes that were published in great numbers in the eighteenth and nineteenth centuries. Many of these are preserved in the modern anthology *Hanashibon taikei* 噺本大系 (1975-79), which, at twenty volumes of several hundred pages each, gives an immediate sense of the sheer quantity of production.

Two jokes from the late eighteenth century locate the *shugenja* at different points on the spectrum between fool and fraud, but in both cases with a gentle touch. The first, from a 1774 collection, hinges on the aural similarity between the jingling bells on the *shugenja*'s staff (*shakujō* 錫杖)—used in the mountains to drive away evil spirits and wild animals—and the sounds of an Edo sex toy known as *rin no tama* りんの玉, or "jingling balls." An itinerant ascetic has hired the services of a courtesan for the night, and he attempts to make conversation by asking her to guess his day job. After running through various possibilities, the courtesan tires of the game and begins preparations for lovemaking, sliding the mattress and pillow into place. As she moves the pillow, a jingling noise emanates from the sex toy inside. "You got it! You got it!" the man cries out in delight (*Waraigusa* 和良井久佐: 77).

The second joke, from a collection prepared by Ōta Nanpo 大田南畝 (1749-1823) only a few years later, tells of a group of farmers who come across a *yamabushi* on a footpath between some rice paddies. The *yamabushi* has been bewitched by a fox spirit and is madly shoveling horse manure into his mouth. After the group carries him to safety and brings him back to his senses, he ostentatiously thanks them with a very special gift: some of the same protective talismans he has just shown to be utterly ineffectual (*Uguisu bue* うぐひす笛: 66).

Mockery was not always so gentle, particularly in lengthier genres with more room for exposition and development. An example of a more cutting depiction of a *shugenja* appears in a collection of satirical essays and short stories published in Kyoto and Osaka under the title *Karasu no tsuibami* 烏之啄 (The Pecking Crow, 1777). The skeptical, confrontational style of the pieces brings to mind the writings of Hiraga Gennai 平賀源内 (1728-80), among others, while the title suggests similarly omnivorous appetites—the author's willingness to peck away, like a crow, at any subject that crosses his path. In other words, it is a sort of grab bag of short pieces on diverse subjects, one of which is the efficacy of magico-religious healing. In a story near the end of the collection, a physician and a *yamabushi* are called in to minister to a sick patient, and the pair ends up in a heated argument over who is better suited to the task. The dispute culminates with the doctor issuing a challenge to test their powers. The *yamabushi* is to strike down the doctor using his incantations, while the doctor will administer his rival a deadly cocktail of drugs. The *yamabushi* flees on the spot (*Karasu no tsuibami*: 93-4).[2]

The common thread in these and many other satirical anecdotes is the desire to expose the *shugenja* as comically impotent or, less benignly, as a fraudulent impostor. Yet it must be remembered that the *shugenja* is hardly unique in this regard. One encounters similar depictions of not only other religious figures but also physicians, teachers, scholars, samurai, daimyō, and others. That is to say, rather than giving particular insight into the *shugenja*, the examples above are perhaps best seen as reflecting a broader tendency toward irreverence and the subversion of traditional sources of authority, a tendency that underlies much of Edo comic fiction.

Defenders of the Downtrodden

The remainder of this chapter focuses largely on two examples from a rather different type of literature, namely late Edo historical fiction, a body of works conventionally referred to as the *yomihon*. Many of the great, sprawling works of (often serialized) historical fiction from the early nineteenth century—narratives like Kyokutei Bakin's 曲亭馬琴 (1767–1848) *Nansō Satomi hakkenden* 南総里見八犬伝 (Legend of the Eight Dogs, 1814–42) and *Chinsetsu yumiharizuki* 椿説弓張月 (Strange Tale of the Crescent Moon, 1807–11), or Santō Kyōden's 山東京伝 (1761–1816) *Mukashigatari inazuma byōshi* 昔話稲妻表紙 (The Straw Sandal, 1806)—feature occasional appearances by *yamabushi* and *shugenja*. In their depiction of such figures, authors often drew on tropes and conventions that originated in earlier visual and literary genres such as picture scrolls (*emaki* 絵巻) and *setsuwa* 説話 anecdotal literature.

Ueda Akinari's 上田秋成 (1734–1809) *Me hitotsu no kami* 目ひとつの神 (The One-Eyed God), from the collection *Harusame monogatari* 春雨物語 (Tales of the Spring Rain, 1808–9), offers a colorful example of the way in which earlier forms are reworked in Edo fiction. A man who is traveling to Kyoto from the east takes refuge one evening at a dilapidated shrine. He awakens in the middle of the night and secretly observes a supernatural procession that includes a Shinto priest, a Buddhist monk, a *yamabushi*, a pair of foxes disguised as a shrine maiden and her servant, and a strange one-eyed creature that turns out to be the manifestation of the shrine god (*Me hitotsu no kami*: 517–25). Nakamura Yukihiko 中村幸彦 observes a resonance between Akinari's rendering of these characters and the anthropomorphized, gently comic depiction of frogs, rabbits, and other creatures in the famous *Chōjū jinbutsu giga* 鳥獣人物戯画 picture scrolls.[3] We might also note similarities with the *hyakki yagyō* 百鬼夜行 processions of monsters illustrated in numerous medieval and early modern picture scrolls. Whatever the exact lineage in which we position Akinari's tale, the *yamabushi* appears as but one member of a larger menagerie of fantastic beings familiar from earlier works.

Although completed around the same time Bakin and Kyōden were writing their longer narratives, conventionally referred to as "late *yomihon*," Akinari's *Harusame monogatari* is in form what is often called an "early *yomihon*"—collections of short stories, typically historical fiction with a strong supernatural element, that had their heyday in the second half of the eighteenth century. The early *yomihon* often has an even clearer relationship with antecedent texts, which are frequently of Chinese origin and consist mainly of classical tales of the strange along with an assortment of vernacular fiction. A number of eighteenth-century *yomihon* stories adapted from Chinese source material feature *shugenja* prominently. Given that Shugendō is not part of the continental religious landscape, this raises some obvious questions: What types of Chinese characters were reimagined as *shugenja* in Japanese adaptations, and how did the depiction of these characters change across the cultural divide? What changes did Japanese authors have to make in assimilating this material to the Japanese context?

More interesting than these questions, though, is the possibility for new meanings and associations that can come into existence through precisely this sort of intertextuality. That is to say, adaptation does not neatly transform one cultural, historical context into another cultural, historical context. Rather, residue from the source text, and its biases and idiosyncrasies, are brought to bear on the adaptation. In other words, where the image of the *shugenja* is concerned, adaptation does not merely map *onto* an *existing* image, but transforms that image, thereby creating a new image. This is something useful to bear in mind more broadly when considering the prominence of adaptation in early modern Japanese fiction. Adaptation does not have to be seen as a derivative or parasitic enterprise. Instead it is something that, through complicated intertextual relationships, can be richly creative and generative of meaning. It follows that the *shugenja* we see in Edo-period historical fiction is not necessarily true to life, nor is it a uniquely Japanese character type. Rather, it is its own thing—like Shugendō itself, a complicated Sino-Japanese hybrid.

For the first of the two main examples in this chapter, I have chosen the seventh tale in Tsuga Teishō's 都賀庭鐘 (1718–c.1794) *Hanabusa sōshi* 英草紙 (A Bouquet of Stories, 1749), titled "Kusunoki Danjōzaemon Defeats His Enemy Without a Fight" (*Kusunoki Danjōzaemon tatakawazu shite teki wo sei-suru koto* 楠弾正左衛門不戦して敵を制する話). The plot centers around the machinations of a band of seven samurai, headed by the eponymous Kusunoki Danjōzaemon 楠弾正左衛門, as they plot to overthrow the tyrant Mutō Yoshiuji 武藤義氏, ruler of a domain in northern Dewa Province near what is now the city of Tsuruoka in Yamagata Prefecture. Toward the end of the story, as Yoshiuji awaits an opportune moment to subdue his rivals, a *shugenja* abruptly appears on the scene. Although Yoshiuji is not inclined to consort with such characters, the man's reputation prompts the ruler to summon him for an audience. After agreeing to read the warlord's palm for the tidy sum of ten gold pieces, the *shugenja* expresses alarm at what he sees, but details a course of action that might allow Yoshiuji to avoid disaster.

The *shugenja*'s name, Sagamibō Sonkai 相模坊尊海, immediately brings to mind another famous figure from Japanese literature, Hitachibō Kaison 常陸坊海尊, who appears in the *Gikeiki* 義経記 (Chronicles of Yoshitsune) and other legends as one of Minamoto no Yoshitsune's 源義経 (1159–89) four indispensable retainers. Before the Edo period, Kaison was a relatively undeveloped figure, and also an ambiguous one. In the *Gikeiki*, he is praised for his learning and rows into battle fearlessly alongside Benkei. Yet as his master's situation grows more dire he is nowhere to be found, prompting the narrator to remark that "such conduct is best passed over in silence" (*Yoshitsune*, McCullough, transl. 1966: 285). In later variations on the Yoshitsune legend, however, Kaison reemerges as a *shugenja*-like figure who heroically aids his master's flight from Yoritomo by means of a variety of magic and sorcery. Hiraga Gennai's puppet play *Genji ōzōshi* 源氏大草紙 (The Great Tale of the Genji, premiered 1770) depicts Kaison leaping across mountains in a single bound and subduing fearsome demons, while an early-nineteenth-century piece of historical fiction by Gennai's student Morishima

Chūryō 森島中良 (1756–1810) has him resurrecting Yoshitsune's men from the dead and conjuring a fleet of ships to carry them off to Tartary in the north.[4]

Teishō's story, which explicitly identifies Sonkai as a *shugenja*, presents an image not unlike that in these slightly later examples, but with certain unique elements that merit further consideration. To understand his vision of the *shugenja*, it will prove useful to delve into the source text behind this section of the narrative. Teishō's tale as a whole draws on multiple sources, both Japanese and Chinese, but the largest among these is the great, sprawling Chinese vernacular narrative *Shuihu zhuan* 水滸伝 (Jp. *Suikoden*; The Water Margin).[5] The section in which Sonkai appears and has an audience with Yoshiuji draws heavily on an episode near the beginning of chapter 61. A side-by-side examination of excerpts from both texts reveals not only Teishō's close adherence to key elements of his Chinese source, but also the ways in which the continental cultural landscape, although projected onto the world of medieval Japan, carries with it a measure of distinctive residue:

Hanabusa sōshi	*Shuihu zhuan*
There was around this time a *shugenja* named Sagamibō Sonkai, who had paid his devotions at all of Japan's tallest peaks, the Three Mountains of Dewa Province, and regions still further north. This *yamabushi* prayed to great effect on behalf of the afflicted, and the common people revered him, calling him a living Immovable One (*iki Fudō* 生不動). Yoshiuji had in the past scorned this sort of thing […]	Wu Yong wore a black crepe scarf around his head, a black Daoist robe edged with white silk, and a multicolored sash about his waist. On his feet were black square-toed cloth shoes, and he carried a golden staff with a bronze bell at the end. […] "It is most amusing! A fortune teller from out of town is selling readings on the street for one tael of silver. Who would waste such a sum on that? […] Children are following him around and laughing."
其の此日本の高山をあまねく巡拝し、出羽国の三山を拝して、尚奥へ通る修験者、相模坊尊海といへる山臥、人の憂をいのりて巧験ありとて、村里の人民、是を崇敬すること、生不動ともいふべし。義氏日来はかかることをあざけりさみせし人なれ共 […]	吳用戴一頂烏縐紗抹眉頭巾，穿一領皂沿邊白絹道服，繫一條雜綵呂公絛，著一雙方頭青布履，手裏拿一副賽黃金熟銅鈴杵。 ［…］ 「端的好笑，街上一個別處來的算命先生，在街上賣卦，要銀一兩算一命，誰人捨的！［…］小的們跟定了笑。」
Nevertheless, [Yoshiuji] invited Sonkai into the castle and had him pray for good fortune for his family. After some conversation, he had him read his palm to determine whether it foretold good or ill. […] "Up until now I have only read two men their fortunes. Although I cannot reveal their names, both are men of great import in neighboring provinces, and it has been customary for me to receive ten gold pieces as my divination fee."	"He talks big, so he must have some knowledge," replied Lu Junyi. "Invite him in right away." […] "My name is Zhang Yong, but I call myself 'The Mouth That Speaks of Heaven.' My ancestral home is in Shandong. I am able to read the fortunes of emperors, and I know when men will be born, when they will die, and whether they will be rich or poor. For a tael of silver, I will read your fortune."

尊海を請うて城中にいたらしめ、家運を祈らせ、対話の上にて、自身の掌文を相せしめて、「吉凶を占ふべし」とある。 [...] 「やつがれ是まで占を施す人、わづかに両人、其の名姓はあらはしがたけれども、俱に近国の大人なり。卜料の式、黄金十枚を収む。」	盧俊義道：「既出大言，必有廣學。當直的，與我請他來。」 [...] 「小生姓張，名用，自號談天口。祖貫山東人氏。能算皇極先天數，知人生死貴賤。卦金白銀一兩，方纔算命。」
He asked Yoshiuji the year of his birth, then prepared the divination rods and made his calculations. Greatly alarmed, his face went pale, and without a word he rose from his seat and began to leave.	Wu Yong produced some iron divination rods and arranged them on the table. After a few calculations, he slapped them down again. [...] [His] face went pale, and he quickly returned the silver. Then he rose and began to leave.
義氏の干支を問ひ、卦を設け、一算するに至つて、大に驚き、面色をちがへ、ことばもなく座を立つて去らんとす。	吳用取出一把鐵算子來，排在桌上，算了一回。拿起算子，桌上一拍，[...] 吳用改容變色，急取原銀付還，起身便走。
"[...] But is there some way to avoid this misfortune?" [Yoshiuji] asked. "The only way to avoid disaster," Sonkai replied, "is for you to move your residence. Each day, starting today, you must secretly move two *ri* away. Cleanse your mind and live peacefully. The world is in turmoil, so you must tell no one. Today you are to head southward, and from there proceed to the northeast."	"Is there any way to avoid [disaster]?" Lu Junyi asked. Wu Yong again made some calculations with his iron rods. He replied as follows: "The only way is if you go to a place one thousand *li* southeast from here. Then you may escape great trouble. There may still be a few scares along the way, but you will not suffer any serious harm."
「[...] ただし此の凶兆を避くるに術ありや」と問ひ給ふ。 尊海云ふ、「禍をさくるの道、唯御座所を別所へ移してさけ給へ。今日をはじめとして、毎日四方二里の外に忍び行きて、心をすまし、安居し給へ。さわがしき世の中なれば、かならず人にしられ給ふな。今日南方よりはじめて、東北にめぐりて出で給ふべし。」 (*Hanabusa sōshi*: 159–61)	盧俊義道：「可以迴避否？」吳用再把鐵算子搭了一回，便回員外道：「則除非去東南方巽地上一千里之外，方可免此大難。雖有些驚恐，却不傷大體。」 (*Shuihu zhuan*: 900–3)

We first observe that the character in *Hanabusa sōshi* is, in the source text, a Daoist priest—or at least someone dressed the part, complete with a Daoist robe (*daofu* 道服) and other accoutrements—who is earning income as an itinerant fortune-teller (*suanming xiansheng* 算命先生). The equation of *shugenja* and Daoist priest as general categories is unsurprising given the analogous cultural niche each occupies, not to mention the element of Daoist practice in Shugendō. Both undertake ascetic training in the mountains, are attributed magical powers including knowledge of divination, and are accordingly afforded a measure of reverence—or irreverence, as the case may be, for as it happens there is a nearly identical counterpart to the Ōta Nanpo joke discussed above in Feng Menglong's 馮夢龍 (1574–1646) *Xiao fu* 笑府 (A Treasury of Laughs), but featuring an ineffectual Daoist priest in place of the *shugenja* (*Chūgoku shōwa sen*: 65–6).

Teishō makes significant changes to the figure as he appears in *Shuihu zhuan*. The source text includes a thorough description of clothing and accessories, but there is no mention at all of Sonkai's physical appearance in *Hanabusa sōshi*, even though detailed accounts of dress are common in Edo fiction. Indeed, the description of a *shugenja* in the slightly later *yomihon* discussed in the final section below features a level of detail comparable to that in *Shuihu zhuan*. Teishō instead emphasizes the *shugenja*'s qualifications, acquired through ascetic training in mountains across Japan. Moreover, where *Shuihu zhuan* gives no indication of the priest's abilities, and the only suggestion of how he is viewed is offered by the children who follow him around laughing, Sonkai is esteemed for his powers among the common folk.

Nevertheless, the source text exerts a powerful pull. The result is the emphasis of elements less commonly associated (if associated at all) with Shugendō, or a sort of layering effect through which practices central to the Chinese and Daoist context leave their trace in Teishō's depiction of Sonkai. One of these is the commercial context of the Daoist priest's services, whereby he is first encountered selling his fortune readings in the marketplace. Indeed, the already sizable fee of one tael of silver—roughly an ounce—becomes the astronomical sum of ten gold pieces in adaptation. A further example of a primarily Daoist practice is Sonkai's use of divination rods to read Yoshiuji's fortune in place of more common Shugendō techniques such as calendrics, astrology, geomancy, or yin-yang divination.[6]

Knowledge of the Chinese source also helps account for the otherwise abrupt appearance of Sonkai in the Japanese narrative, not to mention what proves to be the complete failure of advice that, rather than averting disaster, lures Yoshiuji into the open, delivering him into the hands of Danjōzaemon and his gang a few days later. While this outcome suggests that the *shugenja* is perhaps somehow allied with Danjōzaemon, neither his "true" identity nor the nature of any relationship with Yoshiuji's rivals is overtly spelled out. In *Shuihu zhuan*, however, the Daoist priest in the corresponding scene is not a *real* Daoist priest, but the outlaw Wu Yong in disguise. Readers are fully aware of the deception; in the context of the broader narrative, Wu Yong has disguised himself as a fortune-teller in order to lure his credulous ally Lu Junyi southward to Liangshan Marsh to join forces with the other outlaws. Awareness of this deception puts the character of Sonkai in a different light. He is not a neutral party who happens to lead Yoshiuji astray. Instead, it is implicitly understood that he is in league with Yoshiuji's rivals and appears on the scene in order to entrap Yoshiuji in a larger plot. Thus, in addition to assuming qualities more often associated with a Daoist priest than with a *shugenja*, Sonkai is also imbued with the character of the gallant Chinese vernacular hero, emerging as a valiant protector of the vulnerable and downtrodden.

Seers and Saviors

A related example of the *shugenja* in fiction comes from a somewhat later *yomihon* collection by Morishima Chūryō titled *Tales from the Withering Wind* (*Kogarashi zōshi* 凩草紙, 1792). Like Teishō's tale, the second story in Chūryō's collection, titled "How the Lesser Monk of Yokawa Vanquished an Evil Spirit" (*Yokawa no kohijiri akuryō wo gōbuku suru koto* 横河の小聖悪霊を降伏する話), is set amidst the mountainous terrain of the far north, in this case the district of Shinobu in Mutsu Province, near what is now the city of Fukushima.[7] The protagonist, Kuranuki Koyata 鞍貫小弥太, is a handsome, refined samurai whose family has lived in the area for generations, ever since an ancestor was granted a holding of land as reward for distinguished service in battle at the end of the eleventh century. Koyata, however, has strayed from this exemplary model and, in a nod to the political climate and conservative agenda of the Kansei Reforms (*Kansei no kaikaku* 寛政の改革, 1787–93), during which Chūryō's collection was published, fails to uphold the "twin paths of the brush and the sword" (*bunbu nidō* 文武二道). Or at least he fails to uphold the second of the two. The brush presents no problem, for Koyata is so completely consumed by the pleasures of poetry that he has turned over household affairs to his wife and moved into a mountain cottage where he is able to read and write without distraction.

One autumn evening Koyata is jolted from his musings by the sound of crying. He emerges from his cottage to find an attractive girl, about sixteen years old, huddled outside his gate. She startles at the sight of him, but after a few kind words on his part she opens up and relates her situation. Her name is Uta 歌. Born in Kyoto, at the age of eleven she was indentured to a merchant couple and brought to the east. Far from home, she was forced to endure sexual advances from the husband and daily beatings from his jealous wife. Although she has at last managed to escape, Uta is now homeless and adrift and appears resolved to take her own life. Koyata comforts her, insisting that she stay with him until they are able to find someone to take her back to the capital. Inside, as the two converse by lamplight, Koyata finds himself increasingly captivated by her beauty, and the grateful girl eagerly reciprocates his feelings. In spite of Koyata's strong moral fiber, of which the narrator assures his readers, their conversation soon gives way to intimate whispers. They share a bed for the night.

Although the narrative is scarcely underway, readers familiar with Akinari's *Ugetsu monogatari* 雨月物語 (Tales of Moonlight and Rain, 1776) will already feel a sense of foreboding. Koyata's qualities, after all, are not unlike those of the polished but effete male archetype in that earlier collection, a figure whose shortcomings leave him susceptible to grave danger. As Ōtaka Yōji 大高洋司 has observed, Koyata brings to mind above all Toyoo 豊雄, the protagonist of Akinari's *Jasei no in* 蛇性の婬 (The Serpent's Lust). Uta, for her part, bears a striking resemblance to Manago 真女児, Toyoo's deadly love interest. Both are elegant Kyoto beauties down on their luck in the provinces, and both are in immediate distress (and apparently vulnerable) when the male protagonists first meet them, albeit less direly in the case of Manago, who encounters Toyoo when the two take shelter together during a sudden autumn downpour. In other words, Koyata's precarious situation is apparent to anyone with an awareness of earlier *yomihon*, as well as the conventions and heavy intertextuality of the genre. As if this were not enough, the name Chūryō gives the girl—Uta, meaning "poem" or "song"—offers a further signal of what lies in store. Building on the tale's opening lines, with their account of Koyata's lack of martial preparedness and neglect of the "twin paths," the girl appears at his door as the embodiment of the very weakness that has distracted him from his duties and rendered him vulnerable.

In *Jasei no in*, it is an enigmatic ascetic figure who first recognizes Manago as a demon in disguise and alerts Toyoo to the danger she presents. One fine spring day, Toyoo and Manago join his sister and her husband for some sightseeing in the mountains of Yoshino. As they spread out a picnic beside a crashing waterfall, an old man bounds toward them across the boulders. He glares at Manago and her maidservant and curses them under his breath. "How strange! Evil spirits! Why must you guide men astray? Do you think you can sit there right before my very eyes?" (*Ugetsu monogatari*: 431). The two women leap into the falls and the water boils up after them. Although Toyoo's savior is identified only as an "old man" (*okina* 翁), the mountainous setting, the ease with which he navigates the treacherous terrain, and the fact that he appears beside a powerful waterfall—where he had presumably been performing austerities—are all clues that he is, in fact, a *shugenja*.

A similar encounter occurs in *Kogarashi zōshi* as Koyata hurries back to his cottage, where he has left Uta waiting, after a short trip to his main residence to fetch supplies. Here the seer figure is explicitly identified as a *shugenja*:

As he hurried through town on his way home, a *shugenja* approached from the other direction wearing a tan robe tightly bound with a braided cord, wooden leg-guards, and eight-looped straw sandals. Hair white as snow flowed disheveled from his head. The two passed so close their noses almost touched, and as Koyata hastened on, the man lingered, pacing back and forth. "What a pitiful sight," he murmured to himself. "Shrouded in an evil spirit, he sits at the brink of death." Koyata heard the words clearly enough, but his mind was elsewhere and he gave the incident hardly a second thought. He continued on to his cottage without so much as a backward glance.

忙がはしく立戻る街にて、香染の篠掛に、組糸の貝掛をざつくと結び、櫟の行縢に、八つ目のわらんずを履きしめ、雪を欺むく白髪を乱し懸たる修験者、小弥太と鼻白に行合ひ、道を譲りて行違ひしが、盤桓として立もとをり、「傷しいかな此人。邪気繁続して、性命旦夕に迫りたり」と独言声、さだかに耳へは入れども、心愛に有ざれば、余所事に聞流して、見かへりもせず庵に至り...

(*Kogarashi zōshi*: 165–6)

Readers unfamiliar with Akinari's stories in their original form may nevertheless discern a close resemblance between this passage and a memorable scene from Mizoguchi Kenji's 溝口健二 (1898–1956) 1953 film adaptation. Near the end of the film, as Genjūrō 源十郎, one of the two male protagonists, walks through town on his way back to the estate of Lady Wakasa 若狭, the malignant spirit that has seduced him in the guise of a beautiful noblewoman, he passes an itinerant monk at close distance. The monk is not a *shugenja* but a close counterpart, a Tendai monk from nearby Mount Hiei (the film is set on the shores of Lake Biwa) performing the ascetic practice of *kaihōgyō* 回峰行 ("circling the peaks"); he is recognizable by his distinctive clothing, the most conspicuous item being the "lotus hat" (*renge-gasa* 蓮華傘) whose twin cylinders evoke the rolled-up edges of an unopened lotus leaf. The monk stops and calls out to Genjūrō. "The shadow of death (*shisō* 死相) lies upon your face," he says. "Have you not encountered some strange being (*ayashii mono* 妖しい者)?" Genjūrō initially laughs at the suggestion, but is soon persuaded of the seriousness of his predicament.

Although this encounter has become part of the popular image of *Ugetsu monogatari*, there is no such scene in any of Akinari's tales. Toyoo's encounter with the old man in *Jasei no in*—which, together with *Asaji ga yado* 浅茅が宿 (The Reed-Choked Hut), is one of the two stories cited in the opening credits of Mizoguchi's film—is the closest counterpart, but occurs under very different circumstances. The passage in *Kogarashi zōshi*, however, is remarkably similar and proceeds in like fashion. Like Genjūrō, Koyata is soon persuaded of the truth of the seer's words. Arriving back at the cottage, he decides to play a joke on Uta by sneaking up to the window and surprising her. But as he peers inside he sees instead a terrifying demon with flashing eyes and fearsome fangs. Uta's robes lie in a pile nearby. Koyata's first thought, evoking the famous sixth episode of *The Tales of Ise*, is that Uta has been "swallowed in a single gulp" by a demon. He reaches for his sword. However, as he continues to watch, his gaze transfixed, the demon pulls a human skin over its head, dresses itself in the cast-off garments, and begins to apply makeup. The demon has not eaten Uta; it *is* Uta.

The significance of the encounter in the marketplace at last dawns on Koyata. Fleeing in terror, he resolves to track down the monk to ask for his help. No sooner does the thought occur to him than he discerns the very same man resting in the shadows a short distance away, his backpack on the ground beside him. Koyata throws himself on the ground and begs to be saved. After a few moments of silence, the monk claps his hands together and introduces himself. He is known as the "lesser monk of Yokawa." More than seventy years have passed since he began his annual pilgrimages from Kumano to Yoshino, and with his powers he has never failed to dispel a demon in the past. Yet he fears that this particular demon lies beyond even his ability to contain. Still, the situation is dire and there is no time to find someone else to help. The *shugenja* gives Koyata a protective charm—a yellowed piece of paper with an inscription in cinnabar ink—and instructs him to affix it to his gate.

The title "lesser monk" (*kohijiri* 小聖) simply denotes a monk of ordinary status, while Yokawa indicates one of the three complexes of Enryakuji Temple on Mount Hiei. Taken together, however, the *shugenja*'s title and affiliation carry a more specific association, for it is another "lesser monk of Yokawa" who performs the exorcism of Lady Aoi in the Noh play *Aoi no ue* 葵上 (Lady Aoi).[8] In Chūryō's story, the *shugenja* does not perform the exorcism himself. Rather, after giving Koyata the charm, he leaves him to his own devices. Koyata rushes home to his main residence, affixes the charm to the lintel, and bolts himself in. His wife, Ayase 綾瀬, is appalled as she learns of her husband's predicament for the first time, but the two hunker down for the night and hope for the best. Sometime after midnight a violent storm blows up, and Uta appears at the gate. Enraged that a charm has been positioned to prevent her from passing through the gate, she tears down a section of the earthen wall and enters the compound that way instead. Towering over Koyata as he cowers in his bed, she pulls out his still-beating heart and gulps it down.

The next morning the *shugenja* appears at the door, having sensed a disturbance the night before. Finding Ayase unconscious on the floor, he raises his staff and revives her with an invocation of the protective "nine-character incantation" (*kuji no bun* 九字の文; also known as the *kuji goshinbō* 九字護身法) of Shugendō practice. He then leads Ayase and her servants deep into the forest, where they locate Uta in a noxious pit. After pausing above her to declaim her many sins and defilements, the monk strikes her with his staff. Her body dissolves into thousands of will-o'-the-wisps that slowly trail into the distance.

Here we enter the final section of the narrative. Impressed by the *shugenja*'s extraordinary powers, Ayase begs him to bring her husband back from the dead. With a sigh, he informs her that this lies beyond even his abilities, but after training his ear to the wind in the treetops, he claps his hands and tells her that if she continues along the path home, she will encounter a "strange-looking seeker" (*ayashige naru dōjin* 怪しげなる道人) who will help her, so long as she is willing to swallow her pride and do whatever he asks. He urges Ayase on her way, and when she pauses a few paces later to look back, she spies him atop a peak far in the distance. Ayase eventually comes across a leprous beggar who she is certain must be the seeker. Steeling herself, she accedes to his demands, sucking his sores to ease his pain and forcing down a handful of filthy rice thick with the man's phlegm. In spite of her perseverance, he ultimately rejects her entreaties to help bring back Koyata, and she returns home in humiliation. Then, as she tends to her husband's body, her stomach begins to churn, and she vomits the lump of rice right into the open chest cavity. It is his warm, beating heart. Ayase wraps up the wound, and Koyata slowly returns to consciousness.

Like the section of the tale in Teishō's *Hanabusa sōshi* discussed above, Chūryō's story is also adapted from a Chinese source. The main elements of the plot are taken from the story *Hua pi* 畫皮 (The Painted Skin) in Pu Songling's 蒲松齡 (1640–1715) collection *Liaozhai zhiyi* 聊斎志異 (Strange Tales from Liaozhai Studio, Jp. *Ryōsai shii*). To this is added considerable detail and embellishment, including allusions to diverse Chinese and Japanese texts, that expand the tale to several times its original length. There are also changes in the framing of the story and the motivation of characters beyond those alterations strictly necessary to fit the narrative to the Japanese context.

For present purposes, we are interested in the figure of the *shugenja*. Unsurprisingly, the corresponding character in the Chinese source is again a Daoist priest, this time a legitimate one. The protagonist, Wang 王, encounters the priest in the marketplace and is warned that his life is in jeopardy. After observing the demon in its true form, Wang is convinced, and the priest gives him a protective talisman. Even so, Wang is unable to ward off disaster. That night the demon bursts into his bedroom and tears his heart from his body. The next day, Wang's brother joins forces with the priest. They track down the demon, now in the guise of an old woman, and the priest dispatches her with a swing of his wooden sword. He then sends Wang's wife in search of a beggar in the marketplace who can help bring her husband back to life.

Many aspects of Daoist practice map readily onto Shugendō, making the *shugenja* a convenient counterpart to the Daoist priest in adaptation. The priest's wooden sword, to take one of the most straightforward examples, is transformed into the *shugenja*'s staff. Yet the result of this conversion process may be to overemphasize those elements of Shugendō practice with origins in Daoism, for example, the nine-character incantation—ultimately traceable to the *Baopuzi* 抱朴子—that is used to revive Ayase. At the same time, Buddhist and Shinto elements are layered on top of this Daoist foundation. The *shugenja* does not merely wield his staff to dispel the demon, as the priest does his wooden sword; rather, his assault is preceded by a substantial monologue in which he enumerates Uta's offenses, in the process drawing heavily on the *Kojiki*, *norito*, and other elements of Shinto tradition and ritual. Among her most egregious sins is having circumvented the gate to Koyata's house (thus avoiding the charm affixed to the lintel), an offense against Amenoiwatowake 天石門別, the god of the gate. Later, shortly before he sends Ayase in search of the seeker, the *shugenja* cocks his head and listens to the wind, then explains that a bodhisattva has spoken to him and given hope for Koyata's revival. There is, accordingly, a hint of Buddhist salvation in the final pages of the tale, building on the image of the *shugenja* as an advocate and savior of the downtrodden.

Given the sheer quantity and diversity of early modern Japanese literary production, there is no single image of the *shugenja* that emerges in Edo fiction. Authors were free to represent the *shugenja* as they chose, and clearly did so in the comic literature explored above. There were, moreover, domestic precedents available in *setsuwa*, *emaki*, and other forms, as Akinari is seen to have employed in *Harusame monogatari*. Nevertheless, genre and convention were powerful forces, and an understanding of these factors yields valuable insights. Nowhere is this more the case than in the early *yomihon*, where so many narrative elements are shaped by Chinese fiction. The prevalence of the figure of the Daoist priest in Chinese fiction, whether vernacular narratives or classical tales of the strange, translates into regular cameos by *shugenja*, who were seen as the most natural Japanese counterpart. Adaptation, however, is never a process of one-to-one conversion. Daoist elements inherent to Shugendō are brought to the fore, but so are the peculiar emphases of the source texts, particularly those elements that are critical to the plot. To these are added other elements, so that through the process of adaptation and the intertextual relationship with source text and other antecedents, a sort of hybrid emerges, one that is rooted in the flesh-and-blood *shugenja*, at least as popularly conceived, but onto which are layered new associations and meanings.

Part Four

Materiality and Visual Culture

10

The Cult and Statuary of Zaō Gongen

Fujioka Yutaka
Translation by Andrea Castiglioni

Buddhism has always considered mountains as cultic sites. Starting with the *Kusharon* (Skt. *Abhidharmakośa śāstra*), in numerous Buddhist scriptures the structure of the cosmos is centered around Mount Sumeru where the divine protectors of Buddhism reside. The highest level of the heavenly realm, above this mountain, represents the land of perfect enlightenment. For example, this cosmology is visually displayed in the engravings on the lotus petals of the gilt bronze pedestal for the statue of the Vairocana Buddha at Tōdaiji.[1]

Besides Mount Sumeru, which is a mountain existing only in the scriptures, there are also real sacred mountains such as the Vulture Peak (Skt. Gṛdhrakūṭa) in the present-day state of Bihar in India. This mountain is located to the northeast of Rājagṛha, the capital of the ancient state of Magadha, and here Śākyamuni preached important scriptures such as the *Lotus Sutra* (Skt. *Saddharma puṇḍarīka sūtra*) and the *Sutra of the Meditation on the Buddha of Immeasurable Life* (Skt. *Amitāyur dhyāna sūtra*) during his last rebirth. According to legends, the abode of the Bodhisattva Kannon is located on a floating mountain called Potalaka, which is located somewhere in the sea south of India.[2] The idea of sacred mountains as abodes of buddhas and bodhisattvas is not peculiar to India but is common to every region of Asia. For example, in China, Mount Wutai was considered to be the sacred place of the Bodhisattva Mañjuśrī; Mount Emei of the Bodhisattva Samantabhadra; Mount Putuo was the site where the Bodhisattva Kannon experienced his last rebirth; and Mount Tiantai was a numinous location of *arhat* since ancient times.

Mountains were taken in great consideration not only as places where buddhas manifest themselves but also as ascetic spots for purificatory practices. Mountains became sites for building Buddhist halls, consecrating Buddhist statues, meditating, and reciting scriptures. These circumstances explain why, in Chinese and Korean mountains, there are numerous stone caves and buddha figures carved in natural rocks (*magai butsu* 磨崖仏). Because mountains were perceived as sacred sites in Southeast Asia, they were also considered ideal places to perform rituals. These mountains, before being conceived as abodes for buddhas or places for ascetic practices, were almost invariably sacred territories prior to the arrival of Buddhism and had functioned as *trait d'union* between this religion and preexisting local cults. As Buddhism developed a close relationship with mountains in India, so, too, did the phenomenon occur in Japan. A short time after the transmission of Buddhism, the temple Hisodera 比曽寺 was built on Mount Yoshino, which immediately became a renowned center for meditation and ascetic practices.[3] From that moment, in each region of Japan, various mountain-temples (*yamadera* 山寺) were founded on mountainous sites, which were already venerated in local religious systems and distinguished themselves for peculiar natural features or location in the territory.

Mount Kinpu 金峯山, situated in the southern part of Nara prefecture, can be considered as the most paradigmatic sacred mountain of Japan (Blair 2015). A broad definition of Mount Kinpu includes the mountainous range, which goes from Mount Yoshino to a place called Ozasa 小篠 immediately after Sanjōgatake 山上ヶ岳 on Mount Ōmine 大峰山. The ancient and medieval sources provide a narrow definition of Mount Kinpu, which basically overlaps with Sanjōgatake. Toward the end of the seventh century, En no Gyōja climbed Mount Kinpu. From that moment forward, numerous Buddhist ascetics arrived on the mountain to perform their practices. This chapter is dedicated to the cult of Zaō Gongen 蔵王権現, which is worshiped as the tutelary deity of this site.

According to legends, Zaō Gongen manifested his exterior form as a deity who saves human beings when En no Gyōja was performing ascetic practices on Mount Kinpu. In this chapter, I first take into account discourses about Zaō Gongen, and then discuss statues of Zaō Gongen as concrete elements of the cult to this deity, as a way to explain developments in the relationship between images and doctrines dedicated to Zaō Gongen. I also analyze the techniques and manufacturing processes used to build the numerous gilt bronze statues that were offered to Zaō Gongen on Mount Kinpu, by referring to other Buddhist gilt bronze statues of the same period and by showing the connections between these objects and the ritual pilgrimages to Mount Kinpu.

Discourses on Zaō Gongen[4]

Although Mount Kinpu is said to have been opened by En no Gyōja, it is not clear in fact since when *shugenja* started to consider it a sacred land. According to the *Nihon ryōiki* (824), Kōtatsu 広達 (Shimotsukeno Ason 下毛野朝臣) who had performed ascetic practices on Mount Kinpu during the reign of Emperor Shōmu (724–49) received the title of meditation master (*zenji*) in 772 together with nine monks.[5] In the *Sangō shiiki* (797), Kūkai (774–835) wrote that he had practiced asceticism on the same mountain. In the *Shōryōshū* 性霊集, Kūkai explains that he caught sight of the numinous site of Mount Kōya after walking south for one day from Mount Yoshino and then west for two more days. It is likely that the place reached by Kūkai on the first day of walking was precisely Mount Kinpu. It seems clear that already in the late Nara period (710–84) Mount Kinpu was considered as a suitable site for performing mountain ascetic practices (*sangaku tosō* 山岳抖擻) and worship activities. However, it is impossible to ascertain the presence of a cult specifically dedicated to Zaō Gongen at this early stage.

Table 10.1 Principal Written Sources On Zaō Gongen From The Heian To The Nanbokuchō Period

	Written sources	Year	Nomenclature of Zaō Gongen	Contents
①	*Ribuōki*. 932, second month, fourteenth-day entry	932	Kongō Zaō Bosatsu	Kongō Zaō Bosatsu of Mount Kinpu originally lived on Mount Kinpu in China from which he flew to Japan together with the mountain. Thanks to his divine powers, Kongō Zaō Bosatsu subjugated the dragon that inhabited the mountain
②	*Daigoji konpon sōjō ryakuden*	937	Kongō Zaō Bosatsu	Shōbō made a one meter and eighty centimeters high golden statue of Nyoirin Kannon and two and three meters high colored statues of Tamonten and Kongō Zaō Bosatsu
③	*Yichu liutie* Chapter Twenty-One, story forty-three	954	Kongō Zaō Bosatsu	The first miracle concerns Kongō Zaō Bosatsu, which lives on Mount Kinpu, located almost twenty kilometers on the southern side of a city
④	*Nichizō yume no ki*	Late 10th century	Praise to Zaō Daibosatsu as a manifestation of [Shakya] Muni (Namu Muni *keshin* Zaō Daibosatsu 南無牟尼化身蔵王大菩薩)	In 941 Dōken Shōnin was fasting on Mount Kinpu when he had a dream in which an eminent monk changed his name to Nichizō and guided him through the Tuṣita Heaven and various hells
⑤	*Sanbō ekotoba* Last volume	984	Kane no mitake Zaō カネノミタケノ蔵王	While praying to Kane no mitake Zaō for finding the necessary gold to complete the coating of the Vairocana Buddha statue at Tōdaiji, the deity requests the enshrinement of a Nyoirin Kannon statue at Ishiyamadera upon which a miracle took place and a vein of gold was discovered in the Michinoku region
⑥	*Konshikiji Hokekyō okugaki* 紺紙金字法華経奥書	998	Kongō Zaō	Fujiwara no Michinaga made a copy of the *Lotus Sutra* in order to praise the divine power of Kongō Zaō
⑦	Gilt bronze sūtra box inscription (*Kondōsei kyōzutsu mei* 金銅製経筒銘)	1007	Namu kyōshu Shaka Zaō Gongen	Fujiwara no Michinaga requested the protection of Namu *kyōshu* Shaka Zaō Gongen burying copies of the *Lotus Sutra*, *Amida Sutra*, and *Miroku Sutra* on Mount Kinpu.

(continued)

	Written sources	Year	Nomenclature of Zaō Gongen	Contents
⑧	*Honchō Hokke genki.* Last volume, chapter ninety-three	1044	Zaō Daibosatsu	The monk Tenjō (–849) was performing ascetic practices in front of the statue of Zaō Daibosatsu when the deity manifested in guise of a demon (*yasha* 夜叉) with a dragon-crown on the head and fulfilled Tenjō's vows
⑨	*Dōsei kyōzō mei* 銅製鏡像銘	1056	Kongō Zaō	A mirror-icon of Kongō Zaō that was buried on Mount Kinpu
⑩	*Fujiwara no Moromichi ganmon* 藤原師通願文	1088	Kongō Zaō	Fujiwara no Moromichi buried *sūtra* copies on Mount Kinpu on behalf of Kongō Zaō
⑪	*Go-Nijō Moromichi ki*	1090	Zaō	Fujiwara no Moromichi climbed again on Mount Kinpu and prayed in front of Zaō's boulder
⑫	*Shichidaiji junrei shiki* 七大寺巡礼私記	1140	Kinpusen Zaō	Rōben 良弁 (689–773) built Ishiyamadera after a premonitory dream of Kinpusen Zaō and collected gold for coating the Vairocana Buddha of Tōdaiji traveling to the Dewa, Okuriku, and Shimotsuke regions
⑬	Written vow placed within the Zaō Gongen statue at Sanbutsuji	1168	Zaō Gongen	Thanks to the offerings of the Ōmi 大見 family a statue of Zaō Gongen was enshrined in the Sanbutsuji
⑭	*Konjaku monogatarishū* Volume eleven, chapter three	Late Heain period	Kinpusen no Zaō Bosatsu	Zaō Gongen of Mount Kinpu manifested in front of En no Gyōja
⑮	*Konjaku monogatarishū* Volume eleven, chapter thirteen	Late Heain period	Tutelary deity of the mountain (*sono yama ni mamoru shinrei* 其山ニ護ル神霊)	After praying to the tutelary deity of Mount Kinpu to find the gold for coating the Great Buddha of Tōdaiji, a monk appeared in Rōben's dream and ordered him to enshrine a statue of Nyoirin Kannon at Ishiyamadera. After this event veins of gold were miraculously found in the Okuriku and Shimotsuke regions
⑯	*Shozan engi* 諸山縁起	Early Kamakura period	The original august body of Zaō (Zaō *konpon mishōtai* 蔵王根本御正躰)	The stone statue of the original august body of Zaō, which is located in the cave where En no Gyōja practiced ascesis seven days per month, is three meters high
⑰	*Kinpusen zakki* 金峯山雑記	1262	Kongō Zaō	Thanks to En no Gyōja, Kongō Zaō appeared on Mount Kinpu

	Written sources	Year	Nomenclature of Zaō Gongen	Contents
⑱	*Shasekishū* Chapter One	1283	Zaō Gongen	En no Gyōja performed ascetic practices on the summit of Mount Yoshino and after dismissing Shaka Nyorai and Miroku Bosatsu as unfit to guide the sentient beings of Japan toward salvation, Zaō Gongen appeared in front of him
⑲	*Kinpusen himitsu den* First volume	1337	Kongō Zaō	After En no Gyōja dismissed Shaka Nyorai, Senju Kannon, and Miroku, Zaō Gongen manifested himself in the cave on the top of Mount Yoshino. Zaō had a dark blue body, a three-pronged crown, three eyes, a three-pronged mallet in the right hand, the left foot stumped on the stone and the right one was suspended in the air
⑳	*Kinpusen sōsō ki* 金峯山草創記	Late Kamakura-early Muromachi period	Kongō Zaō	The original grounds (*honji*) of Kongō Zaō are Shaka Nyorai for the past, Senju Kannon for the present, and Miroku Bosatsu for the future. A different explanation says that Dainichi Nyorai and Jizō Bosatsu are also original grounds of Kongō Zaō
㉑	*Taihei ki* 太平記. Chapter twenty-six	Nanbokuchō period	Zaō Gongen	Upon meditating for one thousand days on Mount Kipusen for the salvation of sentient beings, En no Gyōja made a statue of the apparitional body of a deity, which provoked the manifestation of Jizō Bosatsu. After dismissing this god, Zaō Gongen appeared in front of the ascetic.

The title of Gongen, which follows the name of Zaō, indicates a provisional manifestation of a buddha or a bodhisattva as a different deity and is a typical Buddhist title usually granted to Japanese local deities, based on the combinatory system associating original grounds and provisional traces (*honji suijaku*). The first appearance of the name of Zaō Gongen is in the inscription of a gilt bronze sutra box, which Fujiwara no Michinaga (966–1027) buried in a sutra mound (*kyōzuka* 経塚) on Mount Kinpu in 1007 (Table 10.1, point 7). The sentence "Praise to the Dharma-preacher Shaka Zaō Gongen" (*Namu kyōshu* Shaka Zaō Gongen) identifies Zaō as a provisional manifestation or an apparitional body (*keshin* 化身) of the Buddha Śākyamuni. The colophon of a copy of the *Lotus Sutra*, transcribed in 998 and inserted in Michinaga's sutra box, reports the name Kongō Zaō 金剛蔵王, which is also another appellative for Zaō Gongen (Table 10.1, point 6). Because the standardization of the name of Zaō Gongen began only after the Kamakura period (1185–1333), before this time the same deity was variously called "Kongō Zaō Bosatsu," "Zaō Bosatsu," or simply "Zaō."

Another source that mentions the origin of Zaō Gongen is the legend of Tenjō Hōshi 転乗法師, included in the last volume of the *Honchō Hokke genki* (1040–44) (Table 10.1, point 8). The eminent monk Tenjō who died in 849 is said to have made a pilgrimage to worship Zaō Daibosatsu, but this information cannot be historically validated. In contrast, the *Daigoji konpon sōjō ryakuden* (937) reports a legend, reliable from a historical point of view, about the founder of Daigoji and famous Shugendō patriarch, Shōbō 聖宝 (832–909), who built a hall on Mount Kinpu, where the main statue of Nyoirin Kannon was enshrined together with a statue of Tamonten and Kongō Zaō Bosatsu (Table 10.1, point 2). The credibility of this text, which was compiled less than thirty years after the death of Shōbō, is high and it is possible to suppose that the hall mentioned above had actually been built on Mount Kinpu toward the end of the ninth century (Nishikawa 2001: 252).

In 932 on the fourteenth day of the second month Prince Shigeakira 重明親王 (906–54), the fourth son of Emperor Daigo (885–930), annotated in his diary, *Ribuōki* (920–953), a legend transmitted by Jōsū 貞崇 (866–944), who was the monk in charge of ritually protecting (*gojisō* 護持僧) Emperor Daigo.[6] According to this text, Mount Kinpu was originally located in China; Kongō Zaō Bosatsu moved the entire mountain across the ocean after eliminating the dragon who lived in it. Jōsū was a disciple of Shōbō's and there is no doubt that he knew about the statue of Kongō Zaō Bosatsu built and enshrined on Mount Kinpu by his master. It is important to note that the details about the flying mountain and the subjugation of the dragon emphasize a strong faith in this deity, which goes beyond the historical dimension.

Among Buddhist tales about sacred mountains that came flying from China to Japan, the *Yichu liutie* (*Giso rokujō*) 義楚六帖 (954) reports a legend transmitted by a Japanese Buddhist monk called Kanho 寛輔, according to which Kongō Zaō Bosatsu of Mount Kinpu is the most powerful divinity of Japan and corresponds to the apparitional body of Miroku Bosatsu (Table 10.1, point 3).[7] The name of Kongō Zaō Bosatsu was diffused also in China, where it was compared with the bodhisattva Mañjuśrī of Mount Wutai.

The name of Zaō Bosatsu also appears in the *Nichizō yume no ki*, compiled in the mid tenth century (Table 10.1, point 4). In 941, the monk Nichizō 日蔵 (*c*.905–67) had a dream after being close to death due to the intense ascetic practices he had performed on Mount Kinpu. While in this oneiric dimension, Nichizō encountered an ascetic monk who called himself Shukongōjin 執金剛神 (Skt. Vajradhara). Then, another monk of great virtue appeared and introduced himself as Zaō Bosatsu, the apparitional body of Śākyamuni (Muni *keshin* Zaō Bosatsu 牟尼化身蔵王菩薩) who protects the Pure Land of Mount Kinpu. At that moment, Daijōitokuten, the spirit of Sugawara no Michizane (845–903), revealed himself within a blaze of light surrounded by a crowd of acolytes and prostrated on the ground to worship Zaō Bosatsu.

According to the *Sanbōe* (984), in order to find the necessary gold for the external coating of the Vairocana Buddha's statue at Tōdaiji, supplications were addressed to Zaō of Kane no mitake (Zaō of Mount Kinpu), and a statue of Nyoirin Kannon was built at Ishiyamadera 石山寺.[8] Thanks to the divine protection and miraculous power of these two deities, a vein of gold was found in Michinoku province (Table 10.1, point 5).

It is evident that Zaō Gongen began as a Dharma-protector deity (*gohōjin* 護法神) for the statue of Nyoirin Kannon enshrined by Shōbō and immediately became the focus of numerous legends in which he was said to have come flying from China, or was described as a bodhisattva living on Mount Kinpu since ancient times or, again, was interpreted as the apparitional body of Śākyamuni or Maitreiya. Being at the center of such a considerable production of legends, Zaō Gongen immediately surpassed the main deity Nyoirin Kannon in popularity and attracted the devotional interests of large strata of society. The climax of worshiping practices dedicated to Zaō culminated with Michinaga's pilgrimage to Mount Kinpu when, for the first time, the name of Zaō Gongen was used to emphasize the combinatory nature between Buddhist deities and local gods. In the legend about the gold coating of the Vairocana Buddha's statue at Tōdaiji, which is reported in the *Konjaku monogatarishū* (mid-twelfth century), Zaō is defined as a divine spirit (*shinrei* 神霊) that progressively transformed itself into a local deity (Table 10.1, point 15).

The *Konjaku monogatarishū* provides a new narrative of the origin associated with Zaō Gongen, in which the deity is said to have answered the prayers of En no Gyōja, who was then performing ascetic practices on Mount Kinpu, manifesting himself in front of the ascetic (Table 10.1, point 14).[9] After the *Konjaku monogatarishū*, other texts such as the *Shasekishū* (1283) (Table 10.1, point 18) and the *Kinpu himitsu den* (1337) (Table 10.1, point 19), wrote descriptions of the encounter between Zaō Gongen and En no Gyōja, thus marking the definitive consolidation of a cycle of legends dedicated to the epiphany of Zaō Gongen. However, the formation of such legends about the manifestation of Zaō Gongen probably predates the literary sources mentioned above. This can be inferred from the fact that in 1088 Fujiwara no Moromichi (1062–99), the great-grandson of Michinaga, made a pilgrimage to Mount Kinpu where he buried a written vow (*ganmon* 願文) with the expression "divine trace of Kongō Zao" (Kongō Zaō *no shōshi* 金剛蔵王之聖趾). According to the *Go-Nijō Moromichi ki* (1083–99), Moromichi made a new pilgrimage in 1090 to Mount Kinpu in order to bury sutras in the site where Zaō Gongen manifested his presence (Table 10.1, point 11). After this ritual Moromichi made three prostrations in front of the big stone of Zaō. Thus, the "divine trace" of Kongō Zao must refer to the place where the deity appeared and the big stone could be the boulder (*banjaku* 盤石), which was believed had been used by Zaō Gongen as pedestal. Because the pilgrimage of Michinaga to Mount Kinpu took place in 1007 anticipating that of Moromichi, it is possible to suppose that the legend of the epiphany of Zaō Gongen was already in place when Michinaga visited Mount Kinpu. The statue of Zaō Gongen built and enshrined by Shōbō immediately inspired numerous legends, probably because its presence was shielded from the sight and the secrecy increased the attribution of miraculous powers to this artifact.

The Images of Zaō Gongen

While the above-mentioned literary records and Buddhist tales testify to the presence of Zaō Gongen, it is also interesting to take into account how the visual form of this deity was created.

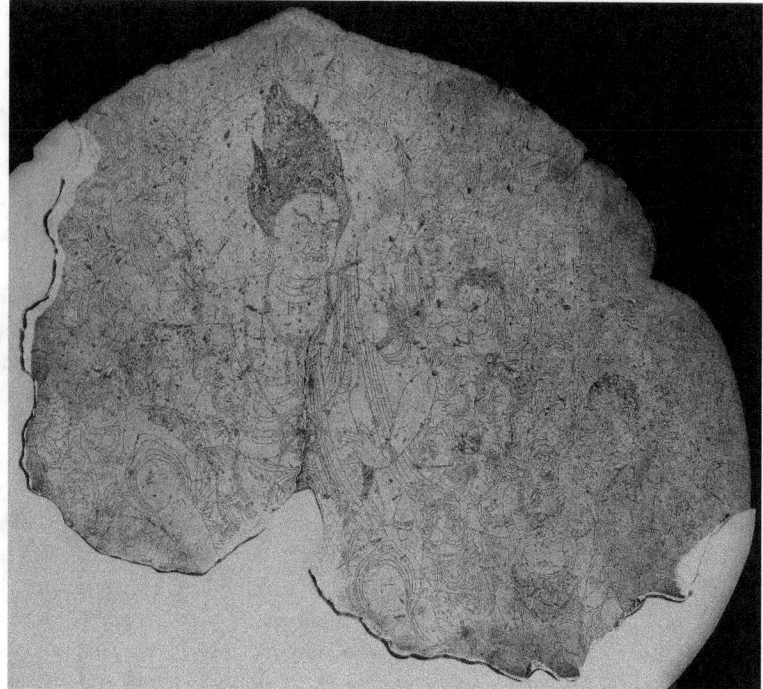

Figure 10.1 Zaō Gongen mirror icon, 1001, Tokyo. Courtesy of Sōjiji Temple.

The oldest extant artifact of Zaō Gongen seems to be a mirror icon (*kyōzō* 鏡像) made in 1001 and preserved among the treasures of Sōjiji 総持寺 in Tokyo (See Figure 10.1) (Ariga 1986: 3–27). This mirror icon has a width of about seventy-six centimeters and the borders are in guise of big petals. According to the *Kinpu kokin zakki* (1783), this mirror icon was transmitted during the Edo period (1600–1868) among the leading monks on top of Mount Kinpu (Tanabe 1983: 18). This Zaō Gongen follows the canons of his classical iconography: it shows the enraged third eye in the middle of the forehead, the right leg raised to kick the enemies, and the right hand gripping a three-pronged mallet.

The striking aspects of this bas relief are the elegance of the outfit and accessories of Zaō Gongen, who is escorted by numerous members of his retinue, each one presenting unusual features. Importantly, this image of Zaō Gongen overlaps with a description provided in the legend of Tenjō Hōshi 転乗法師, which is included in the *Honchō Hokke genki*, where Zaō Gongen appears in a demonic form with various ornaments to adorn his body and a crowd of acolytes as entourage (Table 10.1, point 8).

Images of Zaō Gongen were also made in guise of statues, paintings, mirror icons, and hanging buddhas (*kakebotoke* 懸仏). The *Kinpu himitsu den* reports that Zaō Gongen is usually depicted with dark blue skin to symbolize wrath, three eyes, and a three-pronged diadem; the left hand makes the gesture of the wisdom sword while the right hand holds a three pronged mallet; and the left foot firmly stands on a rock. Although there are other literary descriptions which match this one, the extant artifacts of Zaō Gongen show numerous variations in the rendering of the diadem, the presence or absence of the third eye, the hand gesture, the holding objects, and the type of pedestal (Ishida and Yajima 1937: 72–4). This may be due to the fact that Zaō Gongen was continuously reinvented, thanks to the formation of new legends, and was never considered to be a fundamental deity even in those sutras that were used as textual bases for its iconography and rituals.

Among this great variation in the images dedicated to Zaō Gongen, it is interesting to analyze the backgrounds of the mirror icons and hanging buddhas. For instance, in the mirror icon at Sōjiji, Zaō Gongen is surrounded by various members of the retinue with unusual features. In another mirror icon, Zaō Gongen appears among mountains, clouds, and mist as in the pivotal moment during which he revealed his form in a flash of light on the top of Mount Kinpu. In a third type of mirror icon there is an archway behind Zaō Gongen (See Figure 10.2), and in a different mirror icon Zaō Gongen is escorted by a group of *kami* from Mount Yoshino. It is possible to speculate that these images were influenced by numerous legends.

Figure 10.2 Zaō Gongen mirror icon, twelfth century. Kyoto National Museum Collection. Photographic credit: Mainichi Shinbunsha.

One cannot ignore the relationship between the basic patterns reported in the illustrations about Zaō Gongen and the statue of Kongō Zaō Bosatsu, which was enshrined by Shōbō on Mount Kinpu. This statue is part of a tryptic, together with Nyoirin Kannon, which is the main deity, and Tamonten. Shōbō's tryptic is identical to another one at Ishiyamadera, where Shōbō himself resided for a while. Not only do Kongō Zaō Bosatsu and Tamonten play the role of two tutelary deities, but they also represent the two primordial local gods, which presided over Ishiyamadera, in guise of divine kings. The *Shōsōin monjo* reports that the Ishiyamadera tryptic was made in 762 when a statue of Kanzeon Bosatsu was paired with two other statues of divine kings. According to the *Sanbōe,* this statue was subsequently identified as Nyoirin Kannon; for the *Kakuzenshō,* the two flanking deities were called "Shukongōjin" and "Kongō Zaō." In 1078, a fire burnt Ishiyamadera, and the following years were characterized by a continuous series of calamities and restorations (Tanabe 1989: 217–22). In the *Shō Kannon zuzō,* dated 1078, there is an illustration of the appearance of the statues before this difficult period. The statue of Zaō Gongen was quickly repaired after the fire, and the wooden axle of the original statue could be maintained. Comparing the illustration with the statue's axle, it is possible to establish that Zaō Gongen was represented with the right foot in the kicking position and the right hand with the gripping fist already in the original statue (Iwata 2002: 10–13). On the basis of our discussion so far, we can argue that Kongō Zaō Bosatsu enshrined by Shōbō on Mount Kinpu was probably based on the Ishiyamadera tryptic. There is also the possibility that Shōbō himself or someone from his entourage influenced the creation of Buddhist tales in which Zaō Gongen and the main deity of Ishiyamadera appear together, as in the case of the stories about the miraculous finding of a vein of gold to coat the exterior part of Vairocana Buddha's statue at Tōdaiji.

On the Statues of Zaō Gongen of Mount Kinpu: Ritual Offerings and Manufacturing Techniques[10]

The extant statues of Zaō Gongen can be divided into two groups. The first group includes those bronze or copper statues discovered on Mount Kinpu, that is, close to the main hall of Ōminesanji on the summit of Sanjōgatake. The second group includes those statues of Zaō Gongen mostly made of wood that are located on sacred mountains in various geographical areas with some connections with Mount Kinpu. The statues of the first group were created as offerings to be donated to the divine spirit of Zaō Gongen, which inhabited Mount Kinpu, and were not considered to be objects of worship. The statues of the second group were thought to be alternative bodies of Zaō Gongen's spirit from Mount Kinpu and were separately enshrined as cultic objects. For example, statues of this type can also be found in the Nageiredō 投入堂 of Sanbutsuji 三仏寺 in Tottori prefecture, where they were probably used as offerings for the deity in the same way as those on Mount Kinpu. Some aspects of the devotional practices connected with the statues of Zaō Gongen are still to be fully understood.

Regarding the custom of making statues of Zaō Gongen to be used as offerings, the *Nichizō yume no ki* reports the following dialog between Daijōitokuten and Nichizō: "Because you are a trustworthy ascetic, I want to give you these instructions. Make an image of me and chant my name. If you respectfully pray in front of it, I will certainly respond to your supplications." In this passage, Daijōitokuten orders Nichizō to make a statue with his features and promises to bestow benefits for those who recite his name. It is possible that *shugenja* kept producing statues of Zaō Gongen, basing their devotional behavior on the same logic of this episode.

Most of the statues of Zaō Gongen discovered on Mount Kinpu date from the end of the Heian (794–1185) to the Kamakura periods and show a peculiar color due to the fact that they were made of bronze or copper. Like the sutra boxes used during the ritual burials of Buddhist scriptures, the materiality of Zaō Gongen's statues indicates that they were supposed to last until Miroku's descent on earth.

In spite of this attempt to reach a good degree of durability, every metal statue of Zaō Gongen presents a different level of completeness. Some of them seem to be almost incomplete due to the numerous copper burrs, which formed in correspondence to the matrix's joints during the casting process. Nevertheless, when examined with fluorescent X-rays, even these rough statues suggest that the artists took time to do the external coating with care.

Table 10.2 shows the analysis of the chemical components and casting techniques of the twenty-six statues of Zaō Gongen that were excavated on the top of Sanjōgatake and have been indicated as important cultural properties (see Figure 10.3). Some of these statues are made combining together two casts, one for the front and the other for the back; others are constituted of a single cast, which was probably produced following the lost wax technique.[11] The joints of the mold should not be clearly visible, but in numerous statues there are residual burrs. Some parts of the arms, hair, and garments were separately molded and subsequently added to the statue, even though this seems an unnecessary operation in the case of a standard casting with the lost wax technique. In the majority of cases even the small bumps on the garments are due to fractures in the molds rather than consciously created for aesthetic reasons.

The bronze coating of these statues is usually very thin and the iron core is replaced by a sort of internal scaffolding made of iron nails, which holds the torso, legs, and arms. In numerous statues, the part of the body under the shoulders was created following a process resembling the one used to make wooden statues toward the end of the Heian period. This casting procedure can be summarized as follows:

(1) A wooden matrix is smeared with earth in order to create the shape for the external mold.
(2) The wooden matrix is removed and a sprue is created before firing the external mold.
(3) The external mold is filled with earth in order to create another internal mold to which an iron core and nails are added as structural supports for the statue's body.
(4) The surface of the internal mold is lightly shaved off in order to be placed in the inner part of the statue.
(5) The external and internal molds are joined together thanks to the iron core and nails.
(6) After firing the molds, metal is cast into it.
(7) The sprue is eliminated and accessories are added to the statue's body, which is also polished, gilded, and colored.

Table 10.2 Techniques And Bronze Components Of The Zaō Gongen Gilt Bronze Statues Excavated Around The Main Hall Of Ōminesanji.

No.	Technique	Iron core and nails	Other constructive aspects	Coating, color, and analysis of the adjunctive components	Height (cm)	Period/notes
1	Frontal and back cast	There is an iron core from the head to the left foot and from the mallet in the right hand to the left arm		The tiger skin is gild and painted with ink. The gild was probably made with a metal foil.【Buttocks】Cu81.8 Pb10.9 Sn5.4 As1.6 Fe0.4	34.5	Heian
2	Frontal and back cast	There is an iron core from the head to the left leg and from right armpit to the left shoulder. There are also iron nails in the arms and legs	There are iron nails and patches to secure the ornaments on the garment and head	Probable metal foil gilt.【Left arm】Cu79 Pb8.9 Sn9.3 As1.3 Fe0.4	51.5 (present condition)	Heian
3	Frontal and back cast	There is an iron core from the head to the left leg and from the mallet in the right hand to the wrist of the left hand		Without gilt.【Arm】Cu79.3 Pb10.6 Sn8 As1.7 Fe0.4	33.8	Produced from the same mold of number one
4	Frontal and back cast	There is an iron core from the head to the left leg (partially missing) and from the left part of the waist to the right leg	There is probably a patch for the sprue under the left knee	Without gilt.【Arm】Cu81.7 Pb11 Sn5.9 As1.1 Fe0.2	34.6	Produced from the same mold of number one

Cult and Statuary of Zaō Gongen 179

No.	Technique	Iron core and nails	Other constructive aspects	Coating, color, and analysis of the adjunctive components	Height (cm)	Period/ notes
5	Technique unknown	There are iron cores and nails in the arms, left shank, and legs		Amalgam gilt. 【Left cheek】 Cu70.4 Pb7.8 Sn9 As1 Fe0.2	35.6	Heian
6	Cast and technique unknown	There is an iron core from the halo to the lower part of the body and there are probably iron nails in the neck and waist	The part under the shoulders was separately cast. There are patches under the head, on the left part of the chest, and in the middle of the back	Amalgam gilt. Lapislazuli on the top of the head. 【Left armpit】 Cu78.5 Pb13.5 Sn5.2 As2 Fe0.8	52.2	Heian
7	Probable frontal and back cast.	There is an iron core from the head to the left leg and there are probably iron nails in both armpits, left thigh, and right leg	There are patches under the shoulders	Without gilt. 【Chest】Cu89.4 Pb4.8 Sn2.9 As1.5 Fe0.2	37.6	Heian
8	Technique unknown	There are iron nails in the head, shoulders, right knees, right foot, and left leg	There are patches under the shoulders and a nail hole on the left knee	Amalgam gilt. 【Lower part of the body】Cu81.2 Pb8.4 Sn7.7 As1.7 Fe1.1	47.9	Heian
9	Frontal and back cast.	There are iron cores from the halo to the arms, in the shoulders, waist, and legs. There are iron nails in both thighs	There are patches under the shoulders, on the right foot, and below the tiger mat	Probable metal foil gilt. 【Left shoulder】Cu84.5 Pb5.6 Sn3.5 As4.9 Fe1.2 【Tiger skin】 Cu96.4 As1.5 Fe1	57.6	Heian

(continued)

No.	Technique	Iron core and nails	Other constructive aspects	Coating, color, and analysis of the adjunctive components	Height (cm)	Period/notes
10	Frontal and back cast	There is an iron core in the trunk and arms	There are patches under the shoulders and knees	Without gilt. 【Right shoulder】Cu79.3 Pb10.6 Sn6.6 As3.2	37.1	Heian
11	Technique unknown	There is an iron core from the halo to the lower part of the body. There are probably iron nails in the chest and legs			39.3	Heian
12	Technique unknown	There are iron nails in the arms, waist, and legs	There are patches under the shoulders, knees, and a hole on the left leg	Without gilt. 【Chest】Cu74.9 Pb13.5 Sn8.8 As2 Fe0.7	34.1	Heian
13	Frontal and back cast	There are traces of an iron core and nails in the left knee and right leg. There is an iron plaque under the right knee	The parts under the shoulders and close to the ears were separately cast. The left arm is fixed with a tack and the left heel was attached to the pedestal with a mandrel. There are patches on the top of the head	Without gilt. There is a mottles design painted with ink on the tiger skin and a fur design is painted on the edge of the garment. 【Waist】Cu80.7 Pb8.8 Sn6.3 As2.6 Fe1.4	71.2	Heian
14	Frontal and back cast.	There are traces of an iron core and nails in the left shoulder, right armpit, thighs, and right ankle	There are holes in the lower part of the trunk and left leg	Without gilt. 【left shoulder】Cu79.1 Pb13.6 Sn1 As6 Fe0.2	32.9	Heian

(continued)

No.	Technique	Iron core and nails	Other constructive aspects	Coating, color, and analysis of the adjunctive components	Height (cm)	Period/notes
15	Frontal and back cast	There are traces of an iron core and nails in the head, armpits, thighs, and right knee	There are patches and square holes under the shoulders	Amalgam gilt. 【Chest】Cu71 Pb11.9 Sn7.2 As2.1 Fe0.7	44.4	Heian
16	Technique unknown	There is an iron core from the head to the chest. There are iron nails in the chest and from the right thigh to the left knee	There are patches under the shoulders and the lotus pedestal under the right foot was separately cast	Amalgam gilt. 【Left leg】Cu70.4 Pb5.3 Sn10.1 As2.3 Fe0..2	23.0	Heian
17	Probable frontal and back cast	Solid block	The edge of the garment was separately cast	Without gilt. 【Back】Cu79.2 Pb11.7 Sn7.7 As1 Fe0.3	32.0	Heian
18	Probable frontal and back cast	Solid block	The back is almost flat	Without gilt. 【left knee】Cu87.7 Pb8.1 Sn2.4 As1.5 Fe0.3	35.6	Heian
19	Frontal and back cast	–		Without gilt. 【Chest】Cu83.5 Pb6.5 Sn3.7 As5.4 Fe0.6	16.9 (present condition)	Heian
20	Technique unknown	There are traces of an iron core and nails in the left part of the body, right hand, and right leg	There is a patch under the left shoulder and the left part of the halo was separately cast	Without gilt. Color pigments on eyes, mouth, and hair painted with ink on the back of the head. 【Back】Cu77.5 Pb11.4 Sn7.6 As2.7	35.5	Heian
21	Frontal and back cast	There is an iron core from the head to the left leg and iron nails are placed in the armpits and in the right thigh	There are patches under the shoulders and below the head	Amalgam gilt. Tiger skin decorated with carved lines. 【Back】Cu73.8 Pb14.2 Sn6.8 As1.3 F3.9	39.5	Heian

(continued)

No.	Technique	Iron core and nails	Other constructive aspects	Coating, color, and analysis of the adjunctive components	Height (cm)	Period/notes
22	Technique unknown	There is an iron core in the head and chest. There are empty holes for iron nails in the hands and legs		Amalgam gilt. Color pigments on eyes and mouth. 【Left leg】Cu69 Pb19.7 Sn9 As1.8 Fe0.6	40.0	Produced from the same mold of number eleven
23	Frontal and back cast	There is an iron core in the right shoulder	There are patches up and down the waist, under the left shoulder, and on the buttocks	Amalgam gilt. Carved eyebrows. 【Left shank】 Cu73.4 Pb7 Sn4.3 As0.9 Fe0.4	55.7	Kamakura
24	Frontal and back cast	The iron core is absent but there are numerous iron nails	There are patches under the shoulders and an iron nail under the head	Amalgam gilt. Cinnabar on the top of the head. Belt and tiger skin carved with line designs. 【Left shoulder】Cu70.1 Pb18.8 Sn10.2 Fe0.2	38.2	Kamakura
25	Technique unknown	Numerous iron nails	There are patches under the shoulders and knees. The accessories were created from a bronze plaque	Amalagam gilt. Cinnabar on the top of the head and other color pigments on eyes and mouth. 【Left leg】Cu81.1 Pb11 Sn5.3 As1.8 Fe0.8	36.8	Kamakura
26	Technique unknown	There is an iron core in the head	The tiger mat, garment, waistband, and accessories were created from a bronze plaque	Amalgam gilt. 【Lower part of the body】Cu84.7 Pb7.6 Sn5.2 As1.2 【Tiger skin】Cu97.2 Pb0.7 As0.8	34.1 (present condition)	Kamakura

Figure 10.3 Gilt bronze statue of Zaō Gongen, twelfth century, Nara, Ōminesanji. Photo by Fujioka Yutaka.

While the twenty-six statues of Zaō Gongen present various differences among them, most were made of bronze even though the molding techniques are different. Table 10.2 shows that copper and lead were the principal materials for casting the statues, together with tin and arsenic. Among the fourteen gilded statues, eleven were created following the amalgamation process and three with the golden leaf process. For the remaining twelve statues, the type of gilding cannot be verified. Statue number one presents gilding traces together with forgotten burrs, which testify to a certain inaccuracy in the creation process. Statue number nine completely lost its gilding around the shoulders and has a hole in the back, which was simply repaired with a thin copper foil to patch the scratched area. Although some statues have the hair part of the head decorated with gold leaf and present peculiar decorations on different areas of the skin, most of them seem to be forged in a rough way.

Offering Small Statues of the Buddhas Made with Gilt Bronze in the Late Heian Period

Diaries of aristocrats from the later Heian period include many passages on the production of gilt bronze statues of buddhas. According to these texts, casters were invited to private residences to make these statues in one day. In the case of funerary ceremonies for the forty-ninth day after death or other urgent situations, such statues were also used as main icons for the rituals. In general, these small statues were not permanently enshrined in temples; rather, they were intended as worship objects for individual prayers, used as main icons in special Buddhist ceremonies (*hōe* 法会) or carried to different locations during travels thanks to their portability (Mitsuhashi 2000: 512–38).

Considering the simple finishing that characterizes the statues of Zaō Gongen on Mount Kinpu, it is possible to argue that they were similar to these small gilt bronze statues of buddhas. However, it is important to take into account the fact that most of the Zaō Gongen statues of Kinpusenji required the preparation of a wooden matrix before beginning the actual casting process. It is, therefore, impossible that such statues were created in just one day. For example, the *Taiki* (1155) has an entry on the process for making a gilt bronze statue of Nyoirin Kannon commissioned by Fujiwara no Yorinaga (1120–56) in 1134.

According to this text, in the morning of the twenty-ninth day of the third month "a matrix was prepared to create a statue of Nyoirin [Kannon]. During the night of the same day Kakunin 覚仁 began making offerings for the deity and prayers were offered at the Buddhist ceremony." On the twenty-third day of the fourth month, "A statue of Nyoirin [Kannon] of almost twenty centimeters was created," and on the tenth day of the sixth month "the monk Jitsuhan [or Jichian] 実範 (d. 1144) was summoned to venerate and present offerings in front of the bronze statue of Nyoirin [Kannon]. Because the prayers were fulfilled, the cast of the statue was completed and it was used as the main icon [for the rituals]." It is likely that the first matrix was made of wood. It is interesting to notice that the completion of the statue took place only after the realization of Yorinaga's prayers.

According to the *Midō kanpaku ki* (1021), in 1007 on the second day of the eighth month, Fujiwara no Michinaga began his pilgrimage to Mount Kinpu in preparation for which he had been performing purificatory rituals for one hundred days from the seventeenth day of the fifth month (Moerman 2005). These purificatory practices were considered to be essential preliminary activities before the pilgrimage. As for the Zaō Gongen statues of Mount Kinpu, which were probably created during this pre-pilgrimage period, it seems that they had to be completed in a short amount of time in order to be ready for the beginning of the pilgrimage; this would also explain the rough finishing of many of them. It is also possible to argue that this extremely crude finishing was a prerogative not only of those statues, which were used for a one-time offering ritual, but also of other statues, which were worshipped in a series of itinerant ceremonies such as those performed during the pilgrimage to Mount Kinpu.

Conclusion

In the first part of the chapter we saw that the cult for Zaō Gongen spread, thanks to the diffusion of devotional attitudes and material objects. Based on this, it is possible to individuate two crucial developments.

First, by the time of Michinaga's pilgrimage to Mount Kinpu, the name of Zaō Gongen was clearly used to refer to a combinatory deity. This is also testified by the oldest extant mirror icon of Zaō Gongen, which displays the deity's body as a provisional manifestation of a buddha (Taniguchi 2007: 13–15). The inscription of the mirror icon of Sōjiji indicated that the object was produced in an atelier sponsored by the court (*kan'ei kōbō* 官営工房), which was probably involved in Michinaga's pilgrimage to Mount Kinpu. From this time on, the statues of Zaō Gongen kept displaying a great diversity of external features, which were probably due to the fact that new visual renderings were triggered by the aura of secrecy always associated with this deity.

Second, starting with the Buddhist tale about the manifestation of Zaō Gongen on Mount Kinpu, included in the *Konjaku monogatarishū*, Zaō Gongen came to be gradually associated with En no Gyōja. Most of the artifacts dedicated to Zaō Gongen are concentrated in the late Heian and Kamakura periods. Afterward, besides the statue at Kinpusenji, which was restored two times in the Nanbokuchō (1336–92) and Muromachi (1392–1573) periods, the production of new statues declined. Moreover, from the medieval to the early modern period there was a proliferation of statues exclusively dedicated to En no Gyōja, who was conceived as the patriarch of Shugendō (see Chapter Six by Carina Roth). This was due to the continuous adaptations and dramatizations of the famous episode in which En no Gyōja prays in front of Zaō Gongen as first described in the *Konjaku monogatarishū*. For example, in the *Kinpusen himitsu den* (Table 10.1, point 19), En no Gyōja calls for a buddha suitable for bestowing salvation during the defiled age of degeneration of Dharma (*mappō jokusei* 末法濁世): the Buddha Śākyamuni, One-thousand-arm Kannon, and Miroku appear one after the other, but En no Gyōja dismisses them all as unsuitable; finally, Zaō Gongen manifested himself, to En no Gyōja's approval. Thus, Zaō Gongen came to be newly conceived as a deity able to provide salvation during the final age of the Dharma, but this type of Buddhist narrative is usually focused on the supernatural powers attributed to En no Gyōja. Moreover, the identification of Zaō Gongen as the central deity of Yoshino contributed to the relocation of its cult from the summit of Mount Kinpu to its slope. This aspect probably marks the development of Yoshino as the principal site for the veneration of Zaō Gongen. It seems that these continuous transformations in the cult of Zaō Gongen contributed to preserve a sort of veil around this divine figure.

The second part of the chapter took into account the various techniques and circumstances associated with the production of the statues of Zaō Gongen, which were repeatedly offered to worship at Mount Kinpu. A peculiarity of these statues is that, despite the complexity of the casting techniques, most of them present an extremely approximative finishing. The reason for this probably resides in the fact that these statues were not supposed to be permanently enshrined in temples but were used as temporary objects of worship during the expressions of vows and prayers in one-time offering ceremonies. It is also interesting to keep in mind that these statues were probably produced during the time of the preliminary purification rituals, which anticipated the actual pilgrimage on the mountain, and had to be completed in a limited amount of time in order to be ready for the various ceremonies that accompanied the ascension toward the summit.

11

Religious Culture in Transition: Mt. Fuji

Janine T. Anderson Sawada

Reverence paid to Mt. Fuji in late medieval and early modern Japan was part of a larger universe of rural and increasingly urban practices and beliefs that centered on various deities and perceived sources of spiritual power. As in other parts of the country, religious hopes and attitudes toward the local mountain *kami* were intertwined with preoccupations about ordinary life problems and not clearly differentiated from those directed at buddhas, bodhisattvas, or other deities (see also Chapter Twelve by Andrea Castiglioni). This diffuse form of devotion to Mt. Fuji (*Fuji shinkō* 富士信仰) coexisted with, and for the most part reinforced, the system of organized pilgrimage to the mountain that developed in the medieval period under the auspices of local temples and shrines. In this chapter I offer a visual perspective on the emergence of a new form of Fuji devotionalism, later called Fujikō 富士講, in this socioreligious environment. After a brief sketch of the existing pilgrimage system, I discuss selected religious images of the mountain that appeared in the late Muromachi and early Edo periods with an eye to modulations that may shed light on the nature of the incipient Fuji movement. Conceptualizations of Mt. Fuji continued to draw on existing Buddhist and *kami*-centered paradigms, as well as on traditions of mountain practice, but ordinary people's thinking about the religious meaning of Fujisan evolved in distinctive ways, as rituals associated with the mountain grew in popularity.

Shugendō played a formative role in the development of group devotion to Mt. Fuji.[1] During the medieval period, ritual austerities on the mountain came to be associated with Murayama 村山, a site at the beginning of the frontal trail (*omoteguchi*) on the southern slope that was allegedly favored by Matsudai Shōnin (末代上人, n.d.), the reputed pioneer of Shugendō-type disciplines on Mt. Fuji in the late Heian period.[2] By the late fifteenth century, the temple complex at Murayama, formally titled Fujisan Kōbōji, had been drawn into the line of Shugendō dominated by Shōgoin in Kyoto (Ōtaka 2013: 26–7).[3] The institution became a powerful presence in the world of Mt. Fuji pilgrimage; it possessed rights to the upper reaches of the mountain, above the eighth station (*hachigōme*), and its *yamabushi* supervised most activities along the southern route.

The operation of the pilgrimage was a highly organized affair. The Murayama temples worked in parallel with the nearby Main Sengen Shrine (Fujisan Sengen

Hongū 富士山浅間本宮, also known as Ōmiya 大宮); for the most part, the shrine staff operated the pilgrim hostels while the mountain practitioners took responsibility for the climbers' practices (*gyō*) on the mountain (Horiuchi 1995: 145, 148).⁴ In the late sixteenth century, despite the military turbulence of the time, climbing activities on the slopes of Mt. Fuji expanded considerably;⁵ the *dōsha* 道者 (pilgrims) who used the southern approach began to arrive from an increasingly wide range of geographical locations. Kikuchi Kunihiko's study of *Fujisan danki* and other Murayama pilgrim registers indicates that long before the Fuji movement spread in the late Tokugawa period people from areas such as Ise, Iga, Kyoto, and Ōmi were organized into small cells under the supervision of mountain guides (*sendatsu*) and group leaders, anticipating the later lay-directed *kō* 講 system (Kikuchi 2009: 381, 388). *Yamabushi* (mostly in the Ōmine line of Shugendō) had steadily encouraged groups of prospective pilgrims in several distant locations both to visit the mountain and to participate actively in Fuji devotions close to home (Kikuchi 2009: 387).

The Murayama establishment, nevertheless, lost ground in the increasingly competitive pilgrimage environment of the Edo period. A number of possible factors have been suggested, notably the shifting political winds of the time and related economic challenges, including tensions with the Main Shrine over control of income derived from lodging house and other pilgrim fees.⁶ Mt. Fuji Shugendō did not immediately pass into oblivion, however. The three head priests, accompanied by a number of lower-ranked practitioners, continued to rotate the expected summer disciplines on the mountain every year, with the local villagers sharing responsibility for the expenses involved in these and the associated proxy rituals (*daisan* 代参) (Ōtaka 2013: 111, 113). Murayama-affiliated mountain guides led pilgrims on the trail and paid home visits to their regular patrons (*danna* 檀那), giving out talismanic slips and performing prayer rituals, as before. In 1641 the three temples were also allotted income from shogunal "red-seal" land parcels, which helped defray the cost of building maintenance and activities. Even so, Shugendō-affiliated activities on the southern side of Mt. Fuji dwindled, especially after the late seventeenth century, when the Murayama complex lost status and property in the aftermath of a protracted land-rights dispute. By the late eighteenth century, when the shogunate took up the issue of rights to Mt. Fuji above the eighth station, Murayama was not even in the running (Ōtaka 2013: 118–19).⁷

Another factor in the diminution of Shugendō-supervised activities on Mt. Fuji was competition from pilgrimage enterprises on the other side of the mountain. The great proliferation of visitors on the eastern and especially northern trails in the Tokugawa period is often associated with the establishment of the shogunal headquarters in nearby Edo, but in reality pilgrimage activity was already surging in the north during the late Muromachi and Momoyama periods.⁸ By the late sixteenth century, as in the south, climbers were arriving from an ever-wider range of provenances and the supervisory structure of the system was well established; pilgrimage coordinators (*oshi* 御師) were reportedly operating over eighty lodges at the Yoshida entry by 1572 (Hirano 1987: 127–8, 129–30). In the early years of the Edo period, the catchment area cultivated by Yoshida priests expanded further to include today's Fukushima, Ibaraki, Chiba, and Saitama prefectures (Horiuchi 2009: 282).⁹

Regardless of where they began their climbs, pilgrims of the time were expected to follow a set ritual etiquette. While in the south these protocols were usually monitored by Murayama *sendatsu* in conjunction with the Main Shrine staff, in the north they were administered by the Yoshida Shrine personnel.[10] Contemporary manuals describe these ritual practices in detail. A work drawn up by a Shingon Buddhist priest at the behest of a Yoshida pilgrimage agent includes precise instructions for supervising pilgrim conduct before and during the climb—specifying, for example, the length of periods of abstinence and cold-water purification to be carried out and measures to be followed when pilgrims were exposed to ritual defilements (such as the death of a family member or a menstruating woman). The text also contains diagrams of the purification wands (*gohei* 御幣) that the officiants were to use, the Buddhist surplices they should wear, and descriptions of requisite mandalic and mudric exercises, including notations for reciting the Sanskrit sound syllables correctly while performing the mudras.[11] The ritual activities of the Yoshida *oshi* were evidently grounded in a version of the same Esoteric Buddhist heritage that infused religious protocols at the southern approach to the mountain.[12]

The staff of the Mt. Fuji religious establishment, whether the Murayama *yamabushi* and the Ōmiya priests at the frontal entry, or the Yoshida *oshi* in the north, effectively controlled the ritual knowledge as well as the physical access to the mountain that people needed to complete a legitimate pilgrimage. The priests were authorized to exert this control initially by local warlords and in due course by the newly installed shogunal and domain governments. However, the demand for more informal access to religious experience (which pilgrimage may have seemed to promise) was on the rise in Japan. Even as the Tokugawa authorities solidified mechanisms for regulating and centralizing religious institutions and ritual activities, changes in the social dynamics of pilgrimage were well under way—at Mt. Fuji as at other revered sites throughout Japan.[13]

It was during this time of profound sociopolitical change that a wandering ascetic practitioner called Kakugyō Tōbutsu 角行藤佛 (1541–1646?) is said to have performed extraordinary austerities in the vicinity of Mt. Fuji.[14] In the seventeenth century, villagers and townspeople in eastern Japan who were inspired by reports of this figure's spiritual prowess and his teachings about Mt. Fuji began to form small cells devoted to the worship of the mountain god, Sengen (written 仙元 rather than 浅間). By the end of the Edo period, a network of Fuji *kō*, as these groups came to be known, had spread throughout much of Japan. It is generally assumed that the ideas and practices popularized by Kakugyō and his disciples drew on existing traditions of mountain asceticism in the Kantō area, though not on Shugendō in any formal sense (Suzuki 2015b: 146). In this chapter I do not dispute this view, but seek to complicate it by focusing on the religious content and uses of Fuji visual culture of the time. Contemporary devotional representations of Mt. Fuji, ranging from inspirational pilgrimage maps to talismanic icons, variously emphasize or de-emphasize elements from the existing stock of ideas and symbols depending on the intended use of the particular item. Taken as a whole they suggest an ongoing negotiation between priestly and popular control of mountain devotionalism during the early Edo period. The activism of the Fujikō founding figure and his immediate followers, who were not formal representatives of any religious institution, is emblematic of this broader impulse toward more religious choice combined with realistic adaptation to the new Tokugawa order.

Pilgrimage Imaginaries

Mediated forms of Esoteric Buddhism played a key role in framing the practices and ideas that gave birth to the new Fuji religion. In the aforementioned manuals used by Sengen Shrine priests during the seventeenth century, the crater of Mt. Fuji is identified with Dainichi, the great Buddha who sits in the center of the Eight Lotus Petals of the Womb Realm Mandala. "Eight Petals" was shorthand for the mountain's summit—the fortitudinous pilgrims who reached the peak were said to have "attained the Eight Petals."[15] The detailed correlations between Mt. Fuji and the Buddhist deities of the Diamond and Womb Realms, along with their corresponding *kami* manifestations (*suijaku* 垂迹), are carefully set out in these works.[16] But prescriptive manuals are by no means the only source of evidence that correlative exoteric–esoteric (*kenmitsu* 顕密) patterns of thought and practice loomed large in the culture of Fuji pilgrimage at this time. Pictorial records show that the paradigm of an all-encompassing Buddha-like deity who operates in the form of a powerful *kami* dominated the ritual and aesthetic sensibilities of the emerging Fuji *kō*. The visual culture produced in association with the mountain during the early Edo period suggests that the practitioners who laid the foundations of the later mass movement adapted these combinative patterns of thought to suit the ritual needs of their own time.

Mt. Fuji's image was, of course, idealized long before group pilgrimage to the crater became an identifiable movement in the medieval and early modern periods—whether as a malleable aesthetic object for artists and poets, or as an envisioned source of divine fertility and destruction among the farming communities of the vicinity.[17] But it was particularly in the Edo period that religious interpretations of the mountain's image began to proliferate. These renditions were produced and used by diverse interested parties—mountain ascetics, pilgrimage coordinators, shrine priests, itinerant preachers, and in due course lay consortia of pilgrims and hometown devotees—to inspire prospective visitors, solicit alms, and serve as ritual aids. The visual interpretations of Mt. Fuji generated by these often-overlapping groups suggest both consensus and contestation over the meaning of the shared religious site. I refer here especially to developments in the universe of Fuji religious images after the sixteenth century: most prominent is a transition from spectator-oriented display to ritual utility and hands-on portability. The aim was no longer only to visit the mountain and engage in special practices under the guidance of religious professionals, perhaps in the hope of dissolving karmic impediments to one's future salvation in a Pure Land paradise, but increasingly also to gain personal access to Mt. Fuji's power in order to solve immediate life concerns. At first these new images of the mountain were spontaneously created and employed by a small group of dedicated practitioners, but by the late Edo period they were based on set models and diffused on a large scale by Fujikō members and Sengen Shrine *oshi*.

An important early stratum in the progressive sedimentation of Mt. Fuji's religious image, associated primarily with the Main Sengen Shrine and its Murayama Shugendō wing, is constituted by the distinctive Japanese genre of art known as "pilgrimage mandalas" (*sankei mandara* 参詣曼荼羅). These representations of Japanese religious sites are closely related to an earlier genre called *suijaku* or *miya mandara* ("trace" or "shrine" mandalas), which identify revered places with specific *kami* and buddhas, sometimes indicated in a combinatory fashion following the "essence and trace" (*honji suijaku* 本地垂迹) model. The pilgrimage mandalas, which came into vogue in the late medieval period, distinctively set out not only the pilgrimage venue and its deities but also human figures traveling through and conducting devotions at the site, as well as, in some cases, engaging in entertainment or commercial activities in the immediate vicinity.[18]

During the medieval and early modern periods, itinerant proselytizers carried hanging scrolls and hand scrolls of illustrated Buddhist narratives, hagiographies, popular tales, and origin stories (*engi* 縁起), and unfurled them in public preaching sites as the occasion demanded. They explained the pictures in a narrative fashion (*etoki* 絵解) ostensibly in order to convey the Buddhist teachings and solicit alms, even if the stories were not overtly concerned with Buddhist doctrine—as Ikumi Kaminishi puts it, "*Etoki* narratives […] contain morals explained by Buddhist logic" (Kaminishi 2006: 12). *Sankei mandara* served the same proselytizing and fundraising purposes, though not all lent themselves to narrative performance in the manner of the well-known *Kumano kanshin jikkai mandara* or *Tateyama mandara*. Late medieval pilgrimage views of Mt. Fuji (*Fuji sankei mandara*) are a case in point. These images no doubt excited interest in the pilgrimage, and, in some cases, awe for the deities displayed at the peak, but they did not necessarily lend themselves to moral exposition. The *sankei mandara* served primarily as inspirational itineraries; they suggested the parameters of an envisioned journey and prompted prospective visitors to undertake it (or send a representative in their stead)—and, as part of that commitment, to give donations to the professionals who exhibited these images on behalf of the pilgrimage establishment.[19]

Fuji pilgrimage mandalas began to appear after religious travel to the mountain grew popular in the late medieval period under the influence of Murayama Shugendō and the neighboring Main Sengen Shrine. The images typically center on the precincts of the shrine-temple establishment, through which the pilgrims, dressed in their customary white garb and headgear, are passing on their way up the mountain. The best-known exemplars are a pair of paintings on silk held in the collection of the Main Shrine, both dated to the late Muromachi period.[20] The larger work, *Fuji sankei mandara* 富士参詣曼荼羅, designated a Japanese Important Cultural Property in 1977, measures 186.6 by 118.2 centimeters and bears the seal of Kano Motonobu (1476–1559) (Figure 11.1).[21] The painting is oriented toward the southern side of Mt. Fuji and focuses on the Main Shrine and the Murayama complex, Kōbōji, along with human figures making their way through these facilities and up the mountain. Suruga Bay and the Tōkaidō are indicated in the lower foreground, with the peak rising high in the upper third of the painting. Given the quality and dimensions of this painting, it was probably

Figure 11.1 *Fuji sankei mandara*. Hanging scroll, color on silk. 186.6 by 118.2 cm. Sixteenth century. Courtesy of Fujisan Hongū Sengen Shrine, Fujinomiya-shi, Shizuoka.

not moved around and displayed in public venues in the way we associate with more portable works of this nature.

A smaller *Fuji sankei mandara* (a tangible cultural property of Shizuoka prefecture) similarly exaggerates areas of interest related to the main shrine in the center of the picture, while highlighting lively activity near Suruga Bay in the lower tier of the image, such as pilgrims passing through the toll barrier on their way to the shrine (Figure 11.2).[22] In this version, the peak recedes further into the distance in the top

Figure 11.2 *Fuji sankei mandara*. Hanging scroll, color on silk. 91.5 by 67.3 cm. Sixteenth century. Courtesy of Fujisan Hongū Sengen Shrine, Fujinomiya-shi, Shizuoka.

stratum of the painting, and the climbing path does not appear at all, nor do any travelers making their way along the upper trail; the Murayama Shugendō structures are subtly indicated by their roofs in the upper-central and right-hand portions of the image (just below the tree line) and also by the nearby performing *miko* (Ōtaka 2013: 321–2).[23]

However, most of the figures in the painting (198, by Ōtaka's count) are not pilgrims—several are shrine priests, some are *yamabushi,* and a great number (especially in the lower third of the painting) appears not intrinsically related to the pilgrimage at all.[24] In short, the prefectural painting elides the climb itself, focusing instead on an envisioned experience at or near the Main Sengen Shrine.

Ōtaka has argued on the basis of several discrepancies in the topography and shrine layout that, even though this *sankei mandara* was clearly intended for viewing by prospective pilgrims, it may have been created offsite, or perhaps used at a distance from Mt. Fuji, in order to inspire people to visit or support the shrine rather than actually to climb the mountain (Ōtaka 2013: 319–20, 330–1).[25] The painting's relatively modest dimensions (91.5 by 67.3 centimeters) and the creases along its length indicate that it may have been folded for transportation or storage, though perhaps only occasionally for proselytizing. There is no doubt, in any case, that the itinerant proxies of the hostels at Ōmiya and Murayama used visual displays of this kind as preaching and fundraising tools (Hirano 2004: 49).[26] However, like other medieval Japanese preachers, when traveling in the provinces representatives of the Fuji pilgrimage establishment more likely carried paper-based versions of the *mandara,* which would have been both more portable and more easily reproduced. Extant *Fuji sankei mandara* on paper indeed show signs of having been moved around in this way (Tanaka 1984: 12; Andrei 2016: 149–50).

Regardless of how the Fuji *mandara* were displayed, they invariably aimed not only to give prospective pilgrims a sense of the route and the expected ritual behaviors, but also to persuade them that the journey would bring them, through successive stages, closer to the deities of Mt. Fuji and the realm of salvation. Even viewers who were not very literate could acquire from these imagined landscapes a good sense of how performing ritual disciplines in the shrine precincts and subsequently under Murayama auspices would lead them up into the Buddha realm, which was graphically correlated for them with the peak. Most of the extant pilgrimage views of Mt. Fuji include clear references to the Buddhist deities reigning at the summit, along with other standard *mandara* iconographic elements, such as the sun and moon.[27] The Kano painting is especially effective in conveying the idea of a culminating spiritual experience at the crater that is identifiable with the Amida triad and/or Dainichi Buddha of the Diamond and Womb Realms.[28] These relatively elaborate types of Fuji *mandara* may well have served as a kind of substitute pilgrimage for people, especially women, who could not personally climb the mountain—much as did medieval tales about entering the mountain and/or miniature Fuji replicas built in the Edo area during the late Tokugawa period.[29]

At the same time, if we take the paintings at face value, they confirm that during late Muromachi–early Edo transition the *dōsha* remained fundamentally in a passive position vis-à-vis their mountain guides and pilgrimage coordinators. The *sankei mandara* corroborate indications in textual sources that the people who visited Mt. Fuji on its southern side during this period were expected to carry out their devotions strictly under the auspices of the institutions that controlled the frontal route, namely the Main Shrine and the Shugendō complex. The emphasis in the paintings is on activities at defined spots, notably the ritual cleansing in the Wakutama Pond at Ōmiya and in the Ryūzu Falls at Murayama, and always within the ambit of shrine priests and *yamabushi*. Images like these thus served not only to entice prospective pilgrims and solicit alms but also to structure people's experiences of the mountain—in short, to modulate their expectations and to set boundaries. True to their map-like nature, the paintings obscure or completely omit areas that the makers deemed outside the purview of their target audience, and visually confine representative figures to designated spots on the imagined mountain. The most obvious example in the sixteenth-century paintings is the absence of women from the upper reaches of the mountain, marking the policy of excluding female pilgrims from the climb.[30] The Kano painting does include numerous female pilgrims dressed in white garb proceeding through the initial stages of the pilgrimage, but the only other women (in both *mandara*) seem to be the *miko* (who appear in the proximity of the Murayama center).[31] Formal shrine priests (some of whom wear black *eboshi* hats) also appear for the most part in or near the Sengen Shrine precincts, while aside from the white-clad pilgrims, the lower trail itself (in the Kano painting) is dominated by figures in dark overclothes, presumably Buddhist clergy, indicating the customary division of labor in the operation of the time.

Several pilgrimage images of Mt. Fuji produced in the early Edo period also focus on the details of the Main Sengen Shrine and the initial portion of the southern trail. However, some devotional representations of the frontal approach belong to a *mandara* subgenre that is less oriented toward the pilgrimage process itself. The most distinctive and perhaps earliest extant example is the *Sanzon kuson zu* 三尊九尊図, also issued by the Main Sengen Shrine (Figure 11.3).[32] This image of the mountain, rendered in black ink, may also have been hung for viewing, but it is quite small (38 by 27.5 centimeters) and was probably not intended for display to large groups. It is compact enough to have been rolled up and carried on one's person, much as were the later Fujikō images, discussed below.

The *Sanzon kuson zu* includes neither climbing trails nor pilgrims, and has more the look of a devotional image (*miei* 御影) than a pilgrimage mandala. However, the work conforms with the *miya mandara* and/or *honji suijaku mandara* format insofar as it correlates a revered site with its *kami* and Buddhas deities; and although the *Sanzon kuson zu* does not adopt an elevated perspective (as do many *sankei mandara*), it does suggest an approximate progression from the bottom of the mountain, marked by the shrine, to the deities at the top, as in the full-scale pilgrimage paintings. In the uppermost stratum of the work, we accordingly see the Amida triad, with the accompanying Buddhas and bodhisattvas of the Womb Mandala lined up directly below. Mount Fuji itself occupies the middle third of the picture, flanked, as was common in pilgrimage mandalas, by images of the sun and the moon.[33]

The most striking element of the composition, however, is the large Dharma seal (*hōin* 法印) superimposed on the mountain. It centers on the siddham vaṃ, thus clearly identifying Mt. Fuji with Mahāvairocana (Dainichi) Buddha of the Vajradhātu

Figure 11.3 *Sanzon kuson zu*. Woodblock print on paper. 38 by 27.5 cm. Edo period. Courtesy of Fujisan Myūjiamu (Fujiyoshida-shi Rekishi Minzoku Hakubutsukan), Fujiyoshida-shi, Yamanashi.

(Diamond Realm). The lowest register of the picture adds two monkeys facing each other across a grove of trees that surround the shrine hall, and at the very bottom, a *torii* that marks the approach to the latter. If, as is likely, the *Sanzon kuson zu* dates to the early or mid-Edo period, we can safely regard this complex of religious signifiers as representative of the variegated nature of the devotionalism promoted by the Main Shrine at the time. Indeed, the picture summarizes several key features of the Tokugawa popular religious universe (or a variant of it): a blend of Pure Land and Esoteric Buddhist beliefs; reverence for a central *kami* (in this case, the mountain); a cosmology ordered by the cyclical forces of yang and yin, sun and moon; customary notions of territorial sacrality (marked by the *torii* and tall trees); and due deference to supplementary spiritual powers (in this instance, Kōshin, represented by the monkeys).[34] Iconography of this kind was later popularized by Fujikō, though with the Pure Land and Esoteric Buddhist motifs further abbreviated.

I have noted that the Main Shrine and Murayama establishment dominated the southern pilgrimage during the late medieval period, but that the Shugendō center came to play a diminished role on Mt. Fuji in the Edo period. Late Tokugawa images of Mt. Fuji, often called *zenjō no zu* (literally, "samādhi pictures") or *annai ezu* (pictorial guide maps), still depict the three Murayama temples on the frontal trail, not infrequently in the central portion of the picture (Ogino 1999: 23-4). But as a whole, early modern pilgrimage depictions of Mt. Fuji confirm that the enterprise in the south was gradually overshadowed by pilgrim activity in the north, centered on the Yoshida Sengen Shrine. Most of these views of the northern approach date to the later period, but one extant image, *Hachiyō kuson zu* 八葉九尊図 (again quite small, at 40.5 by 28 centimeters), offers a rare rendition of the *kitaguchi* from 1680, before Fujikō became widespread (Figure 11.4).[35] True to the *sankei mandara* genre, this image adopts an elevated perspective, in this case, beginning with the Yoshida Shrine in the lower register and moving up through natural surroundings, lodges, and other shrine-related structures on the way to the summit. Needless to say, in contrast to the late medieval Fuji paintings, *Hachiyō kuson zu* is a rudimentary drawing, block-printed and probably distributed on a large scale on the occasion of the mountain's special *kōshin* year. The size of the work and the relative simplicity of the production process are comparable to those of the *Sanzon kuson zu*—yet it retains the key features of a pilgrimage-oriented *mandara*, insofar as it displays an actual route and place names as opposed to Fuji iconic symbols per se.[36]

These two block-printed images of Mt. Fuji (*Sanzon kuson zu* and *Hachiyō kuson zu*) emerged from the quite distinct institutional contexts of the south and the north, respectively. Yet they both show that the established pilgrimage aesthetic and its Esoteric Buddhist underpinnings were reiterated in Fuji religious art through the early Edo period. These relatively simple prints, almost schematic in appearance, are quite unlike the enchanting Kano painting, for example, with its exquisite rendition of the ritual procedures required at each stage of the pilgrims' route. The *sankei mandara* scrolls, in general, clearly aimed to inspire in spectators a religious-aesthetic appreciation of the significance of the mountain journey, but these small block prints were portable icons or even talismans, meant for individual and small group use. The contrast between the two types of Fuji art may easily be dismissed as a function of

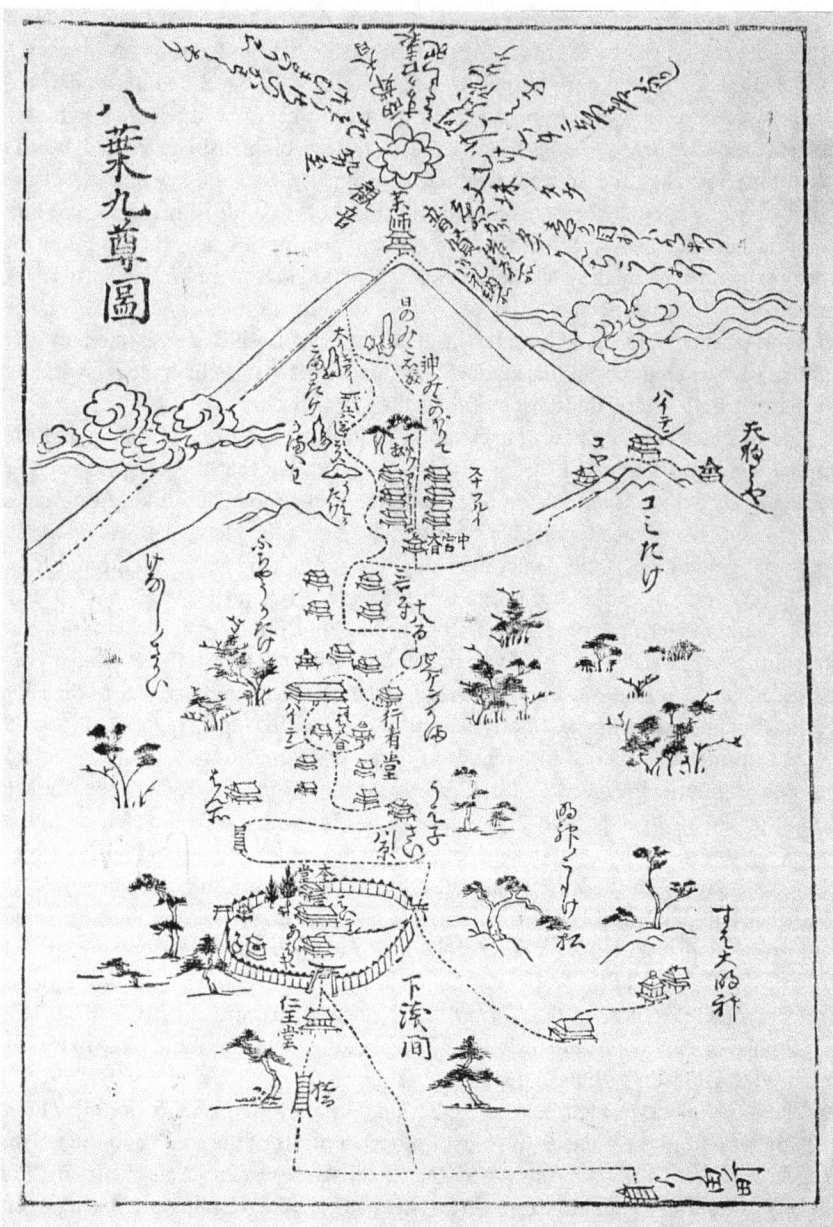

Figure 11.4 *Hachiyo kuson zu*. Woodblock print on paper. 40.5 by 28 cm. 1680. Courtesy of Fujisan Myūjiamu (Fujiyoshida-shi Rekishi Minzoku Hakubutsukan), Fujiyoshida-shi, Yamanashi.

the intended uses and socioeconomic context in each case. However, their relative prominence during different historical moments is nonetheless a valuable indicator of how and why the mountain was being re-imagined during the seventeenth-century transition. The block-printed *mandara* represent another phase in the shifting visual imaginaries of the mountain generated over time by diverse socioreligious interests. They overlapped in aim with the more ostentatious *sankei mandara*—after all, both genres were designed to inspire and inform. But they also document a general Tokugawa trend toward convenient encapsulation of religious meaning. The *kuson* prints in particular preview the cost-effective images that Fujikō members would later disseminate on a wide scale.

The production of visual replicas of Japan's great mountain has been a characteristic feature of Fuji devotionalism throughout its history, and the graphic materials produced by the incipient Fuji *kō* in the seventeenth century are among the most distinctive and intriguing in this corpus. Like the earlier *sankei mandara*, these works were religiously inspired depictions of the mountain, but they were not used as visionary itineraries targeted toward prospective pilgrims and donors. In the later images, the mountain is not a hallowed topography that one might traverse in order to attain religious salvation or enlightenment: the new Fuji devotees were no longer being invited to contemplate a ritual journey that would culminate in Amida's Pure Land, or to conceptualize the mountain as an embodiment of the essential-ground Buddha, Dainichi. The emerging Fuji *"mandara"* for the most part omit or downplay images of Buddhas and bodhisattvas, even as they continue to echo the idea of an all-powerful deity who manifests through multiple auxiliary forms.

Ritual Refigurations

The new genre of Mt. Fuji images originated with the founding figure, Kakugyō Tōbutsu. He is believed to have been active in the Mt. Fuji area during the late medieval and early Edo periods, when, as we have seen, shrine priests and mountain guides affiliated with the well-established Sengen-Murayama complex dominated activities along the frontal approach to Mt. Fuji. It is possible, as Endō Hideo has suggested, that during the late sixteenth century Kakugyō avoided the *omoteguchi* and practiced on the northern side of the mountain because the Murayama *shugenja*, who enjoyed the protection of the domain lord of Suruga, tightly controlled Mt. Fuji's southern trails (Endō 2000: 55). Even after the Tokugawa shogunate was in place, Kakugyō's followers continued to have little to do with the Honzan-line *yamabushi* at Murayama and to favor the northern trail (Miyaji and Hirono 1929: 826–7). Given the paucity of historical documentation of Kakugyō's activities, his precise relationship (or lack of it) with other religious specialists in the Mt. Fuji area must remain unclear for the time being.[37] However, considering the well-regulated nature of the *omoteguchi* enterprise during his lifetime, Endō's insinuation that Kakugyō's own peregrinations were tacitly anti-establishmentarian in this regard is persuasive.

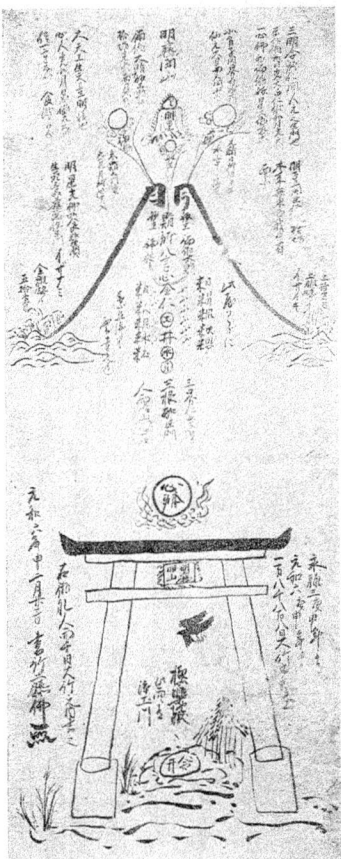

Figure 11.5 *Ominuki*. Hanging scroll, ink on paper. 1620. Source: Murakami Shigeyoshi and Yasumaru Yoshio, eds., *Minshū shūkyō no shisō*, 483.

discussed above, and indeed some scholars refer to Kakugyō's and his followers' works as *mandara* and even, in some cases, *sankei mandara*.[42]

However, unlike pilgrimage artworks, the *ominuki* were understood not primarily to depict the mountain, but to embody it. Their configurations of ideographs, syllabic marks, and elementary drawings were regarded in the movement as living distillations of Mt. Fuji as God. In this sense, too, Kakugyō's works seem to reiterate the esoteric premise that the great Buddha, Dainichi, is directly accessible through graphic presentation. In these Fuji *mandara*, however, rather than Dainichi the group's main deity, Moto no chichihaha or "True Father and Mother" (identified with Sengen) emerges as the mountain's *honji*.[43]

A work produced in the late seventeenth century by Kakugyō's fourth-generation successor, Getsugan 月旺 (Maeno Ribei 前野理兵衛, 1630–89), richly illustrates the commonalities and contrasts between the pilgrimage images associated with

Murayama and Ōmiya, on the one hand, and the devotional works produced by the early Fuji *kō* members, on the other. By this time, the small cells of lay practitioners who took inspiration from Kakugyō's legendary activities had begun to establish lineages and produce their own ritual materials in earnest. *Getsugan ominuki* appears to be a relatively large rendition of the mountain scape and was likely hung for display as a hanging scroll rather than frequently transported. It was created in 1680, most likely to endorse pilgrimage to Mt. Fuji during its *kōshin* year, like the aforementioned *Hachiyō kuson zu*.[44] In contrast to the latter, however, even though the view is from the northern perspective, virtually all sides of the mountain are represented,

Figure 11.6 *Getsugan ominuki*. Hanging scroll; ink and color on paper. 92.0 by 32.0 cm. 1680. Courtesy of Fujisan Myūjiamu (Fujiyoshida-shi Rekishi Minzoku Hakubutsukan), Fujiyoshida-shi, Yamanashi.

from Hito-ana Cave, Ōmiya, and Murayama in the west and south to the Subashiri approach and Kawaguchi Lake in the east and north (Figure 11.6). Given this relatively panoramic interpretation of Mt. Fuji, it seems unlikely that Getsugan's work was sponsored by a single religious establishment. Multiple points of interest on the mountain—not only *torii*, lodges, and prayer halls, but also mountain paths, special crags, and other sites intended to serve the mind's eye of the prospective pilgrim (such as the station beyond which women were not allowed to travel)—are highlighted throughout the scroll. Moreover, the usual sets of Buddhist deities (Amida, Dainichi, and their retinues) are explicitly represented, although by their names rather than images. As was common in mountain *mandara*, they appear in the top stratum of the image, visually identifying the summit with the acme of Buddhist practice.

In all these respects, Getsugan's *ominuki* resembles the medieval and post-medieval *sankei mandara*. On the other hand, we see no human figures carrying out rituals or climbing the slopes, whether priests or pilgrims. Instead, the landscape is replete with the talismanic syllable signs and neo-ideographs inherited from Kakugyō's corpus, which define the *ominuki* genre. Four clusters of ritual text, themselves miniature *ominuki*, are authenticated by Getsugan's signature and in one case (on the lower right) dated. Two additional sets of lines (on either side of the mountain's upper axis beneath the crater) record apotropaic formulae.[45] Numerous other interpretive signs and symbols, most of which would have been familiar to ordinary people of the time, are interspersed throughout the scroll, such as Buddhist swastikas, a *gojūnotō* (five-tiered pagoda), a systematic list of stars, geographical directions, and selected elemental forces (especially water).[46]

In comparison with the *Fuji sankei mandara*, which stress certain areas of the mountain and channel the prospective traveler to selected purification sites, shrine structures, and hostels on the way to a Buddha land at the peak, Getsugan's landscape-like *ominuki* does not single out an itinerary from the bottom of the mountain to its peak. In this regard, it has more in common with Kakugyō's works, which tend to depict all parts of Mt. Fuji on the same plane, as of equal value. Medieval mountain pilgrimages were, to borrow Allan G. Grapard's words, "intimately related to the Buddhist notion that the religious experience was a process (ongoing practice) rather than simply the final goal of practice ... the entirety of the path followed by the pilgrim was seen to be sacred" (Grapard 1982: 205). For the emerging *kō* members as well, all parts of the volcano, whether the wooded areas, lava caves, and bodies of water on its lower slopes, or its gravelly upper reaches and huge crater above, were suffused with religious meaning; one did not absolutely have to reach the peak in order to become one with the Fuji deity. From the perspective of these lay practitioners, attainment of the "final goal" visually suggested by the *sankei mandara* and implicit in the ritual disciplines promoted by the pilgrimage establishment was no longer necessarily their imperative.

In reviewing selected devotional images of Mt. Fuji that circulated in the late sixteenth and seventeenth centuries, I have noted overlapping and shifting interpretations, rather than a linear evolution, of the religious meaning of the mountain—from a venue of salvific pilgrimage supervised by shrine priests and *yamabushi* to the outright revelation of a powerful parental divinity. Growing numbers of people were beginning to visualize Mt. Fuji not predominantly as a trace manifestation of the Esoteric Buddha, or even as a gateway to Amida's Pure Land, but more fundamentally as the creator and caregiver of the universe. Early modern Fuji devotees came to conceive of the mountain less as a site for individual rebirth high on the slopes than as a point of access, even if by proxy, to its healing and protective powers. Kakugyō's and his followers' *ominuki* accordingly functioned in the movement primarily as icons and talismans; they were displayed as hanging scrolls for worship and carried by individuals for apotropaic purposes (see also Chapter Thirteen by D. Max Moerman).[47] Their proliferation in the eighteenth and nineteenth centuries was part of a broader trend in which ordinary people independently created, ritualized, and disseminated their own religious culture.

12

The Shape of Devotion: Mounds, Stelae, and Empowering Ritual Fasting in the Early Modern Cult of Mount Yudono

Andrea Castiglioni

> It is important to stress that this [stone] is not the lodging, the "seat" of the god, but the god himself, consubstantially.
> Not the stone of the genie, but the stone-genie.
> Paul Mus, *India Seen from the East: Indian and Indigenous Cults in Champa*

In the early decades of the Edo period, the veneration of Mount Yudono 湯殿山, which was one of the Three Mountains (Sanzan 三山) of the Dewa province (present-day Yamagata prefecture) together with Mount Haguro 羽黒山 and Mount Gassan 月山, spread among the rural population not only in the northeast region (Tōhoku) but also in the Kantō area around the city of Edo. The god (*kami*) of Mount Yudono, namely Yudono Gongen 湯殿権現, became a so-called "*kami* à la mode" (*hayarigami* 流行神) and started to be worshiped as a protector (*shugojin* 守護神) of villages and crops. Yudono Gongen was associated with the cosmic buddha Dainichi Nyorai, according to the combinatory logic in which buddhas were interpreted as original grounds (*honji* 本地) and *kami* as their provisional traces (*suijaku* 垂迹). Within this religious mindscape, to be a devotee of a sacred mountain such as Yudono meant that its geophysical body functioned as a material *trait d'union* between *kami* and buddhas, whose divine powers were reified by the natural environment of the mountain. Even if Yudono is called a "mountain," it is actually a massive volcanic boulder, called Gohōzen 御宝前, its two craters symbolizing the two mandalas of the Diamond Realm (smaller crater on the right) and Womb Realm (bigger crater of the left). The reddish surface of Gohōzen is permanently covered by a thin layer of hot water, which gushes from the top of the rock and flows away in the Daibonji 大梵字 River below.

The cult of sacred mountains has a double movement: one is "centrifugal" (from the mountain to other geographical areas), and the other one is "centripetal" (from outside areas to the mountain). In this chapter I focus on the centrifugal aspects of the Yudono cult by analyzing practices and discourses associated with this sacred place outside the Dewa province. In particular, I take into account some objects and ascetic practices that were performed by lay devotees members of religious confraternities (*kō* 講) under the guidance of Yudono ascetics (*issei gyōnin* 一世行人) or Shugendō practitioners (*shugenja*) in order to establish positive karmic ties (*kechien* 結縁) with the mountain deities and obtain worldly benefits (*genze riyaku* 現世利益) in this life and salvation after death (see also Chapter Eleven by Janine Sawada). Among the different types of materiality and austerities that characterized the veneration of Mount Yudono among rural classes, I specifically consider the construction of sacred mounds (*tsuka* 塚), the erection of votive stelae (*tō* 塔), and the performance of ritual fasting (*fujiki kuyō* 不食供養).

It is important to keep in mind that mounds and stelae were not conceived as mere reminders or mnemonic aids of a distant mountain but worked instead as living "doubles" or "authentic copies" of Mount Yudono and its divine pantheon, which these sacred objects transposed within the space and time of human society.[1] Thus, mounds and stelae of Yudono did not simply symbolize Mount Yudono. They were worshiped as miniaturized bodies of Yudono Gongen, from which their power derived due to an undifferentiated relationship between the original (Mount Yudono) and its replica (mounds and stelae). These material refractions of the paradigmatic body of the sacred mountain dotted the rural landscape of the Tōhoku and Kantō regions, boosting the faith in Yudono among large strata of subaltern classes.

Borrowing Paul Mus's definition of "mesocosm" or "magic copula," it is possible to say that mounds and stelae worked as material mediators between the ordinariness of human reality and the extraordinariness of gods.[2] In other words, this class of sacred objects allowed, at the same time, an "up-grade" of the devotee toward the deity and a "down-grade" of the deity toward the devotee, setting in motion a mutual fertilization between micro- and macrocosm. As mesocosmic entities, mounds and stelae became zones of complexity where religious discourses, aesthetics, economics, and politics merged together and constituted networks of meanings and symbols with a great socio-religious relevance. Different types of human actors with heterogeneous agendas exploited the materiality of mounds and stelae to reaffirm their roles within the preexistent structures of society or, in certain cases, contest the existing balances of power. To put it in Latourian terms, the mounds and stelae of Yudono were "quasi-objects," which did not limit themselves to an amorphous transmission of meanings from one communicative knot to another but actively modified the contents of the transmitted discourses having a creative impact on the social relationships between human actors (Latour 1993: 55; see also Chapter Six by Carina Roth).

It is also interesting to remember that in order to become a living entity, the stone of which Yudono stelae were made had to be activated through a transfer of ascetic power. In the pages further, we focus in particular, among these empowering practices, on the *fujiki kuyō* performed by lay female devotees in the Kansai region, but it should be underlined that *issei gyōnin*, too, were often requested to directly empower Yudono stelae at the end of their ascetic retreats. In this way, the stelae were transformed into a sort of legal contract, which certified the accomplishment of an ascetic endeavor by lay devotees or religious professionals, while at the same time forcing the deity to take into consideration such human expressions of devotion by granting its protection. It was probably this unspoken blackmail mechanism embedded in the production of the stelae and its empowering rituals that kept this practice flourishing among various social classes at different historical periods.

Chthonian Bodies: The Mounds of Mount Yudono

The cult of Mount Yudono reached a peak of popularity among the rural classes not only in the domains of the Tōhoku region but also in Kantō area around the city of Edo during the Kan'ei era (1624–44). This devotional phenomenon was due to numerous ritual transfers (*kanjō* 勧請) of fragmented parts (*bunshin* 分身) of the main body (*honshin* 本身) of Yudono Gongen. *Kanjō* took place in the guise of ceremonial processions during which the deity was enshrined within a portable palanquin and escorted toward mountains, villages in the countryside, and urban peripheries in order to be worshipped by the local populations. For instance, the *Kaikichō* 開基帳 (1663) reports that in 1624 Yudono Gongen was carried around (*yugyō* 遊行) the Ishizuka village (present-day Ibaraki prefecture) in its palanquin and an ascetic called Kōkai *gyōnin* 光海行人 built a "mountain" on behalf of this deity (Enomoto 1991: 28). What the text refers to with the term "mountain" was actually an artificial mound dedicated to Yudono Gongen. In the Michinoku region (present-day Fukushima and Miyagi prefectures), these devotional mounds were so numerous that they were collectively called "August Tsuka Gongen" (Ontsuka Gongen 御塚権現); they were made on every land spot on which the beanpoles of Yudono Gongen's palanquin were placed to rest. It can be said that the ritual transmission of the cult of Mount Yudono to new territories corresponded to a sort of cultic impregnation of the land during which Yudono Gongen penetrated the soil of the village, which swelled as a maternal belly to give birth to a miniaturized image of Mount Yudono (i.e., the mound). Then, human devotees venerated this chthonian object as a non-anthropomorphic living icon of Yudono Gongen within the ordinary space and time of the village.

The construction of the mound was a fundamental moment marking the official entry of Yudono Gongen into the religious landscape of the village after the *kanjō* ceremony. The mounds dedicated to Mount Yudono were usually square or round and the main body of the structure could be occasionally divided into three levels or steps like a sort of small pyramid, which usually measured two or three meters in height and three or four meters in width. Once the mound was completed, devotional activities could immediately begin, as may be gathered from a short written invocation (*saimon* 祭文) composed in 1636 for Yudono Gongen, which was discovered inside a small shrine built on the top of a Yudono mound in the city of Sōma 相馬 (present-day Fukushima prefecture). On the front side of the text, Yudono Gongen is evoked through honorific names such as "saint master" (*shōshu* 聖主) or "god among gods with a wonderful voice like the bird of paradise [*karyōbinga*, Sk. *kalavinka*]" (*ten chū ten karyōbinga* 天中天迦陵頻伽) (Iwasaki 1963: 277). At the end of the text, the name of a Shugendō practitioner is reported: a certain Chōei 長栄 of the temple Juōzan Kōmyōin, who presented the written invocation to Yudono Gongen on behalf of the lay members of a religious confraternity, the head of the village, and the head of the district. This source is relevant because it shows that there were three different types of social actors usually involved in the worship of Mount Yudono. First, there were religious professionals such as the *shugenja* Chōei or Yudono ascetics (*issei gyōnin*) who were extremely active in these religious practices associated with mounds. Second, there were lay devotees who were officially affiliated with religious confraternities for the veneration of Mount Yudono's pantheon. Third, there were representatives of the political institutions of the village such as the two public officials of Sōma. It is probable that the confraternity members and the two Sōma supervisors asked the *shugenja* Chōei to act as a sort of mediator between themselves and Yudono Gongen, which was conceived as a protector deity that bestowed prosperity on the village from its sacred mound.

Another type of Yudono mound was called *bontenzuka* 梵天塚 and served as a funerary tumulus for the ritual staffs (*bonten* 梵天) that the pilgrims brought back to their villages after visiting Mount Yudono in summer. These old staffs were completely buried within the earth of the mound on the top of which three big poles were usually stuck into the ground to represent the Three Mountains of Dewa. *Bontenzuka* were not simply funerary monuments to pray for the pilgrims who were symbolically represented by their old staffs, but were also ritual platforms or altars for the performance of ceremonies in praise of the Three Mountains deities.[3] For example, the gigantic *bontenzuka* of Bōdaira, which was built around 1678 in the village of Ichihara in Shimōsa 下総 province (present-day Chiba prefecture), attracted many pilgrims from various domains of the Kantō region. According to a description provided by one such pilgrim who visited the *bontenzuka* of Bōdaira in 1855, on the top level of the mound there were three hundred and four *bonten* stuck into the ground, among which the tallest three symbolized Mount Haguro, Mount Yudono, and Mount Gassan; these *bonten* were covered with long paper strips. In the middle and lower levels of the *bontenzuka*, there were another hundred twenty *bonten* donated by the people of nearby villages. On each side of the three levels of the mound, the divine bodies of the Three Dewa Mountains were separately venerated in the guise of three *bonten*. The *bontenzuka* of Bōdaira was so massive that by climbing on it pilgrims could perform a veneration from afar (*yōhai* 遥拝), gazing at the numerous sacred peaks of the region.[4] The symmetric structure of the *bontenzuka* of Bōdaira and the repetition of the three *bonten* pattern, which served as a visual reminder of the Three Dewa Mountains, in the internal and external zones of each level transformed the entire structure into a sort of tridimensional mandala made of earth and wooden poles. By accessing this mound, pilgrims were ritually transmogrified into the sacred geography of Haguro, Yudono, and Gassan and, at the same time, could pay their homages to other sacred mountains in the Kantō area.

Another type of mound dedicated to the worship of Mount Yudono were the "mounds for the ascetics" (*gyōninzuka* 行人塚), which were regarded as funerary monuments. Their purpose was to commemorate either famous lay pilgrims (*gyōnin* 行人) who belonged to local confraternities venerating the Three Mountains of Dewa, or eminent *issei gyōnin* who provided rural communities with their religious services. The fact that both practitioners were often simply defined as *gyōnin* makes it sometimes difficult to establish whether the *gyōninzuka* was a funerary mound for a part-time ascetic as in the case of the pilgrim or full-time ascetic as in the case of the *issei gyōnin*. In some cases, the *gyōninzuka* actually contains the human remains of the ascetic; in other cases, it is empty. For example, the *gyōninzuka* at Kakegawa village in Tōtōmi province (present-day Shizuoka prefecture) was probably built in the early seventeenth century to preserve the corpse and the ritual implements of an important local ascetic of Yudono; in 1827, members of a Yudono confraternity restored it to perpetuate his memory (Matsuzaki 1994: 57). When the *gyōninzuka* actually hosted the ascetic's corpse, those human remains transformed into a sort of "foundation material" or "organic brick," which overlapped with the architectonic body of the mounds that was, in its turn, equivalent to the sacred geophysical body of Mount Yudono. Like a matryoshka, the *gyōninzuka* enabled the body of the ascetic to establish an everlasting mystical union with the body of the mountain. At the same time, the human remains of the ascetic triggered an animation process that added a biological dimension to the materiality of the mound, which thus became a living entity.

Astral Bodies and Climbing Dragons: The Yudono Stelae in the Kan'ei Era

In many cases, the semiotic and semantic sphere of the sacred mounds was enhanced by the erection of a stele on its top. These stelae were often decorated with a bas-relief of Yudono Gongen, whose outward appearance was displayed in the shape of the body of the cosmic buddha Dainichi Nyorai of the Two Realms of Diamond and Womb (Kontai ryōbu Dainichi Nyorai). This amalgamation between the *kami* of Yudono (Yudono Gongen) and Dainichi Nyorai allowed this powerful buddha to undertake a process of localization in which his Pure Land (*mitsugon jōdō* 密厳浄土) came to be localized within the mandalized landscape of Mount Yudono. The Dainichi Nyorai of Mount Yudono erased the elitist patina that characterized the image of Dainichi Nyorai in the esoteric schools and began to be perceived as a familiar deity with a clear location in Japan. In particular, Kantō peasants worshiped the Dainichi Nyorai of Yudono as a sort of cosmic ruler—literally, a "big sun" (*dai nichi*)—under whose power clouds, rain, hail, wind, and celestial bodies all interacted harmoniously. As a consequence of these two processes of localization and ruralization, the Dainichi Nyorai of Mount Yudono became a protective god of rural villages and was specifically invoked to secure a balanced transition from the dry to the wet seasons before harvest time. It is also possible to observe that the creation of Yudono stelae increased in intercalary years, in which a supplementary month was added to the lunar calendar in order to avoid calendrical distortions. This was due to the fact that peasants wanted to express their gratitude for the prolonged presence of the sun in the sky.[5]

A peculiarity of these stelae is that images of Yudono Dainichi Nyorai show an unusual prominence of the nose, lips, and eyebrows' arches; the ears and jaws of this cosmic buddha are also overemphasized and give to the face a calm, but extremely solid, expression.[6] This Dainichi Nyorai is often represented in a seated position on a lotus throne surrounded by the solar and lunar disks, stars, and a heavenly canopy. It seems clear that the aesthetic arrangement of the visual elements transforms these stelae into authentic stone mandalas, which were enshrined within the space syntax of the rural villages in Kantō region. Among these there is a group of twelve stelae, erected in rural areas around the city of Tsukuba 筑波 between 1629 and 1642, where the bas-relief shows the triad (Dainichi sanzon-zō 大日三尊像) composed of Dainichi Nyorai, Fudō Myōō, and Gōzanze Myōō (Tokuhara 2004: 320). Four stelae display

Dainichi Nyorai of the Womb Realm (Taizōkai Dainichi Nyorai) as the central deity, while all the others have Dainichi Nyorai of the Diamond Realm (Kongōkai Dainichi Nyorai) (Figure 12.1).

The iconographical choice to locate the Dainichi Nyorai of the Diamond Realm at the center, Fudō Myōō on the right side, and Gōzanze Myōō on the left follows the iconographical pattern of the Victorious One mandala (*Sonshō mandara*).

The basic structure of the *Sonshō mandara* derives from the Central Dais Eight Petal Hall (Chūdai hachiyō-in) of the Womb Realm mandala (*Taizōkai mandara*), but replaces the Dainichi Nyorai of the Womb Realm with the Dainichi Nyorai of the Diamond Realm and leaves unchanged the two Myōō, that is, Fudō and Gōzanze. Concerning the replacement of Dainichi Nyorai of the Womb Realm with

Figure 12.1 Stele of Dainichi Sanzon-zō. 1639. Mitsukaidō, Chūtsuma, Ibaraki prefecture. Photo by Tokuhara Satoyuki.

(Diamond Realm). The lowest register of the picture adds two monkeys facing each other across a grove of trees that surround the shrine hall, and at the very bottom, a *torii* that marks the approach to the latter. If, as is likely, the *Sanzon kuson zu* dates to the early or mid-Edo period, we can safely regard this complex of religious signifiers as representative of the variegated nature of the devotionalism promoted by the Main Shrine at the time. Indeed, the picture summarizes several key features of the Tokugawa popular religious universe (or a variant of it): a blend of Pure Land and Esoteric Buddhist beliefs; reverence for a central *kami* (in this case, the mountain); a cosmology ordered by the cyclical forces of yang and yin, sun and moon; customary notions of territorial sacrality (marked by the *torii* and tall trees); and due deference to supplementary spiritual powers (in this instance, Kōshin, represented by the monkeys).[34] Iconography of this kind was later popularized by Fujikō, though with the Pure Land and Esoteric Buddhist motifs further abbreviated.

I have noted that the Main Shrine and Murayama establishment dominated the southern pilgrimage during the late medieval period, but that the Shugendō center came to play a diminished role on Mt. Fuji in the Edo period. Late Tokugawa images of Mt. Fuji, often called *zenjō no zu* (literally, "samādhi pictures") or *annai ezu* (pictorial guide maps), still depict the three Murayama temples on the frontal trail, not infrequently in the central portion of the picture (Ogino 1999: 23–4). But as a whole, early modern pilgrimage depictions of Mt. Fuji confirm that the enterprise in the south was gradually overshadowed by pilgrim activity in the north, centered on the Yoshida Sengen Shrine. Most of these views of the northern approach date to the later period, but one extant image, *Hachiyō kuson zu* 八葉九尊図 (again quite small, at 40.5 by 28 centimeters), offers a rare rendition of the *kitaguchi* from 1680, before Fujikō became widespread (Figure 11.4).[35] True to the *sankei mandara* genre, this image adopts an elevated perspective, in this case, beginning with the Yoshida Shrine in the lower register and moving up through natural surroundings, lodges, and other shrine-related structures on the way to the summit. Needless to say, in contrast to the late medieval Fuji paintings, *Hachiyō kuson zu* is a rudimentary drawing, block-printed and probably distributed on a large scale on the occasion of the mountain's special *kōshin* year. The size of the work and the relative simplicity of the production process are comparable to those of the *Sanzon kuson zu*—yet it retains the key features of a pilgrimage-oriented *mandara*, insofar as it displays an actual route and place names as opposed to Fuji iconic symbols per se.[36]

These two block-printed images of Mt. Fuji (*Sanzon kuson zu* and *Hachiyō kuson zu*) emerged from the quite distinct institutional contexts of the south and the north, respectively. Yet they both show that the established pilgrimage aesthetic and its Esoteric Buddhist underpinnings were reiterated in Fuji religious art through the early Edo period. These relatively simple prints, almost schematic in appearance, are quite unlike the enchanting Kano painting, for example, with its exquisite rendition of the ritual procedures required at each stage of the pilgrims' route. The *sankei mandara* scrolls, in general, clearly aimed to inspire in spectators a religious-aesthetic appreciation of the significance of the mountain journey, but these small block prints were portable icons or even talismans, meant for individual and small group use. The contrast between the two types of Fuji art may easily be dismissed as a function of

It is not implausible that Kakugyō operated as a *kanjin hijiri* 勧進聖 or wandering religious mendicant earlier in his life, whether to make a subsistence living on his own or on behalf of an organized alms campaign. Given the preponderance of mendicant performers and ritual professionals who circulated in late medieval Japan, we can at least surmise that he was exposed to the various ceremonial skills and tools that made up the *kanjin* repertoire of the time, including the aforementioned pictorial performances (*etoki*). Certainly, Kakugyō's Fuji-related works suggest that he was familiar with the general appearance of pilgrimage mandalas. His innovation was to create, in effect, his own mountain mandalas and to use them in outreach activities among the rural population in the Mt. Fuji catchment area as well as further afield.[38]

Kakugyō's ritual works, called *ominuki* 御身抜, were allegedly revealed to him by Sengen, the god of Mt. Fuji, during or directly after he completed specified regimens of fasting, cold-water ablutions, continuous standing, and other disciplines. "*Minuki*" literally means "body extraction." The implication may be that after uniting with Mt. Fuji through self-emptying austerities, Kakugyō was able to extract Sengen's truth from his own now-sanctified person (*mi*) and condense it in his writings and drawings.[39] In any case, his "extractions" present an intriguing contrast to the *sankei mandara* that promoted the Sengen-Murayama version of the Fuji experience during the same period. The *ominuki* are, in fact, closer in appearance to the block-printed *kuson* images issued in the early Edo period, which as noted were more akin to devotional pictures than inspirational itineraries. Like the *Sanzon kuson zu* in particular, Kakugyō's works direct our gaze, not to the physical mountain qua terrain to be traversed as a religious exercise, but to the "content" of Mt. Fuji, represented as both image and special text.

Most *ominuki* are composed of clusters of ideographs and cursive marks, and, in some cases, simple drawings. The strings of characters often do not form coherent thoughts and some individual ideographs are entirely outside the Japanese lexical stock of the time.[40] However, the way in which the text is arranged and the overall visual design of the *ominuki* is clearly indebted to Japanese mandalic culture. A key aesthetic strategy of Kakugyō's works is the placement of the text in such a way as to evoke an image of the mountain. Several exemplars consist of vertical lines of characters loosely organized, often with the help of a rudimentary outline drawing, into the shape of the volcano. The calligram-like layout is a fascinating, if elemental, echo of the well-known Buddhist genre of pagoda texts, in which images of religious architecture are composed of sutra passages. In viewing these works, the spectator may focus on the image-texts either close up, as distinct lines of characters or, stepping back, from a distance, as iconic pictures. In the *ominuki*, the stylized triple peak of the great volcano further resembles Buddhist pagoda-stupa texts in that it encloses within itself the "relics" of the teaching—left behind in this instance by a distinctly Japanese deity.

Although many of the *ominuki* preserved today are composed almost entirely of text, some also include pictorial elements. Kakugyō's own versions often display small drawings of a few recurring motifs. In one example, in addition to the bare outline of the mountain itself, we see at its base a *torii*, indicating entry into the Fuji god's territory in the foothills; a three-legged crow, flying right to left; and on either side of the summit, spheres representing the moon and sun (Figure 11.5).[41] These elements together with the general format reiterate the iconography of the pilgrimage mandalas the Dainichi Nyorai of the Diamond Realm in the *Sonshō mandara*, a passage in the *Henkushō* 遍口鈔 (thirteenth century) explains that: "The cosmic buddha Dainichi of the Diamond Realm [of the *Sonshō mandara*] corresponds to the Dainichi of the non-duality between the Womb and the Diamond (Ryōbu funi Dainichi); the two side attendants, Fudō and Gōzanze, correspond to the alternation of the teachings [of the Womb and Diamond mandalas]" (Park 2000: 55). In other words, in the *Sonshō mandara* the Dainichi Nyorai of the Diamond Realm symbolizes the non-duality, or the stable synthesis, between the Womb and Diamond mandala while Fudō, alias the *Taizōkai mandara*, and Gōzanze, alias the *Kongōkai mandara*, represent the perpetual motion and circulation of these two teachings. Because Dainichi Nyorai of Yudono was specifically defined as Dainichi of the Two Realms of the Womb and Diamond, it is evident that the *issei gyōnin* relied on the iconographical and doctrinal characteristics of the *Sonshō mandara* to materially display the ultimate nature of the cosmic buddha of Yudono.

It is important to note that the appropriation of the basic pattern of the *Sonshō mandara* for the Yudono stelae was not a mere duplication of the original, but included numerous innovative elements. For instance, the sacred triad is always located in the lower part of the stele. Dainichi Nyorai of the Diamond Realm sits on a bipartite lotus throne placed on the top of an incense burner and makes the hand gesture of the knowledge fist. Fudō and Gōzanze stand on gem thrones that reproduce the bases of two platforms for the fire ritual. The entire body of Dainichi Nyorai of the Diamond Realm is enveloped in the extremely long pendants of an enormous jewel crown that resembles a placental membrane surrounding an embryo. In the middle of the jewel crown there is a small cross that symbolizes the stars and, in particular, Ursa Major, which regulates the life and death of sentient beings. Over the jewel crown there is a heavenly canopy that ensures additional protection for Dainichi Nyorai's body. The entire space of the triad is studded with small stylized triangles that represent wish-fulfilling jewels and, by extension, the relics of the buddha. On the upper part of the stele there is a representation of celestial bodies and meteorological phenomena: the sun, the moon, and a big cross that represents the stars. This big cross is placed over the fire halo of Gōzanze, while a big swastika rotated in the clockwise direction appears over the head of Fudō. The shape of the clouds is extremely interesting because it creates an inter-visual effect of the body of a dragon (*ryū*) that is intent on devouring the sun while a half-moon rests on its tail. From the perspective of this dragon the solar disk is not only the sun but also the magic pearl of the Daoist tradition that bestows immortality.

Moreover, the *Sadaaki kushō rokuza nenbutsu* 定敬口称六座念仏 (eighteenth century) of Shida village in Hitachi province (present-day Ibaraki prefecture) reports that one of the names of Yudono Gongen was Dainichi Dairyū [great dragon] Gongen, another proof of the dragon-like aspect of this deity.[7] The clouds, which were fundamental elements for the fertility of the crops, became, at the same time, the body of a celestial dragon and of Yudono Gongen. Thanks to this visual conflation, the provisional trace *kami* (*suijakushin*) of Dainichi Nyorai of the Two Realms of Diamond and Womb—namely, Yudono Gongen—could be represented disguised as a dragon extending its claws over the jewel crown of Dainichi Nyorai of the Diamond realm.

In a stele dedicated to Mount Yudono that was erected in Akenomachi village (Hitachi province), there are two anthropomorphic figurines dancing in the space immediately below the sacred triad. These dancers are called Shudaeten 須陀会天 in reference to the highest level of the Brahmā's world (Skt. Śuddhāvasa), their actual residence. They pay homage to the sacred triad while shaking an ornamental fan. Shudaeten appear also in the illustration of the *Sonshō mandara* reported in the *Kakuzenshō* (1213), but in this stele the head of the heavenly god is replaced with a crow's head in one case and a rabbit's head in the other. Thanks to the visual mixture between Shudaeten, the solar crow (Yatagarasu), and the lunar rabbit (Tsuki no usagi), these celestial deities were all summoned together to pay homage to Dainichi Nyorai of Mount Yudono (Tokuhara 2004: 188–91).

At this point, it may be relevant to ask the reason why the Kan'ei era saw such a proliferation of stelae dedicated to Mount Yudono among village communities in the Kantō region. A possible answer could be that the early decades of the seventeenth century registered enormous changes in the social structures of the rural classes. The cadastral survey ordered by Tokugawa Ieyasu (1542–1616) in 1612 led to the promulgation of a new fiscal legislation according to which peasants who were registered as landowners had to pay regular taxes to the lord of their domain. Social tensions skyrocketed, because the political offices within the village were entirely monopolized by the titled peasants (*hon'yakunin* 本役人), who constituted an older class of peasant aristocracy that had inherited their ruling privileges from pre-seventeenth-century political concessions. The result was that in the early seventeenth century small peasants (*kobyakushō* 小百姓) shared with titled peasants the majority of the internal revenue but, differently from the latter, could not participate in the political life of the village (Ooms 1996: 76–7, 81). At the same time, titled peasants legitimated their dominant position claiming for themselves the exclusive right to sit on the "shrine council" (*miyaza* 宮座) as residents of the village since old times (*zakata* 座方), whose ancestors were venerated as protective gods of the entire rural community (*ujigami*). It goes without saying that the political ostracism of small peasants was strongly reverberated in their exclusion from the organization of the religious festivals for the *kami* of the village (Smith 1959: 58–9, 194–6).

Being completely cut off from this religio-political circulation of power, small peasants tried to connect their fiscal contribution to the right to hold administrative offices among the bureaucratic circles of the village. At the same time, small peasants attempted to make up their status of non-seat holders (*hirakata* 平方) in the shrine council (due to the fact that their ancestors did not belong to the *ujigami* group), by performing alternative religious practices. It was precisely in this turbulent socioeconomic panorama that the construction of mounds and stelae dedicated to the cult of Mount Yudono reached its apogee. Such religious micro-practices, the devotional protocols of which did not require devotees to be members of the shrine council or have his ancestors recognized as *ujigami*, allowed small peasants to carry out their political claims and to legitimize them through alternative devotional discourses. Toward the end of the seventeenth century, most of the legal disputes ended with the actual inclusion of small peasants among the political echelons of the village; the sociopolitical motivations, which were associated with the cultic objects of Mount Yudono in the Kan'ei era, took then different directions.

Fujiki kuyō: Empowering Ritual Fasting

The erection of a stele always constituted the final step of a complex devotional and ascetic endeavor that began much earlier and served to empower or ritually "switch on" the natural stone. In other words, mounds and stelae of Yudono, far from being neutral objects, were connected to specific ritual procedures and doctrinal discourses that could not be replaced with others at will. For instance, Miura Jōshin (1565-1644) reports in the *Keichō kenmonshū* (1614) that in 1613 a monk of the Pure Land school, a certain Kikurenji 菊蓮寺, installed a stūpa on a mound for the veneration of Mount Yudono in the Mito domain (Hitachi province). An enraged crowd of about 3,000 Yudono devotees, which Miura calls "Shingon practitioners," gathered in that place, threw down Kikurenji's stūpa, and proclaimed that the ritual procedures for making offerings to the Yudono mound must follow the ritual protocol of their congregation. According to the legend, those liturgical procedures had been transmitted by Dainichi Nyorai to Kūkai (774-835) during his pilgrimage to Mount Yudono in the Daidō era (806-810). Crestfallen Kikurenji commented: "This Mount Yudono represents the perfection of the three bodies [of the Buddha].⁸ So why does it hate the Pure Land school ceremony for offerings?" (*Keichō kenmonshū*: 64).

Following up this clash on ritual matters between lay members of a Yudono confraternity and a Pure Land monk of the Mito domain, it is interesting to identify the social and religious networks that allowed lay Yudono devotees to materially sponsor the stelae and the ritual practices they adopted to empower these sacred stones. The creation of a votive stele, which was often called "tower" (*tō*) or stūpa (*tōba*), usually required a synergetic interaction of three groups of social actors. First, lay devotees of Mount Yudono who generally—not necessarily—belonged to Yudono confraternities (Yudonosan *kō*) formed a devotional assembly (*ikkesshū* 一結衆) to accumulate financial resources and legal permits for purchasing the stone, paying the specialized workers, and selecting the plot of land on which the stele could be erected. These persons became the donors (*seshu* 施主) of the stele. They took upon themselves not only the economic and legal tasks for the material construction of the sacred object but also the ascetic practices that were necessary to charge the inert matter with religious merit. Donors made a vow (*gangyō* 願行) to keep performing specific types of ascetic practices to empower their stele, without interruption, for a stipulated amount of time, which usually lasted for three years and three months (*sennichigyō* 千日行). From the point of view of the temporal duration, the austerities made by the lay devotees of Mount Yudono within the ordinariness of their lives as peasants or small artisans perfectly mirrored those made by the *issei gyōnin* within the extraordinariness of their ascetic seclusions in the Valley of the Immortals (Senninzawa 仙人沢) on Mount Yudono. The last day of practice marked at the same time the accomplishment of the ascetic endeavor (*mangyō* 満行), the inauguration of the stele, and the consequent realization of the vows (*gan jōju* 願成就).

Second, an *issei gyōnin* or a Haguro *shugenja* played the role of religious sponsor (*hongan* 本願) and served as guarantor of the devotional authenticity and ascetic commitment of the donors. Even if the religious sponsor did not directly participate in the financial operations to materially produce the stele, he followed the lay devotees during the ascetic and ritual practices that took place between the expression of the vow and the enshrinement of the stele. The religious sponsor worked as spokesman for confraternity members before the deity, making sure that their vows were safely communicated to Dainichi Nyorai of Yudono once the stele was finished.

Third, groups of highly specialized artisans such as the stone-engravers (*sekkō* 石工) used their creative and artistic skills to give aesthetic shape to the devotional practices performed by the lay donors and supervised by the religious sponsors.[9] In the case of the Yudono stelae erected in the Kantō area, the donors very often used biotite stones quarried from Mount Tsukuba, which played a pivotal role in the material and logistical diffusion of the Yudono cult in the provinces around Edo. A network of irrigation canals around the quarry was also necessary to transport the stele as close as possible to the village where it was requested. Very often the passage of heavy stone slabs through the canals damaged the banks of the rice fields, creating tensions among the peasants. Therefore, the team of donors, religious sponsors, and stone-engravers had to constantly cooperate with each other in order to take care of all the religious procedures as well as the logistical issues related to the erection of a stele.

What kind of ascetic practices were specifically associated with the ritual activation of the votive stelae dedicated to Mount Yudono? For instance, there was a special type of ritual fasting and offering ceremony called *fujiki kuyō*. The term *fujiki* did not indicate a total abstention from food, but a selective elimination of certain foodstuffs, such as the ten grains (*jukkoku-dachi* 十穀断ち), meat, and the five pungent roots (*gokun* 五葷) on a specific day of each month (Okumura 1979: 2). The *fujiki kuyō* usually lasted for three years and three months, at the end of which the practitioner could obtain various benefits for the present and future life. Analyzing the names of the confraternity members that were carved on the stelae built after the completion of the *fujiki kuyō*, it is evident that this type of *kuyō* was originally practiced by mixed groups of male and female devotees, but toward the second half of the seventeenth century it became an almost exclusive practice for the female devotees.

The oldest ascetic manual about this practice is the *Fujiki no nikki* 不食ノ日記, dated 1610, which was used by a female practitioner—Osaka オサカ—who belonged to a *fujiki* confraternity of Kokawachō village in Kii Province (present-day Wakayama Prefecture). The incipit reads:

> The ritual fasting, which [was transmitted from] Yudono Gongen ユトノコンケン and Dainichi Nyorai [to] Kōbō Daishi [Kūkai], takes place one day per month. Thanks to this practice it is possible to obtain peace in the present world and rebirth in the Pure Land after death. First month, fifteenth day. [This *fujiki*] corresponds to the creation of sixty-five thousand statues of buddhas [...].
>
> (Sakamoto 1988: 185)

It is interesting to note that independently from the deity on behalf of which the *fujiki kuyō* was practiced, this type of ritual fasting was always conceived as a secret transmission that Kūkai received from Yudono Gongen, alias Dainichi Nyorai, after arriving at Mount Yudono. Therefore, already in the early Edo period the name of Yudono was used to legitimize ritual abstention from food that was performed by lay devotees in conjunction with the recitation of the *nenbutsu* before making a votive stele.

An extremely interesting aspect of this text is that Osaka was a lay female practitioner of the Kansai region and this detail shows that the geographical extension of the cult of Yudono was not limited to Kantō and Tōhoku, but also extended to religious practices of devotees who lived in very distant locations. The ritual logic of the *fujiki kuyō* was that abstention from food, which was undertaken by the lay practitioner once a month, corresponded to an imaginary offering of precious gifts, such as 65,000 statues of Buddhas, ten nine-storied stūpas, or twenty-one Buddhist monasteries. The *fujiki kuyō* allowed individual lay devotees who would never have been able to make such expensive donations with their limited economic means to accumulate merit by transforming their ritual fasting into precious gifts. It is relevant to underline that the ritual fasting and offering ceremony was not a practice without risks. For instance, a different *Fujiki no nikki* dated 1681 reports that an incorrect or irregular performance of the *fujiki kuyō* would cause the practitioner and all her relatives to be reborn at the bottom of hell (*muken jigoku*) (Okumura 1979: 7–8). In other words, the female devotees who performed the *fujiki kuyō* were responsible not only for the accumulation of positive karma for themselves and six generations of relatives but also, in case of failure, for the ruin of the entire family. This aspect shows that ascetic practices by female devotees were perceived to be as momentous in soteriological terms as those by male devotees.

A stele empowered via *fujiki kuyō* was located in the precinct of Fukutokuji and was sponsored in 1567 by a group of female lay donors who belonged to a sorority of Yudono Gongen (Yudono Gongen *shū* 湯殿権現衆), both located in Sakai village on the southern outskirts of Ōsaka.¹⁰ In the lower part of the stele there is a bas-relief of Kūkai in a seated position making the hand gesture of the bestower of fearlessness (*semui'in*) with the right hand and holding a lotus flower in the left. At the top, above the head of Kūkai, Mount Yudono is represented through the lines of a written invocation, carefully disposed to form the silhouette of the sacred mountain. The inscription says: "Praise to the buddha Amida and the original vow to seek enlightenment of the buddha Mida (Mida *butsu*). We, members of the congregation of Yudono Gongen, erected [this stele]. The members of our congregation [abstained from] food (*jikishū* 食衆) and on the last day of our practice (*kechigan* 結願) our vows were realized" (Okumura 1973: 341–2).

Although the inscription of this stele does not clearly mention the term *fujiki* but instead substitutes the expression "food congregation" (*jikishū* 食衆) for it, this lexical choice could be due to the fact that the *fujiki kuyō* was a ritual practice divided into two halves: the *fujiki* part that corresponded to a devotional abstention from specific foods once a month for three years, and the *kuyō* part that corresponded to an offering ceremony during which the practitioners actually presented purified food offerings (*saijiki* 斎食) to the deities (Miyashima 1993: 1277). Therefore, the term *jikishū* could indicate a congregation of female devotees who abstained from certain foods, made *nenbutsu* recitations, and finally built a votive stele in front of which they presented food offerings to Amida and Yudono Gongen. It is clear that the *fujiki kuyō* was an adaptive and porous ceremony that could be performed in various devotional contexts and on behalf of different deities such as Amida Nyorai and not necessarily Yudono itself. Nevertheless, in every case the legitimacy of this practice was based on the secret transmission that Kūkai received from Yudono Gongen. Thanks to this semiotic link between *fujiki kuyō* and Mount Yudono, some important elements of the cult of this site reached devotees located in territories extremely distant from Dewa Province.

Conclusion

The analysis of mounds and stelae dedicated to the cult of Mount Yudono in the early decades of the Edo period reveals, first of all, a double process of ruralization and localization of beliefs in Dainichi Nyorai, understood as a celestial governor of all atmospheric phenomena for the protection of crops whose Pure Land matched with the territory of Mount Yudono. This highly localized form of Danichi Nyorai of Yudono became a guardian deity for numerous villages in the countryside around Edo. Sacred objects such as mounds and stelae played a pivotal role in the diffusion of religious practices for the veneration of Mount Yudono among rural classes especially in the Kantō region.

Votive stelae were erected thanks to the mutual collaboration of three different groups of social actors: lay donors (*seshu*), religious sponsors (*hongan*), and stone-engravers (*sekkō*). This fact demonstrates that in the Edo period the structure of religious networks for the veneration of sacred mountains such as Mount Yudono was built on the continuous interactions of religious professionals like *issei gyōnin* or Shugendō practitioners and groups of lay devotees who gathered together in religious confraternities. Village officials could also participate in the ritual procedures for the recitation of textual invocations on behalf of Yudono Gongen after the construction of mounds or stelae. The same was also true for members of the emerging rural class of the small peasants (*kobyakushō*), who often patronized the erection of Yudono stelae in the Kan'ei era in order to create a religious legitimization for their political claims against titled peasants (*hon'yakunin*). From this point of view, it can be said that mounds and stelae embraced multidirectional instances of power, which could manifest themselves in a descending direction from the top of society to the bottom or, vice versa, in an ascending direction from subaltern classes toward the privileged ones. Mounds and stelae were flexible and porous entities characterized by a polyphonic authority that could be favorable to institutional elites as in the case of the two officials of Sōma, or, on the contrary, be against the status quo as in the case of those stelae built by the small peasants who did not hold a seat in the shrine council of the village.

With regard to the empowering mechanisms of the votive stelae, it is clear that the stele per se meant nothing if it was not ritually charged. In the case of Mount Yudono cult, special importance was given to a type of ritual fasting and offering ceremony—*fujiki kuyō*—, which was practiced by female and male lay devotees until the second half of the seventeenth century, when it turned into an ascetic practice specifically designated for female practitioners. The sources related to *fujiki kuyō* testify that the cult for Yudono Gongen was already diffused even in the Kansai region toward the end of the sixteenth century and was often associated with devotional discourses related to other Buddhist deities such as the Buddha Amida. Therefore, it is possible to suppose that in the sixteenth century the cult of Yudono Gongen functioned as a sort of legitimizing seal for certain ascetic practices such as the ritual fasting performed by lay devotees on behalf of deities that were not necessarily limited to the Mount Yudono pantheon. Although the empowering rituals for Yudono mounds and stelae in the seventeenth century seem to strictly follow a specific liturgical protocol that was transmitted among the members of Yudono confraternities, in the previous century it is likely that the diffusion of the cult of Yudono Gongen in areas far away from the Dewa province was due to the symbiotic character of these devotional practices, which could be easily integrated with different liturgies for venerating other deities in heterogeneous religious contexts.

The analysis of the ritual fasting and offering ceremony demonstrates that ascetic practices could begin as shared activities between female and male lay practitioners and progressively become polarized toward one gender with the exclusion of the other. As soon as the *fujiki kuyō* became a practice suitable only for female practitioners, male devotees who gathered in male-only religious confraternities began performing a peculiar version of *nenbutsu*, called *toki nenbutsu* 時念仏, for the worship of Mount Yudono. Like *fujiki kuyō*, *toki nenbutsu* was also performed only on specific days of the month, called "six purified days" (*rokusai nichi* 六斎日), namely, the eighth, fourteenth, fifteenth, twenty-third, twenty-ninth, and thirtieth day of the month. During these days male lay devotees were supposed to follow the eight pure precepts (*hassai kai* 八斎戒) that characterized the moral conduct of the monks. Among these precepts, the eighth, the prohibition to eat food after noon (*hiji jiki* 非時食), was considered the most important and was specifically associated with the eighth day of the month that marked the start of the practice. This was probably the reason for the great diffusion of the name Yōka-kō 八日講,[11] which can be translated as "religious confraternity of the eighth day," among the various appellatives of the Yudono confraternities.

13

Shugendō as Social Practice: Kumano Talismans and Inscribed Oaths in Premodern Japan

D. Max Moerman

As the title of this book suggests, we are at a very different place in the study of Shugendō than we were only a few decades ago. No longer marginalized as mere "folk religion," Shugendō has become recognized as a religious tradition central to Japanese culture, during all historical periods, in all geographic regions, and for people of all social classes. Our task is no longer simply to recognize Shugendō; it is to define and reposition it. My contribution to this task is to examine the position of Shugendō within Japan's social order across time, place, and class. The temples and shrines associated with Shugendō, and, in particular, with the Three Kumano Shrines, one of the earliest centers of Shugendō and headquarters of the Honzan-ha, supplied the documentary infrastructure for the most public and private protocols of Japan's social institutions. My argument is that the materials and methods of Japanese religion, and of Shugendō, in particular, defined and sustained, from the thirteenth through the nineteenth centuries, the methods of trust and truth observed and enacted within juridical, political, and sexual relations. I understand these relations not as separate domains but as overlapping fields of practice, which relied on a common corpus of documentary and ritual forms. Because these documents and rituals have been treated in only piecemeal fashion, and in terms of narrow disciplinary interests, we have failed to understand their shared networks of meaning and agency.

Such documentation and implementation operated through the most ephemeral of objects: religious oaths inscribed on paper talismans, signed in blood, enforced by the gods, and tested by physical ordeals. Such talismans were, and continue to be, produced at major Shugendō centers throughout Japan, such as Ōmine, Kinpusen, Yoshino, Kurama, Dorogawa, Atagosan, Shigisan, Hakusan, Kubotesan, and Togakushisan. The longest and most extensive history of production and use, however, belongs to those of the three Kumano shrines of Hongū, Shingū, and Nachi. Oaths inscribed on Kumano talismans operated at every level of the social order: they were used by farmers to complain of mistreatment by local authorities, to resolve land disputes, and to justify rebellions; they were used by shogunal courts to adjudicate land claims, designate administrative authority, and resolve inheritance disputes; they were used by military clans to guarantee fealty from vassals, swear allegiance to superiors, and cement political alliances; and they were used by aristocrats, warriors, and townspeople to prove their emotional devotion and sexual fidelity. Such talismanic oaths were used by people of all classes in marriages, adoptions, last wills and testaments, commercial transactions, civil procedures, and judicial appointments (Kanda 1974). The breadth and range of such use—across divisions of time, region, faith, class, and gender—reveal the profound role of Shugendō, and of its material culture, with the social domain. Oaths inscribed on Kumano talismans constituted the media and the mechanism by which social bonds were established and by which the economic, legal, and political order was secured.

The talismans of Kumano, and of many other temples and shrines as well, are known by the term *goō hōin* 午王宝印, or "jewel seal of the ox king." They first appear in the thirteenth century and continue to be produced and used to this day. A single sheet of paper, generally smaller that 30 × 50 cm, with a woodblock design printed in black and vermillion ink, the *goō hōin* is the material ground and visible impression of the enshrined deity: both sign and presence of its authority and power. The woodblocks are themselves venerated as sacred objects. *Goō hōin* are printed, consecrated, and distributed at temples and shrines most commonly at ceremonial assemblies held in the first or second month of the lunar year. Their production is ritualized as well. At the Kumano Hongū and Nachi Shrines, for example, the woodblocks are carved from the trunks of trees growing within the shrine compound and the talismans are printed on the second, seventh, and eighth days of the first month. The *goō hōin* are then offered before the deities by the shrine priests and ritually consecrated with ceremonial water and pine torches before they are distributed to parishioners (Yoshii 1988: 139).

The name of the temple or shrine issuing the *goō hōin* is generally written in black ink in the center of the print and is flanked by the four characters: "jewel 宝," "seal 印," "ox 牛," and "king 王." On top of these characters are secondary impressions, made in vermillion ink, of wish-fulfilling jewels (Jp. *nyoi hōju* 如意宝珠; Skt. *cintamāṇi*) and/or seed syllables (Jp. *shūji* 種子; Skt. *bīja*) of the enshrined deities. Both the wish-fulfilling jewel and the seed syllable are images common to the visual and ritual culture of Shugendō, and Japanese Esoteric Buddhism in general. The semantics of the characters for jewel and seal are thus reinforced by the vermillion impressions with which they are superscribed. Scholars have speculated variously on the meaning of the other two characters: "ox" and "king" (Aida 1976: 192). The seventeenth-century *Jakushōdō kokkyōshū* 寂照堂谷響集 by the Shingon monk Unshō 運敞 (1604–93), however, identifies the term as "ox yellow" (*goō* 牛黄) or bezoar, a highly valued substance within the East Asian *materia medica*, derived from the gallstones of cattle and used in Japanese Buddhist rites of healing since at least the Heian period (*Jakushōdō kokkyōshū*: vol. 1, 1a, 4).[1]

Although inscribed calligraphically in their earliest form, the woodblock-printed *goō hōin*, produced from the fifteenth century onward, are written in a cryptic zoomorphic orthography. Such hybrid "image-texts" are common to East Asian Buddho-Daoist visual culture, and, in particular, to the "heavenly scripts" of Chinese talismans (see Robson 2008). In the Japanese case, however, the zoomorphic characters on *goō hōin* represent the animal messengers specific to the deities of each temple or shrine. The characters of Kumano talismans are composed of crows, the animal messenger of the

Kumano deities.² The talismans of Hachiman shrines include doves, the messenger of the Hachiman deity; those of Mt. Hiko contain eagles; those of Tōji, Tōdaiji, and Dorogawa are composed of snakes; and those of Kyoto's Bishamondō, centipedes.

Such talismans were put to a wide range of apotropaic uses. In addition to the use for the inscription of oaths, *goō hōin* were, and continue to be, planted in rice fields to protect the crops from insects, worn on the person for protection against all manner of demonic forces, and affixed to the eaves of houses to defend residents from evil spirits. In early fourteenth-century illustrated handscrolls, such as the *Kasuga gongen genki e* 春日権現験記絵 of 1309 and the *Matsuzaki Tenjin engi* 松崎天神縁起 of 1311, *goō hōin* in black and vermillion ink are shown pasted on the walls of bedrooms, sickrooms, and kitchens to protect inhabitants from malevolent forces, illness, and fire.³ In early seventeenth-century folding screens depicting the pleasure quarters of Kyoto, *goō hōin* from the Gion and Iwashimizu Hachiman Shrines are shown posted above the doorway of brothels.⁴ And in his *Kansō sadan* 閑窓瑣談, Tamenaga Shunsui 為永春水 (1818–86) reports that young women of the early eighteenth century affixed Kumano *goō hōin* to doors to keep demons from entering their rooms at night.⁵

The use of talismans for protection is, of course, found in many religious traditions. Less common, however, is their role in the performance of oaths. The reverse side of the Kumano talisman was used for inscribing a pledge or an attestation of truth, known as a *kishomōn* 起請文, a "written vow" between humans witnessed and enforced by the gods. The *kishomōn*, performed both orally and in writing, consists of two parts. The first, the *maegaki* 前書き, states the facts of the claim or the details of the pledge. The second, the anathema clause, referred to as *shinmon* 神文 or *batsubun* 罰文, calls down the punishments of the gods—generally meted out as leprosy in the present life and rebirth in the lowest realm of Buddhist hell in the next—if the claim is untrue or the pledge not kept. The *kishomōn* is thus both a promise and a curse, a statement of truth and the public invocation of divine punishment.⁶ Holding both constitutive and instrumental force, a *kishomōn* is at once an assertion of truth and the means by which the veracity of the assertion was determined. Blood was often used to sign these documents and occasionally to write them out as well.⁷

Oaths inscribed on talismans were instrumental to forming and proving the bonds of trust and obedience that constituted the institutional structure of premodern Japan. The earliest evidence of their use dates from the Kamakura period, the age of Japan's first military government, a time in which pledges of allegiance and loyalty were indispensable to the social and political order. The *Azuma kagami* 吾妻鏡, the official history of the Kamakura Bakufu, provides an example marking the very genesis of warrior rule. In 1185, Minamoto no Yoritomo 源頼朝 (1147–99), the provincial warrior who was soon to become the leader of Japan's first military government, began to doubt the loyalty of his brother, Minamoto no Yoshitsune 源義経 (1159–89). Yoshitsune defended himself, according to the *Azuma kagami*, in a famous letter written from Koshigoe, stating, "I have gathered all sorts of *goō hōin* from various shrines and temples and have written a *kishōmon* on their reverse, swearing upon all of the greater and lesser deities of Japan that I harbor no ambition against you" (*Azuma kagami*, 1185.5.24). The *kishōmon*, however, failed to convince his brother and Yoshitsune remained an adversary until he was killed by Yoritomo's forces in 1189. An oath of loyalty by another brother of Yoritomo, Minamoto no Noriyori 源範頼 (1150–93), fared equally poorly. In 1193, Yoritomo suspected him, too, of harboring disloyalty and ordered him executed—but not before Noriyori submitted the following oath of loyalty:

> Having taken part in all of the battles delegated to me, I have destroyed the enemies of the Emperor and proven my fidelity. I have never once been disloyal to you and pledge to continue this loyalty to your descendants. [...] I do not have the slightest disloyal intention in the present or future and have admonished my descendants should they ever have such thoughts. If any of these statements are false, may the divine punishments of Brahmā, Indra, the deities of Ise, Kasuga, and Kamo Shrines, and especially the tutelary deity of our clan, the Great Bodhisattva Hachiman be visited upon me.
>
> (*Azuma kagami*, 1193.8.2)

As with Noriyori's pledge, the first deities listed in *kishōmon* are usually the Indian gods Brahmā (Bonten 梵天) and Indra (Taishakuten 帝釈天), who together with the Four Deva Kings (Shitennō 四天王), dwell on Mount Sumeru at the center of the Buddhist world and oversee and protect the entire realm. Listed next are the various gods and Buddhas of major shrines and temples throughout the country, and finally the deities particular to the local region, community, or religious institution of the person making the oath. The distribution of deities, like the distribution of the talismans themselves, suggests a historical demography of Japanese religion. Some deities are invoked throughout the country, whereas others are specific to province, region, temple, shrine, or even a single agricultural estate. Talismans from the Kumano Shrines enjoyed country-wide distribution and use. The standardization of the pantheon invoked in *kishōmon* has been identified by Satō Hiroo as a shared cosmology of medieval Japan, extending from the gods of pre-Buddhist India to the most local of Japanese deities (Satō 2006).

Whereas the contents of the pledge were various, the anathema clause followed a common pattern and was standardized early on in thirteenth-century document manuals, law codes, and oaths of office. According to the written guides for the composition of official documents, such as the *Zappitsu yōshū* 雑筆要集 (*ZGR*, item no. 66, vol. 11b: 830) and the *Jurin shūyō* 儒林拾要 (*ZGR*, item no. 56, vol. 31b: 376), a *kishōmon* should begin by stating the subject of the oath. This initial statement should be followed by the promise that if the signatory ever violates their word, they will suffer

> divine punishment, in every pore of their body, from each of the great deities of Kumano 熊野, Kinpusen 金峯山, Ryōgoku Chinju 両国鎮守, Hinokuma 日前, Ōjō Chinju Sho Daimyōjin 王城鎮守諸大明神 and the other deities, great and small, of the more than sixty provinces of Japan.

This is followed by the date and, at the bottom of the document, the name and seal of the signatory.

This formulation of divine punishment, characteristic of all such oaths, lay at the very foundation of medieval law. The *Institutes of Judicature* (*Goseibai shikimoku* 御成敗式目) law code of the Kamakura government promulgated in 1232, applied to all warriors under Bakufu rule, and established the model for Japanese legal codes for centuries thereafter. The code of fifty-one articles concludes with the following oath to which all warriors, whether lords or vassals, were bound to swear:

> If even in a single instance we swerve from these laws, either to bend or to break them, may the deities Brahmā, Indra, the Four Great Deva Kings, and all the gods great and small, celestial and terrestrial of the more than sixty provinces of Japan and especially the two Avatars (*gongen* 権現) of Izu and Hakone, the Great Deity (*daimyōjin* 大明神) of Mishima, the Great Bodhisattva Hachiman, and the Celestial Deity of Great Power Filling Heaven (Tenman Daijizai Tenjin 天満大自在天神), punish us and all our house, connections, and possessions.
>
> (*Goseibai shikimoku*: 29–30; translated in Hall 1906: 17–18)

All officials and magistrates within the law courts of the Kamakura Bakufu (*hyōjōsho* 評定所) were required to swear the same, as oath of office (Steenstrup 1980: 434).

Vows by warriors, officials, and magistrates to obey, uphold, and carry out the law were public acts and a similar ritual context applied to the performance of all talismanic oaths no matter how private their content. Presenting a *kishōmon* was often preceded and followed by a period of seclusion or purification at the temple or shrine where it was performed, with the deities serving as witness, judge, and jury (Aida 1976: 183). In some cases, the oath was accompanied by an ordeal: a painful or dangerous test of the veracity of the assertion. The pairing of oaths and ordeals in Japan appear in the accounts of Japan's origins collected in the eighth-century *Nihon shoki* and the patterns and practices described in these chronicles continued to be invoked and applied into the nineteenth century. In one example, when the sovereign Ōjin (r. 270–310) found it "impossible to ascertain the right and the wrong" between the statements of two ministers, he "gave orders to ask the gods of heaven and earth for an ordeal by boiling water" (*NKBT* vol. 67a: 367; translated in Aston 1956: 258). In another passage, to adjudicate the authenticity of genealogical claims, the sovereign Ingyō (r. 410–53) ordered the claimants to "wash themselves and practice abstinence, and have each one, calling on the gods, to plunge their hands in boiling water … saying, 'he who tells the truth will be uninjured; he who is false will suffer harm.'" The chronicle also notes a variant method in which, "an axe is heated red-hot and placed on the palm of the hand" (*NKBT* vol. 67a: 439; translation in Aston 1956: 316–17).

Such early Japanese examples seem to have much in common with a kind of oath, or performative utterance, commonly found in Buddhist literature: the Truth Act (Skt. *satyakriyā*), a ritual declaration of fact "in which the truth inherent in the words generates magical or protective powers" (*Princeton Dictionary of Buddhism*: 789). Such self-confirming acts of truth are articulated most commonly by bodhisattvas in Mahayana sutra literature and in accounts of the Buddha's former lives in *jātaka* tales, both of which were part of the literary, visual, and religious culture of medieval Japan.[8] Acts of truth in Buddhist literature are similarly often accompanied by ordeals to prove their veracity. In the *Lotus Sutra*, the bodhisattva "Gladly Seen by all Beings" (Issai-shujō-kiken-bosatsu 一切衆生喜見菩薩) burns his arms as an offering and declares, "I have thrown away both my arms. May I now without fail gain the buddha's gold-colored. If this oath is reality and not vanity, then may both my arms be restored as before!" (Hurvitz 2009: 273). In a famous *jātaka*, in which the Buddha is born as a king in a former life, the bodhisattva plucks out his eyes, gives them to a blind beggar, and declares, "All beggars are dear to me. If this statement is true, let my eyes be restored" (Burlingame 1917: 430).

Yet in both the early Japanese and Buddhist accounts, the ordeal confirms a *spoken* oath. It is only in medieval Japan that the ordeal is accompanied by an oath written on a printed talisman. In some cases, the talisman on which the oath was inscribed would be burned and the ashes drunk. If the individual was lying, it was said that the oath would be regurgitated or that the victim would vomit blood (Yoshii 1988: 138). In other cases, the person swearing the oath would plunge a hand into boiling water or remove stones from a boiling cauldron, an ordeal similar to those mentioned in the *Nihon shoki*. Such ordeals were performed at temples or shrines under clerical supervision and in the presence of a government magistrate. After writing out a *kishōmon*, the person taking the oath would undergo an ordeal by fire or boiling water, and remain in retreat at the temple or shrine for a period of three days before being inspected for burns, the severity of which would indicate falsity or truthfulness of his oath (Longrais 1950: 397–98). In another form of judgement, the author of a *kishōmon* would be similarly confined to a temple for a period of observation to divine the ruling of the gods. The written oath would be judged false if the signatory suffered from, among other things, a nose bleed, choking while eating, having their clothing eaten by rats, or if they were the target of bird dropping from either a kite or crow.[9]

Kishōmon inscribed on *goō hōin* served a wide range of purposes. They operated as instruments of communication, control, and resistance within the medieval *shōen* 荘園 system, an agricultural and economic order which has been recognized as one of ideological as well as material domination. Historians of medieval Japan have long argued that provincial governors (*kokuga* 国衙), proprietors (*ryōshū* 領主), and land stewards (*jitō* 地頭) used *kishōmon* to threaten estate residents.[10] Yet *kishōmon* also served as a ritual and documentary means by which peasants asserted and inscribed their own agency and autonomy and a mechanism of negotiation, and even coercion, by farmers against proprietors. In 1213, farmers on a Tōdaiji 東大寺-held estate in Iga Province sought an exemption from annual taxes because of drought damage to the fields and ended their request with a *kishōmon* stating, "if this is false, may we be punished in every pore of pour bodies by Brahmā, Indra, the Great Buddha, Hachiman, the deities of Kasuga and Kumano, the tutelary deities of this estate and all of the greater and lesser gods of the more than sixty provinces of Japan" (Irumada 1986: 39). In 1309, Tōdaiji exempted a different estate in Wakasa Province 若狭国 from their annual tribute, but only after the farmers proved the truth of their claims with a *kishōmon* attesting the actual condition of agricultural loss (Irumada 1986: 37). In other *kishōmon*, peasants complained of exploitation by estate stewards or threatened to abandon their fields if their demands were not met.

Kishōmon were also central to early warrior governance and served as the means by which loyalties were expressed and enforced, especially at moments of political transition and crisis. In addition to the twelfth-century examples cited above, in which the first Shogun Yoritomo received oaths of loyalty from his brothers, envoys of the Bakufu in Kyoto were ordered to collect *kishōmon* swearing fealty from all of the vassals in the capital and the Kinai region when the third Kamakura shogun, Minamoto no Sanetomo 源実朝 (1192–1219), was appointed in 1203 (*Azuma kagami*, 1203.10.19). During the Jōkyū Rebellion of 1221, when the former emperor Go-Toba sought to overthrow the Kamakura government, partisans of both the court and the Bakufu were forced to produce *kishōmon* to document their allegiance. During another attempted coup in 1331, by the former emperor Go-Daigo, which marked the fall of Kamakura and the origin of Ashikaga rule, Ashikaga Takauji was forced to produce an oath of loyalty to the government he was soon to betray.

Even though the talismanic oaths of Yoshitsune, Noriyori, and Takauji failed to have their desired effect, the use of *kishōmon* inscribed on *goō hōin* only increased, in the fourteenth and fifteenth centuries, among provincial lords (*shugo daimyō* 守護大名) and their retainers. Indeed, *kishōmon* oaths inscribed on *goō hōin* became particularly important as testimonies of allegiance in the wars of the late fifteenth and sixteenth centuries. When Toyotomi Hideyoshi rose to power at the end of the sixteenth century, he forced all vanquished clans to sign such talismanic oaths recognizing and authorizing his supremacy. After Tokugawa Ieyasu established military hegemony in the early seventeenth century, *kishōmon* on *goō hōin* came into even wider use. Indeed, the disproportionate use of talismans from the Kumano shrines may be due to Ieyasu's own religious allegiances. The Tokugawa shogun was a devotee of a particular sub-temple at Nachi from which he received Kumano talismans. Before Ieyasu's rise to power, the talismans of Hakusan were those most commonly used in Eastern Japan, but the first decades of the seventeenth century saw a marked switch to Kumano *hōin*.[11] Under Tokugawa rule, oaths written on the back of Kumano *hōin* were used by members of each military house to swear allegiance to their lord and, by the mid-seventeenth century, they were used by these same lords to swear their fealty to the Tokugawa shogun (Ravina 1995: 1008). They were also used in the oath of office (*yakunin seishi*) by all appointed to the Council of Elders (*rōjū*) of Conference Chamber (*hyōjōsho*; Umeki 2012: 179).

Oaths written on Kumano *hōin* were also used to adjudicate local disputes. In one case from 1653, two groups of villages in Echigo Province could not agree on a common border. The village headmen of the respective groups drafted an agreement on the back of a Kumano *hōin*, which was signed and sealed in blood by ten village representatives. They then burned the talisman, mixed the ashes with earth from the disputed border, and ingested the mixture. It was agreed that first to get sick would lose the boundary claim of their group. In an earlier case from 1619, two villages in Aizu domain requested an ordeal by fire to resolve a similar dispute over village boundaries. It was performed at the shrine of a neighboring village in the presence of a domain official and villagers from the area. A representative from each side stepped forward, both donned ceremonial robes, received a Kumano talisman, and approached the fire. Each representative was to grasp a rod-hot iron with only the paper talisman protecting their hand. The representative of one side grasped it three times and then put it aside. But when the villager from the other side tried to pick up the iron, the talisman instantly burst into flames, and he dropped the iron from his burning hand. The loser's hands and feet were then cut off and his grave was used to mark the new boundary between the two villages (Ooms 1996: 230-4).

If such village disputes represent the juridical use of talismanic oaths at the local level, the following example suggests the extent of their territorial reach and political force. In 1609, the Lord of the Satsuma domain, Shimazu Iehisa 島津 家久 (1547-1587), dispatched over a hundred ships and three thousand troops to invade and conquer the sovereign island kingdom of the Ryūkyū. In a matter of months, the Satsuma forces occupied the king's castle, looted the palace and temples, and returned to Japan with the king and more than a hundred of his officers as prisoners. But if the Lord of Satsuma took control of the Ryūkyū through military force, he had his authority over the islands confirmed through ritual performance. He allowed the King Shō Nei 尚寧 (1564-1620) and his officers to return to the Ryūkyū only after they signed, and sealed in blood, a Divine Punishment Oath (*tenbatsu kishōmon* 天罰起請文) inscribed on the back of seven talismans from the Kumano Nachi Shrine, performed within the sacred precincts of a Kagoshima shrine (Tokyo Kokuritsu Hakubutsukan and Tokyo Daigaku Shiryō Hensanjo 2001: 129, 133). (See Fig. 13.1) The talismanic oath granted Satsuma the Ryūkyū kingdom's valuable monopoly on foreign trade with China as well as control of all of its economic affairs. The king and his ministers were forced to swear to "forever be the humble servants of Satsuma, and obedient to all its commands and never be traitors to our Lord" and also to "preserve and hand down to posterity a written copy of this oath." When one of the king's ministers refused to sign, he was beheaded on the spot: offering rather dramatic evidence that the oath was less than voluntary and the punishment less than divine. This document of surrender,

Figure 13.1 1609 oath signed by Ryūkyū King Shō Nei. Tōkyō Daigaku Shiryō Hensanjo.

forced on a vanquished sovereign kingdom, took the form of an oath, inscribed of the back of Kumano talismans, and performed on the grounds of a shrine.

The content of the pledge is relatively brief: just thirteen lines of text inscribed on a single sheet of plain paper at the beginning of the document. The anathema vow, however, comprises ninety-eight lines of text extending across seven sheets of Kumano talismans glued together to form a document over two meters long, listing the names of the hundreds of gods who will visit divine punishment on the king should he or his descendants fail to uphold their promises. Signed, sealed in blood, and delivered in the presence of the gods, it valorized a military attack on a sovereign state, the capture of its rulers, the expropriation of its wealth, the control of its maritime trade, and institutionalized in perpetuity the economic and political subjugation of an independent kingdom. This oath of subjugation, moreover, was not limited to the single moment of conquest. From the time of the invasion until the late nineteenth century, the king of the Ryūkyū, the Regent (sesshō 摂政), and the Council of the Three (sanjikan 三司官) were forced to regularly submit kishōmon—inscribed on Kumano hōin and sealed in blood—to the reigning Lord of Satsuma in which they called down upon themselves, if they ever failed "serious illness, pain and agony day and night, and white and black leprosy in all of the 84,000 pores and 42 joints of the body."[12] Some two hundred and seventy years after it was signed, King Shō Nei's Divine Punishment Oath of 1609 was translated into English by the Japanese government and presented to international representatives attending the Sino–Japanese sovereignty disputes of the 1870s (Kerr 1958: 160). The translation was published in the *Japan Weekly Mail* of October 18, 1879, which notes that it was "laid before General Grant by the Japanese Ministers, in July last." The contents of a religious oath, calling down divine punishment, written on seven talismans from the Nachi Shrine, and signed in blood in the presence of the gods, remained a crucial evidentiary document in matters of international trade, diplomacy, sovereignty, into the late nineteenth century.

Oaths inscribed on Kumano talismans applied to relations both distant and intimate, from the political and economic aspects of foreign trade and statecraft to the intimate territory of the human heart. In her diary, *Towazugatari* とはずがたり (*An Un-Asked for Tale*), composed around 1307, a woman in service to the royal court, commonly known as "Lady Nijō" (Go-Fukakusa-in no Nijo 後深草院二条, 1258 to after 1307), illustrates the role of oaths in sexual life of the aristocracy. She describes receiving a letter from one of her lovers, Imperial Priest Shōjo 性助, abbot of Shingon temple Ninnaji, whom she refers to as Ariake, in which he confesses the depth of his feelings for her. "I fell in love with you," he writes "Night after night I wept out of longing for you; whenever I chanted sutras in front of sacred images it was your words that came to mind, I offered your letters before the *goma* altar as I would a sutra; I opened them by the light of sacred lamps to sooth my heart" (*Towazugatari*: 87; translation Brazell 1973: 90). Nijō notes that the letter included "*goō* from Kumano and several other major temples, on the back of which he had listed all of the gods and Buddhas of the more than sixty provinces of Japan, starting with Bonten and Taishaku" (*Towazugatari*: 87; translation Brazell 1973: 89–90). She is shocked that "he had written the names of a forbiddingly large number of gods, starting with Amaterasu and Hachiman. Seeing this made my hair stand on end and struck terror and grief into my heart" (*Towazugatari*: 88; translation Brazell 1973: 91). Nijō later recounts how another of her lovers, the retired sovereign Go-Fukakusa (1234–1304), pledged to Ariake, his own half-brother, that Ariake, not himself, was the father of Nijō's child. "If what I say is untrue," he swore to Ariake, "may the gods of Ise, Iwashimizu, Kamo, Kasuga, and all of the gods that guard this country, withhold their protection" (*Towazugatari*: 126; translation Brazell 1973: 132). And when years later, after completing a period or religious pilgrimage, Go-Fukakusa questions her fidelity, she exclaims:

> I swear to you that though I traveled eastward as far as the Sumida River in Musashino, I did not so much as make a single night's pledge to any man. If I did, may I be excluded from the original vow of Amida Buddha, the *honji* of Hachiman, and may I fall into the uninterrupted suffering of the Avici hell. And if any bond of love attracted me when I visited the pure waters of the sacred river at Ise, may I be punished by [Dainichi,] the ruler of the Diamond and the Womb Realm Mandalas. ... If there is a man from the slope of Nara southward to whom I have pledged my troth, may the four *daimyōjin* of Kasuga Shrine withdraw their protection, leaving me to the sufferings of the three paths and the eight difficulties.
>
> (*Towazugatari*: 208–9; translation Brazell 1973: 222–3)

Intimate oaths of love as well as personal promises of sexual discipline were sworn on Kumano talismans and similarly underwritten by invocations divine punishment by the gods and buddhas.

Such pledges of romantic devotion and sexual fidelity, however, were not limited to the affairs of aristocrats. Similar love oaths appear among the *kishōmon* of warrior elites. One such oath, dated 1546, was inscribed by Takeda Shingen 武田信玄 (1521–75), the daimyo of Kai, who would become one of the most powerful military rulers of sixteenth-century Japan. In it, Shingen swears to his younger male lover, the page Gensuke 源助, that he did not have sexual relations with another youth, named Yashichirō 弥七郎. Shingen adamantly denies the charge of infidelity: "I did not sleep with Yashichirō at that time, nor did I do so before then, let alone sleep with him all day and night. I especially did not think of sleeping with him tonight."[13] Shingen swear to the truth of his assertion on the local deities of his clan and region: "If there are any lies contained within these articles, may I be punished by the Great Shining Deities (*daimyōjin*) of the Ichinomiya, Ninomiya, and Sannomiya of this province, Fuji, Hakusan, and above all else, the Great Bodhisattva Hachiman and the Great Shining Deities of the upper and lower shrines of Suwa." The Ichinomiya, Ninomiya, and Sannomiya refer to the three highest ranked shrines of Kai Province: Asama Shrine, Miwa Shrine, and Tamamuro Shrine, which were all generously patronized by Shingen and his family, as were the deities of the Suwa and Hachiman, the tutelary deity of the Takeda family. The sacred mountains of Fuji and Hakusan, moreover, were both major Shugendō centers which also produced their own *gōo hōin*.

Shingen's oath is also notable as it reveals that oaths of love between warrior elites relied on the same format, language, and pantheon as oaths of military allegiance. Shingen himself demanded hundreds, if not thousands, of similar worded oaths of military loyalty—enforced by the same local pantheon and inscribed on the back of Kumano *goō hōin*—from his vassals.[14] Shingen's love oath, however, was inscribed on a blank sheet of paper, rather than a Kumano talisman. He explains this deviation from standard practice in a postscript that precedes the oath's signature, date, and addressee: "I intended to write this on a *hōin*, but as there were many people staying awake for [Kō]shin, I wrote it on a blank sheet of paper. Because of this, even if I must do so again tomorrow, I will convey this information to you." Shingen explains that he was unable to obtain a Kumano *goō hōin* because of the number of people awake throughout the night observing religious ceremonies, but promises to repeat the oath using a talisman the following day.[15] Shingen's love oath to his young page also documents an inversion of the relations of power that normally define the bond between lord and vassal and reveals that *kishōmon* inscribed on Kumano *goō hōin* were multivalent tools of social power, which could be used to turn the tables on traditional hierarchies of authority and, as in earlier examples of estate residents challenging administrators, allow subordinates to coerce superiors.

Oaths on Kumano talismans were also used by partners within the urban sex trade of seventeenth- and eighteenth-century Japan to establish, enforce, and even subvert bonds of obligation, loyalty, and fidelity. The *Great Mirror of the Erotic Way* (*Shikidō ōkagami* 色道大鏡), a seventeenth-century guide to the customs and etiquette of the sex trade, describes how Kumano talismans were used in what the author describes as "the symbolic act that expresses the fidelity of a man and a woman to each other and their ties of deepest intimacy" (Rogers 1994: 40). The *Great Mirror of the Erotic Way* locates the origin of the lover's vow in the same classical sources of history and law with which we are now familiar: it lists the antecedents in the *Nihon shoki* accounts of "the ordeal by fire and the ordeal by boiling water" in which one was made "to grope about with his hand in boiling water or grasp a broad axe that had been heated in the fire." The sex manual goes on to note, "the style that enjoys universal usage is that of the written oath of the *Goseibai shikimoku*"—the law code of the Kamakura Bakufu quoted earlier, which ends with a standardized divine punishment oath. *The Great Mirror* continues: "An oath written on paper is called an attestation (*kōbun* 告文) because it is an appeal to the gods informing them of a person's innocence [and] contains the language of the covenant, it has been called a vow document (*seijō* 誓状) and a vow paper (*seishi* 誓紙)." The *Great Mirror* specifies that "the paper stock on which the oath is written is principally the paper talismans of Kumano, but the paper talismans of one's tutelary deity can also be used." The guide then lists a number of exemplary courtesans of the past: one who "joined together seven charms from the Nigatsudō and did not use any blank paper"; another who wrote hers on "nine charms from the Three Kumano Shrines," and the most impressive of all, written on the back of "a total of 31 joined pieces: 8 charms from various shines and 23 amulets." The vows are to be sealed in blood, and the author described the best methods in great detail. As with all other official documents, "it is customary to have the name of the house written under the reign title and date, next to the woman's name." And, as in pledges between vassal and lord, such oaths were mutually exchanged. "When, at a man's urging, a courtesan writes out an oath, she in turn requests an oath from him. In some cases, they pledge their troth and compose their oaths together. In other instances, the man writes out his after he has received the woman's." The guide also notes, as in juridical practice, "a man will often have the courtesan burn the oath she wrote and swallow the ashes" (Rogers 1994: 44–7).

The bonds (and conflicts) of loyalty, duty, and love between prostitutes and patrons lie at the heart of the popular culture of the period. Perhaps the most famous of Chikamatsu's puppet plays, *Love Suicide at Amijima* (*Shinjū Ten no Amijima* 心中天網島), written in 1720, tells the tragic tale of Kamiya Jihei 紙屋治兵, an impoverished and married merchant, and Koharu 小春, a prostitute with a heart of gold. The two swear their love for each other on the backs of Kumano talismans, and Jihei pledges to buy her out of her contract with the brothel. But when their bond is discovered, Jihei is forced to renounce his beloved in front of his family. To prove that he will end his relations with Koharu, Jihei agrees to write a second vow, one that overturns his previous oath.

> On a talisman from the Kumano Shrines, Jihei reverses his previous vows of eternal love. Composing a Divine Punishment Vow, he writes, "I promise to sever my relations with and cease thoughts of Koharu. If this is a falsehood, may I be punished by Brahma and Indra and by the Four Great Deva Kings." To this text, in which are enumerated other Buddhas and *kami*, Jihei boldly writes his name and firmly affixes his seal in blood.
>
> (Shively 1953: 79)

Love and war, loyalty and law, property and politics, all required and were empowered by religious documentation. Such documentation was, for more than six hundred years, produced at centers of Shugendō such as Kumano. It was the talismanic presence and punitive power of the deities of these sites that rendered such instruments "legal tender." *Goō hōin* and *kishōmon*, on paper and in practice, show us that religious belief and ritual action are at the core of the social practices that express and enforce all acts of truth and trust, faith and fidelity, duty and devotion, covenant and contract. They suggest that if we are to reposition Shugendō, it should be within the history of social practice: at the intersection of religious culture and juridical procedure, military action and diplomatic form, and economic faith and sexual labor.

Notes

Introduction

1. In 1975, Wakamori Tarō became the chief editor of a monumental research project in eighteen volumes on the most relevant Shugendō groups, which were associated with different mountainous centers localized on the entire territory of the Japanese archipelago. See Wakamori ed. (1975–84).
2. Murayama Shūichi was one of the first Japanese scholars who took into account the relationships between Shugendō and Onmyōdō (The Way of Yin and Yang). See Murayama (1997).
3. Suzuki Shōei wrote about the interactions between *sendatsushū* and Daigoji Sanbōin in the three seminal articles: "Tōzan-ha no kyōdan keisei" 当山派の教団形成 published in 1964 (now in Suzuki 2003 vol. 1, 184–135), "Tōzan sendatsushū to Daigoji Sanbōin" 当山先達衆と醍醐寺三宝院 published in 1965 (now in Suzuki 2003 vol. 1, 136–235), and "Tōzan sendatsushū Yamato Matsuodera no Shugendō" 当山先達衆大和松尾寺の修験道 published in 1977 (now in Suzuki 2003 vol. 1, 236–67).
4. Kuroda Toshio focused on the genesis of Shugendō in the article "Hakusan shinkō" 白山信仰 published in 1981 (now in Kuroda 1995 vol. 3, 242–310).
5. Nagamatsu Atsushi demonstrated that in the Edo period the alleged opposition between agricultural and hunting communities was less marked because hunters were also used to cultivate lands in conjunction with hunting activities. See Nagamatsu (2005).
6. Kuroda Toshio mentioned the role of Shugendō within the Buddhist exo-esoteric system in the article "Mikkyō taisei ron to Nihon shūkyōshi ron" 密教体制論と日本宗教史論 published in 1990 (now in Kuroda 1995 vol. 2, 325–340) and in another article of the same year "Bukkyō kakushin undō no rekishiteki seikaku" 仏教革新運動の歴史的性格 (now in Kuroda 1995 vol. 2, 232–83).
7. For an excellent overview of the new trends in Shugendō studies, see Tokieda, Hasegawa, Hayashi (2015).
8. For the original text, see *Nihon sandai jitsuroku*, in *Kokushi taikei* (revised edition) vol. 8: 234.
9. Heather Blair underlines that early textual evidence of the link between *yamabushi* practices and mountainous landscapes can be already detected in a passage of the *Shinsarugakuki* (eleventh century). See Blair (2015: 273–4).
10. In a different perspective, Pfoundes also inaugurates a small lineage of Western practitioners *cum* researchers, each with their own idiosyncrasies, who get ordained in a *shugen* tradition in Japan, and often set up their own site of practice in their respective countries (e.g. Sylvain Guintard in France, John M. Evans in the UK, Neville G. Pemchekov Warwick and V. K. Leary in California, etc.).
11. For a different aspect of Shugendō material culture, see Jonathan Thumas's enquiry into the history of *horagai* 法螺貝, the conch shells that are perhaps the most recognizable feature of *yamabushi* equipment (Thumas 2016).

12 Both volumes are composed of chapters translated from diverse articles and lectures; hence, they lack a truly comprehensive character.
13 See, for instance, Helena Blavatsky (1890: 301), Tokuzawa (1896: 421–2).
14 For recent research on *nyonin kinsei* in English, see Lindsey (2015 and 2016), mentioned earlier in the introduction.
15 In a similar vein, Bernard Faure had already underscored that a serious study of gender differences in religious traditions cannot set aside other fundamental elements of social distinction between male and female agencies, such as social class, race, and age, according to which there is a constant renegotiation of gender discourses (Faure 2003: 10).
16 Perhaps the most famous illustration of this association is the Nō play *Ataka* 安宅, in which Minamoto no Yoshitsune 源義経 (1159–89) flees the capital disguised as a *yamabushi* and is saved from arrest by his vassal Benkei 弁慶 (1155–89).
17 For examples of thorough comments on two important Edo period documents, see Bouchy (1993) (*En no Gyōja hongi* 役行者本紀), Klonos (2019) (*Konohagoromo* 木羽衣). For an example of an annotated translation, see Swanson (1999) (*Bussetsu sanshin juryō muhen kyō* 仏説三身寿量無辺経), Roth (2014) (*Shozan engi* 諸山縁起).

Chapter 1

1 "With the abolition of all mixed elements from shrines large and small throughout the nation, it is required that those called *bettō* 別当 or *shasō* 社僧 be known as *kannushi* 神主 and *shajin* 社人, giving up Buddhism and making Shinto their occupation." Dajōkan 280 (Keiō 4. int. 4.4 [May 25, 1868]). This was the clarification of kami–buddha admixture, not necessarily the "separation" of kami and buddhas.
2 According to the Cabinet Statistics Bureau in 1930, the population of Japan in 1868 was 34,806,000. If the male population was around 17 million, then at the beginning of the Meiji period approximately one in ten males must have been a *yamabushi*. In the survey on Japanese religion conducted by the Agency for Cultural Affairs (2013), shrine priests affiliated to the Jinja Honchō (Association of Shinto Shrines) alone numbered 21,690 and the total number of shrines was 78,954. Incidentally, Buddhist priests at present number 220,000.
3 Fenollosa studied philosophy at Harvard University and after graduating entered the art school recently established by the Boston Museum of Fine Arts. He was appointed by the Meiji government in 1878 to teach at the Imperial University of Tokyo. He created a large collection of Japanese art and in his travels around the country experienced firsthand the effects of the destruction of Buddhist temples and sacred objects. From 1881 he began working to preserve Japanese art and in 1884 went to Nara and conducted the first proper survey of the Yumedono 夢殿 at Hōryūji 法隆寺.
4 An order from the Council of State to Honganji and other head temples dated June 22, 1868, states that the government's action aimed at reestablishing the Jingikan and clarifying kami and buddhas; the court had no intention of destroying Buddhism. The word used here for *haibutsu* was 排仏 (exclude Buddhism) not the more commonly used 廃仏 (abolish and destroy Buddhism). This order was issued to quell false rumors that Buddhism was to be banned.

5 For the anti-Buddhist critique (*haibutsuron*), see Klautau (2008: 269–70; 2012: 191–6). The nativist scholar Hirata Atsutane actively developed it, and his school was continued by the ethnologist and folklorist Yanagita Kunio.

6 Adachi is known as the person who introduced Ishida Baigan's Shingaku 心学 to the modern readership. He worked as chief editor for Nihon kōdōkai 日本弘道会 between 1904 and 1918.

7 Here, Adachi saw *shūgō* as deriving from the theory of *honji suijaku*. Yoshida Kanetomo divided Shinto into his own original *genpon sōgen shinto* 元本宗源神道, that is, Yoshida Shinto, and two less original forms, *honjaku engi no shintō* 本迹縁起神道 (Shinto in which kami are avatars of Buddhist deities) and *ryōbu shūgō no shintō* 両部習合神道 (Ise Shinto based on Esoteric Buddhism). At that point, the influence of Buddhism was very strong, and it was in that sense that *shūgō* was used.

8 *Shigaku zasshi*, nos. 1, 4, 5, 8, 9, 12 (1907).

9 The concept of "religion" that lay behind this dichotomy had taken root in Japan by then.

10 The first mention of a New Year's shrine or temple visit (*hatsumōde*) to Kawasaki Daishi appeared in an article on railways in the *Tōkyō nichinichi shinbun* of January 2, 1885 (Hirayama 2015: 28).

11 In the prewar period, Meiji Jingū gradually strengthened its connection with Ise Jingū.

12 The Japan Youth Hall featured performances of regional folk dances and folk songs in its inauguration celebrations. It was the first time that local youth associations had been invited to Tokyo to perform. In the postwar period, this grew into the National Convention of Folk Performing Arts (*Zenkoku minzoku geinō taikai*) (Suzuki 2015: 24–43).

13 The first use of the term *Bukkyō darakuron* 仏教堕落論 (Corruption of Buddhism) to describe this discourse appears in Tamamuro (1971: 1).

14 Orikuchi Shinobu 折口信夫 (1887–1953) formed the Folklore Society following the closure of the journal *Minzoku* and edited its journal *Minzokugaku* 民俗学 (1929–33), while also contributing to the journal *Minzoku geijutsu* 民俗藝術 (1928–32). Yanagita Kunio's main works *Minkan denshōron* 民間伝承論 (1934) and *Kyōdo seikatsu no kenkyūhō* 郷土生活の研究法 (1935) were published subsequently.

15 Oka Shoin published important works on ethnology, folklore, mythology, linguistics, and archaeology by authors such as Torii Ryūzō (1870–1953), Takagi Toshio (1876–1922), Matsuoka Shizuo (1878–1936), Minakata Kumagusu (1876–1941), Kon Wajirō (1888–1973), Shinmura Izuru (1876–1967), Hamada Kōsaku (1881–1938), Kiyono Kenji (1885–1955), Fujita Toyohachi (1869–1929), and Hasebe Kotondo (1882–1969). In the field of ethnography, it published Minakata Kumagusu's *Minakata zuihitsu* (1929), Yanagita Kunio's *Yukiguni no haru* (1928), and *Hanamatsuri* (1930) by Hayakawa Kōtarō (1889–1956), as well as translations of works by Augustus Pitt Rivers (1827–1900) and Ferdinand de Saussure (1857–1913).

16 For Gorai Shigeru, *shinbutsu shūgō* was not a combination of Shinto and Buddhism as equals but "a historical process whereby Buddhism was absorbed into the fundamental culture and came to be accepted by the common people (*jōmin* 常民)," a position that helps us understand what that fundamental culture was (Gorai 2007b: 145). This is a productive suggestion.

17 In recent years, Japanese scholars have extended the concept of *shinbutsu shūgō* to Asia as a whole in an attempt to discuss Japan in comparison with other countries (Yoshida 1996: 30–35). However, *shinbutsu shūgō* is a modern Japanese concept,

a mere interpretation of ancient, medieval, and early modern discourses. Finding similar examples in China, the Korean peninsula, and Vietnam and drawing comparisons can be considered an irrational line of argument, since it ignores place, time, and context. It dilutes cross-cultural understanding and the awareness of historical change, regional diversity, and the multidimensional relationship between kami and buddhas. To translate *shūgō* as "syncretism" is a mistranslation.

18 Founders often had the terms *yori* (possessed) or *waka* (youth) in their names, such as Ariyori in Tateyama and Yorimichi at Hōki Daisen. Yanagita Kunio argued that names like "Toranni" and "Tora" were general appellations of female shamans who were believed to have broken the prohibition against female access and climbed the mountain.

19 According to *Jōgū Shōtoku hōō teisetsu* (a biography of Shōtoku Taishi) and *Gangōji garan engi narabini ruki shizaichō* (History of Gangōji temple and catalog of its possessions), the date of the transmission was the year of the horse, earth-*yang* (*tsuchinoe-uma*) of Kinmei's reign. This year of the sexagenary cycle did not, however, occur during Kinmei's reign, but the year before (538). The date 552 (Kinmei 13) appears in the *Nihon shoki*.

20 Monmu reigned in the years 697–707, before the move to Nara (Heijōkyō). He was the grandson of Tenmu (r. 673–86) and Jitō (r. 686–97), and the oldest son of Crown Prince Kusakabe (662–89). The Taihō Code was promulgated during his reign (701). He was followed as sovereign by his mother Genmei (r. 707–15), Kusakabe's consort. During her reign the capital was moved from Fujiwarakyō (710). She was succeeded by her daughter Genshō (r. 715–24) and her grandson Shōmu (r. 724–49).

21 Of the gazetteers, the *Harima fudoki* commemorated the 1300th anniversary of its compilation in 2015 and the *Hitachi fudoki* in 2013. There was no commemoration for the *Izumo, Hizen,* and *Bungo fudoki*.

22 The year 2020 will be the 1300th anniversary of the compilation of the *Nihon shoki* (Yoshida 2016).

23 Following advances in mountain archeology, sites on Mt. Nantai, Sanjōgatake, Misen, Mt. Hōman, and other mountains have been excavated. The anecdote about the surveyor Shibazaki Yoshitarō discovering a *shakujō* (monk's staff) on Tsurugidake in 1907 is well known. Scientific analysis dates it to the Heian period, not as far back as the Nara period.

24 People from Etchū 越中 province secluded themselves in the Tamadono cave and those from outside the province did so in the Kokūzō cave.

25 The seventh century was the time of the final stage of *kofun* construction. The paintings on the walls of the late-seventh-century/early-eighth-century Takamatsuzuka *kofun* imitate the Goguryeo style of Korea. According to an interpretation, that tomb was built for Prince Osakabe (d. 705), a son of the Emperor Tenmu who had inaugurated the Korean style.

26 The *Honchō Hokke genki* (本朝法華験記, 1040) records cases of Lotus practitioners (*jikyōsha* 持経者) in the mountains of Kumano throwing themselves off cliffs to their deaths or burning themselves to death.

27 The *gumonjihō* is associated with the bodhisattva Kokūzō 虚空蔵菩薩 (Skt. Ākāśagarbha), and it is surely no coincidence that so many mountains in Japan bear this name.

28 Gyōki was the only known person to have been punished according to the regulations of the Sōniryō of 701.

29 Hinata Yakushi (Hinatasan Ryōzenji) in Sagami is an ancient temple whose main image is one of Yakushi carved in the *natabori* method, which retains round chisel marks in the completed work. Gyōki is considered to have "opened" the mountain in 716; a bell inscription dated 1340 and an entry on the temple in the *Azuma kagami* date its foundation at least back to the Kamakura period. Other mountain temples associated with Gyōki as founder include Unzendake in Kyushu (701), Nokogiriyama in Chiba prefecture (725), and Takaosan (744) and Jakushōji in Yamagata prefecture (708). Some six hundred temples in Japan claim Gyōki as their founder.

30 A post mountain-entry ritual tablet (*hiden* 碑伝) at Mt. Hasuge (Sagami) records that in 1291 a *nagatokoshū* from Hongū in Kumano completed the Autumn Peak mountain-entry ritual (Atsugi-shi hishobu shishi hensan, ed. 1999: 979–80). According to the *Kōshōji saikō kanjinchō* (1419), the founder was Gyōki, but according to the *Sagami no kuni Hasugesan engi* (1786), it was En no Gyōja who founded the temple in 703.

31 An entry about En no Gyōja appears in the *Shosan engi* (late twelfth century). In his *Gōki* (*Gozōnutsu narabini shinbitsu gokyō kuyōbu ruiki*), Ōe no Masafusa (1041–1111), who traveled with retired emperor Shirakawa (1053–1129) on his pilgrimage to Kinpusen in 1092, mentioned the active participation of a monk trained in *shugen* and a ritual at a spot where sutras were buried, known as the site of En no Gyōja's practice. See Kawasaki (2016: 69) and Blair (2015).

32 "If we ask the origin of *yamabushi* practice, it began with the activities of En no Gyōja": *Shijū hyaku innenshū* (1257).

33 En no Gyōja statue at Shikkakuzan Enrakuji (former Gosha Gongen), Kōfu, Yamanashi Prefecture. This was a center of Shugendō activity in Kai province. An inscription about repairs placed inside the statue is dated 1309. The *Kai kokushi* (1814) says that it was placed in the En no Gyōja Hall at the second stage of Mt. Fuji, which was under the administration of Enrakuji.

34 Its earliest appearance is in the *Nihon sandai jitsuroku*, Jōkan 10 [868] 7.9 in an entry evaluating the powers of an esoteric monk (*genja* 験者): "A *shamon* called Dōju entered into the mountains of Yoshino in Yamato province as a young man and is still there. The emperor heard that he had miraculous powers (*shugen*)."

35 *Konjaku monogatarishū* vol. 11, 3, "How En no Ubasoku recited spells and employed demonic deities" (Ury 1979: 82–83).

36 Themes for future research are how to deal with the ambiguity of the definition of Shugendō and how to separate chronologically *yamabushi* and *shugen*/Shugendō.

37 Published by Oka Shoin, whose editor, Oka Shigeru, the elder brother of Oka Masao, was also involved with the publication of the journal *Minzoku*. Oka Shoin published a large number of important works on ethnology, folklore studies, mythology, linguistics, and archaeology.

38 His main theoretical works were *Shūkyōgaku* (The Study of Religions, 1931), *Shūkyōgaku no shijitsu to riron* (History and Theory of the Study of Religions, 1931), *Minzoku seishin no shūkyōmen* (Religious Aspect of the Ethnic Spirit, 1935), and *Shūkyōgaku tsūron* (General Theory of the Study of Religions, 1943).

39 Akamatsu Chijō, who had studied in Europe and the United States at the same time as Uno, became active in Korean studies on his return to Japan. He was appointed to the Religious Studies Seminar at the Seoul Imperial University (which started in 1926) and later returned to Japan and took Uno's place as a professor at the Institute of Oriental Culture, severing his connections with the colonial administration. After Uno, ethnology of religion was continued by Sugiura Ken'ichi (1905–54) and Tanase

Jōji (1910–64), based on the twin pillars of theory and fieldwork, and later modified by Furuno Kiyoto (1899–1979) and Sasaki Kōnan (b. 1930) as the anthropology of religion.

40 Kume used the words *jinshu* 人種 (race) and *minzoku* 民族 (ethnic group) once each. Before that, in his *Bunmeiron no gairaku* (An Outline of the Theory of Civilisation, 1875), Fukuzawa Yūkichi 福沢諭吉 (1834–1901) used *kokutai* 国体 to translate "nationality", based on J. S. Mills's *Considerations of Representative Government* (1861). He also used *shuzoku* 種族, but not *minzoku*.

41 During fourteen years of exile in Japan after 1898, the Chinese journalist and reformer Liang Qichao (梁啓超, 1873–1929) became familiar with the term *minzoku*; its spread in China is thought to date from 1899. It may be presumed that *minzoku* was in general use at that period (Yokoyama 1989: 265).

42 In two lectures, "Jinshu tetsugaku kōgai" (Outline of the Philosophy of Race, 1904) and "Kōkaron kōgai" (Outline of the Idea of Yellow Peril, 1903), Mori Ōgai used the terms *Rasse* (*jinshu* 人種) and *shuzoku* 種族. Even Yanagida Kunio, who tended to use *jinshu* and *minzoku* interchangeably, defined "different race" (*iminzoku* 異民族) as black people.

43 Abe Jirō 阿部次郎 (1883–1959), a Taishō-period intellectual, used the expressions *minzokuteki kyōyō* 民族的教養 (ethnic education) and *minzokuteki jikaku* 民族的自覚 (ethnic awareness) in his 1922 book *Jinkakushugi* 人格主義 (Personalism) (Abe Jirō 1961: 429).

44 Uno studied under Wilhelm Schmidt, who taught the theory of "Kulturkreis" in Vienna, and is said to have introduced Oka Masao to him when Oka went to study in Germany.

45 He translated "Volk" (in the singular) as *waga minzoku* (our ethnic group) and "Völker" (in the plural) as *ōku no minzoku* (many ethnic groups). He also translated "Volkskunde" as *minzokugaku* 民族学 (ethnology).

46 For example, Yanagita Kunio, Oka Masao, Uno Enkū, Minakata Kumagusu, and Orikuchi Shinobu. Publications included: Iha Fuyū, "Nantō kodai no sōgi", *Minzoku* 2, 5 (1926), Oka Masao, "Ijin sono ta", *Minzoku* 3-6 (1928) and Orikuchi Shinobu, "Tokoyo oyobi marebito", *Minzoku* 4-2 (1929).

47 Published by Bukkyō jihōsha as Volume 3 of the monograph series *Bukkyō shinkō sōsho*.

48 In 1930, the Nakazai-ke *hanamatsuri* from Hongō-chō (Tōei-chō) in Aichi Prefecture was invited to the celebrations marking the completion of the structure built by the industrialist Shibusawa Keizō, an enthusiastic student of folklore, at his residence in Mita Tsunamachi (Tokyo) to house his collection of folk articles. Those associated with Shibusawa's "commoners' scholarship" (*minkangaku* 民間学) came in large numbers to watch it. In 1935, Shibusawa and Uno Enkū took Wilhelm Schmidt, then visiting Japan, to see the *hanamatsuri in situ* (Suzuki 2010: 170–82).

49 The official designation of this society is now the Japanese Society of Cultural Anthropology (changed April 1, 2004).

50 Yanagita Kunio distanced himself from the journal *Minzoku*. There was discord between him and Oka Masao, and he felt envy toward Orikuchi Shinobu over his theory of *marebito*. At that time Yanagita referred to ethnology (*minzokugaku*) as the "*minzokugaku* of folklore," and used expressions such as "the conflict between the study of *minzokugaku* 民俗学 and folklore" (*Kyōdo kenkyū no shōrai*, 1931), not differentiating between ethnology 民族学 and folklore 民俗学. Subsequently, he addressed this when he corrected the definition in his book *Kokushi to minzokugaku*

国史と民俗学 (1944). The definition *minzokugaku* 民族学 = folklore studies was established in his *Minkan denshōron* 民間伝承論 (1934) and *Kyōdo seikatsu no kenkyūhō* 郷土生活の研究法 (1935). This is confirmed by the questionnaire items in the Survey of Mountain Villages (1934–36).

51 Republished in Tōyō bunkō (Heibonsha) in 1972. According to some accounts the book was first published in 1942, but the correct date is January 1943.

52 There is a large number of articles reviewing the book. For an overview, see Miyake (1982).

53 It was also thought of as a martial art linked to Bushidō.

54 Hans Naumann, *Grundzüge der Deutsche Volkskunde*, Leipzig: Quelle & Meyer, 1922. Gorai Shigeru, too, used the expression "fundamental culture" many times. Some mutual influence can be presumed. Naumann, however, is known for his fascist tendencies.

55 Hiking, from the English Boy Scout movement, and *Wandervogel*, from Germany, were introduced as ways to cultivate "civic spirit" and led to a boom in walking trips in the 1930s. Mountain climbing as a mass phenomenon was used by the public authority (Takaoka 1993: 17–23).

56 Born in 1906. In the postwar period, he was a professor at Tokushima University, Kobe University, and Kobe Women's University.

57 The Law for National Economic Mobilization (*kokka sōdōinhō*) and the Electricity Management Law (*denryoku kanrihō*) were promulgated in 1938; the National Service Draft Ordinance (*kokumin chōyōrei*), the Rice Distribution Control Law (*beikoku haikyū tōseihō*), the Wages Regulation Ordinance (*chingin tōseirei*) and the Land Rent Control Ordinance (*chidai yachin tōseirei*) in 1939; the Ordinance Controlling Basic Necessities (*seikatsu hitsuju busshi tōseihō*) and the Agricultural Production Control Ordinance (*nōgyō seisan tōseirei*) in 1941; and the Food Management Law (*shokuryō kanrihō*) and the Bank of Japan Law (*Nihon ginkōhō*) in 1942. With the creation of the Ministry of Munitions from 1943, there was growing integration of the consumer goods industry and a strengthening of control over private enterprise. It was a time when the state had precedence. The textile and publishing industries were also strictly controlled. The import of wood pulp was capped and domestic pulp was diverted to making bullets and other munitions purposes. There was no provision for publishing books.

58 After the war, he published *Shinbutsu shūgō shichō* (Heirakuji shoten, 1957) and *Yamabushi no rekishi* (Hanawa shobō 1970).

59 This was based on a series of lectures given at the Imperial University of Tokyo from June 26, 1941. Many of the attendees were science students. Yanagita also gave a lecture entitled "Shinto and Folklore Studies" on July 5 the same year at the Jinja Seishin Bunka Kenkyūjo.

60 There is a continuity between these works and works the two authors published after the war: Yanagita Kunio, *Senzo no hanashi* (Chikuma Shobō 1946; About the Ancestors) and Matsudaira Narimitsu, *Matsuri: honshitsu to shosō* (Nikkō shoin 1946).

61 The influence of the "Japanese spirit" is also apparent in the names of the various publishing companies associated with these works: Murakami published *Shugendō no hattatsu* with Unebi Shobō 畝傍書房, Uno republished *Shūkyō minzokugaku* with Yaesu Shobō, and Matsudaira published *Matsuri* with Nikkō Shoin.

62 This idea of national spirit goes back to the Imperial Rescript *Kokumin seishin sakkō shōsho* of November 10, 1923, following the Kantō Earthquake. It sought to deal with

the growing organization and influence of popular movements that had emerged out of the Rice Riots of 1918—the rise of individualism, democracy, and socialism. Its overall purpose was to promote and strengthen the national spirit in order to quell social unrest after the earthquake.

63 The Japanese spirit is "the living spirit that strives with all its might to make Japan a truly good country both at an individual and a state level, through true love of country and combining nationalism and internationalism" (Tosaka 1979: 289–90).

64 On Gorai, see also Ōmi (2016: 232).

65 An advisory body of the Ministry of Education, the Committee to Investigate the Problem of Student Thought (Gakusei shisō mondai chōsa iinkai, instituted in 1931) advised to take measures against left-leaning students by "setting up a powerful research facility whose purpose was to make clear the principles of our national polity and national spirit, promote national culture, criticise foreign thought, and build a body of theory sufficient to combat Marxism." This was the basis upon which the institute was established.

66 Controversy had risen in 1935 over the theory of the emperor as an organ of the state, as put forward by Minobe Tatsukichi, a professor of law at the University of Tokyo. In response to it, the government declared "clear evidence of the national polity" (kokutai meichō) and the Ministry of Education compiled *Kokutai no hongi* as a teaching material about *kokutai*. It asked what kind of country Japan was, and began with a discussion of the "unbroken imperial line." It is said that Shida Nobuyoshi (1906–2003), a scholar of Japanese literature, wrote it with the help of other scholars.

67 He was a professor at the Nishōgakusha Senmon Gakkō, a vocational school in Tokyo teaching classical and modern Japanese language, from 1939, and became an assistant at the institute the same year.

68 For a discussion of his *Nihon bukkyōshiron* (Meguro shoten, 1940) and *Nihon jōdai bunka to bukkyō* (Hōzōkan, 1940), see Matsuoka (2010).

69 *Indo minzokuron–Sensō bunka sōsho* (Ajia mondai kenkyūjo 1940). He coauthored *Tōa shūkyō no kadai–Daitōa bunka kensetsu kenkyū* (Kokumin seishin bunka kenkyūjo 1942) with Masuda Fukutarō. Masuda is known for his *Taiwan no shūkyō: nōson o chūshin to suru shūkyō kenkyū* (Yōkentō 1939).

70 Hori Ichiro, *Folk Religion in Japan: Continuity and Change*, edited by Joseph M. Kitagawa and Alan L. Miller (Chicago: University of Chicago Press, 1983). The book has a number of problems.

71 For Gorai's theories, see Hayashi (2008) and Ōmi (2007, 2016).

72 Wakamori Tarō also spoke of the purpose of folklore studies as a clarification of "Ethnos."

73 "Ethnic religion" refers to a religion grounded in a particular ethnic group or community that does not extend beyond its boundaries. Examples are Hinduism, Shinto, and Judaism. Hinduism though is not based on a specific ethnic group and its content is complex. The concept of ethnic group is vague yet it continues to circulate. A "world religion" is one that transcends the framework of ethnic group, state, or community and has expanded all over the world. Examples include Christianity, Islam, and Buddhism. It is also referred to as a "universal religion." The term was coined in German as *Weltreligion* in an article entitled "Von der Landesreligion und der Weltreligion" (On the Religion of a Country and the Religions of the World), published in 1827 by a Catholic priest and theologian, Johann Sebastian von Drey. The English translation of "world religion" was used by J. Estlin Carpenter in

1877 when he translated C. P. Tiele's *Geschiedenis van den godsdienst, tot aan de heerschappij der werldgodsdiensten* (Outline of the History of Religion: To the Spread of the Universal Religions), and it became widely accepted. Gustav Mensching's *Die Religion: Erscheinungsformen, Strukturtypen und Lebensgesetze* (1959, translated in English as *Structure and Patterns of Religion*) argued that "we investigate the historical circumstances of some religions which are confined to a single ethnic group and which we term ethnic religions, and others which have spread among many people and are called world religions. The difference inherent among historical religions does not concern geographic diffusion alone. Rather it is based on a deeper structural differentiation of religion itself" (Mensching 1976: 45). Ethnic religions seek the happiness and stability of the community while world religions seek the salvation of the individual and how to overcome tribulation. A move from ethnic to world religion is seen here as a historical inevitability.

74 When people can travel by car to the fifth or seventh stages (out of ten) of the mountain, the meaning of a pilgrimage path is lost and the consciousness of making a pilgrimage is greatly changed. Changes in confraternities have accelerated with each generation.

75 Gowland, also known as the father of Japanese archaeology, popularized the term "Japanese Alps." Sir Rutherford Alcock climbed Mt. Fuji in 1860. See Takeya (2011).

76 Besides being a place for people of all ages to enjoy themselves, mountains have seen the presence of the "*yama* girl" ("a young urban woman who enjoys doing outdoor activities in her free time, but wants to look good while doing so") since 2009–10. A topic worth consideration is that mountain climbing is popular only in relatively few countries (the UK, Germany, Italy, Korea and Japan, to name some).

77 On May 5, 2017, the International Council on Monuments and Sites (ICOMOS) recommended to the Japanese government the registration of Okinoshima as a world heritage site. However, it excluded certain areas that the government had included, notably the *yōhaisho* (the site where worship from afar of the sacred island took place) since it was distant from the island and not deemed to have global value. After remonstrations were made, the UNESCO committee turned down the ICOMOS advice and included all the excluded sites. Okinoshima was added to the world heritage list in July 2017. It was difficult from a European perspective to include sites that could not physically be seen.

78 Regarding intangible cultural heritage, there have been significant changes since the Proclamation of Masterpieces of the Oral and Intangible Heritage of Humanity 2001–2005. Beginning with the proclamation of 2001, and with the coming into effect of the Convention for the Safeguarding of the Intangible Cultural (2003) in 2006, the range of activities eligible for listing has broadened considerably to include music, dance, theatre, customs, rituals, festivals, handicrafts, and cultural spaces. In Japan, Hayachine kagura, *washi* (Japanese paper), Japanese food, and decorative festival floats have been listed. In 2018 efforts are continuing to have visiting deities (*raihōshin*) listed. There is a possibility that *kagura* will also be listed in the near future.

79 The participation of local authorities has increased with the association of the festivities with sports events such as the National Sports Festival.

80 Japanese language website: "Mt. Daisen 1300 Years of History Festival" website (Festival Committee, Yonego) http://www.daisen1300.org.

81 English language website: https://www.daisen1300.org/user/common/pdf/pamphlet_en.pdf.

82 English language website (Natadera): http://www.natadera.com/EN/.
83 Japanese language website (Hakusan city): http//hakusan1300.info.
84 Japanese language website (Shirayamahime Shrine): http://www.shirayama.or.jp/news/year1300.html.
85 Ecoparks and geoparks are a UNESCO designation.
86 This article is a companion piece to Suzuki Masataka, *Sangaku shinkō: Nihon bunka no kontei o saguru* (Tokyo: Chūō Kōronsha, 2015). I have taken a more theoretical approach here than in the book. The present chapter is inspired by Mabuchi Tōichi, "Toward the Reconstruction of Ryukyuan Cosmology" (1968).

Chapter 2

1 For a discussion and contextualization of Shozan engi, see Kawasaki (2004), Kawasaki and Chikamoto (2005), and Roth (2014).
2 Depending on time periods and Buddhist branches, the title 和尚 can be pronounced *kashō*, *wajō*, or *oshō*. In general, the Tendai and Kegon schools use *kashō*, the others *wajō* or *oshō*. In this case, since Nin'ei's affiliation is unclear, I chose to use *wajō*, whereas in the case of Sōō, a Tendai monk, I use *kashō*.
3 Dictionaries and encyclopedias generally report *sendatsu* and not *sendachi*. There is no actual difference in meaning between the two, and both pronunciations are attested in the medieval period. Because the *Nippo jisho* 日葡辞書 (*Japanese-Portuguese Dictionary*) compiled by Jesuit missionaries bears *sendachi*, it appears that in the Sengoku period, the latter was preferred. In the Edo period, *sendatsu* clearly prevails. In medieval documents pertaining to the Kumano shrines, several documents show *furigana* explicating the reading as *sendachi*, so it seems that in the context of medieval Kumano beliefs and Shugendō vocabulary, the pronunciation *sendachi* was consciously used.

Chapter 3

1 The scholarship of Marylin Ivy, Carol Gluck, George Figal, and others have dealt at length with the twentieth-century rise of these ideas through figures like Yanagita Kunio and Yanagi Sōetsu.
2 Susan Burns, Mark McNally, Peter Nosco, and others have written extensively on these movements.
3 For representative scholarship on Jōin, see Sonehara's various works (collected in a recent volume, 2018), Bodiford (2007), and Carter (2018).
4 As examples from other regional peaks, see Ambros (2008: 34) on his appearance at Ōyama in the *Ōyamadera engi* (1532); Thal (2005: 67) on mention of him in respect to Mount Zōzu (now Mount Kotohira) in the mountain's seventeenth-century origin account *Sanshū michi Zōzusan engi* (*c.*1656).
5 The texts, the *Shugen sanjūsan tsūki* (Thirty-three transmissions of Shugen-[dō]) and the *Sanbu sōjō hossoku mikki* (Secret record of the transmissions and regulations concerning the Three Peaks [practice]), became especially influential with their inclusion in the *Shugen gosho*.

6 The original manuscript of the *Shugen mondō* was lost to a fire in 1942, but a transcription from 1931 exists.
7 See: *Sanbu sōjō hossoku mikki*, 488.
8 Extant registers of "treasured possessions" (*hōmotsu* 寶物) of the three main temples reveal that each held a pair of the statues.
9 This language was reinterpreted in the *Togakushisan Kenkōji ruki* (1458) as a proper name (Gakumon Gyōja) with one change from *mon* 問 to *mon* 門.
10 For example, see Miyake's (2001a) chapter devoted to Daoist influences in Shugendō.
11 As one example, Jōin cites the *Shengxuan jing* 昇玄經 (non-extant) but seems to be borrowing from Falin's 法琳 *Poxie lun* 破邪論, which quotes the same passage from the *Shengxuan jing*.

Chapter 4

1 *Gyokuteki inken* (Shiseki kenkyūkai 1985). Its date and author are unknown, but from the cut-off date it can perhaps be placed at the late seventeenth century. The episode about Otake, entitled "Strange incident concerning the Buddhist power of the servant Take," is contained in vol. 10, in the section dealing with the Kan'ei era (1624–43). This episode is quoted by Yamazaki Yoshishige (1797–1856?) in his *Kairoku* (1820–37). The description of the triad suggests a slight similarity with the *osugata* of the Zenkōji Amida triad featuring Honda Yoshimitsu and his wife kneeling before it.
2 For example, in Hashimoto Sadahide's print in the *Kōtei Onna Kagami* series (*c.*1843–6) "Takejo" later left Edo and went to do religious training at Yudonosan (Edo Tokyo Hakubutsukan collection), and in the *Otake Dainichi Nyorai osanai emaki* (*c.*1815) she is said to have been born at the foot of Yudonosan, a child granted by Dainichi (Ideha Bunka Kinenkan, Togawa Archive).
3 See *Kojidan*: 303–4. For the *Senjūshō* version and its relation to the Noh play *Eguchi*, see Tyler (1992: 68–70).
4 *Ogen Otake Dainichi Nyorai ryaku engi* (1777) Hinoto tori shichigatsu (seventh month) (Togawa 2005: 264–6). Pamphlet *Ushū Hagurosan Koganedō Otake Dainichi Nyorai ryaku engi* (Yamagata Museum No. 5C000566).
5 This *engi* was presented at a gathering organized by Kyokutei Bakin (1767–1848) in the third month of 1825 by Yamazaki Yoshishige, and appeared in volume 3 of Bakin's *Toen shōsetsu*. It is also mentioned in the *Dōchō tosetsu* of Ōsato Shinsai which records events from 1825 to 1830. It may well have been used in the 1812 *kaichō* too, since there is no evidence Genryōbō composed a separate one (unless it was the "*engi* in poor condition" reproduced in 1849).
6 *Shin Chomonjū* (1749), a *setsuwa* collection of 377 tales (8 vols.) attributed to Kamiya Yōyūken (*Shinchō monjū*: 389–90). "Sakuma no Take Ōgonkyū no shōzu" (Ōjōhen).
7 *Dewa Sanzan shiryōshū* vol. 3 (2000: 841–53).
8 Ibid., 843.
9 *Otake Dainichi Nyorai engi emaki* (3 vols.) 1849. Shozen'in. Roll 3 section 2. Text by Kurokawa Harumaru (1799–1867), Edo *kokugakusha* and poet, illustrations by Kita Busei (1776–1857), his son Kita Buichi (active 1817, 1849), Yamazaki Tomoo (1798–1861) and six others. It is now in the possession of Shōzen'in, the administrative temple of Haguro Shugendō, which took over responsibility for the Otake Dainichidō

from Genryōbō in the 1870s. The scroll has been digitized by Nichibunken http://www.nichibun.ac.jp/graphicversion/dbase/otake/index.html.

10 *Otake Dainichi Nyorai engi narabi mizu nagashi ita no yuraiki*. Handwritten copy, undated. Togawa Archive, Ideha Bunka Kinenkan no. 5–26. May have been copied by Togawa Anshō when he visited Shinkōin in 1920 (Togawa 2005: 260).

11 *Ogen Otake monogatari*. Novel, published 1849. Text by Gyokutei Senryū, illustrations by Kuniyoshi. Illustration of the drainboard (*nagashi*): "Hagurosan Genryōbō, precious object, Otake Dainichi's drainboard", p. 2 verso. An illustration of the three mountains (p. 1 recto) shows them inside a frame that suggests a tray or drainboard. Original in the possession of Kongōjuin, Tōge, copy in the Ideha Bunka Kinenkan. Another original in the Mitsuoka Bunko, Sakata, digitized by the National Institute of Japanese Literature (340–1).

12 Zentokuji, another former branch temple of Zōjōji located in Asakusa, also lays claim to Otake. It was the funerary temple of the Magome family, the *nanushi* of Ōdenmachō, who took responsibility for the memorialization of the Sakuma family after it died out in 1698. Perhaps some graves, including Otake's, were moved from Shinkōin at this time. Yamazaki Yoshishige describes the gravesite in his Kairoku, noting it was surmounted, as today in Zentokuji's postwar location, by a statue of Nyoirin Kannon.

13 For details of Nishikawa Sugao and the implementation of the "clarification" policy at Hagurosan, see Sekimori (2005: 197–234).

14 Shōzen'in possesses an apron, a drainboard section, and a cloth bag said to have belonged to Otake. These Genryōbō had displayed in 1849. They have been exhibited in recent times at Itabashi Kuritsu Kyōdo Shiryōkan (1992) and Ideha Bunka Kinenkan (2016). Photographs appear on the Nichibunken website: http://www.nichibun.ac.jp/graphicversion/dbase/otake/data/data01/index.html.

15 *Otake Dainichi Nyorai engi emaki, kan* 3 *dan* 2.

16 Personal communication from Shimazu Kōkai of Shōzen'in. The hall was moved to its present location when the road in front was widened to make it accessible to vehicular traffic in the mid-twentieth century. A postcard dated 1931 of the Koganedō clearly shows a space where the hall now stands and one from 1935 shows the stone, steps leading up to the Ichi no torii with what appears to be the hall (from its distinctive roof) further beyond on the left (author's collection).

17 *Haguro mōde sode kagami* published *c*.1702 (but date is disputed) by Iseya, a lodging house in Nanokamachi, Tsurugaoka; republished 1936 by Abe Masaki. Original (in color) deposited at Zenpōji near Tsuruoka (but a search in 2006 failed to find it).

18 *Sanzan sōezumen* (1791). An official map on a flat projection showing the location of buildings. Its afterword states it was compiled as a result of the renewed hostility between Hagurosan and the Yudonosan temples in the Kansei era (1789–1801) and sent to the shogunate. Dewa Sanzan Hakubutsukan collection.

19 *Shintō taikei, Jinja-hen, Dewa Sanzan* (1982: 563–75). Genryōbō appears on p. 574, one of 195 signatories. Since Sen'an died in 1678–79, he himself may have been the signatory.

20 *Shintō taikei, Jinja-hen, Dewa Sanzan* (1982: 364–418).

21 *Goonbun hiramonzen e ōsedasaresho* (1816). See *Dewa Sanzan shiryōshū* vol. 1 (1994: 737–42).

22 Bettō map, undated, Dewa Sanzan Jinja archive. This also identifies Genryōbō as the *bettō* of the Dainichidō.

23 *Fumoto kenbetsu aratamechō* (1854). See *Dewa Sanzan shiryōshū* vol. 1 (1994: 278).

24 The Bettō and the three senior *sendatsu* temples took it, in turn, to act as the *daisendatsu* for the annual Akinomine mountain-entry practice. Each lodged at one of the four *onbun* residences on Matoba kōji: Shōon'in at Raifukubō, Chiken'in at Myōkōbō, Kezōin at Tōrinbō and the Bettō (Hōzen'in) at Genryōbō from at least 1780 (*Kakujun bettō nikki*, 1816. See *Dewa Sanzan shiryōshū* vol. 1, 1994: 846). This permitted him to have a *nagayamon* (long house gate) with *kannon-biraki* doors.
25 These were the Bettō (Hōzen'in), the three *sendatsu* temples (Kezōin, Shōon'in, Chiken'in) and the three Arasawa temples (Kitanoin, Hijirinoin, Kyōdōin).
26 *Ushū Hagurosan chūkō oboegaki* (*Shintō taikei, Jinja-hen, Dewa Sanzan* 1982: 139). By the early nineteenth century, the Kan'eiji sub-temple Senryūin was the liaison office (*furegashira*). Gyōchi, *Suzukakegoromo* (*Konohagoromo, Suzukakegoromo, Tōun rokuji, Shugendō shuryō*: 288).
27 "Edo jūrō kaiki" (*Shintō taikei, Jinja-hen, Dewa Sanzan* 1982: 461–2).
28 *Haguro-ha matsuji narabi shugen inseki aisū torishirabe-chō* (*Dewa Sanzan shiryōshū* vol. 1, 1994: 223).
29 For example, for a *kaichō* held at Ekōin in the fifth month of 1852, Kōmyōji, a temple from Tateyama, paid twenty *ryō* ground rent and 150 *ryō* to erect pavilions, and total outlay came to around 200 *ryō* (Yoshihara 1978: 150–1).
30 *Otake Dainichi rishōki* 於竹大日利生記, *kibyōshi* published in 1777, illustrated by Hōraisanjin Kiyū, publisher Matsumuraya Yabei. Republished under a different name the following year.
31 Print in collection of Ideha Bunka Kinenkan (Togawa Archive).
32 (1) "Degaichō yakusho todoke." Shōzen'in archive. Reproduced at http://www.nichibun.ac.jp/graphicversion/dbase/otake/data/data05/02.html. (2) Kongōjuin archive. Reproduced in Ushijima (1992: 32, Ill 72). (3) Ideha Bunka Kinenkan, Togawa Archive 5–28. Saitō Ichizō described a further document in the collection of the Dewa Sanzan Hakubutsukan signed by Genryōbō Kōdō, "Otake Dainichi Nyoraidō shūfuku, kifusha shōmeiryoku," which included more than a thousand signatures from supporters (Saitō 1965: 29–30).
33 A print of this scene is in the possession of Kongōjuin (Tōge). This temple also has a copy of the *Hoke senbō* used for services during the *kaichō*, and a wooden admission ticket (*kidofuda*) from it. They were in the possession of Jibō (Koseki) Shunyū, who was the officiating priest at the *kaichō*, and who took full Tendai ordination in 1872 and was later associated with Kongōjuin, which, like Shōzen'in, remained Buddhist. They are illustrated in Itabashi Kuritsu Kyōdō Shiryōkan, 1992, 10, Ill 18.
34 The copper tablet is kept at Kōtakuji and the wooden one hangs at the front of the Otake Dainichidō. The latter, which hangs over the front of the Dainichidō, became the basis for *osugata* subsequently printed by Genryōbō and later Shōzen'in.
35 This is in the possession of Genryōbō and purportedly shows Sen'an.
36 The *Bukō nenpyō* gives details of 107 *misemono* that took place in the nineteenth century; of these 86 occurred after 1840. See Markus (1985: 499–541).
37 Itabashi Kuritsu Kyōdō Shiryōkan, 1992, 31, Ill 68, 69.

Chapter 5

1 Throughout the chapter, quotations from the journals *Meikyō shinshi* 明教新誌, *Jinben* 神変, and *Shugen kenkyū* 修験研究 report the issue number, page number, and publication year in brackets at the end of the passage.

2   Translator's note: The Shingi branch is divided into the Chizan branch, which is administered by Chishakuin in Kyoto, and the Buzan branch, which is controlled by Hasedera in Nara Prefecture.
3   Around 1909, at Daigoji, the balance between membership fee payers and exempts chief monks showed that there were 602 chief monks divided into 376 payers and 226 exempts. The self-nominated *shugenja* were 2,450 divided into 1,385 payers and 1,065 exempts. See *Jinben* 13, 1910.
4   A digitalized version of *Shugendō* by Uno Enkū is available on the National Diet Library website: http://dl.ndl.go.jp/info:ndljp/pid/1092195.

Chapter 6

1   This expression, also commonly used among *shugen* followers, figures in the title of the first large-scale exhibition of Shugendō heritage at Osaka Municipal Museum in 1999.
2   *Shoku Nihongi* (797), *Nihon ryōiki* (822), and so on.
3   *Shinsarugakuki*, c.1050, is one early example of this appellation.
4   On Zaō Gongen, see Fujioka Yutaka's contribution to this book, as well as Suzuki Shōei (2011), Blair (2015), and Morris (2018).
5   In 1169, the cult was transferred to the bottom of the mountain (Nishikawa 1999: 167).
6   According to 1814 *Kaikokushi* 甲斐国誌 vol. 35 and 80, Enrakuji was founded by En no Gyōja, and was a subtemple of Daigoji. *Yamabushi* used to live on the premises, which featured an oratory dedicated to the worship of En no Gyōja, along with other temple buildings attributed to celebrated Buddhist sculptor Unkei 運慶 (1150–1223). There are no pre-medieval remains (Nishikawa 1999: 166).
7   According to Anne Bouchy, the first document to name them is *Ōmine shugyō kanjōshiki, Zenki no koto* 大峰修行灌頂式前鬼事 (Initiatory Rite of Ōmine Practice, Zenki). Zenki and Goki are often, but not always, described as a couple, sometimes with children, whom En no Gyōja encounters on Ikoma, where he subdues them, and makes them his disciples. Zenki and Goki's "descendants," to this day, are said to take care of *shugen* practitioners both in the Ōmine and the Katsuragi range (Bouchy 2005: 163ff.).
8   Several scholars have suggested that En no Gyōja's appearance may be related to that of Shinra Myōjin 神羅明神, Onjōji's tutelary deity (Miyake 2000a; Ishikawa and Ozawa 2000; Ishikawa 2015). Although it is difficult to determine whether the iconographic features of Shinra and of En no Gyōja are indeed related, and in that case, which one preceded the other, it is clear that both emerge in the common context of Tendai *jimon* Buddhism, at the beginning of the Kamakura period. In certain Kumano mandalas, they are also both represented, usually differentiated by their clothing (Shinra Myōjin is dressed in Chinese style) and their seats (folding chair vs. rock or cave) (Ishikawa 1999: 191). This resemblance may also be considered as one of the elements of a tradition on the verge of constituting and asserting itself. On the constitution of the cult of Shinra Myōjin, see Kim 2018.
9   Little is known about this term, despite its widespread usage in the context of the Ōmine range (*Shugendō jiten* 2000: 179). The verb *nabiku* literally means to float in the wind like a flag or a banner.

10 In older sources, such as *Shozan engi* or *Daibodaisantō engi* (twelfth century), though the name Gyōsen no shuku appears, it refers to a different place, close to Ozasa no shuku 小笹の宿 (cf. Figure 12.2).
11 See website: http://syamabiko.web.fc2.com
12 The Shingū Yamabiko group was nominated "citizen of the year" in 2004 for their work in rending the southern part of the Okugake accessible (https://www.citizen.co.jp/coy/archive/2004_01.html).
13 Maeda had founded another association, the *Okugake Hagoromokai* 奥駈羽衣会, for the specific purpose of restoring the southern part of the Okugake. At the end of the 1970s, Maeda was terminally ill with cancer, and he urged Tamaoka and the Shingū Yamabiko Group to take over his life's work, knowing that his own association was likely to dissolve after his death (which it did). The Yamabiko Group took his wish to heart and organized several campaigns of what Maeda had named the practice of "One Thousand Days of Grass Cutting on the Mountain" (*Sennichi karimine gyō* 千日刈り峰行). The first campaign took place in 1984. After the second campaign, a member of the Kumano *shugen* group, who had taken part in the practice, observed that, even with a restored trail, the distance between Tamaki jinja and Jikyō no shuku is too far for beginners. Moreover, if the path remained underused, it would soon end up being overgrown again. These observations created the incentive to build a mountain hut between Tamaki and Jikyō no shuku, at Gyōsen no shuku (http://syamabiko.web.fc2.com/introduction.html).
14 By Kyoto Buddhist sculptor Sagawa Jōkei 佐川定慶 (Miyagi 2017, my interview).
15 See website: http://syamabiko.web.fc2.com/introduction.html.
16 Onjōji, or Miidera, is the founding temple of the *jimon* branch of Tendai Buddhism. In 1090, its head was named as the Supervisor of the Three Mountains of Kumano (*Kumano Sanzan Kengyō* 熊野三山検校), thus officializing a *shugen* lineage within the temple hierarchy.
17 On the rituals of animation and de-animation of a statue, see Brinker (2011), Lamotte (2013), and Sharf and Sharf (2001).
18 In doing this, Miyagi followed a millenary tradition of copying and adding new comments and colophons to copied documents, which is particularly apparent in *engi* literature (foundation narratives of temples and shrines).
19 Despite its dynamism, the Yamabiko Group suffers a lack of continuity in the younger generations. Its current representative, Kawashima Isao 川島功, is now in his late seventies, and overtly concerned about the to find younger people willing to commit themselves seriously in the association (Kanai 2018).
20 As duly consigned in the Yamabiko group's records, a gift of sixteen kilograms of raw tuna had been carried up, plus ice, to the hut.
21 The village of Zenki, situated below the mountain saddle of Jinzen, used to be populated by five families, called "Goki" 五鬼 (Lit. "Five demons"), who claim to be the descendants of the initial couple of demons tamed by En no Gyōja (Bouchy 2005: 164). Similarly, in the village of Nakatsugawa, at the foot of the Katsuragi range, five families named Zenki or Goki used to take care of practitioners, and still do today, welcoming and hosting Shōgoin groups on their spring mountain entry (Wakayama kenritsu hakubutsukan 2011: 3).
22 The altar in a *shugen* temple is often filled to the brim with statues and figures of different times, styles, and origins, often gifts by followers or passersby, and revered along with the main deities.

23. In that particular case, it turned out that a single person was responsible for most of the thefts around Wakayama (Ōkōchi 2016).
24. The main statue was later recovered, but not those of Zenki and Goki.
25. Along similar lines, the bronze statue of En no Gyōja in Tateishi Kōshō's temple is made by a sculptor rated as a Living national treasure, but Tateishi forgot his name, and has misplaced the paper on which it was written (Tateishi 2017, my interview).
26. Kawasaki Tsuyoshi has worked extensively on the development of this textual tradition, which seems to have emerged within the context of *Minoodera engi*, much as En no Gyōja's initiation by Ryūmyō (Kawasaki 2007, 2010, 2013).
27. For a summary of such accounts, see Miyake (1992: 50–8; 2001a: 44–7).

Chapter 7

1. Shingon Buddhism uses two lists of eight founding patriarchs (*hasso* 八祖). The Shingon Denji 真言伝持 tradition, in which Ryūmyō is the first patriarch, and the Shingon Fuhō 真言付法 tradition, in which he appears as the third patriarch.
2. Also known as *Tengu zōshi* 天狗草子, see Wakabayashi (2012).
3. *Tengu*, "celestial dogs," are ambivalent beings traditionally depicted with a long nose or a bird's beak, wings, and a human body. Generally described as opponents to Buddhism, or transformations of eminent monks who fell prey to their own conceits, which is how *Tengu zōshi* describes them.
4. This expression denotes the Shingon lineage before Kūkai.
5. List of eight eminent Japanese monks who traveled to China in the early Heian period to study Esoteric Buddhism, starting with Kūkai and Saichō.
6. Probably a misspelling for Daisoku 大足.

Chapter 8

1. Compiled in 1325, *Shingonden* begins with the presentation of the seven Shingon patriarchs. It then combines the account of the transmission of Esoteric Buddhism to Japan with biographies of eminent monks. The edition used here is *Taikō Shingonden* 対校真言伝.
2. Neither *Honchō monzui* 本朝文粋 nor *Honchō zoku monzui* 本朝続文粋 present such an example, and, while going through *Nihon shiki* 日本詩紀, I only found one instance in which the expression *kōkaku* 礦确 appears (in *Jukkai kochōshi ippyaku'in* 述懐古調詩一百韻 by Ōe no Masahira 大江匡衡; 952–1012).
3. *Sangō shiiki chūshū* by the monk Jōan is an annotation of Kūkai's *Sangō shiiki* 三教指帰.
4. The manuscript bears the character *rō* 磙, which conveys the sound of stones rolling in a stream, so that I changed it to its homonym *rō* 浪 (wave), which is closer to the meaning expressed here.
5. Although the character used in the manuscript is *tō* 藤 (wisteria), I followed a marginal note suggesting that the correct character should rather be *tō* 騰 (to leap up).
6. The manuscript has a character composed of 舍＋并, but with regard to both meaning and graphism, I replaced it with *hen* 骿.

7   The manuscript bears the character *hyō* 憑, but I followed a marginal note and replaced it with the character *utsumaki* 憑. Both characters mean "depend," "trust."
8   The character *o* 於 is missing in the manuscript, but needed for the couplet.
9   The character *sha* 者 is missing in the manuscript, but needed for the couplet.

Chapter 9

1   Some of these elements emerge from the image of the *shugenja* established in literature before the Edo period. See, for example, Morley (1993).
2   A synopsis of *Karasu no tsuibami* 烏之啄 (1777) by Koinshi 古隠子 is included in Mizutani Futō's 水谷不倒 *Sentaku kosho kaidai* 選擇古書解題 (1937), in Mizutani (1974: 93–4).
3   Nakamura first noted the similarity in "Kaidai" (Nakamura ed. 1947). The similarity is also observed in the annotation to the text in Nakamura ed. (1973: 521), which similarly features a reproduction of an image from the picture scrolls.
4   In an homage to his mentor, Chūryō authored the work, a *yomihon* titled *Izumi no Chikahira monogatari* 泉親衡物語 (The Tale of Izumi Chikahira, 1809), using the same penname under which Gennai had written his puppet plays.
5   On Teishō's use of vernacular Chinese sources in *Hanabusa sōshi*, see Ogata (1966, reprinted in Ogata 2011: 489–503), and Rai (1974). The use of chapter 61 in particular is observed in the annotation in Nakamura ed. (1973: 161). A recent analysis of two stories from Teishō's *Shigeshige yawa* 繁野話 (A Thicket of Tales, 1766) shows that he drew on both the 100-chapter recension (of which the 1610 Rongyutang edition is best known) and the longer 120-chapter recension. See Liu (2017: 33–7).
6   On Shugendō divination techniques, see Miyake (1985: 245–313).
7   For an extended discussion of the tale, focusing on its didactic and intertextual elements, along with a complete annotated translation, see Fleming (2013: 75–115).
8   No character by this name appears in the "Aoi" chapter of *The Tale of Genji*, although it is the similarly named Prelate of Yokawa (*Yokawa no sōzu*), a monk of higher rank, who oversees the exorcism of Ukifune in the chapter "Tenarai."

Chapter 10

1   On written sources at the basis of the idea of Mount Sumeru as *axis mundi* on the lotus pedestal of the Vairocana Buddha at Tōdaiji, see Sotomura (2016: 21–40).
2   In the *Lotus Sutra* as well as in the *Daitō saiiki ki*, the Potalaka is located in the southern direction.
3   The *Nihon shoki* entry for the fifth month of 552 reports that two shining planks of Camphor Tree were retrieved in the trait of sea between Izumi and Awaji and were used to create two statues of Buddhas, which were enshrined in a temple at Yoshino.
4   This section is based on Fujioka (2004: 234–54; 2011: 193–8; 2015: 207–9).
5   For the original text, see *Nihon ryōiki* (1996: 249).
6   For the original text, see *Ribuōki* (1974: 60).
7   About the deeds of Kanho, see Wang Yong (2000: 459).
8   Translator's note: for a study and a translation of *Sanbōe*, see Kamens (1988).

9 Translator's note: for an English translation of the *Konjaku monogatarishū*, see Dykstra (2014).
10 The contents of this section are mostly based on Fujioka (2016: 338–48).
11 This technique consists in creating a primary model made of wax, which has to be smeared with earth and heated up until the wax melts. At this point, the cavity of the mold can be filled with a cast of liquid bronze.

Chapter 11

1 I use the term "Shugendō" throughout this chapter to refer to organized mountain asceticism, although the rubric was not necessarily in use during the periods in question.
2 It was the outreach efforts of an early-thirteenth-century practitioner, Raison, which reportedly led to regular religious practice on the mountain. See Ōtaka (2013: 27–28), Hayakawa (1997: 324c, 325), and Earhart (2015: 26–8).
3 By the Edo period, Murayama was centered on three main temples—Tsujinobō, Chiseibō, and Daikyōbō—each of which, in accordance with the combinatory thinking of the time, correlated its main deity with another god or Buddha and the religious institution in which the latter was enshrined (Hayakawa 1997: 324c). Tsujinobō was the *bettō* or affiliate of the Sengen Shrine, Chiseibō was the affiliate of Dainichidō, and Daikyōbō was identified with Daitōryō Gongen.
4 Ōtaka Yasumasa concludes that the Murayama practitioners and the priests of the Main Shrine enjoyed close relations during this period; members of the Fuji family, head priest of the Shrine, had either joined the Shugendō community or held blood ties with the temple residents (Ōtaka 2013: 29). See also Ōtaka (2012: 241).
5 The numbers of pilgrims soared especially after medieval domain barriers were lifted; Shinjō (1982: 659–61).
6 The Murayama practitioners were discredited by association with the domain lord, Imagawa Yoshimoto (1519–60), who was defeated by Oda Nobunaga (1534–82) in 1560, whereas the Ōmiya priests had prudently aligned themselves with Nobunaga's forces and received special treatment under the Tokugawa regime (Endō 2000: 55–6; Hayakawa 1997: 326). Talia J. Andrei argues on the basis of the shifting composition and content of *Fuji sankei mandara* that the Murayama and Main Shrine were at loggerheads over the channeling of pilgrims through the shrine (rather than proceeding directly to Murayama) and that the Shugendō center was already well in decline during the second half of the sixteenth century. See her "Mapping Sacred Spaces: Representations of Pleasure and Worship in *Sankei mandara*," Ch. 3. Based on her survey of guide maps (*annai ezu*), Ogino Yūko shows that in the late Edo period Murayama guides were still being pressured to direct pilgrims coming from the west to pass through the Main Shrine (Ogino 1999: 26–9).
7 By the early nineteenth century, Mt. Fuji *yamabushi* was greatly reduced in number and *shugen* disciplines at the peak had fallen off almost entirely.
8 The recent discovery on Fuji's northern slope of two 1482 plates engraved with devotional images and the names of sponsoring patrons tallies with reports of increased ritual practice in the area from at least the late fifteenth century (Horiuchi 2009: 283). For a photograph of one example, see *Fujiyoshida-shi shi, shiryō hen 2: kodai chūsei* 1992: 166 (n. 104). Judging from the *Katsuyama-ki*, a Nichiren Buddhist

record, religious travel on the northern slopes of the mountain surged from the late fifteenth to early sixteenth centuries. See, for example, the 1500 and 1518 entries in "Katsuyama-ki," in Sasuga Hō, ed., *Katsuyama-ki to genpon no kōshō*, 104 and 116, respectively.
9   See also Horiuchi's map of the geographical distribution of the Yoshida *danna* sites (Horikuchi 2009: 286).
10 Regarding the latter see Horiuchi (2009: 281); and for the rituals, esp. 294–5.
11 The text is *Fuji mono-imi narabini naishō no oboe*, dated 1612. The author belonged to Sen'yōin, a branch temple of the Shingon temple, Enchōji, in Shimōsa. The priests of this temple apparently also served as *sendatsu* for the climbers in the north (Horiuchi 2009: 287, 292). Another manual, *In-musubi* (likely from the same period), similarly describes the practices required of pilgrims, as well as the mudras and mantras that the priests were expected to use at the northern Sengen Shrine. For the text, see Horiuchi (2009: 309–15).
12 The Yoshida *oshi* guild's resistance to enrollment of their members in the Yoshida and Shirakawa Shinto denominations, a position taken as early as 1711, may have been related to this combinative self-identity (Hirano 2004: 154–5, 158–9).
13 See, for example, Barbara Ambros (2008: Chs. 1–3). The *oshi*'s eventual dominance of the Ōyama pilgrimage system that Ambros describes bears striking parallels to developments at Mt. Fuji. See also Sarah Thal (2005: Ch. 4).
14 For a thorough discussion of biographical materials related to Kakugyō, see Royall Tyler (1993: 251–83).
15 *Hachiyō mesareru* (Horiuchi 2009: 282). "Hachiyō" is also a generic designator for Amida Buddha's Pure Land.
16 For a list of the *kami* and their original essences (*honji*), see Horiuchi (2009: 288–9).
17 Much has been published on artwork that depicts Mt. Fuji. For a treatment of the mountain's aesthetic idealization over time, see, for example, Hirose 2005.
18 The definition of *sankei mandara* and its related genres varies widely. See, for example, Miyake (2000: 434). A good recent discussion of the various defining criteria appears in Talia Andrei's "Mapping Sacred Spaces: Representations of Pleasure and Worship in *Sankei mandara*," Ch. 1. With regard to mountain mandalas in particular, in English see the now-classic essays by Seidel (1992) and Grapard (1982); as well as ten Grotenhuis (1999: 172–9); and (especially regarding the Nachi *sankei mandara*) Moerman (2005).
19 Fuji pilgrimage mandalas were not treated as such until Kondō Yoshihiro's seminal discussions in the mid-twentieth century. See his "Fuji mandara to shinkō" and a later expanded treatment in "Fuji Sengen mandara zusetsu." Also see Tanaka (1984), Miyake (2000: esp. 421–35), and Ōtaka (2013: 313–37). The last work contains a list of studies of Fuji pilgrimage mandalas on pp. 332–3 (n. 3). Scholars have dated at least six *Fuji sankei mandara* to the late medieval and early modern periods. In addition to the two mentioned below, another exemplar on silk, known as the Takeuchi version, and two on paper, originated in the early Edo period. Andrei expertly discusses all three in her "Mapping Sacred Spaces," 135–50.
20 Ōtaka disagrees with Kondō on the relative dating of the two *mandara* (Ōtaka 2013: 329–31).
21 See *Fujiyoshida-shi shi, shiryō hen 2: kodai chūsei*, 651ff. (n. 704), for a color reproduction and details. Ōtaka speculates that this work was originally commissioned by a person or institution of high rank, perhaps the Suruga daimyo

and/or Shōgōin, but that later changes to the picture may have been sponsored by Murayama *shuto* and/or shrine priests at Ōmiya (Ōtaka 2012: 244–5).

22 This *Fuji sankei mandara*, also in the collection of the Main Shrine, is reproduced in color in *Fujiyoshida-shi shi, shiryō hen 2: kodai chūsei*, 652 (n. 705).

23 *Miko* were female ritual practitioners who sometimes worked collaboratively with *yamabushi* in providing exorcistic and other services.

24 See Ōtaka (2013: 319–21) for a detailed analysis of the identities of these figures.

25 The prefectural *mandara* appears not to have come into the possession of the Main Shrine until 1942, when it was acquired in Kyoto.

26 *Fuji sankei mandara* have, in fact, been classified as *etoki* paintings (Kaminishi 2006: 12).

27 The prefectural *Fuji sankei mandara* is the outlier in this regard. It displays neither deities nor celestial bodies.

28 There is no consensus on the identity of the depicted deities, however; see Andrei (2016: 121, including n. 278).

29 The popular *Tale of Fuji no Hito-ana* (*Fuji no hito-ana zōshi*) explicitly invited this sort of interpretation, as I discuss elsewhere. I thank Caleb Carter for stressing to me the comparability of the *mandara* and the later *fujizuka*.

30 On the prohibition of women climbers from Mt. Fuji, see Miyazaki (2005).

31 Ōtaka theorizes that images of female pilgrims were later added to the Kano painting to help promote visits to the shrine in the special *ennen* (*kōshin* year) of 1560 (Ōtaka 2012: 234–6, 241). For his analysis of the figures in the prefectural *mandara*, see Ōtaka (2013: 319–24).

32 *Sanzon kuson zu*, literally, "Picture of the Three and Nine Revered Figures," is reproduced in Fujiyoshida-shi Rekishi Minzoku Hakubutsukan, ed., *Fujisan tozan annaizu*, 17, plate 35; and idem., *Fujisan no efuda*, 16, plate 57. It is undated, but the two-story structure of the main shrine building depicted in the image (a style not in use earlier) indicates that this mandala postdates the shrine's 1604 restoration and was likely issued to commemorate the project's completion. *Efuda*, 25. Ogino Yūko argues that it postdates 1757 (quoted in *Annaizu*, 72).

33 The "sun and moon" motif in Japanese art and archaeological remains dates at least to the seventh century; for a study of its role in Japanese screen paintings, see Bambling (1996).

34 The monkeys were associated with the great pilgrimage waves that took place in *kōshin* 庚申 or *kanoe-saru* years, which were marked in the traditional calendar by the ninth position of the twelve-year cycle, *saru* 申, a homophone of *saru* 猿, monkey. However, the visual correlation between the monkeys and Mt. Fuji's *kōshin* years was likely not fully established until 1800, when commemorative picture cards (*efuda*) displaying the monkeys were distributed for the first time. See Fujiyoshida-shi, ed., *Efuda*, 12.

35 *Hachiyo kuson zu* is reproduced in Fuji Yoshida-shi, ed., *Efuda*, 13; and idem, *Annaizu*, 27 (Figure 6.1), with commentary on 69.

36 Another wood-block print (52 by 28.5 centimeters), probably also produced in 1680, *Fujisan hachiyō kuson*, depicts discrete images of Dainichi and his mandalic retinue (rather than simply their names), but is devoid of reference to the pilgrimage landscape. See Fujiyoshida-shi, ed., *Efuda*, 24; idem, *Annaizu*, 28 (plate 2) for a larger reproduction, and 69 for brief commentary; as well as Horiuchi (2009: 301). It is worth noting that the blocks used to print both of these works are held by Shōfukuji,

a True Pure Land temple in Fujiyoshida that was reportedly Esoteric Buddhist at the time of the blocks' production; Fujiyoshida-shi, ed., *Efuda*,13.

37 Kakugyō's hagiographical biography, the *Go-taigyō no maki*, probably did not appear until the late eighteenth century at the earliest and as such must be used with great caution, and perhaps most fruitfully as a record of the interests of the Fujikō members of that later time. Royall Tyler has discussed in detail the nearly intractable problem of the historicity of the founding figure in his Introduction to "The Book of Great Practice," esp. 256–64.

38 For a sampling of reproductions of Kakugyō's signed *ominuki* and related works, see *Fujiyoshida-shi shi, shiryō hen* 5, *kinsei* III: frontispiece n. 2 and *shiryō* n. 32, "Kakugyō ominuki," 451; Iwashina (1977: 43, 61, 301); and Ōtani (2011: 23).

39 Itō Kenkichi and Yasumaru Yoshio suggest that the *ominuki* functioned as a *yorishiro* or substitute object of faith (see *Ominuki* 1971: 483, headnote).

40 Okada Hiroshi lists several sets of the revealed words (*monku*) and apotropaic formulae (*fusegi*) that Kakugyō inscribed in these works (Okada 1987: 196). See also Iwashina (1977: 59–60).

41 Kakugyō Tōbutsu, *Ominuki*, reproduced and annotated in Murakami and Yasumaru (1971: 482–3). Sometimes an additional sphere appears in the *ominuki*, symbolizing the stars. The crow motif harks back to Kumano symbology; see Moerman (2005: 158).

42 See, for example, *Fujiyoshida-shi shi, shiryō hen* 5:III: 1132, and document nos. 33 and 35.

43 The neo-ideographs for *Moto no chichihaha* appear on either side of the summit in most *ominuki*.

44 *Fujiyoshida-shi shi, shiryō hen* 5, *kinsei* III, 453 (n. 33, foldout), from the Fujii Yosaburō family collection. No dimensions are cited.

45 In three of the four miniature *ominuki* clusters signed "Getsugan, fourth-generation," the names and positions of his predecessors in the movement also appear, beginning with Kakugyō. Fuji *kō* leaders used their ritual texts (not only the *ominuki*) to certify succession lineage within the group.

46 The formal title of the Fuji deity, "Myōtō kaisan," here initiates the central lines of the small *ominuki* in the upper right and lower left sections of the scroll, but is replaced by "Myōjōten" (Venus) in the upper axis (where "Myōtō kaisan" ordinarily appears in Kakugyō's *ominuki*).

47 From late Tokugawa times the *ominuki* were revered alongside *miei*, devotional portraits that superimpose images of the group's leaders on the mountain and completely omit the pilgrimage trails. See, for example, Fujiyoshida-shi, ed., *Efuda*, 16; and for two larger *miei*-like *mandara*, Hirano (1987: 60–2). Miyake Toshiyuki says small versions of these "*Fuji mandara*" circulated widely after Fujikō spread, anticipating Fuji picture cards (*efuda*) (Miyake 2000: 433–5; see also Iwashina 1977).

Chapter 12

1 On the concepts of living doubles and authentic copy in Esoteric Buddhism, see Rambelli (2013: 12).

2 Analyzing the religious meaning of the *stūpa*, Paul Mus defines it as a "mesocosm" or a "magic copula" that favors a mystic union between the Buddha and the practitioner. This union was based on a breaking of communicative levels, namely the *stūpa*

allowed the Buddha "to descend" to the real world of human beings and the officiant "to ascend" to the divine universe (Mus 1998: 55–6). See also Faure (1996: 254–6, 280).

3   It is interesting to consider that in the rural context the *bonten* was also associated with the god Bonten (Skt. Brahmā) and the idea of "aim high" (*takaku medatsu*) or "stand out" (*hote* ホテ), which characterized the ritual poles (*sao* 竿) used to build the ceremonial stage during the village festivals for the gods (*matsuri*) (Konishi 1990: 152).

4   Shiota Kazunori 塩田一則 made this description in the *Bonten kuyō ikkenki* 梵天供養一見記 (1855). For the original text see Tsushima (2011: 93).

5   See, for instance, the inscription of the stele located in the Community Center of the Iritsubo district of Tsukuba. For the original text see Tokuhara (2004: 9, 308).

6   Because of this intense facial expression, the local scholar Tokuhara Satoyuki 徳原聰行 (1929–2002) proposed to call the Dainichi Nyorai carved on the Yudono stelae as "Big-nose Dainichi-sama" (*hana no ōkina Dainichi sama*). See Tokuhara (1982: 28–9).

7   The character *taki* 滝 means "waterfall" and was purposely used to replace the character *ryū* 龍 "dragon" in order to evoke the water element, which is normally associated with the dragon. For the original text see Sakamoto (1988: 184).

8   According to the theory of the three bodies, the Dharma-body (*hosshin*) of Dainichi Nyorai also comprises Amida Nyorai, which represents his reward-body (*hōshin*), and Shaka Nyorai, which corresponds to his apparitional-body (*keshin*). Kikurenji implies that, since Amida Nyorai is part of the cosmic body of Dainichi Nyorai, the Yudono mound could also be worshiped according to Pure Land school rituals.

9   For a study on the *sekkō* in late Muromachi (1336–1573) and early Edo period see Kanamori (1986: 421–432). For a historical analysis of the diffusion of the stelae among the lay population see Chijiwa (1988: 183).

10 A black-and-white picture of the Fukutoki stele is reported in Okumura (1973: 341). In September 2018, I did fieldwork at Fukutokuji but I was not able to find it. The son of the head priest told me that Fukutokuji remained without an official head priest from the late eighties to the early years of this century when it was also destroyed by a fire. It is possible that the Yudono stele went missing or was stolen because of the state of neglect or the occurrence of unlucky events.

11 For a detailed analysis of the religious meanings attributed to the eighth day of the month during the Edo period and a reference to the Yōka-kō, see Suzuki (2006: 120–6).

Chapter 13

1   I am grateful to Benedetta Lomi for bringing this text to my attention. Human yellow (*ninnō* 人黄), the essential life force described in Esoteric Buddhist ritual texts, which is often compared to ox yellow, is similarly associated with the wish-fulfilling jewel and the seed syllable. See Faure (2016: 183).

2   Kumano *goō hōin* composed of crow-script date only from the late fifteenth century. Those of an earlier date are written in standard script (Chijiwa 2010: 263).

3   See Komatsu Shigemi, ed., *Kasuga gongen genki e*, in *Zoku Nihon no emaki* vols. 13–14 (Tokyo: Chūō Kōronsha, 1991), and idem, ed., *Matsuzaki Tenjin engi*, in *Zoku Nihon no emaki* vol. 22 (Tokyo: Chūō Kōronsha, 1992).

4   See, for example, the pair of six-panel folding screens, entitled "Scenes of Pleasure Quarters" (*Yūri fūzoku zu*), in the Museum of Fine Arts, Boston.
5   Tamenaga Shunsui, *Kansō sadan*, in *Nihon zuihitsu taisei* vol. 1, no. 14, 381–2.
6   Fabio Rambelli has discussed the curses and punishment that appear in *kishōmon* in "The Buddha's Wrath: Esoteric Buddhism and the Discourse of Divine Punishment," *Japanese Religions* 27 (1): 41–68.
7   See, for example, *Hashiba Hideyoshi Keppan kishōmon*, Tenshō 1 (1582).7.11 (羽柴秀吉血判起請文 天正 1 .7.11) in the Hosokawa Collection, Eisei Bunko (細川コレクション 永青文庫).
8   Many of the *jātaka* tales were included in such early collections as the twelfth- to thirteenth-century *Konjaku monogatarishū* and *jātaka* illustrations appear on sources such as the seventh-century *Tamamushi no zushi* and in the twelfth-century *Heike nōkyō*.
9   See, for example, *Kamakura ibun* vol. 7, 190 (doc.nr. 4784).
10 The work of Kawane Yoshiyasu is perhaps most representative of this view (e.g. Kawane 1977).
11 After Ieyasu gained independence from Imagawa Uchizane at Mikawa, he wrote a *kishōmon* on a *Hakusantaki hōin*. Only after the fall of Hideyoshi did he begin using *Kumano hōin*. After the establishment of the Tokugawa bakufu, it became customary to submit *kishōmon* to the bakufu on *Kumano hōin* (Chijiwa 2010: 263).
12 The last *kishōmon* from the king is dated 1854, the last *kishōmon* from the Regent is dated 1861, and the last *kishōmon* from the Council is dated 1862 (Umeki 2012: 187).
13 "Takeda Harunobu (Shingen) seishi kaidai," 1546 [Tenbun 15]/7/5. *Ashina Moritaka shojō ika jūhachitsū*, 14–16. University of Tokyo Historiographical Institute. I am grateful to Alexander Kaplan-Reyes for introducing me to this document and for allowing me to cite his careful translation and analysis.
14 The Ikushimatarushima Shrine houses a collection of loyalty oaths submitted to Shingen by more than a hundred vassals, dating from 1566 and 1567. See *Shingen bushō no kishōmon*.
15 Kōshin, the ceremony to which Shingen refers, is celebrated on the fifty-seventh day of the sexagenary cycle when it is believed that performing rituals throughout the night will keep the three worms that reside in the human body from reporting one's misdeeds to the gods. See Kohn (1993–1995).

Bibliography

Abbreviations

DNBZ *Dai Nihon bukkyō zensho* 大日本佛教全書. Bussho kankōkai 仏書刊行会, eds. 150 vols. Tokyo: Meicho fukyōkai, 1978 (original ed. 1912-1922).

KT *Kokushi taikei* 国史大系. Kuroita Katsumi 黒板勝美, ed. Revised edition. 57 vols. Tokyo: Kokushi taikei kankōkai, 1929-1940.

NKBT *Nihon koten bungaku taikei* 日本古典文學大系. Takagi Ichinosuke 高木市之助 *et al.*, eds. 102 vols. Tokyo: Iwanami shoten, 1957-1968.

NKBZ *Nihon koten bungaku zenshū* 日本古典文学全集. 51 vols. Tokyo: Shōgakukan, 1970-1976.

NST *Nihon shisō taikei* 日本思想大系. Ienaga Saburō 家永三郎 *et al.*, eds. 67 vols. Tokyo: Iwanami shoten, 1970-1982.

SNKBT *Shin Nihon koten bungaku taikei* 新日本古典文学大系. 100 vols. Tokyo: Iwanami shoten, 1989-2005.

SNKBZ *Shinpen Nihon koten bungaku zenshū* 新編日本古典文学全集. 88 vols. Tokyo: Shōgakukan, 1994-2002.

ST *Shintō taikei* 神道大系. Shintō taikei hensankai 神道大系編纂会, ed. 120 vols. Tokyo: Shintō taikei hensankai, 1977-1994.

T *Taishō shinshū Daizōkyō* 大正新修大蔵経. Takakusu Junjirō 高楠順次郎 and Watanabe Kaigyoku 渡邊海旭, eds. 85 vols. Tokyo: Issaikyō kankōkai. Also, *Taishō shinshū Daizōkyō bekkan* 別巻: Shōwa hōbō sōmokuroku 昭和法寶總目錄. 3 vols. Tokyo: Taishō Issaikyō kankōkai and Daizō shuppan, 1924-1932/1934.

ZGR *Zoku Gunsho ruijū* 續群書類從. Zoku Gunsho ruijū kanseikai 續群書類従完成会, ed. Tokyo: Zoku Gunsho ruijū kanseikai, 1923-1972.

ZNE *Zoku Nihon no emaki* 續日本の絵巻. 27 vols. Komatsu Shigemi 小松茂美, ed. Tokyo: Chūō kōronsha, 1990-1993.

Collections and Reference Works

Chūgoku shōwa sen: Edo kobanashi to no majiwari 中国笑話選—江戸小咄との交わり. 1964. Matsueda Shigeo 松枝茂夫 and Mutō Sadao 武藤禎夫, eds. Tokyo: Heibonsha.

Dai Nihon shiryō 大日本史料. 1971. vol. 4/10. Tōkyō daigaku shiryō hensanjo 東京大学史料編纂所, ed. Tokyo: Tōkyō daigaku shuppankai.

Dewa Sanzan shiryōshū: Gassan, Hagurosan, Yudonosan 出羽三山史料集—月山、羽黒山、湯殿山. 1994-2000. 3 vols. Umezu Keihō 梅津慶豊, ed. Haguro-chō: Dewa Sanzan Jinja musho.

Edo kobanashi shū 江戸小咄集. 1971. Miyao Shigeo 宮尾しげを, ed. Tokyo: Heibonsha.

Hanashibon taikei 噺本大系. 1975-1979. Mutō Sadao 武藤禎夫 and Oka Masahiko 岡雅彦, eds. 20 vols. Tokyo: Tōkyōdō shuppan.

Heian ibun 平安遺文. 1947-1967. Takeuchi Rizō 竹内理三, ed. *Komonjo hen* 古文書編. 11 vols. Tokyo: Tōkyōdō shuppan.

Kamakura ibun 鎌倉遺文. 1971-1995. Takeuchi Rizō 竹内理三, ed. *Komonjo hen, komonjo hen hoi* 古文書編・古文書編補遺. 46 vols. Tokyo: Tōkyōdō shuppan.

Minzokugaku jiten 民俗学事典. 1972. Ōtsuka minzoku gakkai 大塚民俗学会, ed. Tokyo: Kōbundō.

Princeton Dictionary of Buddhism. 2017. Robert E. Buswell, Donald S. Lopez Jr., and Juhn Ahn, eds. Princeton: Princeton University Press.

Shugendō jiten 修験道辞典. 2000. Miyake Hitoshi 宮家準, ed. 6th reprint. Tokyo: Tōkyōdō shuppan (or. ed. 1986).

Shugendō shōso 修験道章疏. 1973. Suzuki gakujutsu zaidan 鈴木学術財団. Tokyo: Kōdansha.

Shugendō shōso 修験道章疏. 1985. In Nihon daizōkyō 日本大蔵経. Nihon daizōkyō hensankai 日本大蔵経編纂会, ed. Tokyo: Meicho shuppan (or. ed. 1916-1919).

Shugendō shōso 修験道章疏. 2000. Nihon daizōkyō hensankai 日本大蔵経編纂会 and Miyake Hitoshi 宮家準, ed. 3 vols [facsimile]. Tokyo: Kokusho kankōkai.

Primary Sources

Ataka 安宅. 1968. By Kanze Nobumitsu 觀世信光 and Kanze Motoshige 観世左近. Tokyo: Hinoki shoten.

Azuma kagami 吾妻鏡. 2000. Kuroita Katsumi 黒板勝美, ed. *Azuma kagami* 吾妻鏡 (*Shintei zōho Kokushi taikei* 新訂増補国史大系 vol. 32). Tokyo: Yoshikawa Kōbunkan.

Bukō nenpyō 武功年表 (1882). 1968. By Saitō Gesshin 斎藤月岑. In Kaneko Mitsuharu 金子光晴, ed. *Bukō nenpyō* (Tōyō bunko 東洋文庫 vol. 116). Tokyo: Heibonsha.

Chūmonjō 仲文章. 1993. Gakugyōhen yōgaku no kai 学業篇幼学の会, ed. *Shohon shūsei Chūmonjō bunshō chūkai* 諸本集成仲文章注解. Tokyo: Bensei shuppan.

Dainipponkoku Hokkekyō genki 大日本国法華経験記 (also *Honchō Hokke genki*). In NST vol. 7.

Edo meisho zue 江戸名所図絵 (1834). 1975. By Saitō Yukio 斎藤幸雄. In Suzuki Tōzō 鈴木棠三 and Asakura Haruhiko 朝倉治彦, eds. *Edo meisho zue* 江戸名所図会. 3 vols. Tokyo: Kadokawa shoten.

En no Gyōja hongi 役行者本記. In *Shugendō shōso* 修験道章疏 vol. 3.

Fujiokaya nikki 藤岡屋日記. 1987-1995. By Fujiokaya Yoshizō 藤岡屋由蔵. In Suzuki Tōzō 鈴木棠三 and Koike Shōtarō 小池章太郎, eds. *Fujiokaya nikki*. 15 vols. Tokyo: San'ichi shobō.

Futsū shōdōshū 普通唱導集. 2006. Murayama Shūichi 村山修一, ed. *Futsū shōdōshū, honkoku, kaisetsu* 普通唱導集—翻刻・解説. Kyoto: Hōzōkan.

Genji monogatari 源氏物語. By Murasaki Shikibu 紫式部. In SNKBZ vol. 21.

Genkō shakusho 元亨釈書. 1965. By Kokan Shiren 虎関師錬. Kuroita Katsumi 黒板勝美 ed. *Nihon kōsōden yōmonshō; Genkō shakusho* 日本高僧伝要文抄 元亨釈書 (*Shinpen zōho Kokushi taikei* 新編増補国史大系 vol. 31). Tokyo: Yoshikawa Kōbunkan.

Geschichte und Beschreibung von Japan. By Engelbert Kaempfer. 1964 [1777-1779]. Christian Wilhelm Dohm, ed. 2 vols. Stuttgart: Brockhaus.

Getsugan ominuki 月旺御身抜. 1680. By Getsugan 月旺 (Maeno Ribei 前野理兵衛). In Fujiyoshida-shi Shi hensan iinkai 富士吉田市史編纂委員会, ed. *Fujiyoshida-shi* 富士吉田市史, *shiryō hen* 史料編 vol. 5: *Kinsei* 近世 vol. 3, 1997.

Gogumaiki 後愚昧記. 1980. Tōkyō daigaku shiryō hensanjo 東京大学史料編纂所, ed. *Dai Nihon kokiroku, Gogumaiki* 大日本古記録, 後愚昧記 1. Tokyo: Tōkyō daigaku shuppankai.

Goseibai shikimoku 御成敗式目. 1955–1965. In Satō Shin'ichi 佐藤進一 *et al.*, ed. *Chūsei hōsei shiryōshū* 中世法制史料集 vol. 3. Tokyo: Iwanami shoten.

Gyokuteki inken 玉滴隠見 (1573–1680). 1985. In Shiseki kenkyūkai 史籍研究会, ed. *Dankai, Gyokuteki inken* 談海・玉滴隠見 (Naikaku Bunko shozō shiseki sōkan 內閣文庫所蔵史籍叢刊 vol. 44). Tokyo: Kyūko shoin.

Haguro Gassan Yudono Sanzan gashū 羽黒・月山・湯殿 三山雅集. (1710). 1974. By Tōsui 東水. Togawa Anshō 戸川安章 and Tōhoku shuppan kikaku 東北出版企画, eds. Tsuruoka: Tōhoku shuppan kikaku.

Hanabusa sōshi 英草紙. In NKBZ vol. 48.

Harusame monogatari 春雨物語. In NKBZ vol. 48.

Heihanki/Hyōhanki 兵範記. 1981. Zōho Shiryō taisei kankōkai 増補史料大成刊行会, ed. *Zōho Shiryō taisei* 増補史料大成 vol. 18, *Hyōhanki* 兵範記 vol. 1. Kyoto: Rinsen shoten.

Heutiges Japan. 2001. By Engelbert Kaempfer. Wolfgang Michel and Barend J. Terwiel, eds. München: Iudicium.

The History of Japan, Giving an Account of the ancient and present State and Government of that Empire; [...] By Engelbert Kaempfer. 1727. Translated by J.G. Scheuchyer, F.R.S. and a member of the College of Physicians. 2 vols. London.

Jakushōdō kokkyōshū 寂照堂谷響集. By Unshō 運敞. In DNBZ vol. 149.

Jien kishōmon (Daisenpōin jōjō kishō no koto) 慈円起請文 (大懴法院条々起請事). 1971. Tōkyō daigaku shiryō hensanjo 東京大学史料編纂所, ed. *Dai Nihon shiryō* 大日本史料 vol. 4/10. Tokyo: Tōkyō daigaku shuppankai.

Jinben 神変. 1909–. Seiyaku kyōkai 聖役協会, ed. Kyoto: Jinbensha.

Jitokushū 寺徳集. In ZGR vol. 26/1.

Jurin shūyō 儒林拾要. In ZGR vol. 31b.

Kaikichō 開基帳. 1663. In Enomoto Minoru 榎本実, "Kan'ei shoki no Yudono Gongen ni tsuite: Mito hanryō no baai" 寛永初期の湯殿権現について−水戸藩領の場合, 28–33. *Ibaraki no minzokugaku* 茨城の民俗学 30, 1991.

Kairoku 海緑 (1820–1837). 1915. By Yamazaki Yoshishige 山崎美成. Kokusho kankōkai 国書刊行会, ed. 20 vols. Tokyo: Kokusho kankōkai gyōsho.

Kansō sadan 閑窓瑣談. 1993. By Tamenaga Shunsui 為永春水. In *Nihon zuihitsu taisei* 日本随筆大成 vol. 1, no. 14: 381–2. Tokyo: Yoshikawa Kōbunkan.

Karasu no tsuibami 烏之啄 (1777). 1974. By Koinshi 古隠子. In *Mizutani Futō* 水谷不倒. *Mizutani Futō chosakushū* vol. 7. (Sentaku kosho kaidai 選擇古書解題 [1937]). Reprint Tokyo: Chūō kōronsha.

Kasuga gongen genki e 春日権現験記絵. In ZNE vols. 13–14.

Katsuragawa no jirei 葛川の事例. 1984. Tōkyō daigaku shiryō hensanjo 東京大学史料編纂所, ed. *Dai Nihon shiryō* 大日本史料 vol. 7/1.

Keichō kenmonshū 慶長見聞集 (1614). 1969. By Miura Jōshin 三浦浄心. In Nakamaru Kazunori 中丸和伯, ed. *Keichō kenmonshū* (Edo shiryō sōsho 江戸資料叢書). Tokyo: Shinjinbutsu ōraisha.

Keiran shūyōshū 渓嵐拾葉集. T vol. 76.

Kinpusen sōsō-ki 金峰山創草記. In *Shugendō shōso* vol. 3.

Kogarashi zōshi 凩草紙. 1994. In *Morishima Chūryō shū*.

Kojidan 古事談 (1215). 1981. Compiled by Minamoto no Akikane 源顕兼. In Kobayashi Yasuharu 小林保治, ed. *Kojidan* vol. 1 (Koten bunko 古典文庫 vol. 60). Tokyo: Gendai shichōsha.

Konjaku monogatarishū 今昔物語集. In SNKBT 36.

Suzukakegoromo 鈴懸衣. 1975. By Gyōchi 行智. In Gorai Shigeru 五来重, ed. *Konohagoromo, Suzukakegoromo, Tōun rokuji* 木葉衣・鈴懸衣・踏雲録事 (Tōyō bunko 東洋文庫 vol. 273, Shugendō shiryōshū 修験道史料集 vol. 1). Tokyo: Heibonsha.

Masuzaki Tenjin engi 松崎天神縁起. In ZNE vol. 22.

Meikyō shinshi 明教維新. 1874–1901. Daikyōin 大教院, ed. Tokyo: Meikyōsha.

Me-hitotsu no kami 目ひとつの神. By Ueda Akinari 上田秋成. NKBZ 48.

Minoodera engi 箕面寺縁起. In *Shoji engishū* 諸寺縁起集 (n. 21).

Morishima Chūryō shū 森島中良集. 1994. In Takada Mamoru 高田衛, Hara Michio 原道生 and Ishigami Satoshi 石上敏, eds. (Sōsho Edo bunko 叢書江戸文庫 vol. 32). Tokyo: Kokusho kankōkai.

Myōtsūji shuto sōjōan (Myōtsūji monjo) 明通寺衆徒等奏状案 (明通寺文書). 1976. Obama-shi shi hensan iinkai 小浜市史編纂委員会, ed. *Obama-shi shi, shajimonjo hen* 小浜市史、社寺文書編. Obama-shi: Obama shiyakusho, 1994.

Nihon ryōiki 日本霊異記. SNKBT 30.

Nihon sandai jitsuroku 日本三代実録. 1955. Kuroita Katsumi 黒板勝美, ed. In *Kokushi taikei* 国史大系 3 (2 vols.). Revised edition. Tokyo: Yoshikawa Kōbunkan.

Nihon sandai jitsuroku 日本三代実録. 2000. Kuroita Katsumi 黒板勝美, ed. *Nihon sandai jitsuroku* 日本三代実録, special edition (*Shintei zōho Kokushi taikei* 新訂増補国史大系 vol. 4). Tokyo: Yoshikawa Kōbunkan.

Nihon shoki 日本書紀. NKBT vol. 67 (2 vols).

Ōmine shugyō kanjō shiki 大峰修行灌頂式. In *Shugendō shōso* 修験道章疏 2.

Ominuki 御身抜. 1971. By Kakugyō Tōbutsu 角行藤佛. In NST vol. 67 (*Minshū shūkyō no shisō* 民衆宗教の思想).

Otake Dainichi Nyorai engi emaki (3 vol.) 1849. http://www.nichibun.ac.jp/graphicversion/dbase/otake/index.html.

Ribuōki 吏部王記, by Shigeakira Shinnō 重明親王. 1974. In Yoneda Yūsuke 米田雄介 and Yoshioka Masayuki 吉岡真之, eds. *Ribuōki* 吏部王記. Tokyo: Zoku Gunsho ruijū kanseikai.

Ryōjin hishō 梁塵秘抄. In SNKBT vol. 56.

Saitō Gesshin nikki 斎藤月岑日記 (1830–1875). 2003. By Saitō Gesshin 斎藤月岑. In Tōkyō daigaku shiryō hensanjo 東京大学史料編纂所, ed. *Dai Nihon kokiroku* 大日本古記録 vol. 4. Tokyo: Iwanami shoten.

San'in shuto shingi hōshiki nanjū ni tsuki bettō meshikae gan 三院衆徒新儀法式難渋につき別当召替願 (abbrev. *San'in shuto shingi*). 1738. In *Nagano kenshi* 長野県史 vol. 1, no. 480. Nagano: Nagano kenshi kankōkai.

Sanbu sōjō hossoku mikki 三峰相承法則密記 (c. 1525). 2000. Compiled by Akyūbō Sokuden 阿吸房即伝. In *Shugendō shōso* 修験道章疏 2: 453–97.

Shasekishū 沙石集. In NKBT 85.

Shichi tengu'e 七天狗絵. 2003. Takahashi Shūei 高橋秀榮. *Shichitengu'e no kotobagaki hakken* 七天狗絵の詞書発見, *Bungaku* 文学 4(6),.

Shijū hyaku innenshū 私聚百因縁集. By Jūshin 住信. In DNBZ 148.

Shijū hyaku innenshū 私聚百因縁集. 1969–1970. By Jūshin 住信. Yoshida Kōichi 吉田幸一 ed. Tokyo: Koten bunko.

Shin Chomonjū 新著聞集 (1749). 1994. In Nihon zuihitsu taisei henshūbu 日本随筆大成編集部, ed. *Nihon zuihitsu taisei* 日本随筆大成, series 2 vol. 5. Tokyo: Yoshikawa Kōbunkan.

Shingen bushō no kishōmon: jūyō bunkazai Ikushima Tarushima jinja monjo 信玄武将の起請文: 重要文化財・生島足島神社文書. 1988. Ikushima Tarushima jinja, Tōshin shigakkai, Shioda bunkazai kenkyūjo 生島足島神社, 東信史学会, 塩田文化財研究所編, ed. Nagano: Shinmai shoseki shuppan sentā.

Shingonden 真言伝. 1988. Setsuwa kenkyūkai 説話研究会, ed. *Shingonden taikō* 真言伝対校. Tokyo: Benseisha.

Shinsarugakuki 新猿楽記. 1979. In NST vol. 8.

Shinsarugakuki (Shinsarugōki) 新猿楽記, 1983. By Fujiwara no Akihira 藤原明衡. Tokyo: Heibonsha.

Shoji engishū (Fushimi Miya-ke Kujōke kyūzō Shojiengishū 伏見宮家九条家旧蔵諸寺縁起集). 1970. Kunaichō shoryūbu 宮内庁書陵部 ed. *Kokushoryō sōkan* 図書寮叢刊. Tokyo: Meiji shoin.

Shokoku ikken hijiri monogatari 諸国一見聖物語. 1981. Kyōto daigaku bungakubu kokugogaku kokubungaku kenkyūshitsu 京都大学文学部国語学国文学研究室, ed. *Shokoku ikken hijiri monogatari* 諸国一見聖物語. Manshuin zō, Kokawadera zō 曼殊院蔵・粉河寺蔵 (Kyōto daigaku kokugo kokubun shiryō sōsho 京都大学国語国文資料叢書 vol. 29). Kyoto: Rinsen shoten.

Shoku Nihongi 続日本紀. SNKBT vols. 12–16.

Shozan engi 諸山縁起. In NST 20.

Shugen kenkyū 修験研究. 1921–1923. Shugen kenkyūsha 修験研究社, ed. Morioka: Shugen kenkyūsha.

Shugen mondō 修験問答. 1561. In ST, *Jinja hen* 神社編 vol. 24.

Shugen shūyō hiketsushū 修験修要祕決集. Compiled by Akyūbō Sokuden 阿吸房即伝. *Shugendō shōso* vol. 2.

Shuihu zhuan 水滸傳 (*Rongyutang ben Shuihu zhuan* 容與堂本水滸傳). 1988. Ling Geng 凌賡, Heng He 恒鶴, and Diao Ning 刁寧, eds. vol. 2. Shanghai: Shanghai guji cubanshe.

Sō Kakuken denchi kishinjō (Katsuoji monjo) 僧覚賢田地寄進状 (勝尾寺文書). 1972. Minoo-shi shi henshū iinkai 箕面市史編集委員会, ed. In *Minoo-shi shi shiryō hen* 箕面市史史料編 2. Minoo: Minoo shiyakusho.

Tengu zōshi 天狗草紙. In ZNE vol. 26.

Tōdaiji sanjū sojōan 東大寺三重訴状案. 2008. Kokubungaku kenkyū shiryōkan 国文学研究資料館 ed. *Tōdaiji honmatsu sōron shiryō* 東大寺本末相論史料 (*Shinpukuji zenpon sōkan* 真福寺善本叢刊, second series vol. 10). Kyoto: Rinsen shoten.

Togakushisan daigongen engi 戸隠山代権現縁起. 1736?. By Jōin. In ST, *Jinja hen* 神社編 vol. 24.

Togakushisan Kenkōji ruki (narabi ni jo) 戸隠山顯光寺流記 (並序). 1458. Compiled by Jikkokusō Utsū 十穀僧有通. In ST, *Jinja hen* 神社編 vol. 24.

Togakushisan shinryōki 戸隠山神領記 (c. 1727–1738). Compiled by Jōin. In ST, *Jinja hen* 神社編 vol. 24.

Towazugatari 問わず語り. By Go-Fukakusa-in no Nijō 後深草院二条. In SNKBT 50.

Ugetsu monogatari 雨月物語. By Ueda Akinari 上田秋成. In NKBZ 48.

Uguisu bue うぐひす笛 (late 1770s-early 1780s). Ōta Nanpo 大田南畝. Quoted in *Chūgoku shōwa sen*.

Ushū Hagurosan chūkō oboegaki 羽州羽黒山中興覚書. In ST, *Jinja hen* 神社編 vol. 32.

Ushū Hagurosan Koganedō Otake Dainichi Nyorai ryaku engi 羽州羽黒山黄金堂お竹大日如来畧縁起. Yamagata Museum No. 5C000566.

Utsubo monogatari うつほ物語. In SNKBZ 1.

Wakan sansai zue 和漢三才圖會. 1712. vol. 3. National Diet Library Digital Collections.

Waraigusa 和良井久佐. 1774. in *Edo kobanashi shū* vol. 1.

Wahrhafftiger Bericht von den neuerfundenen japponischen Inseln und Königreichen. 1586. By Renward/Renwart Cysat. Fribourg: Abraham Gemperlin.

Yichu liutie (Giso rokujō) 義楚六帖. 1990. Makita Tairyō 牧田諦亮, Yamaji Yoshinori 山路芳範 (ed.). Kyoto: Meiyū shoten.

Zappitsu yōshū 雜筆要集. In ZGR vol. 11b.

Secondary Sources

Abe Jirō 阿部次郎. 1961. *Jinkakushugi* 人格主義. In *Abe Jirō zenshū* 阿部次郎全集 vol. 6, 5–324. Reprint. Tokyo: Iwanami shoten (or. ed. 1922).

Abe Yasurō 阿部泰郎. 2003. "*Shichi tengue* to sono jidai." 『七天狗絵』とその時代. *Bungaku* 文学 4 (6): 60–84.

Aceval, Hakim. 2011. *Engelbert Kaempfer (1651–1716) beschreibt die Yamabushi*. München: Grin Verlag.

Aida Nirō 相田二郎. 1976. "Kishōmon no ryōshi goō hōin ni tsuite." 起請文の料紙牛王宝印について. In *Aida Nirō chosakushū* 相田二郎著作集 1, 181–352. Tokyo: Meicho shuppan.

Ambros, Barbara. 2001. "Localized Religious Specialists in Early Modern Japan: The Development of the Ōyama Oshi System." *Japanese Journal of Religious Studies* 28 (3–4): 329–72.

———. 2008. *Emplacing a Pilgrimage: The Ōyama Cult and Regional Religion in Early Modern Japan*. Cambridge, MA: Harvard University Asia Center.

Andrei, Talia J. 2016. "Mapping Sacred Spaces: Representations of Pleasure and Worship in Sankei mandara." Ph.D. dissertation. Columbia University.

Ariga Yoshitaka 有賀祥隆. 1986. "Chūzō kokkaku Zaō Gongen zakkō. 鋳銅刻画蔵王権現雑攷." *Kokka* 國華 1094: 3–26.

Aston, W.G. 1956. *Nihongi: Chronicles of Japan from the Earliest Times to A.D. 697*. London: George Allen and Unwin.

Atsugishi hishobu shishi hensan 厚木市秘書部市史編纂, ed. 1999. *Atsugi-shi shi: Chūsei tsūshi-hen* 厚木市史―中世通史編. Atsugi: Atsugi-shi.

Averbuch, Irit. 2011. "Discourses of the Reappearing: The Reenactment of the 'Cloth-Bridge Consecration Rite' at Mt. Tateyama." *Japanese Journal of Religious Studies* 38 (1): 1–54.

Bambling, Michele. 1996. "The Kongō-ji Screens: Illuminating the Tradition of Yamato-e 'Sun and Moon' Screens." *Orientations* 27 (8): 70–82.

Blacker, Carmen. 1986. *The Catalpa Bow: A Study of Shamanistic Practices in Japan*. London: G. Allen & Unwin.

———. 1995. *Azusa yumi: Nihon ni okeru shāman teki kōi* あずさ弓: 日本におけるシャーマン的行為. Translated by Akiyama Satoko 秋山さと子. Tokyo: Iwanami shoten.

Blair, Heather. 2015. *Real and Imagined: The Peak of Gold in Heian Japan*. Harvard East Asian monographs 376. Cambridge, MA and London: Harvard University Asia Center.

Blair, Heather and Kawasaki Tsuyoshi, eds. 2015. "Forging Accounts of Sacred Origins" Special issue of *Japanese Journal of Religious Studies* 42 (1): 1–26.

Blavatsky, Helen. 1890. "Recent Progress in Theosophy." http://www.katinkahesselink.net/blavatsky/articles/v12/y1890_033.htm: 292–308. *The North American Review* vol. CLI (405): 173–86.

Bocking, Brian. 2013. "Flagging up Buddhism: Charles Pfoundes (Omoie Tetzunostzuke) among the International Congresses and Expositions, 1893–1905." *Contemporary Buddhism* 14 (1): 17–37.

Bodiford, William M. 2007. "Matara: A Dream King between Insight and Imagination." *Cahiers d'Extrême-Asie* 16: 233–62.

Bond, A. Kevin. 2009. "Forcing the Immovable One to the Ground: Revisioning a Major Deity in Early Modern Japan." Ph.D. dissertation. Hamilton: McMaster University.

Bouchy, Anne. 1977. *Shashin gyōja Jitsukaga no shugendō* 捨身行者実利の修験道. Tokyo: Kadokawa shoten.

———. 1978. "Jitsukaga, yamabushi des premières années de Meiji, et le shugendô." *Revue de l'histoire des religions* 193 (2): 187–211.

———. 1993. "Otogizōshi En no Gyōja monogatari emaki no En no Gyōja den" お伽草子『役行者物語絵巻』の役行者伝. In *Bukkyō minzokugaku taikei* 仏教民族体系 vol. 1, 251–76. Tokyo: Meicho shuppan.

———. 2000. "La Cascade et l'écritoire [Dynamique de l'histoire du fait religieux et de l'ethnologie du Japon: le cas du shugendō]." *Bulletin de l'Ecole Française d'Extrême-Orient* 87 (1): 341–66.

———. 2005. "Du légitime et de l'illégitime dans le shugendō ou 'Sang de buddha', 'sang des êtres des montagnes'?" In *Légitimités, légitimations - la construction de l'autorité au Japon*, 111–73. Paris: Ecole française d'Extrême-Orient (EFEO).

———. 2011. "Transformations, Rupture and Continuity: Issues and Options in Contemporary Shugendō." *Cahiers d'Extrême-Orient* 18 (2009): 17–45.

———, ed. 2013. *Le vivre ensemble à Sasaguri, une communauté de Kyushu. Dans l'entrelacs des dynamiques du dedans et du dehors*. Special issue of *Cahiers d'Extrême-Asie* 22.

Brazell, Karen. 1973. *The Confessions of Lady Nijō*. Stanford: Stanford University Press.

Brinker, Helmut. 2011. *Secrets of the Sacred: Empowering Buddhist Images in Clear, in Code and in Cache*. Lawrence and Seattle: Spencer Museum of Art and University of Washington Press.

Burlingame, Eugene Watson. 1917. "The Act of Truth (Saccakiriya): A Hindu Spell and Its Employment as a Psychic Motif in Hindu Fiction." *Journal of the Royal Asiatic Society*: 429–67.

Bynum, Caroline Walker, Stevan Harrell and Paula Richman, eds. 1986. *Gender and Religion: On the Complexity of Symbols*. Boston: Beacon Press.

Carter, Caleb. 2014. "Producing Place, Tradition and the Gods: Mt. Togakushi, Thirteenth through Mid-Nineteenth Centuries." PhD. dissertation. Los Angeles: University of California, Los Angeles.

———. 2017. "Constructing a Place, Fracturing a Geography: The Case of the Japanese Tendai Cleric Jōin." *History of Religions* 56 (3): 289–310.

———. 2018. "Power Spots and the Charged Landscape of Shinto." *Japanese Journal of Religious Studies* 45 (1): 145–73.

———. Forthcoming. *A Path into the Mountains. Tracing the History of Shugendō through the Case of Mount Togakushi*. Honolulu: University of Hawai'i Press.

Castiglioni, Andrea. 2015. "Ascesis and Devotion: The Mount Yudono Cult in Early Modern Japan." Ph.D. dissertation. New York: Columbia University.

———. 2017a. "Edo jidai no Yudonosan shinkō to issei gyōnin no sokushin-butsu." 江戸時代の湯殿山信仰と一世行人の即身仏. *Tōyōgaku kenkyū* 東洋学研究 54: 105–19.

———. 2017b "Shika, sekibutsu, engi ga kataru Yudonosan shinkō: Muromachi makki kara Edo shoki made." 詩歌、石仏、縁起が語る湯殿山信仰—室町末期から江戸初期まで.

In *Shūkyō bungei no gensetsu to kankyō* 宗教文芸の言説と環境 (*Nihon bungaku no tenbō wo hiraku* 宗教文芸の言説と環境 vol. 3), 313-29. Tokyo: Kasama shoin.

———. 2019. "Devotion in Flesh and Bone: The Mummified Corpses of Mount Yudono Ascetics in the Edo Period." *Asian Ethnology* 78-1: 25-51.

Chijiwa Itaru 千々和到. 1988. *Itabi to sono jidai: tejikana bunkazai, mijikana chūsei* 板碑とその時代 てじかな文化財みじかな中世. Tokyo: Heibonsha.

———. 2010. "Gofu no chōsa" 護符の調査. In Chijiwa Itaru, ed. *Nihon no gofu bunka* 日本の護符文化. 251-78. Tokyo: Kōbundō.

Chŏn Kyŏng-su 全京秀. 2008. "Shūkyō jinruigaku to shūkyō minzokugaku no seiritsu katei: Akamatsu Chijō no gakushiteki igi ni tsuite no hikaku kentō." 宗教人類学と宗教民族学の成立過程—赤松智城の学史的意義についての比較検討. *Kikan Nihon shisōshi* 季刊日本思想史 72: 107-29.

Clements, Frank. 2019. "The Fall Peak, Professional Culture, and Document Production in Early Modern Haguro Shugendō." *Japanese Journal of Religious Studies* 4 (2): 219-45.

DeWitt, Lindsey. 2015. *A Mountain Set Apart: Female Exclusion, Buddhism, and Tradition at Modern Ōminesan, Japan*. Ph.D. dissertation. Los Angeles: University of California, Los Angeles.

———. 2016. "Envisioning and Observing Women's Exclusion from Sacred Mountains in Japan." *Journal of Asian Humanities at Kyushu University* 1: 19-28.

Dykstra, Yoshiko. 2014. *Buddhist Tales of India, China, Japan: A Complete Translation of the* Konjaku Monogatarishū. 3 vols. Honolulu: Kanji Press.

Earhart, Harry Byron. 1970. *A Religious Study of the Mount Haguro Sect of Shugendo: An Example of Japanese Mountain Religion*. Tokyo: Sophia University.

———. 1985. *Haguro Shugendō* 羽黒修験道. Translated by Suzuki Masataka 鈴木正崇 and Miyake Hitoshi 宮家準. Tokyo: Kōbundō.

———. 1989. "Mount Fuji and Shugendō." *Japanese Journal of Religious Studies* 16 (2-3): 205-26.

———. 2011. "Mount Fuji: Shield of War, Badge of Peace." *The Asia-Pacific Journal, Japan Focus* 9 (20): 1-15.

———. 2015. *Mount Fuji: Icon of Japan*. Columbia, SC: University of South Carolina Press.

Endō Hideo 遠藤秀男. 2000. "Fuji shinkō no seiritsu to Murayama Shugen." 富士信仰の成立と村山修験. In Suzuki Shōei 鈴木昭英, ed. 1978. *Fuji, Ontake to chūbu reizan* 富士御嶽と中部霊山, 26-57. Reprint. Tokyo: Meicho shuppan.

Enomoto Minoru 榎本実. 1991. "Kan'ei shoki no Yudono Gongen ni tsuite: Mito hanryō no baai." 寛永初期の湯殿権現について--水戸藩領の場合. *Ibaraki no minzoku* 茨城の民族 30 (December): 28-33.

Faure, Bernard. 1996. *Visions of Power: Imagining Mediaeval Japanese Buddhism*. Princeton: Princeton University Press.

———. 2003. *The Power of Denial: Buddhism, Purity, and Gender*. Princeton: Princeton University Press.

———. 2016. *The Fluid Pantheon*. Honolulu: University of Hawai'i Press.

Faure, Bernard, D. Max Moerman and Gaynor Sekimori, eds. 2009. *Shugendō. The History and Culture of a Japanese Religion/L'histoire et la culture d'une religion japonaise*. Special issue of *Cahiers d'Extrême-Asie* 18.

Fleming, D. William. 2013. "Strange Tales from Edo: Liaozhai zhiyi in Early Modern Japan." *Sino-Japanese Studies* 20: 75-115.

Formanek, Susanne. 1998. "Pilgrimage in the Edo Period: Forerunner of Modern Domestic Tourism? The Example of the Pilgrimage to Mount Tateyama." In Sabine Frühstück and Sepp Linhart, eds. *The Culture of Japan as Seen through Its Leisure*, 165-93. Albany, NY: SUNY Press.

Fujimura Midori 藤村みどり. 2015. "Shigo sekai o kakushū wa dō toku (2)" 死後世界を各宗はどう説く. *Gekkan Jūshoku* 月刊住職 17: 120–9.

Fujiyoshida-shi rekishi minzoku hakubutsukan 富士吉田市歴史民俗博物館, ed. 1996. *Fujisan no efuda: goō to miei o chūshin ni* 富士山の絵札―牛玉と御影を中心に. Fujiyoshida-shi: Fujiyoshida-shi kyōiku iinkai.

———, ed. 2000. *Fujisan tozan annaizu* 富士山登山案内図. Fujiyoshida-shi: Fujiyoshida-shi kyōiku iinkai.

Fujiyoshida-shi shi hensan iinkai 富士吉田市史編纂委員会, ed. 1992. *Fujiyoshida-shi shi* 富士吉田市史. *Shiryō hen* 史料編 vol. 2: *kodai chūsei* 古代中世. Fujiyoshida-shi: Fujiyoshida-shi.

———. 1997. *Fujiyoshida-shi shi* 富士吉田市史. *Shiryō hen* 史料編 vol. 5: *kinsei* 近世 vol. 3. Fujiyoshida-shi: Fujiyoshida-shi.

Fujioka Yutaka 藤岡穣. 2004. "Zaō Gongen: sono seiritsu to tenkai 蔵王権現―その成立と展開―." In Zōho Yoshinochōshi henshū iinkai 増補吉野町史編集委員会, ed. *Zōho Yoshino-chō shi* 増補吉野町史, 234–54. Yoshino-chō: Yoshino-chō.

———. 2011. "Densetsu no sonzō, Zaō Gongen 伝説の尊像、蔵王権現." In Osaka-shi bijutsukan 大阪市美術館編, ed. *En no Gyōja to Shugendō no sekai: Sangaku shinkō no hihō* 役行者と修験道の世界―山岳信仰の秘宝, 193–8. Osaka: Mainichi Shinbunsha.

———. 2015. "Zaō Gongen no shinkō to imēji 蔵王権現の信仰とイメージ." In *Nihon bijutsu zenshū: Shinkō to bijutsu* 日本美術全集　信仰と美術 11, 207–9. Tokyo: Shōgakkan.

———. 2016. "Zaō Gongen wo meguru sho mondai 蔵王権現をめぐる諸問題." In Kubo Tomoyasu 久保智康, ed. *Nihon no kodai yamadera* 日本の古代山寺, 321–52. Tokyo: Kōshi shoin.

Fukuda Kyūya 深田久弥. 1964. *Nihon hyaku meisan* 日本百名山. Tokyo: Shinchōsha.

Futazawa Hisaaki 二澤久昭. 1997. "Togakushi no engi to kiroku" 戸隠の縁起と記録. In Futazawa Hisaaki, Hisayama Katsuhiko 久山勝彦, Kyōgoku Okikazu 京極興一, and Oshi Norito 越志徳門, eds. *Togakushi shinkō no rekishi* 戸隠信仰の歴史, 99–108. Togakushi (Nagano Ken): Togakushi Jinja.

Goossaert, Vincent. "Shangqing gong." 2011. In Fabrizio Pregadio, ed. *The Encyclopedia of Taoism* vol. 2, 867–8. London and New York: Routledge.

Gorai Shigeru 五来重. 1970. *Yama no shūkyō, Shugendō* 山の宗教―修験道. Tankōsha.

———. 1975. "Shugendōshi kenkyū to Shugendō shiryō" 修験道史研究と修験道史料. In Gyōchi 行智 and Gorai Shigeru, ed. *Konohagoromo, Suzukaka-goromo, Tōun rokuji* 木葉衣・鈴懸衣・踏雲録事 (*Shugendō shiryō* 修験道史料 vol. 1), 1–44. Tokyo: Heibonsha.

———. 1977. "Hori Ichirō hakushi no Nihon Bukkyōshi kenkyū" 堀一郎博士の日本仏教史研究. In Kusunoki Masahiro 楠正弘, ed. *Hori Ichirō chosakushū* 堀一郎著作集 vol. 1, 589–605. Tokyo: Miraisha.

———. 1980. *Shugendō nyūmon* 修験道入門. Tokyo: Kadokawa shoten.

———. 2007a. "Nihon Bukkyō no minzokusei" 日本仏教の民俗性. In Hinonishi Shinjō 日野西真定, ed. *Nihon Bukkyō minzokugaku no kōchiku* 日本仏教民俗学の構築, 126–37. Kyoto: Hōzōkan (or. ed. 1961).

———. 2007b. "Nihon Bukkyō minzokugaku ronkō" 日本仏教民俗学論攷. In Hinonishi Shinjō 日野西真定, ed. *Nihon Bukkyō minzokugaku no kōchiku* 日本仏教民俗学の構築, 141–390. Kyoto: Hōzōkan (or. ed. 1962).

Grapard, Allan G. 1982. "Flying Mountains and Walkers of Emptiness: Toward a Definition of Sacred Space in Japanese Religions." *History of Religions* 21 (3): 195–221.

———. 1986. "Lotus in the Mountain, Mountain in the Lotus: Rokugō Kaizan Nimmon Daibosatsu Hongi." *Monumenta Nipponica* 41 (1): 21–50.

———. 1989. "The Textualized Mountain – Enmountained Text: The Lotus Sutra in Kunisaki." In George Tanabe and Willa Jane Tanabe, eds. *The Lotus Sutra in Japanese Culture*, 159–89. Honolulu: University of Hawai'i Press.

———. 2011. "Japan's Ignored Cultural Revolution: The Separation of Shinto and Buddhist Deities in Meiji (*shinbutsu bunri*) and a Case Study: Tōnomine." In Lucia Dolce, ed. *Japanese Religions: The Critical Discourse on Japanese Religions* vol. 1, 187–209. Los Angeles, London, New Delhi, Singapore, Washington, DC: Sage (or. ed. 1984).

———. 2016. *Mountain Mandalas: Shugendō in Kyushu*. London and New York: Bloomsbury.

Hall, John Cary. 1906. "Japanese Feudal Laws I: The Institutes of Judicature." *Transactions of the Asiatic Society of Japan* 34: 1–44.

Hasegawa Kenji 長谷川賢二. 1990. "Chūsei kōki ni okeru jiin chitsujo to Shugendō" 中世後期における寺院秩序と修験道. *Nihonshi kenkyū* 日本史研究 336: 31–59.

———. 1991. "Shugendōshi no mikata, kangaekata: kenkyū no seika to kadai wo chūshin ni" 修験道史のみかた・考え方—研究の成果と課題を中心に. *Rekishi kagaku* 歴史科学 123: 17–27.

———. 1994. "Chūsei ni okeru Kumano sendatsu shihai ni tsuite" 中世における熊野先達支配について. *Sangaku shugen* 山岳修験 14: 70–85.

———. 2015. "Yamabushi shūdan no keisei" 山伏集団の形成. In Tokieda Tsutomu 時枝務, Hasegawa Kenji 長谷川賢二 and Hayashi Makoto 林淳, eds. *Shugendōshi nyūmon* 修験道史入門, 533–50. Tokyo: Iwata shoin.

———. 2016. *Shugendō soshiki no keisei to chiiki shakai* 修験道組織の形成と地域社会. Tokyo: Iwata shoin.

Hayakawa Tōru 早川徹. 1997. "Fujisan" 富士山. In Miyake Hitoshi 宮家準, ed. *Shugendō jiten* 修験道辞典, 324–25. Reprint. Tokyo: Tōkyōdō shuppan (or. ed. 1986).

Hayashi Makoto 林淳. 2008. "Gorai Shigeru to Bukkyō minzokugaku no kōsō" 五来重と仏教民俗学の構想. *Shūkyō minzoku kenkyū* 宗教民俗研究 18: 47–62.

Hayashi Mitsuhiro 林三博. 2010. "Nihon seishinshugi no seisui: senzen Nihon ni okeru nejireta shisō gengo no jōken" 日本精神主義の盛衰—戦前日本における捩れた思想言語の条件. *Soshiorogosu* ソシオロゴス 34: 43–64.

Higo Kazuo 肥後和男. 1959. *Nihon ni okeru sangaku shinkō no rekishi* 日本における山岳信仰の歴史. Tokyo: Jinja shinpōsha.

Hirano Eiji 平野榮次, ed. 1987. *Fuji Sengen shinkō* 富士浅間信仰. Tokyo: Yūzankaku shuppan.

———. 2004. "Fuji shinkō to mandara" 富士信仰と曼荼羅. In Hirano Eiji, ed. *Fuji shinkō to Fujikō* 富士信仰と富士, 47–68. Tokyo: Iwata shoin.

Hirasawa, Caroline. 2013. *Hell-Bent for Heaven in Tateyama Mandara*. Leiden: Brill.

Hirayama Noboru 平山昇. 2015. *Hatsumōde no shakaishi, tetsudō ga unda goraku to nashonarizumu* 初詣の社会史—鉄道が生んだ娯楽とナショナリズム. Tokyo: Tōkyō daigaku shuppankai.

Hirose Fujio 広瀬不二雄. 2005. *Fujisan no kaigashi* 富士山の絵画史. Tokyo: Chūō Kōron Bijutsu Shuppan.

Hiruma Hisashi 比留間尚. 1980. *Edo no kaichō* 江戸の開帳. Tokyo: Yoshikawa Kōbunkan.

Hori Ichirō 堀一郎. 1940. *Indo minzokuron* 印度民族論. Tokyo: Ajia mondai kenkyūjo.

———. 1951. *Minkan shinkō* 民間信仰. Tokyo: Iwanami shoten.

———. 1953. *Waga kuni minkan shinkō rekishi no kenkyū* 我が国民間信仰史の研究. Osaka: Sōgensha.

———. 1959. *Nihon ni okeru sangaku shinkō no gensho keitai* 日本における山岳信仰の原初形態. Tokyo: Jinja shinpōsha.

———. 1963. *Folk Religion in Japan: Continuity and Change*. Edited by Joseph M. Kitagawa and Alan L. Miller. Chicago: University of Chicago Press.

Horiuchi Makoto 堀内真. 1995. "Fuji ni tsudou kokoro: omoteguchi to kitaguchi no Fuji shinkō" 富士に集う心—表口と北口の富士信仰. In Amino Yoshihiko 網野善彦 and Ishii Susumu 石井進, eds. *Kyōkai to hina ni ikiru hitobito* 境界と鄙に生きる人々 (Chūsei no fūkei o yomu 中世の風景を読む vol. 3), 129–71. Tokyo: Shinjinbutsu ōraisha.

———. 2009. "Fujikō seiritsu izen no Fuji shinkō: Yoshida oshi shozō no sahōsho o moto ni" 富士講成立以前の富士信仰—吉田御師所蔵の作法書を元に. In Takano Toshihiko 高埜利彦 and Kōshū Shiryō Chōsakai 甲州史料調査会, eds. *Fujisan oshi no rekishiteki kenkyū* 富士山御師の歴史的研究, 281–322. Tokyo: Yamakawa shuppansha.

Hur, Nam-lin. 2000. *Prayer and Play in Late Tokugawa Japan: Asakusa Sensōji and Edo Society*. East Asian Monographs 185. Cambridge, MA: Harvard University Press.

Hurvitz, Leon, trans. 2009. *Scripture of the Lotus Blossom of the Fine Dharma*. New York: Columbia University Press.

Inaba Nobumichi. 稲葉伸道. 2008. "Kaidai" 解題. In *Shinpukuji Zenpon sōkan*, second series vol. 10 真福寺善本叢刊第二期第十巻 (*Tōdaiji honmatsu sōron shiryō* 東大寺本末相論史料), 747–77. Kyoto: Rinsen shoten.

Inoue Mitsusada 井上光貞. 1971. *Nihon kodai no kokka to bukkyō* 日本古代の国家と仏教. Tokyo: Iwanami shoten.

Irumada Nobuo 入間田宣夫. 1986. *Hyakushō shinjō to kishōmon no sekai* 百姓申状と起請文の世界—中世民衆の自立と連帯. Tokyo: Tōkyō daigaku shuppankai.

Ishida Mosaku 石田茂作, Yajima Kyōsuke 矢島恭介. 1937. "Kinpusen kyōzuka ibutsu no kenkyū" 金峯山経塚遺物の研究. *Teishitsu hakubutsukan gakuhō* 帝室博物館学報 8: 1–173.

Ishiguro Tomonori 石黒智教. 2009. "Senkyūhyaku nijū nendai no Shugen: zasshi *Shugen kenkyū* o sozai ni" 一九二〇年代の修験—雑誌『修験研究』を素材に. In Ōtani daigaku Nihon bukkyō bunka kenkyūkai 大谷大学日本仏教文化研究会, eds. *Bukkyō bunka shisō* 仏教文化史叢 vol. 5, 122–9. Kyoto: Ōtani Daigaku Nihon bukkyō bunka kenkyūkai.

Ishikawa Jun 石川淳. 1990. "Edojin no hassōhō ni tsuite" 江戸人の発想法について. In *Ishikawa Jun zenshū* 石川淳全集 vol. 12, 328–39. Tokyo: Chikuma shobō (or. ed. 1943).

Ishikawa Tomohiko 石川知彦. 1999. "En no Gyōja-zō: iwaza ni koshikakete suwaru to iu koto" 役行者像・岩座に腰掛けて座るという事. In Ōsaka shiritsu bijutsukan 大阪市立美術館, ed. *En no Gyōja to shugendō no sekai: sangaku shinkō no hihō* 役行者と修験道の世界—山岳信仰の秘宝, 188–92. Tokyo: Mainichi shinbunsha.

———. 2015. "Genealogies of En no Gyōja, Zengoki and Hachi dai dōji Images, En no Gyōja Zengoki and Hachi dai dōji zō no keifu" 役行者前後鬼・八大童子系譜. In Ryūkoku daigaku, Ryūkoku Museum 龍谷大学、龍谷ミュージアム, eds. *Treasures of Shōgo-in Monzeki Temple, Shōgo-in monzeki no meihō* 聖護院門跡の名宝, 161–4. Kyoto: Yomiuri Shimbun.

Ishikawa Tomohiko 石川知彦 and Ozawa Hiromu 小澤弘. 2000. *Zusetsu En no Gyōja: Shugendō to En no Gyōja emaki* 図説役行者：修験道と役行者絵巻. Tokyo: Kawade shobō shinsha.

Iwasaki Toshio 岩崎敏夫. 1963. *Honpō shōshi no kenkyū: Minkan shinkō no minzokugakuteki kenkyū* 本邦小祠の研究--民間信仰の民俗学的研究. Sendai: Iwasaki hakase gakui ronbun shuppan kōenkai.

Iwashina Kōichirō 岩科小一郎. 1977. "Fujisan no efuda" 富士山の絵札. *Ashinaka* あしなか 156: 18–20.

———. 1983. *Fujikō no rekishi: Edo shomin no sangaku shinkō* 富士講の歴史—江戸庶民の山岳信仰. Tokyo: Meichō shuppan.

Iwata Shigeki 岩田茂樹. 2002. "Ishiyamadera no chōkoku: Honzon Nihi Jōroku Kannon zō wo chūshin ni" 石山寺の彫像—本尊二臂丈六観音像を中心に—. In Nara kokuritsu hakubutsukan 奈良国立博物館, ed. *Tokubetsu ten: Kannon no mitera Ishiyamadera* 特別展観音のみてら石山寺: 10–13. Nara: Nara kokuritsu hakubutsukan.

Kaempfer, Engelbert. 1999. *Kaempfer's Japan; Tokugawa Culture Observed*. Translated by Beatrice M. Bodart-Bailey. Honolulu: University of Hawai'i Press.

Kamens, Edward. 1988. *The Three Jewels: A Study and Translation of Minamoto Tamenori's Sanbōe*. Ann Arbor: Center for the Japanese Studies the University of Michigan.

Kaminishi, Ikumi. 2006. *Explaining Pictures: Buddhist Propaganda and Etoki Storytelling in Japan*. Honolulu: University of Hawai'i Press.

Kanai Tōrō 金居遠郎. 2018. "Kunan no fukkō tsunagu kokorozashi" 苦難の復興つなぐ志. *Asahi Shimbun Wakayama*, March 18, 2018. https://www.asahi.com/articles/CMTW1803163100001.html.

Kanamori Atsuko 金森敦子. 1986. "Sekkō" 石工. In *Nihon sekibutsu kyōkai* 国書刊行会, eds. *Nihon sekibutsu zuten* 日本石仏図典. Tokyo: Kokusho kankōkai.

Kanda, James. 1974. "Japanese Feudal Society in the Sixteenth Century as Seen Through the Jinkaishū and Other Legal Codes." PhD dissertation. Harvard University.

Kanda Yoriko 神田より子. 2011. "Nyonin Ōjō wo negatte Nunohashi wo wataru" 女人往生を願って布橋を渡る. In Miyake Hitoshi 宮家準, ed. *Sangaku shugen e no shōtai: Reizan to shugyō taiken* 山岳修験への招待–霊山と修行体験, 184–93. Tokyo: Shinjibutsu Ōraisha 新人物往来社.

Kawane Yoshiyasu 河音能平. 1977. *Chūsei hōkensei seiritsu shiron* 中世封建制成立史論. Tokyo: Tokyo daigaku shuppankai.

Kawahashi Noriko 川橋範子 and Kobayashi Naoko 小林奈央子. 2017. "Editors' Introduction: Gendering Religious Practices in Japan Multiple Voices, Multiple Strategies." *Japanese Journal of Religious Studies* 44–1:1–13.

Kawasaki Tsuyoshi 川崎剛志. 2004. "*Shozan engi* shoshi kō" 『諸山縁起』書誌攷. *Shūjitsu gobun* 就實語文 25: 23–31.

———. 2006. "*Kongōsan engi* no kisoteki kenkyū" 『金剛山縁起』の基礎的研究. *Kanazawa bunko kenkyū* 金沢文庫研究 307: 1–16.

———. 2007. "Nihonkoku 'Kongōsan'-setsu no rufu: Inseiki, nanto o chūshin ni" 日本国『金剛山』説の流布・院政期、南都を中心に. *Denshō bungaku kenkyū* 伝承文学研究 56: 12–22.

———. 2010. "Inseiki ni okeru Yamato no kuni no reizan kōryū jigyō to engi" 院政期における大和国の霊山興隆事業と縁起. In Abe Yasurō 阿部康朗, ed. *Chūsei bungaku to jiin shiryō: shōgyō* 中世文学と寺院資料・聖教, 401–25. Tokyo: Chikurinsha.

———. 2011. *Shugendō no Muromachi bunka* 修験道の室町文化. Tokyo: Iwata shoin.

———. 2013. "Reizan no jikū to saikōchiku: *Minoodera engi* no shutsugen to sono yoha" 霊山の時空と再構築－『箕面寺縁起』の出現とその余波. Unpublished paper presented at the international symposium on "Religious Performance, City and Country in East Asia", University of Illinois, Chicago.

———. 2015. "The Invention and Reception of the *Minoodera engi*." *Japanese Journal of Religious Studies* 42 (1): 133–55.

———. 2016. "Kinpusen maikyō to En no Gyōja no gyōdō" 金峯山埋経と役行者の行道. *Setsuwa bungaku kenkyū* 説話文學研究 49: 69–72.

———. 2017. "*Minoodera engi* no senjutsu to juyō" 『箕面寺縁起』の撰述と受容. *Shūjitsu hyōgen bunka* 就実表現文化 11: 1–15.

Kawasaki Tsuyoshi 川崎剛志 and Chikamoto Kensuke 近本謙介. 2005. "Ōmine no kuden: engi keisei ni kan suru bunkengakuteki kenkyū, *Shozan engi* o chūshin ni" 大峰の口伝・縁起形成に関する文献学的研究—「諸山縁起」を中心に. Kagaku kenkyūhi hojokin, kiban kenkyū 科学研究費補助金、基盤研究 (C) (2). *Kenkyū seika hokokusho* 研究成果報告書.

Keenan, Linda K. 1989. *En no Gyōja: The Legend of a Holy Man in the Twelve Centuries of Japanese Literature*. Ann Arbor: University Microfilms International.

———. 1999. "En no Gyōja". In George Tanabe J., ed. *Religion of Japan in Practice*, 343–353. Princeton Readings in Religion. Princeton: Princeton University Press.

Kerr, George H. 1958. *Okinawa: The History of an Island People*. Tokyo: Tuttle.

Kihira Tadayoshi 紀平正美. 1930. *Nihon seishin* 日本精神. Tokyo: Iwanami shoten.

———. 1936. *Chi to gyō* 知と行. Tokyo: Kōbundō shobō.

Kikuchi Hiroki 菊地大樹. 2011. *Kamakura bukkyō e no michi* 鎌倉仏教への道. Tokyo: Kōdansha.

Kikuchi Kunihiko 菊池邦彦. 2009. "Chūsei kōki kara kinsei zenki ni okeru Fujisan Murayama-guchi no tozansha: *Fujisan danki* o chūshin ni" 中世後期から近世前期における富士山村山口の登山者—『富士山檀記』を中心に. In Tanaka Toshihiko 高埜利彦, ed. *Fujisan oshi no rekishiteki kenkyū* 富士山御師の歴史的研究, 341–93. Tokyo: Yamakawa shuppansha.

Kim, Sujun. 2018. "Frogs Looking Beyond a Pond: Shinra Myōjin in the 'East Asian Mediterranean' Network." In Fabio Rambelli, ed. *The Sea and the Sacred in Japan: Aspects of Maritime Religion*, 79–88. London and New York: Bloomsbury.

Kinenshi shuppan iinkai 記念誌出版委員会, eds. 1995. *Denpōgakuin sōritsu rokujū shūnen kinenshi* 伝法学院創立六十周年記念誌. Kyoto: Daigosan Denpōgakuin.

Klautau, Orion. 2008. "Against the Ghosts of Recent Past, Meiji Scholarship and the Discourse on Edo-Period Buddhist Decadence." *Japanese Journal of Religious Studies* 35 (2): 263–303.

———. 2012. *Kindai Nihon shisō to shite no bukkyō shigaku* 近代日本思想としての仏教史学. Kyoto: Hōzōkan.

Klonos, George. 2012. "Shugendō in the Tokugawa Period: Mount Ōmine as Imaginary Space and Place of Practice." Ph.D. dissertation. Stanford: Stanford University.

———. 2019. "The *Robe of Leaves*: A Nineteenth Century Text of Shugendō Apologetics." *Japanese Journal of Religious Studies* 46–1:103–28.

Kobayashi Keiichirō 小林計一郎. 1993. "Togakushi shiseki meguri no ki" 戸隠史跡めぐり記. *Nagano* 長野 171: 55–67.

Kobayashi Naoko 小林奈央子. 2017. "Sacred Mountains and Women in Japan: Fighting a Romanticized Image of Female Ascetic Practitioners." *Japanese Journal of Religious Studies* 44 (1): 103–22.

———. 2019. "Minzokugaku ni okeru jendā shiten no hitsuyōsei: josei gyōja wo chūshin ni" 民俗学におけるジェンダー視点の必要性—女性行者を中心に. *Shūkyō kenkyū* 395 93 (2): 57–78.

Kohn, Livia. 1993-1995. "Kōshin: A Taoist Cult in Japan." *Japanese Religion* 18 (2): 113-39, 20 (1): 34-55, and 20 (2): 123-42.

Koizumi Takeei 小泉武栄. 2001. *Tōzan no tanjō: hito wa naze yama ni noboru yō ni natta no ka* 登山の誕生―人はなぜ山に登るようになったのか. Tokyo: Chūō kōronsha.

Kojima Norihiro 小嶋教寛. 2013. "Tōnan-in Shōchū to Daigoji: sono raireki to honmatsu sōron shiryō ni okeru hyōka o chūshin ni" 東南院聖忠と醍醐寺―その来歴と本末相論史料における評価を中心に. *Rengeji bukkyō kenkyūjo kiyō* 6: 5-31.

Komine Kazuaki 小峯和明監 and Hara Katsuaki 原克昭, eds. 2017. *Shūkyō bungei no gensetsu to kankyō* 宗教文芸の言説と環境 (Nihon bungaku no tenbō wo hiraku 宗教文芸の言説と環境 vol. 3). Tokyo: Kasama shoin.

Kondō Yoshihiro 近藤喜博. 1951. "Fuji mandara to shinkō" 富士曼荼羅と信仰. *Shintō shigaku* 神道史學 2: 24-9.

———. 1972. "Fuji Sengen mandara zusetsu" 富士浅間曼荼羅図説. *Shintō shūkyō* 神道宗教 65-66: 97-110.

Kondō Yūsuke 近藤祐介. 2005. "Sengokuki Kantō ni okeru Satte Fudōin no taitō to Kamakura Getsurin'in: Go-Hōjō-shi to Koga kubō no kankei kara" 戦国期関東における幸手不動院の台頭と鎌倉月輪院―後北条氏と古河公方の関係から. *Chihōshi kenkyū* 地方史研究 55 (3): 1-19.

———. 2010. "Shugendō Honzan-ha ni okeru sengokukiteki kōzō no shutsugen" 修験道本山派における戦国期的構造の出現. *Shigaku zasshi* 史学雑誌 119 (4): 445-78.

———. 2015. "Honzan-ha" 本山派. In Tokieda Tsutomu 時枝務, Hasegawa Kenji 長谷川賢二 and Hayashi Makoto 林淳, eds. *Shugendōshi nyūmon* 修験道史入門, 109-29. Tokyo: Iwata shoin.

———. 2017a. "Shōgoin monzeki no seiritsu to tenkai" 聖護院門跡の成立と展開. In Nagamura Makoto 永村眞, ed. *Chūsei no monzeki to kōbu kenryoku* 中世の門跡と公武権力, 126-72. Tokyo: Ebisu kōshō shuppan.

———. 2017b. *Shugendō Honzanha seiritsushi no kenkyū* 修験道本山派成立史の研究. Tokyo: Azekura shobō.

Konishi Masatoshi 小西正捷. 1990. "Funabashi no tentō nenbutsu gyōji" 船橋の天道念仏行事. In Funabashi-shi kyōiku iinkai 船橋市教育委員会, eds. *Funabashi no tentō nenbutsu: Daisanji Funabashi-shi minzoku geinō chōsa hōkoku* 船橋の天道念仏――第3次船橋市民俗芸能調査報告, 3-166. Funabashi: Funabashi-shi kyōiku iinkai.

Kubota Nobuhiro 久保田展弘. 2005. *Shugen no sekai: Genshi no seimei uchū* 修験の世界始原の生命宇宙. Tokyo: Kōdansha (or. ed. 1988).

Kume Kunitake 久米邦武, ed. 1878. *Tokumei zenken taishi Bei-ō kairan jikki* 特命全権大使米欧回覧実記. Tokyo: Hakubusha.

Kuno Takeshi 久野健. 1962. "Gyōja-kei no chōkoku" 行者系の彫刻. *Museum* 130: 2-4.

Kuroda Toshio 黒田俊雄. 1980. *Jisha seiryoku* 寺社勢力. Tokyo: Iwanami shoten.

———. 1995. *Kuroda Toshio chosakushū* 黒田俊雄著作集 5 vols. Kyoto: Hōzōkan.

Laqueur, Thomas. 1990. *Making Sex: Body and Gender from the Greeks to Freud*. Cambridge, MA: Harvard University Press.

Lamotte, Charlotte. 2013. "La pierre qui vit - Naissance et mort des statues dans une ville de pèlerinage -." *Cahiers d'Extrême-Asie* 22: 424-72.

Latour, Bruno. 1993. *We Have Never Been Modern*. Massachusetts: Harvard University Press (or. ed. 1991).

Ling Geng 凌賡, Heng He 恒鶴, and Diao Ning 刁寧, eds. 1988. *Rongyutang ben Shuihu zhuan* 容與堂本水滸傳 vol. 2. Shanghai: Shanghai guji cubanshe.

Liu Feifei 劉菲菲. 2017. "Tsuga Teishō yomihon ni okeru *Suikoden* no juyō" 都賀庭鐘読本における『水滸伝』の受容. *Kinsei bungei* 105: 33-7.

Lobetti, Tullio Federico. 2014. *Ascetic Practices in Japanese Religion*. London: Routledge.

Longrais, F. Joüon des. 1950. *Âge de Kamakura; sources* (1150–1333). Tokyo: Maison franco-japonaise.

Mabuchi Tōichi 馬淵東一. 1968. "Toward the Reconstruction of Ryukyuan Cosmology." In Matsumoto Nobuhiro 松本信広 and Mabuchi Tōichi, eds. *Folk Religion and the Worldview in the Southwestern Pacific*, 119–40. Tokyo: The Keio Institute of Cultural and Linguistic Studies, Keio University.

Markus, L. Andrew. 1985. "The Carnival of Edo: Misemono Spectacles from Contemporary Accounts." *Harvard Journal of Asiatic Studies* 45 (2): 499–541.

Maruyama Shōei 村山正榮. 1934. *Chishakuin shi* 智積院史. Kyoto: Kōbō Daishi onki jimukyoku.

———. 1942. *Shinbutsu shūgō to Nihon bunka* 神仏習合と日本文化. Tokyo: Kōbundō shobō.

Masuda Fukutarō 増田福太郎. 1939. *Taiwan no shūkyō: nōson o chūshin to suru shūkyō kenkyū* 台湾の宗教—農村を中心とする宗教研究. Tokyo: Yōkendō.

Masuda Fukutarō 増田福太郎 and Hori Ichirō 堀一郎, eds. 1942. *Tōa shūkyō no kadai: Daitōa bunka kensetsu kenkyū* 東亜宗教の課題−大東亜文化建設研究. Tokyo: Kokumin seishin bunka kenkyūjo.

Matsudaira Narimitsu 松平斉光. 1943. *Matsuri* 祭. Tokyo: Nikkō shoin.

———. 1946. *Matsuri: honshitsu to shosō* 祭—本質と諸相. Tokyo: Nikkō shoin.

Matsuoka Hideaki 松岡秀明. 2010. "Nihon Bukkyō to kokumin seishin: Shoki Hori Ichirō no bunka shigaku hihan josetsu" 日本仏教と国民精神—初期堀一郎の文化史学批判序説. *Tōkyō daigaku shūkyōgaku nenpō* 東京大学宗教学年報 27: 17–29.

Matsuzaki Kenzō 宮崎憲三. 1994. "Gyōninzuka saikō: tsuka o meguru fōkuroa (1)" 行人塚再考−−塚をめぐるフォークロア（一）. In Yoshihara Ken'ichirō 吉原健一郎, ed. *Nihon jōmin bunka kiyō* 日本常民文化紀要, 44–89. Tokyo: Chūō kōronsha.

McCormick, Melissa. 2012. "Mountains, Magic, and Mothers: Envisioning the Female Ascetic in a Medieval Chigo Tale." In Gregory P. A. Levine, Andrew Watsky, and Gennifer Weisenfeld, eds. *Crossing the Sea: Essays on East Asian Art in Honor of Professor Yoshiaki Shimizu*, 107–33. Princeton, NJ: P. Y. and Kinmay W. Tang Center for East Asian Art, Princeton University.

McCullough, Helen Craig, transl. 1966. *Yoshitsune: A Fifteenth-Century Japanese Chronicle*. (UNESCO Collection of Representative Works: Japanese Series). Stanford: Stanford University Press.

McGuire, Mark P. 2013. « What's at Stake in Designating Japan's Sacred Mountains as UNESCO World Heritage Sites? Shugendō Practices in the Kii Peninsula. » *Japanese Journal of Religious Studies* 40 (2): 323–54.

Mensching, Gustav. 1976. *Structure and Patterns of Religion*. Translated by Hans F. Klimkeit, V. Srinivasa Sarma. Reprint. Delhi, Varanasi, Patna: Motilal Banarsidass (or. ed. 1959).

Miki Masahiro 三木雅博. 2017. "Chūsei kanbun sakuhin ni okeru yōgakusho *Chūmonjō* no riyō ni tsuite: *Kamakura ibun* o taishō to shita chōsa to kōsatsu" 中世漢文作品における幼学書『仲文章』の利用について—『鎌倉遺文』を対象とした調査と考察. *Kyōto gobun* 京都語文 25.

Minowa Kenryō 箕輪顕量. 2015. *Nihon Bukkyōshi* 日本仏教史. Tokyo: Shunjūsha.

Mitsuhashi Tadashi 三橋正. 2000. *Heian jidai no shinkō to shūkyō girei* 平安時代の信仰と宗教儀礼. Tokyo: Zoku Gunsho ruijū kanseikai.

Miyaji Naokazu 宮地直一. 1959. *Sangaku shinkō to jinja* 山岳信仰と神社. Tokyo: Jinja shinpōsha.

Miyaji Naokazu 宮地直一 and Hirono Saburō 廣野三朗. 1929. *Sengen Jinja no rekishi* 浅間神社の歴史 (*Fuji no kenkyū* 富士の研究 vol. 2). Tokyo: Kokin shoin.

Miyake Hitoshi 宮家準. 1982. "Wakamori Tarō kyōju no Shugendō, sangaku shūkyō kenkyū" 和歌森太郎教授の修験道・山岳宗教研究. In *Wakamori Tarō chosakushū* 和歌森太郎著作集 vol. 2, 473–82. Tokyo: Kōbundō.
———. 1985. *Shugendō shisō no kenkyū* 修験道思想の研究. Tokyo: Shunjūsha.
———. 1992. *Kumano shugen* 熊野修験. Tokyo: Yoshida Kōbunkan.
———. 1994. *Nihon no minzoku shūkyō* 日本の民俗宗教. Tokyo: Kōdansha.
———. 1996. *Shugendō to Nihon shūkyō* 修験道と日本宗教. Tokyo: Shunjūsha.
———. 1999a. *Shugendō girei no kenkyū* 修験道儀礼の研究. Expanded edition. Tokyo: Shunjūsha.
———. 1999b. *Shugendō soshiki no kenkyū* 修験道組織の研究. Tokyo: Shunjūsha.
———, 宮家準. 2000a. *En no Gyōja to shugendō no rekishi* 役行者と修験道の歴史. Tokyo: Yoshikawa Kōbunkan.
———. 2000b. *Shugendō shōso kaidai: fukkoku "Shugendō shōso" bekkan* 修験道章疏解題：復刻『修験道章疏』別巻. Tokyo: Kokusho kankōkai.
———. 2001a. *Shugendō: Essays on the Structure of Japanese Folk Religion*. Translated by H. Byron Earhart. Ann Arbor: Center for Japanese Studies, University of Michigan.
———. 2001b. "Shugendō." In Kazuo Kasahara, ed. *A History of Japanese Religion*. Translated by Paul McCarthy and Gaynor Sekimori. Tokyo: Kosei Publishing Co.
———. 2005. *The Mandala of the Mountain: Shugendō and Folk Religion*. Translated by Gaynor Sekimori. Tokyo: Keio University Press.
———. 2012a. *Shugendō no chiikiteki tenkai* 修験道の地域的展開. Tokyo: Shunjūsha.
———. 2012b. *Shugendō* 修験道. Kyoto: Hōzōkan.
Miyake Setsurei 三宅雪嶺. 1985. *Shinzenbi Nihonjin* 真善美日本人. Tokyo: Kōdansha.
Miyake Toshiyuki 三宅敏之. 2000. "Fuji mandara to kyōten mainō" 富士曼荼羅と経典埋納. In Gorai Shigeru 五来重, ed. *Shugendō no bijutsu geinō bungaku* 修験道の美術芸能文学 vol. 1 (Sangaku shūkyōshi kenkyū sōsho 山岳宗教史研究叢書 vol. 14), 420–48. Tokyo: Meicho shuppan (or. ed. 1970).
Miyamoto Kesao 宮本袈裟雄. 2010. *Sato shugen no kenkyū* 里修験の研究. Reprint. Tokyo: Iwata shoin (or. ed. 1984).
Miyashima Junko 宮島潤子. 1993. "Tanzei ippa ni okeru Dainichi shinkō" 弾誓一派における大日信仰. In Miyasaka Yūshū 宮坂宥勝, ed. *Indogaku mikkyōgaku kenkyū: Miyasaka Yūshō hakase koki kinen ronbunshū* インド学密教学研究――宮坂宥勝博士古希記念論文集 vol. 2, 1271–300. Kyoto: Hōzōkan.
Miyazaki, Fumiko. 2005. "Female Pilgrims and Mt. Fuji: Changing Perspectives on the Exclusion of Women." *Monumenta Nipponica* 60 (3): 339–91.
Mizutani Futō 水谷不倒. 1974. "Sentaku kosho kaidai" 選擇古書解題. In *Mizutani Futō chosakushū* 水谷不倒著作集 vol. 7, 5–352. Tokyo: Chūō kōronsha (or. ed. 1937).
Moerman, D. Max. 2005. *Localizing Paradise: Kumano Pilgrimage and the Religious Landscape of Premodern Japan*. Harvard East Asian Monographs 235. Cambridge, MA.: Harvard University Asia Center.
Monbushō 文部省, ed. 1937. *Kokutai no hongi* 国体の本義. Tokyo: Monbushō.
Morley, Carolyn Anne. 1993. *Transformation, Miracles, and Mischief: The Mountain Priest Plays of Kyōgen*. Cornell East Asia, no. 62. Ithaca: East Asia Program, Cornell University.
Morris, Augustine Jonathan. 2005. *Buddhist Hagiography in Early Japan: Image of Compassion in the Gyōki Tradition*. London, New York: Routledge Curzon.
Morris, Yaara. 2018. "The *Kinpusen Himitsuden*: Space, Myth and Ritual in a Medieval Cultic Site." PhD dissertation. London: School of Oriental and African Studies (SOAS).

Murakami Senshō 村上専精, Tsuji Zennosuke 辻善之助 and Washio Junkei 鷲尾順敬, eds. 1926–29. *Meiji Ishin shinbutsu bunri shiryō* 明治維新神仏分離史料. 3 vols. Tokyo: Tōhō shoin.

Murakami Shigeyoshi 村上重良 and Yasumaru Yoshio 安丸良夫, eds. 1971. *Minshū shūkyō no shisō* 民衆宗教の思想 (Nihon shisō taikei 日本思想体系 vol. 67). Tokyo: Iwanami shoten.

Murakami Toshio 村上俊雄. 1978. *Shugendō no hattatsu* 修験道の発達. Tokyo: Meicho shuppan (or. ed. 1943).

Murayama Shūichi. 村山修一. 1957. *Shinbutsu shūgō shichō* 神仏習合思潮. Kyoto: Heirakuji shoten.

———. 1997. *Shugen, Onmyōdō to shaji shiryō* 修験・陰陽道と社寺史料. Kyoto: Hōzōkan.

———. 1970. *Yamabushi no rekishi* 山伏の歴史. Tokyo: Hanawa shobō.

Mus, Paul. 1998. *Borobuḍur: Sketch of a History of Buddhism Based on Archeological Criticism of the Texts*. Translated by Alexander W. Macdonald. New Delhi: Sterling Publishers (or. ed. 1935).

———. 2010. *India Seen from the East: Indian and Indigenous Cults in Champa*. Translated by Ian Mabbett. Victoria: Monash University Press.

Nagamatsu Atsushi 永松敦. 2005. *Shuryō minzoku kenkyū: kinsei shuryō no jitsuzō to denshō* 狩猟民族研究—近世狩猟の実像と伝承. Kyoto: Hōzōkan.

Nagamura Makoto 永村眞. 1988. "'Shingonshū' to Tōdaiji" 『真言宗』と東大寺. In Chūsei jiinshi kenkyūkai 中世寺院史研究会, ed. *Chūsei jiinshi no kenkyū* 中世寺院史の研究 vol. 2, 3–47. Kyoto: Hōzōkan.

Nagano Kenshi Kankōkai 長野県史刊行会, ed. 1987. *Nagano ken shi* 長野県史 vol. 4, no. 1 (Kinsei 近世). Nagano Shi: Nagano Kenshi Kankōkai.

Nakamura, Kyōko Motomachi, transl. 1997. *Miraculous Stories from the Japanese Buddhist Tradition: The Nihon Ryōiki of the Monk Kyōkai*. Harvard-Yenching Institute monograph series vol. 20. Richmond: Curzon.

Nakamura Yukihiko 中村幸彦, ed. 1947. *Harusame monogatari* 春雨物語. Ōsaka: Sekizenkan.

Nakamura Yukihiko 中村幸彦, Takada Mamoru 高田衛, and Nakamura Hiroyasu 中村博保, eds. 1973. *Hanabusa sōshi, Nishiyama monogatari, Ugetsu monogatari, Harusame monogatari* 英草紙・西山物語・雨月物語・春雨物語. In Nihon koten bungaku zenshū vol. 48. Tokyo: Shōgakkan.

Nakayama Tarō 中山太郎. 1984. *Nihon fujoshi* 日本巫女史. Tokyo: Parutosusha (or. ed. 1930).

Nakazawa Shin'ichi 中沢新一. 2006. "Yamabushi no hassei 山伏の発生," in *Geijutsu jinruigaku* 芸術人類学, 220–49. Tokyo: Misuzu Shobō.

Naruhito Shinnō 徳仁親王. 2016. "Rekishi to shinkō no yama o tazunete" 歴史と信仰の山を訪ねて. *Sangaku* 山岳 111: 7–36.

Naumann, Hans. 1992. *Grundzüge der Deutsche Volkskunde*. Leipzig: Quelle & Meyer.

Nishikawa Shinji 西川新次. 1999. "En no Gyōja kara mita shugen no sekai" 役行者から見た修験の世界. In Ōsaka shiritsu bijutsukan 大阪市立美術館, ed. *En no Gyōja to shugendō no sekai: sangaku shinkō no hihō* 役行者と修験道の世界—山岳信仰の秘宝, 166–70. Tokyo: Mainichi shinbunsha.

———. 2001. *Nihon chōkoku shi ronshū* 日本彫刻史論集. Tokyo: Chūō kōron bijutsu shuppan.

Ōba Iwao 大場磐雄. 1958. *Nihon ni okeru sangaku shinkō no kōkogakuteki kōsatsu* 日本における山岳信仰の考古学的考察. Tokyo: Jinja shinpōsha.

Ogata Tsutomu 尾形仂. 1966. "Chūgoku hakuwa shōsetsu to *Hanabusa sōshi*" 中国白話小説と『英草紙』. *Bungaku* 文学 34 (3): 11–20. Reprinted in *Ogata Tsutomu kokubungaku ronshū* 尾形仂国文学論集. Kadokawa gakugei shuppan, 2011: 489–503.

Ogino Yūko 荻野裕子. 1999. "Fujisan Minamiguchi annai ezu: Murayama shugenja to nanroku Fuji tozan" 富士山南口案内絵図—村山修験者と南麓富士登山. *Fuji shiritsu hakubutsukan chōsa kenkyū hōkoku* 富士市立博物館調査研究報告 4: 23–30.

Okada Hiroshi 岡田弘. 1987. "Fujikō to jujutsu" 富士講と呪術. In Hirano Eiji, ed. *Fuji Sengen shinkō* 富士浅間信仰, 195–209. Tokyo: Yūzankaku.

Okamoto Tarō 岡本太郎. 2011a. "Shinpi Nihon 神秘日本." Reprinted in *Nihon saishinbu e* 日本最深部へ (*Okamoto Tarō no uchū* 岡本太郎の宇宙 vol. 4). Tokyo: Chikuma Shobō.

———. 2011b. "Bi no juryoku 美の呪力." Reprinted in *Sekai bijutsu e no michi* 世界美術への道 (*Okamoto Tarō no uchū* 岡本太郎の宇宙 vol. 5). Tokyo: Chikuma Shobō.

Okano Kōji 岡野浩二. 2017. "Heian jidai no sangaku shugyōsha" 平安時代の山岳修行者. *Kokushigaku* 国史学 221: 1–35.

Ōkōchi Tomoaki 大河内智之. 2012. "Nakatsugawadō (Gokurakuji) no Shugendō kankei shiryō" 中津川堂(極楽寺)の修験道関係資料. *Wakayama kenritsu hakubutsukan kenkyū kiyō* 和歌山県立博物館研究紀要 18: 1–24.

———. 2016. "Butsuzō ga tairyō ni nusumareta no wa nazeka kyōjun!" 仏像が大量に盗まれたのはなぜか教順！ *Gekkan Jūshoku* 月刊住職 506: 32–9.

Okumura Takahiko 奥村隆彦. 1973. "Fujiki kuyō no kenkyū (3)" 不食供養の研究（下）. *Shiseki to bijutsu* 史跡と美術 439: 339–45.

———. 1979. "Fujiki kuyō: shinkō no yōsō o chūshin to shite" 不食供養—信仰の様相を中心として. *Nihon bukkyō* 日本仏教 48: 1–18.

Ōmi Toshihiro 碧海寿広. 2007. "Bukkyō minzokugaku no kōsō: Gorai Shigeru ni tsuite" 仏教民俗学の構想—五来重について. *Shūkyō kenkyū* 宗教研究 352: 117–41.

———. 2016. "Gorai Shigeru: Bukkyō minzokugaku to shomin shinkō no tankyū" 五来重—仏教民俗学と庶民信仰の探究. In Orion Klautau, ed. *Sengo rekishigaku to Nihon Bukkyō* 戦後歴史学と日本仏教, 227–47. Kyoto: Hōzōkan.

Ooms, Herman. 1996. *Tokugawa Village Practice: Class, Status, Power, Law*. Berkeley and Los Angeles: University of California Press.

———. 2009. *Imperial Politics and Symbolics in Ancient Japan: The Tenmu Dynasty, 650–800*. Honolulu: University of Hawai'i Press.

Ōsaka shiritsu bijutsukan 大阪市立美術館, ed. 1999. *En no Gyōja to shugendō no sekai: sangaku shinkō no hihō* 役行者と修験道の世界—山岳信仰の秘宝. Tokyo: Mainichi shinbunsha.

Ōsawa Kōji 大澤広嗣. 2015. *Senjika no Nihon Bukkyō to nanpō chiiki* 戦時下の日本仏教と南方地域. Kyoto: Hōzōkan.

Ōtaka Yasumasa 大高康正. 2012. *Sankei mandara no kenkyū* 参詣曼荼羅の研究. Tokyo: Iwata shoin.

———. 2013. *Fujisan shinkō to Shugendō* 富士山信仰と修験道. Tokyo: Iwata shoin.

Ōtani Masayuki 大谷正幸. 2011. *Kakugyō-kei Fuji shinkō: dokusō to seisui no shūkyō* 角行系富士信仰—独創と盛衰の宗教. Tokyo: Iwata shoin.

Ōuchi Fumi 大内典. 2009. "The Lotus Repentance Liturgy of Shugendō: Identification from Vocal Arts." *Cahiers d'Extrême-Asie* 18 (2009): 169–93.

———. 2011. "The Somatic Nature of Enlightenment: Vocal Arts in the Japanese Tendai Tradition." Ph.D. dissertation. London: School of Oriental and Asian Studies.

———. 2016. *Bukkyō no koe no waza: satori no shintaisei* 仏教の声の技—悟りの身体性. Kyoto: Hōzōkan.

Padoan, Tatsuma. 2011. "Actors, Networks, and Languages of the Religious Experience. Semiotic Investigations on the Strategies of Enunciation in Japanese Religious Discourse." Ph.D. dissertation. Venice: Università Ca' Foscari.

Park Hyounggook 朴亨國. 2000. "Ōsaka Kongōji Kongōdō no Kongōkai Dainichi, Fudō, Gōzanze no sanzon keishiki ni kansuru ikkōsatsu" 大阪金剛寺の金剛界大日・不動・降三世の三尊形式に関する一考察. Ars Buddhica 252: 35–72.

Penny, Benjamin. "Zhang Liang." In Fabrizio Pregadio, ed. *The Encyclopedia of Taoism* vol. 2, 1230–1. London: Routledge.

Pfister, Patricia. 1988. "The Impact of Shugendō on the Painting of Yokoi Kinkoku." *Ars Orientalis* 18: 163–95.

Rai Momosaburō 頼桃三郎. 1974. "Hanabusa sōshi shutten tsuikō" 英草紙出典追考. *Kinsei bungei kō* 近世文芸稿 19: 1–9.

Rambelli, Fabio. 2013. *A Buddhist Theory of Semiotics*. London, New York: Bloomsbury.

———. 2019. "Introduction: The Invisible Empire: Spirits and Animism in Contemporary Japan." In Fabio Rambelli, ed., *Spirits and Animism in Contemporary Japan: The Invisible Empire*, 1–15. London and New York: Bloomsbury.

Ravina, Mark. 1995. "State-Building and Political Economy in Early-modern Japan." *Journal of Asian Studies* 54 (4): 997–1022.

Renondeau, Gaston. 1965. *Le Shugendō. Histoire, doctrine et rites des anachorètes dits Yamabushi*. Paris: Imprimerie Nationale.

Robson, James. 2008. "Signs of Power: Talismanic Writing in Chinese Buddhism," *History of Religions* 48 (2): 130–69.

———. 2014. "The Buddhist Image Inside-Out: On the Placing of Objects Inside Statues in East Asia." In Tansen Sen, ed. *Buddhism Across Asia: Networks of Material, Intellectual and Cultural Exchange* vol. 1, 291–307. Singapore: Institute of Southeast Asian Studies.

Rogers, Lawrence. 1994. "She Loves Me, She Loves Me Not: Shinjū and Shikidō Ōkagami." *Monumenta Nipponica* 49 (1): 31–60.

Rotermund, Hartmut O. 1965. "Wahrfafftiger Bericht von den Neuerfunden Japponischen Inseln und Königreichen." *Nachrichten der Gesellschaft für Natur und Völkerkunde Ostasiens*: 45–56.

———. 1968. *Die Yamabushi: Aspekte ihres Glaubens, Lebens und ihrer Sozialen Funktion im Japanischen Mittelalter*. Monographien zur Völkerkunde 5. Hamburg: Kommissionsverlag Cram and Berlin: De Gruyter.

Roth, Carina. 2014. "Au-delà des montagnes: une étude de l'imaginaire religieux dans le Japon médiéval à travers le Shozan engi (fin XIIe siècle)." Ph.D. dissertation. Geneva: University of Geneva.

———. 2019. "Essays in Vagueness: Aspects of Diffuse Religiosity in Japan." In Fabio Rambelli, ed., *Spirits and Animism in Contemporary Japan: The Invisible Empire*, 95–108. London and New York: Bloomsbury.

Saitō Iwazō 斎藤岩蔵. 1965. *Otake Dainichi Nyorai* お竹大日如来. Haguro-chō: Haguro-chō kankō kyōkai.

Sakamoto Gen'ichi 坂本源一. 1988. *Hitachi no kuni nanbu no Dainichi shinkō: Dainichizuka, nenbutsu kōshu no kenkyū* 常陸国南部の大日信仰--大日塚・念仏講衆の研究. Ushiku: Sakamoto Gen'ichi.

Sakamoto Koremaru 阪本是丸. 2005. "Shinbutsu bunri, haibutsu kishaku no haikei ni tsuite" 神仏分離・廃仏毀釈の背景について. *Meiji seitoku kinen gakkai kiyō* 明治聖徳記念学会紀要 41: 22–43.

———. 2007. *Kinsei kindai Shintō ronkō* 近世・近代神道論考. Tokyo: Kōbundō.

Sakamoto Shōjin 坂本正仁. 1982. "Kinsei Shingonshū Shingi-ha ni okeru furegashira seido" 近世真言宗新義派における触頭制度. *Buzan kyōgaku shinkōkai* 豊山教学振興会 10: 123–44.

Sakurai Tokutarō 櫻井徳太郎. 1998. "Kōshūdan seiritsu katei no kenkyū" 講集団成立過程の研究. In Sakurai Tokutarō, ed. *Kōshūdan no kenkyū* 講集団の研究. Reprint. Tokyo: Yoshikawa Kōbunkan (or. ed. 1962).

Sasuga Hō 流石奉, ed. 1985. *Katsuyama-ki to genpon no kōshō* 勝山記と原本の考証. Tokyo: Kokusho kankōkai.

Satō Ayumi 佐藤愛弓. 2015. *Chūsei shingonsō no gensetsu to rekishi ninshiki* 中世真言僧の言説と歴史認識. Tokyo: Bensei shuppan.

Satō Hiroo 佐藤弘夫. 2006. *Kishōmon no seishinshi: chūsei sekai no kami to hotoke* 起請文の精神史―中世世界の神と仏. Tokyo: Kōdansha.

Sawa, Ryūken. 1989. "Shugendo Art." *Japanese Journal of Religious Studies* 16 (2–3): 195–204.

Sawada, Janine. 1993. *Confucian Values and Popular Zen: Sekimon Shingaku in Eighteenth-century Japan*. Honolulu: University of Hawai'i Press.

———. 2014. *Practical Pursuits: Religion, Politics, and Personal Cultivation in Nineteenth-Century Japan*. Honolulu: University of Hawai'i Press.

———. Forthcoming. *Refiguring Mount Fuji: A New Religion in Early Modern Japan*. Honolulu: University of Hawai'i Press.

Schurhammer, P.G. 1922. "Die Yamabushis." *Zeitschrift für Missionswissenschaft und Religionswissenschaft* XII: 206–28.

———. 1965. "Die Yamabushis." *Mitteilungen der Gesellschaft für Natur- und Völkerkunde Ostasiens* XLVI: 47–83.

Seidel, Anna. 1992. "Mountains and Hells: Religious Geography in Japanese Mandara Paintings." *Studies in Central and East Asian Religions: Journal of the Seminar for Buddhist Studies* 5–6: 122–33.

———. 1996. "Descente aux enfers et rédemption des femmes dans le bouddhisme populaire Japonais—Le pélerinage du Mont Tateyama." *Cahiers d'Extrême-Asie* 9 (1): 1–14.

———. 2003. "Datsueba." *Hōbōgirin* 8: 1159–69.

Sekiguchi Makiko 関口眞規子. 2009. *Shugendō kyōdan seiritsu shi: Tōzan-ha o tōshite* 修験道教団成立史―当山派を通して. Tokyo: Bensei shuppan.

———. 2015. "Tōzan-ha" 当山派. In Tokieda Tsutomu 時枝務, Hasegawa Kenji 長谷川賢二 and Hayashi Makoto 林淳, eds. *Shugendōshi nyūmon* 修験道史入門, 131–50. Tokyo: Iwata shoin.

Sekimori, Gaynor. 2005. "Paper Fowl and Wooden Fish: The Separation of Kami and Buddha Worship in Haguro Shugendō, 1869–1875." *Japanese Journal of Religious Studies* 32 (2): 197–234.

———. 2009. "Shugendo: Japanese Mountain Religion: State of the Field and Bibliographic Review." *Religion Compass* 3 (1): 31–57.

———. 2015. "Foetal Buddhahood: From Theory to Practice—Embryological Symbolism in the Autumn Peak Ritual of Haguro Shugendō." In Anna Andreeva and Dominic Steavu, eds. *Transforming the Void: Embryological Discourse and Reproductive Imagery in East Asian Religions*, 522–57. Leiden: Brill.

Sharf, Elizabeth H. and Robert H. Sharf. 2001. *Living Icons: Japanese Buddhist Icons in Context*. Stanford: Stanford University Press.

Shinjō Mieko 新城美恵子. 1999. *Honzanha shugen to Kumano sendachi* 本山派修験と熊野先達. Tokyo: Iwata shoin.

Shinjō Tsunezō 新城常三. 1982. *Shaji sankei no shakai keizaishiteki kenkyū* 社寺参詣の社会経済史的研究. Tokyo: Hanawa shobō (or. ed. 1964).

Shively, Donald H., trans. 1953. *The Love Suicide at Amijima (Shinjū Ten no Amijima): A Study of a Japanese Domestic Tragedy by Chikamatsu Monzaemon*. Cambridge, Ma.: Harvard University Press.

Simon, Pierre. 2008. "Le parcours rituel des Monts Katsuragi au Japon (Printemps 2004–2005–2006–2007–2008): Approche ethnographique du shugendô contemporain." Mémoire de diplôme EHESS. Paris: Ecole des hautes études en sciences sociales.

Smith, Thomas C. 1959. *The Agrarian Origins of Modern Japan*. Stanford: Stanford University Press.

Sonehara Satoshi 曽根原理. 2001. "Kaidai" 解題. In ST, *Jinja hen* 神社編 24: 3–33.

———. 2010. "Togakushisan bettō Jōin no deshi-tachi" 戸隠山別当乗因の弟子たち. *Sangaku shugen* 山岳修験 45: 31–42.

———. 2018. *Tokugawa jidai no itanteki shukyō: Togakushisan bettō Jōin no chōsen to zasetsu* 徳川時代の異端的宗教: 戸隠山別当乗因の挑戦と挫折. Tokyo: Iwata shoin.

Sonoda Kōyū 薗田香融. 1981. "Kodai Bukkyō ni okeru sanrin shugyō to sono igi: toku ni Jinenchishū o megutte" 古代仏教における山林修行とその意義—特に自然智宗をめぐって. In Sonoda Kōyū. *Heian bukkyō no kenkyū* 平安仏教の研究: 27–52. Kyoto: Hōzōkan (or. ed. 1957).

Sotomura Ataru 外村中. 2016. "Shumisen sekai ni kan suru shosetsu to Tōdaiji daibutsu rendai Shumisen zu ni tsuite 須弥山世界に関する諸説と東大寺大仏蓮弁須弥山図について." In Inamoto Yasuo 稲本泰生, ed. *Higashi Ajia Bukkyō bijutsu ni okeru seichi hyōshō no shoyōtai* 東アジア仏教美術における聖地表象の諸様態, 1–32. Kyoto: Kyōto daigaku Jinbun kagaku kenkyūjo.

Steenstrup, Carl. 1980. "Sata Mirensho: A Fourteenth-Century Law Primer." *Monumenta Nipponica* 35 (4): 405–35.

Steineck, Raji C. 2012. "The 44th Tōzan-Ha Okugake Shugyō: A First-Hand Report." In Günther Distelrath, Ralph Lützeler, Barbara Manthey, eds. *Auf der Suche nach der Entwicklung menschlicher Gesellschaften. Festschrift für Hans Dieter Ölschleger zu seinem sechzigsten Geburtstag von seinen Freunden und Kollegen*, 595–618. Berlin: EB Verlag.

Stone, I. Jacqueline. 1999. *Original Enlightenment and the Transformation of Medieval Japanese Buddhism*. Honolulu: University of Hawai'i Press.

Sueki Fumihiko 末木文美士. 2012. *Gendai bukkyō ron* 現代仏教論. Tokyo: Shinchōsha.

Suzuki Masataka 鈴木正崇. 2002. *Nyonin kinsei* 女人禁制. Tokyo: Yoshikawa Kōbunkan.

———. 2006. "Nenbutsu to shugen: Chiba-ken Funabashi-shi no tentō nenbutsu no jirei kara" 念仏と修験—千葉県船橋市の天道念仏の事例から. In Fukuda Akira 福田晃 and Yamashita Kin'ichi 山下欣一, eds. *Fugeki mōsō no denshō sekai* 巫覡盲僧の伝承世界 vol. 3, 86–135. Tokyo: Miyai shoten.

———. 2007. "'Sangaku shinkō to jendā" 山岳信仰とジェンダー. *Sangaku shugen: Nihon ni okeru sangaku shinkō to Shugendō* 山岳修験—日本における山岳信仰と修験道 (Special issue): 39–54.

———. 2010. "'Shibusawa minkangaku' no seisei: Shibusawa Keizō to Oku Mikawa" 『澁澤民間学』の生成—澁澤敬三と奥三河—. *Kokusai jōmin bunka kenkyū kikō nenpō* 国際常民文化研究機構年報 vol. 1, 170–82.

———. 2015a. *Ajia no bunka isan* アジアの文化遺産. Tokyo: Keiō gijuku daigaku shuppankai.

———. 2015b. *Sangaku shinkō: Nihon bunka no kontei wo saguru* 山岳信仰: 日本文化の根底を探る. Tokyo: Chūō kōron shinsha.

———. 2015c. "Minzoku geijutsu no hakken: Kodera Yūkichi no gakumon to sono igi"『民俗藝術』の発見―小寺融吉の学問とその意義. *Meiji seitoku kinen gakkai kiyō* 明治聖徳記念學會紀要 52: 24–43.
———. 2017. "'Kegare' to nyonin kinsei" <穢>と女人禁制. *Shūkyō minzoku kenkyū* 宗教民族研究 27: 102–28.
———. 2018a. "Meiji ishin to Shugendō" 明治維新と修験道. *Shūkyō kenkyū* 宗教研究 92 (2): 353–79.
———. 2018b. "Nihon no yama no seishinshi: kaisan denshō kara sekai isan made" 日本の山の精神史：開山伝承から世界遺産まで. *Nihon sangaku bunka gakkai ronshū* 日本山岳文化学会論集 16: 3–12.
Suzuki Shōei 鈴木昭英. 2003. *Shugendō kyōdan no keisei to tenkai* 修験教団の形成と展開 (Shugendō rekishi minzoku ronshū 修験道歴史民俗論集 vol. 1). Kyoto: Hōzōkan.
———. 2011. "The Development of Suijaku Stories about Zaō gongen." *Cahiers d'Extrême-Asie* 18 (2009): 141–68.
Swanson, Paul L. 1981. "Shugendō and the Yoshino-Kumano Pilgrimage: An Example of Mountain Pilgrimage." *Monumenta Nipponica* 36 (1): 55–84.
———. 1999. "A Japanese Shugendō Apocryphal Text." In George J. Tanabe, ed. *Religions of Japan in Practice*, 246–53. Princeton: Princeton University Press.
Takahashi Nobuyuki 高橋伸幸. 1990. "En no Gyōja no koto" 役行者事. In *Shijū hyaku innenshū no kenkyū: honchō-hen*『私聚百因縁集』の研究本朝篇 vol. 1, 107–52. Osaka: Izumi shoin.
Takahashi Shūei 高橋秀栄. 2003. "*Shichi tengu'e* no kotobagaki hakken"『七天狗絵』の詞書発見. *Bungaku* 文学 4 (6): 85–112.
Takano Toshihiko 高埜利彦 and Kōshū Shiryō Chōsakai 甲州史料調査会, eds. 2009. *Fujisan oshi no rekishiteki kenkyū* 富士山御師の歴史的研究. Tokyo: Yamakawa shuppan.
Takaoka Hiroyuki 高岡裕之. 1993. "Kankō, kōsei, ryokō" 観光・厚生・旅行. In Akazawa Shirō 赤澤史朗 and Kitagawa Kenzō 北河賢三, eds. *Bunka to fashizumu* 文化とファシズム, 9–52. Tokyo: Nihon keizai hyōronsha.
Takeya Yukie 竹谷靱負. 2011. *Fujisan to nyonin kinsei* 富士山と女人禁制. Tokyo: Iwata shoin.
Tamamuro Fumio 圭室文雄. 1971. *Edo bakufu no shūkyō tōsei* 江戸幕府の宗教統制. Tokyo: Hyōronsha.
———. 1977. *Shinbutsu bunri* 神仏分離. Tokyo: Kyōikusha.
Tanabe Saburōsuke 田邊三郎助. 1983. "Sōjiji Zaō Gongen kyōzō no shūhen: kyōzō kara mishōtai e 総持寺・蔵王権現鏡像の周辺―鏡像から御正躰へ." *Museum* 392: 12–20.
———. 1989. "Yama no Bukkyō to sono zōkei 山の仏教とその造形." In Watanabe Saburō 渡辺三郎助, ed. *Zusetsu Nihon no Bukkyō 6: Shinbutsu shūgō to Shugendō* 図説日本の仏教六 神仏習合と修験, 201–52. Tokyo: Shinchōsha.
Tanaka Fumio 田中文雄. 1984. "Fuji mandara zu" 富士曼荼羅図. *Shizuoka kenritsu bijutsukan kiyō* 静岡県立美術館紀要 3 (1): 8–18.
Taniguchi Kōsei 谷口耕生. 2007. "Shinbutsu shūgō bijutsu ni kan suru oboegaki 神仏習合美術に関する覚書." In Nara kokuritsu hakubutsukan 奈良国立博物館, ed. *Tokubetsu ten. Shinbutsu shūgō: kami to hotoke ga orinasu shinkō to bi* 特別展 神仏習合―かみとほとけが織りなす信仰と美, 6–16. Tokyo: Asahi shinbunsha.
Teeuwen, Mark, and Fabio Rambelli, eds. 2003. *Buddhas and Kami in Japan: Honji Suijaku as a Combinatory Paradigm*. London: Routledge Curzon.
Ten Grotenhuis, Elizabeth. 1999. *Japanese Mandalas: Representations of Japanese Mandalas*. Honolulu: University of Hawai'i Press.

Thal, Sarah. 2005. *Rearranging the Landscape of the Gods: The Politics of a Pilgrimage Site in Japan, 1573–1912*. Chicago: University of Chicago Press.

Thomas, B. Jolyon. 2019. "Spirit/Medium: Critically Examining the Relationship between Animism and Animation." In Fabio Rambelli, ed., *Spirits and Animism in Contemporary Japan: The Invisible Empire*, 157–70. London and New York: Bloomsbury.

Thumas, Jonathan. 2016. "The Lion's Roar: Imagining Conch Shell Trumpets in Early Modern Japan." *Material Religions BlogProject*. January 13, 2016. Republished in *The Jugaad Project*. July 27, 2019 (thejugaadproject.pub/home/the-lions-roar-imagining-conch-shell-trumpets-in-early-modern-japan).

Togawa Anshō 戸川安勝. 2005. "Hagurosan no katarimono: Otake Dainichi etoki wo chūshin ni" 羽黒山の語りもの—お竹大日絵解きを中心に. In *Togawa Anshō chosakushū* 戸川安勝著作集 vol. 1 (*Dewa Sanzan to Shugendō* 出羽三山と修験道), 249–71. Tokyo: Iwata shoin.

Tokieda Tsutomu 時枝務. 2005. *Shugendō no kōkogakuteki kenkyū* 修験道の考古学的研究. Tokyo: Yūzankaku.

———. 2013. "Shugendōshi ni okeru sato shugen no isō" 修験道史における里修験の位相. In Tokieda Tsutomu, Yoshitani Hiroya 由谷裕哉, Kubo Yasuaki 久保康顕, and Satō Kikuichirō 佐藤喜久一郎, eds. *Kinsei Shugendō no shosō* 近世修験道の諸相, 7–26. Tokyo: Iwata shoin.

———. 2016. *Sanchō shūkyō iseki no kenkyū* 山頂宗教遺跡の研究. Tokyo: Iwata shoin.

Tokieda Tsutomu 時枝務, Hasegawa Kenji 長谷川賢二 and Hayashi Makoto 林淳, eds. 2015. *Shugendōshi nyūmon* 修験道史入門. Tokyo: Iwata shoin.

Tokuhara Satoyuki 徳原聡行. 1982. "Hana no ōkina Dainichi-sama, hana no takai Dainichi-sama" 鼻の大きな大日様・鼻の高い大日様. *Ibaraki no minzoku* 茨城の民族 21 (December): 27–33.

———. 2004. *Jōsō Kan'ei-ki no Dainichi sekibutsu* 常総寛永期の大日石仏. Tsuchiura: Tsukuba shorin.

Tokunaga Seiko 徳永誓子. 1998. "Shugendō Tōzan-ha to Kōfukuji dōshu" 修験道当山派と興福寺堂衆. *Nihonshi kenkyū* 日本史研究 435: 27–50.

———, 2001. "Shugendō seiritsu no shiteki zentei: shugenja no tenkai" 修験道成立の史的前提—修験者の展開. *Shirin* 史林 84-2 (1): 97–123.

———, 2002a. "Shugendō seiritsu katei no kenkyū 修験道成立過程の研究." Ph.D. Dissertation. Kyoto University.

———, 2002b. "Kumano sanzan kengyō to Shugendō" 熊野三山検校と修験道. *Nenpō chūseishi kenkyū* 年報中世史研究 27: 75–100.

———, 2003. "Shugendōshi kenkyū no shikaku" 修験道史研究の視角. *Atarashii rekishigaku no tame ni* 新しい歴史学のために 252: 1–9.

———, 2014. "Chūsei ni okeru 'Shugendō' no sōtaika" 中世における「修験道」の相対化. *Sangaku shugen* 山岳修験 53: 17–30.

———, 2015. "Shugendō no seiritsu" 修験道の成立. In Tokieda Tsutomu 時枝務, Hasegawa Kenji 長谷川賢二 and Hayashi Makoto 林淳, eds. *Shugendōshi nyūmon* 修験道史入門, 77–92. Tokyo: Iwata shoin.

Tokuzawa, C. 1896. "Jugglers and Sorcerers." *The Theosophist* 17: 421–2.

Tokyo Kokuritsu Hakubutsukan 東京国立博物館 and Tokyo Daigaku Shiryō Hensanjo 東京大学史料編纂所, ed. 2001. *Toki o koete monogataru mono: shiryō to bijutsu no meihō* 時を超えて物語るもの—史料と美実の名宝 (Voice from the Past: Historical Sources and Art Treasures). Tokyo: Tokyo Daigaku Shiryō Hensanjo.

Tosaka Jun 戸坂潤. 1979. "Nihon ideorogīron" 日本イデオロギー論. In *Tosaka Jun zenshū* 戸坂潤全集 vol. 2, 223-412. Tokyo: Keisō shobō (or. ed. 1935).
Tsuchiya Takahiro 土屋貴裕. 2005. "*Tengu-zōshi* no fukugenteki kōsatsu"「天狗草紙」の復元的考察. *Bijutsushi* 美術史 55 (1): 49-64.
Tsushima Ikuo 對馬郁夫. 2011. *Bōsō ni ikizuku Dewa Sanzan shinkō no shosō* 房総に息づく出羽三山信仰の諸相. Awa: Tsushima Ikuo.
Tsutsumi Kunihiko 堤邦彦. 2008. *Edo no kōsō densetsu* 江戶の高僧伝説. Tokyo: Miyai Shoten.
Tyler, Royall. 1989. "Kōfuku-ji and Shugendō." *Japanese Journal of Religious Studies* 16 (2-3): 143-80.
———. 1990. "Kōfuku-ji and the Mountains of Yamato." *Japan Review* (1): 153-223.
———, ed. and transl. 1992. *Japanese Noh Dramas*. Reprint. London, New York: Penguin Books (or. ed. 1970).
———, transl. 1993. "'The Book of the Great Practice': The Life of the Mt. Fuji Ascetic Kakugyō Tōbutsu: Introduction and Translation." *Asian Folklore Studies* 52: 251-331.
Tyler, Royall and Paul Swanson. 1989a. "Editors' Introduction to Shugendō and Mountain Religion in Japan," *Japanese Journal of Religious Studies*, vol. 16 (2-3): 93-100.
Tyler, Royall and Paul L. Swanson, eds. 1989b. "Shugendō and Mountain Religion in Japan," Special Issue *Japanese Journal of Religious Studies* 16 (2-3).
Umeda Yoshihiko 梅田義彦, ed. 1971. *Kaitei zōho Nihon shūkyō seido shi [kindai hen]* 改訂増補 日本宗教制度史 ［近代篇］. Tokyo: Tōsen shuppan.
Umeki Tetsuto 梅木哲人. 2012. "Ryūkyūkoku no kishōmon ni tsuite" 琉球国の起請文について. In Yamamoto Hirofumi kanreki kinen ronshū kankō inkai 山本博文還暦記念論集論刊行員会, ed. *Ryūkyū no rekishi to bunka* 琉球の歴史と文化, 179-96. Kyoto: Kōyō shobō.
Uno Enkū 宇野圓空. 1929. *Shūkyō minzokugaku* 宗教民族學. Tokyo: Oka shoin.
———. 1931. *Shūkyōgaku* 宗教学. Tokyo: Iwanami shoten.
———. 1931. *Shūkyōgaku no shijitsu to riron* 宗教学の史実と理論. Tokyo: Dōbunsha.
———. 1934. *Shugendō* 修験道. Tokyo: Tōhō shoin.
———. 1935. *Minzoku seishin no shūkyōmen* 民族精神の宗教面. Tokyo: Bukkyō jihōsha.
———. 1941. *Maraisha ni okeru tōmai girei* マライシヤに於ける稲米儀礼. Tokyo: Tōyō bunko.
———. 1943. *Shūkyōgaku tsūron* 宗教學通論. Tokyo: Yaesu shobō.
Ury, Marion. 1979. *Tales of Times Now Past*. Berkeley: University of California Press.
Ushijima Fumihiko 牛島史彦, ed. 1992. *Edo no tabi to hayaribotoke: Otake Dainichi Nyorai to Dewa Sanzan* 江戸の旅と流行仏—お竹大日如来と出羽三山. Tokyo: Itabashi kuritsu kyōdo shiryōkan.
Wakabayashi, Haruko. 2012. *The Seven Tengu Scrolls: Evil and the Rhetoric of Legitimacy in Medieval Japanese Buddhism*. Honolulu: University of Hawai'i Press.
Wakamori Tarō 和歌森太郎. 1972. *Shugendōshi kenkyū* 修験道史研究. Tokyo: Heibonsha (or. ed. 1943).
———. 1980. "Togakushi no Shugendō" 戸隠の修験道. In *Wakamori Tarō chosakushū* 和歌森太郎著作集 vol. 2. Tokyo: Kōbundō. Originally in *Togakushi: Sōgō gakujutsu chōsa hōkoku* 戸隠—総合學術調査報告, 394-431. Nagano: Shinano Mainichi Shinbunsha (or. ed. 1971).
———, ed. 1975-84. *Sangaku shūkyōshi kenkyū sōsho* 山岳宗教史研究叢書. 18 vols. Tokyo: Meicho shuppan.
Wakayama kenritsu hakubutsukan 和歌山県博物館, ed. 2011. *Katsuragi shugen no seichi, Nakatsugawa Gyōjadō no bunkazai* 葛城修験の聖地・中津川行者堂の文化財. Wakayama: Wakayama kenritsu hakubutsukan tomo no kai 和歌山県立博物館友の会.

Wang Yong 王勇. 2000. "Dōken wo meguru ningen kankei wo chūshin to shite 道賢をめぐる人間関係を中心として." *Ajia yūgaku* アジア遊学 22: 36–49.

Yamaguchi Makoto 山口真琴. 2015. "Shoshūron tekusuto to *Shichi tengu'e* no seisei wo megutte" 諸宗論テクストと『七天狗絵』の生成をめぐって. *Kokugo to kokubungaku* 国語と国文学 92 (5): 101–13.

Yamamoto Yasumasa 山本恭匡. 2010. "Sekai isan 'Kumano kodō' ni okery 'bunka' gainen no saikentō: bunkateki keikan 'shinkō no yama' wo meguru rinen to jissen" 世界遺産『熊野古道』における『文化』概念の検討—文化的景観『信仰の山』をめぐる理念と実践. *Hakusan jinruigaku* 白山人類学 13: 93–115.

Yanagita Kunio 柳田國男. 1942. *Nihon no matsuri* 日本の祭. Tokyo: Kōbundō.

———. 1946. *Senzo no hanashi* 先祖の話. Tokyo: Chikuma Shobō.

———. 1990. "Zoku yamabushi" 俗山伏. In *Yanagita Kunio zenshū* 柳田國男全集 vol. 11, 394–431. Tokyo: Chikuma shobō (or. ed. 1916).

Yōgaku no Kai 幼学の会, ed. 1993. *Shohon shūsei Chūmonjō chūkai* 諸本集成仲文章注解. Tokyo: Bensei shuppan.

Yokoyama Hiroko 横山廣子. 1989. "Taminzoku kokka e no dōtei 1" 多民族国家への道程. In Uno Shigeaki 宇野重昭, ed. *Shizukana shakai hendō* 静かな社会変動 (Iwanami kōza Gendai Chūgoku 岩波講座　現代中国 vol. 3), 263–84. Tokyo: Iwanami shoten.

Yoneyama Kazumasa 米山一政. 1971. "Gaisetsu" 概説. In Shinano Mainichi Shinbunsha Togakushi Sōgō Gakujutsu Chōsa Jikkō Iinkai 信濃毎日新聞社戸隠総合学術調査実行委員会, ed. *Togakushi: Sōgō gakujutsu chōsa hōkoku* 戸隠：総合學術調査報告, 15–59. Nagano: Shinano Mainichi Shinbunsha.

Yoshida Kazuhiko 吉田一彦. 1996. "Shinbutsu shūgō: higashi Ajia no naka no Nihon shinbutsu shūgō" 神仏習合—東アジアの中の日本神仏習合. In Nihon Bukkyō kenkyūkai 日本仏教研究会, eds. *Nihon no Bukkyō* 日本の仏教 vol. 6, 30–5. Kyoto: Hōzōkan.

———. 2016. *Nihon shoki no jubaku*「日本書紀」の呪縛. Tokyo: Shūeisha.

Yoshihara Ken'ichirō 吉原健一郎. 1978. *Edo no jōhōya: bakumatsu shomin no sokumen* 江戸の情報屋—幕末庶民の側面. Tokyo: Nihon hōsō shuppan kyōkai.

Yoshii Takao 芳井敬郎. 1988. "Kumano goō ni tsuite" 熊野牛王について. In Wada Atsumu 和田萃, ed. *Kumano gongen* 熊野権現, 133–56. Tokyo: Chikuma shobō.

Zitterbart, Susan. 2008. "Kumano Mandara: Portraits, Power, and Lineage in Medieval Japan." Pittsburgh: University of Pittsburgh.

Documentariess

Abela, Jean-Marc and Mark Patrick McGuire. 2010. *Shugendo Now*. Montréal, Canada, Enpower Pictures.

Kitamura Minao 北村皆雄. 2005. *Shugen: Hagurosan aki no mine* 修験—羽黒山秋の峯. DVD video (NTSC). Tokyo: Visual Folklore Inc. Documentary.

Roth, Sandra, and Carina Roth. 2010. *Là où les montagnes volent/Where Mountains Fly*. 4/3, PAL. Umeda, Switzerland.

Websites

Introduction
http://www.katinkahesselink.net/blavatsky/articles/v12/y1890_033.htm
Chapter One
http://www.daisen1300.org
https://www.daisen1300.org/user/common/pdf/pamphlet_en.pdf
http://hakusan1300.info
http://www.natadera.com/EN/
http://www.shirayama.or.jp/news/year1300.html
Chapter Four
http://www.nichibun.ac.jp/graphicversion/dbase/otake/index.html
http://www.nichibun.ac.jp/graphicversion/dbase/otake/data/data01/index.html
Chapter Six
https://www.citizen.co.jp/coy/archive/2004_01.html
http://syamabiko.web.fc2.com
http://syamabiko.web.fc2.com/introduction.html

Index

ajari 阿闍梨 (esoteric masters) 7
aki no mine 秋の峰 (Autumn Peak ritual) 24
Akyūbō Sokuden 阿吸房即伝 (fl. 1509–58) 78, 82
Ambros, Barbara 15
Amida Nyorai 阿弥陀如来 37, 65, 91, 194, 203, 215, 252
Anesaki Masaharu 姉崎正治 (1873–1949) 47
animism 22
annai ezu 案内絵図 (pictorial guide maps) 197
ayaigasa 斑蓋 (ritual cap) 24
Azuma kagami 吾妻鏡 (1266) 67, 221–2, 225, 235n29

Bellah, N. Robert (1927–2013) 53
bettō 別当 (chief administrator) 89, 93, 95, 142, 232n1, 242n22, 243n24 and 25, 248n3
Blacker, Carmen (1924–2009) 13
Blair, Heather 14, 231n9
bontenzuka 梵天塚 (funerary tumulus for the ritual staffs) 208, 252n3
Bouchy, Anne 13, 16–17, 23, 244n7
Buddhist folklore studies (*bukkyō minzokugaku* 仏教民俗学) 53, 54, 63
bukkyō kakushin undō 仏教革新運動 (Buddhist reformation movements) 6
Butsumyōin shoshi meyasu-an (thirteenth century) 仏名院所司目安案 69, 70
Bynum, Carolyn 23–4

Carter, Caleb 16
Castiglioni, Andrea 15
Chishō Daishi 智証大師 (Enchin 円珍, 814–91) 139
Chūbunshō 仲文章 (eleventh century) 150, 151

Clements, Frank 15
Conlan, D. Thomas 15
Cysat, Renward (1545–1614) 12

Daigoji and Daigoji Sanbōin 醍醐寺三宝院 5, 9–10, 16, 26–7, 71, 103–4, 106–9, 111–20, 135, 140, 172, 232n3, 2445n3, 244n6
Daigoji sōgō daihōsshira mōshijōan 醍醐寺僧綱大法師等申状案 69, 70
Daigoji-ha *shugenja* 醍醐寺派修験者 (Daigoji branch *shugenja*) 107
Dainichi Nyorai 大日如来 2, 29, 190, 203, 205, 209–14, 216, 252
Daisendatsu 大先達 (group leaders) 24
Dajōkan 太政官 (Council of state) 37, 103, 105, 253
danna 檀那 (lay patrons) 188
Dewa Sanzan 出羽三山 15, 20, 57, 124, 205, 208
Dewa Sanzan *honjibutsu* (triad of Dewa Sanzan buddhas) 90
DeWitt, Lindsey 15
dhūta (alt. Jp. tsuta, zuda, tosō 斗藪, self-discipline) 5, 47. See also *tosō*
dōgyō 同行 ("co-practitioners") 9
Dōju 道珠 7, 67, 235n34
dōsha 道者 (pilgrims) 188
dōshu 堂衆 ("those of the halls") 8, 9–10
Dōzō 道増 (1508–71) 9

E no Kimi keiseiki 役君形生記 (1684) 76
Earhart, H. Byron 13, 15
Ein bu 恵印部 (Shugendō "Ein division" at Daigoji) 107–8, 112–15
Ein-ryū 恵印流 (Ein lineage) 10, 107
En no Gyōja 役行者 (alt. En no Ozunu 役小角, En no ubasoku 役優婆塞) (mid-seventh to mid-eighth centuries) 7, 27, 45, 69, 71, 78–80, 111, 123–37, 139–40, 147

as Jinben Daibosatsu 神変大菩薩 111, 113, 117, 125, 133–4, 139
  and Zaō Gongen 185
ena 胞衣 (placenta) 24
engi 縁起 (also *jisha engi* 寺社縁起) (origin narratives of temples and shrines) 27, 41–3, 76–7, 137, 191
Enryakuji 延暦寺 72, 139, 162
ethnology 4. *See also* Shugendō and ethnology
etoki 絵解 (pictures explained in a narrative fashion) 191, 200
exo-esoteric Buddhist system (*kenmitsu taisei* 顕密体制) 1, 5–6, 17, 45, 63–5, 71–3, 190

Faure, Bernard 17, 232n15
Fenollosa, Ernest (1853–1908) 38, 232n3
folklore and folklore studies 2, 4, 25, 26, 40, 49, 54, 117, 120. *See also* Shugendō and folklore studies
forest bathing (*shinrin'yoku* 森林浴) 18
fu 巫 (female mediums) 24
Fudō Myōō 不動明王 209–11
Fudōin 不動院 9
Fudoki 風土記 (713) 42
Fuji sankei mandara 富士参詣曼荼羅 191–195, 203
Fuji 富士山, Mt. 15, 28–9, 56, 187–99, 203–4
fujiki kuyō 不食供養 (ritual fasting) 206, 214–16
Fujioka Yutaka 藤岡穣 11
Fujiwara no Michinaga 藤原道長 (966–1027) 184–5

Gachirin'in 月輪院 9
gagen 臥験 (ascetic practitioner with powers) 45
Gakumon Gyōja 学問行者 79, 80, 82, 83
gakuryo 学侶 (scholar-monks) 8
Genkō shakusho 元亨釈書 (1322) 139
genriki 験力 (empowerment) 2, 7, 45
Genryō-bō family 玄良坊 27, 89, 91, 93–7, 98, 100
gesō 下僧 (low-rank monks) 8
Getsugan 月旺 (Maeno Ribei 前野理兵衛, 1630–89) 201–4

geza 験者 (alt. *genja*, *genza*, person with powers, Esoteric Buddhist practitioner) 7, 66–7, 72, 235n34
Gien 義演 (1558–1626) 10
Gōdanshō 江談抄 (eleventh century) 150
gohōjin 護法神 (Dharma-protector deity) 173
Gohōzen 御宝前 205
Goiseibai shikimoku 御成敗式目 legal code (1232) 223
gongen 権現 (alt. Gongen, avatar) 35, 37
goō hōin 牛王宝印 (printed *shugen* talismans) 29, 219–30
Gorai Shigeru 五来重 (1908–93) 4, 5, 21–2, 52–4
goshintai 御神体 (physical objects embodying the *kami*) 33
Gōzanze Myōō 降三世明王 209–11
Grapard, Allan G. 13–14, 16, 203
gumonjihō 求聞求法 (ritual for the attainment of a perfect memory) 44, 234n27
gyōja kō 行者講 (confraternities of ascetics) 8
Gyōki 行基 (668–749) 45, 123
gyōnin 行人 ("practitioners") 8
gyōninzuka 行人塚 (mounds for the ascetics) 208–9

Hachiyō kuson zu 八葉九尊図 197–8
Haguro 羽黒山, Mt. 13, 15, 42, 57, 89–93, 95–7, 205
Haguro-ha 羽黒派 (Haguro-style Shugendō) 4, 24, 87–103, 115
haibutsu kishaku 排仏毀釈 ("exclude Buddhism and destroy Śākyamuni") 39, 109, 129, 232n4
Hakusan 白山, Mt. 5, 42, 58–9
Hanabusa sōshi 英草紙 (1749) 156–9, 163, 247n5
hansō hanzoku 半僧半俗 (ordained priests leading a family life) 6, 41
Harusame monogatari 春雨物語 (1808) 155, 164
Hasegawa Kenji 長谷川賢二 7–8, 45
hayarigami 流行神 ("kami à la mode") 205
Hayashi Makoto 林淳 11

Index

Hayashi Jitsukaga 林実利 (1843–84) 13, 128–9, 133
Heihanki (also *Hyōhanki*) 兵範記 (eleventh century) 67
Hiei, Mt. 比叡山 45, 57
Higashi Kondō 東金堂 8
hiji jiki 非時食 (prohibition to eat food after noon) 217
hijiri 聖 (itinerant holy men) 5, 41, 65, 68
Hiko, Mt. 彦山 16, 42, 44, 78
Hikosan ruki 彦山流記 (1213) 45
Hikosan Shugen (Hiko-style Shugendō) 英彦山修験 4, 45–46
hōin 法印 ("Dharma seal", also used as appellative for *yamabushi*) 36, 195
hon'yakunin 本役人 (titled peasants) 212, 216. See also *kobyakushō*
Honchō mudaishi 本朝無題詩 (twelfth century?) 145, 146
hongan 本願 (religious sponsors) 213–14
Hongū 本宮 8, 24. See also Kumano Sanzan
honji suijaku 本地垂迹 (original grounds and provisional traces) 33, 35, 171, 191, 205
Honzan-ha 本山派 (Tendai-style Shugendō) 4, 9, 79, 103
Honzan-ha *sendatsu* (Honzan-ha leaders) 10
horagai 法螺貝 (ritual conch shell) 80, 130–3, 231n11
Hori Ichirō 堀一郎 (1910–74) 4, 52

Indian gods 222, 224
intonsha 隠遁者 (recluse monks) 5, 7
Ishikawa Jun 石川淳 (1899–1987) 89
issei gyōnin 一世行人 ("lifetime ascetics") 29, 206, 208, 213
isseisō 一世僧 (self-nominated *shugenja*) 104, 112–13, 115, 118

Japanese spirit 18–22
Jesuit missionaries 11, 240n3
Jien kishōmon 慈円起請文 (1206) 69
jikkai 十界 (progressions or regressions within the ten realms) 2
Jimon-ha 寺門派 (Onjōji Tendai branch) 8, 119

Jinben 神変 (1909–) 4, 109
Jingikan 神祇官 (Office of Kami Affairs) 38
Jingishō 神祇省 (Ministry of Kami Affairs) 38
Jingūji 神宮寺 (temples dedicated to the *kami*) 33
jisha engi 寺社縁起. See *engi*
Jōin 乗因 (1682–1739) 76, 79–86. See also Togakushi, Mt., Shugendō and Daoism
Jōjōin 乗々院 9
jōmin 常民 (common people) 4, 54
jukkoku-dachi 十穀断ち (elimination of the ten grains) 214

Kaempfer, Engelbert (1651–1716) 12
kaichō 開帳 (public displays of icons) 77, 89, 91, 97–102
kaizan 開山 ("opening of the mountain") 41–2
kaji kitō 加持祈禱 (magico-religious prayer rituals) 7, 36, 112
kakebotoke 懸仏 (hanging images of buddhas) 174
Kakugyō Tōbutsu 角行藤佛 (1541–1646?) 28, 189, 199–201, 204, 251n37
kami and buddhas 33–6, 38–40, 55, 109, 129, 171, 191, 205. See also *individual kami and buddhas*
kami 神 (local gods) 2, 33–6
Kan'eiji 寛永寺 79, 80
Kanda Yoriko 神田より子 23
kanjin 勧進 (fundraising) 191, 200
kanjō 勧請 (ritual transfers of divinities from one temple to another) 207
kanjō 灌頂 (Skt. *abhiṣeka*, Buddhist consecration) 138
Kantō gechijō 関東下知状 68
Kasuga, Mt. 春日山 9
kasumi 霞 (local communities, parishes) 7, 9–10
Katsuragi, Mt. 葛城山 14, 16, 45, 68–9, 134, 139
Kawahashi Noriko 川橋範子 23
Kawasaki Tsuyoshi 川崎剛志 11, 25, 145–6, 246n26
Keichō kenmonshū 慶長見聞集 (1614) 213

kengyō 検校 (superintendent) 8
Kihira Tadayoshi 紀平正美 (1874-1949) 40, 49-50, 52
Kinpu, Mt. 金峰山 14, 28, 168, 172, 185
Kinpusen himitsuden 金峰山秘密伝 (1337) 45
Kinpusen sōsōki 金峰山創草記 (fourteenth century) 45, 126
kishōmon 起請文 (written oaths) 29, 221-30
Klonos, George 14
kō 講 (religious confraternities of lay devotees, also *kōsha* 講社) 1, 6, 24, 53, 55, 112, 188-9, 206, 213.
Kobayashi Naoko 小林奈央子 23
kobyakushō 小百姓 (small peasants) 212, 216. See also *hon'yakunin*
Kōfukuji 興福寺 8-9, 14, 138-9
Kogarashi zōshi 凩草紙 (1792) 160
Kogi Shingonshū 古義真言宗 (Kogi branch of the Shingon school) 104, 106-9, 119, 244n2
Kojidan 古事談 (1215) 89
Kojiki 古事記 (712) 42
Kōken 高賢 (1639-1707) 10
Kokutai no hongi 国体の本義 (1937) 51-2, 238n66
Kondō Yūsuke 近藤祐介 8-9, 65
Kongōkai mandara 金剛界曼荼羅 (Diamond Realm Mandala) 189, 205, 211
Kongōsan engi 金剛山縁起 11, 137
Konjaku monogatarishū 今昔物語集 (twelfth century) 45, 67, 235n35
Kōya, Mt. 高野山 45
Kubota Nobuhiro 久保田展弘 (1941-2016) 18-19
Kūkai 空海 (also Kōbō Daishi 弘法大師) 45, 111, 123-4, 133, 168, 213-14
Kumano pilgrimage (Kumano sankei 熊野参詣) 14, 69
Kumano Sanzan 熊野三山 (Three Kumano Shrines) 8, 26, 42, 57, 72
Kumano Sanzan *Kengyō* 熊野三山検校 (Supervisor of the Three Kumano Shrines) 72
Kumano *sendatsu* 熊野先達 (Kumano leaders) 8-9
Kumano talismans 29, 220-1, 225-30

Kuroda Toshio 黒田俊雄 (1926-93) 5-6, 17, 64
Kuzuryū no Ōkami 九頭龍大神 80-81
Kyōbushō 教部省 (Ministry of Religion) 38, 105
kyōzō 鏡像 (mirror icon) 174

Lady Nijō 二条 227-8
Latour, Bruno 206
Liaozhai zhiyi 聊斎志異 (Jp. *Ryōsai shii*, 1740) 163
Lobetti, Tullio 15
Lotus Sutra (Skt. *Saddharma puṇḍarīka sūtra*) 224

mappa shugenja 末派修験者 (un-affiliated shugenja) 9. See also *dōgyō*
materiality of religion 28, 206, 209. See also specific objects and ritual tools
Matsudai Shōnin 末代上人 187
McGuire, Mark 16
miei 御影 (devotional images) 195, 251n47
Minamoto no Yoshitsune 源義経 (1159-89) 221
mineiri 入峰り. See *nyūbu*
Minoodera 箕面寺 145
Minoodera engi 箕面寺縁起 (compiled before 1173) 11, 27-8, 134, 137-44, 145-52
minzoku 民族 (ethnicity), definitions 47-9
  as Ethnos 49-52, 54
minzoku shūkyō 民俗宗教 (folk religion) 53-4
Miyagi Tainen 宮城泰年 124, 129, 130
Miyake Hitoshi 宮家準 4, 18, 25, 53-4, 124
Miyamoto Kesao 宮本袈裟雄 (1945-2008) 5
Miyata Noboru 宮田登 (1936-2000) 53
miyaza 宮座 (shrine council) 212
Moerman, D. Max 14
Morishima Chūryō 森島中良 (1756-1810) 156-157, 160
Moto no chichihaha 元の父母 (Mt. Fuji deity) 201
Murakami Toshio 村上俊雄 (b. 1906) 4, 51

Murayama Shūichi 村山修一 (1914–2010) 4, 25, 231n2
Murayama 村山 187–188, 248n6
Mus, Paul (1902–69) 206, 251n2

nabiki 靡 (station) 128, 244n9
Nachi 那智 8, 24. *See also* Kumano Sanzan
Nakano Tatsue 中野達慧 (1871–1934) 3, 110, 117–18
Nakazawa Shin'ichi 中沢新一 19–20
nature, discourses on 18–22
Naumann, Hans (1886–1951) 50, 237n54
nenbutsu 念仏 (recitation of the Buddha's name) 112, 215
Neo-Nativism (Shin-Kokugaku 新国学) and *minzokugaku* 19, 21–2
New Age spirituality 22
Nihon daizōkyō 日本大蔵経 3, 27, 108, 110
Nihon ryōiki 日本霊異記 (824) 124, 168
Nihon sandai jitsuroku 日本三代実録 (tenth century) 7, 67
Nihon sangaku kai 日本山岳会 (The Japanese Alpine Club) 55
Nihon seishin 日本精神 (1930) 49
Nihon shoki 日本書紀 (720) 42
Nihonjinron 日本人論 (discourses on Japanese cultural identity) 19–20
Nihonshugi 日本主義 ("Japanism") 52
Niki Natsumi 仁木夏実 11
Nishi Kondō 西金堂 8
Nōjo Taishi 能除太子 41, 124
Nyaku ōji 若王子 9
nyonin kinsei 女人禁制 (exclusion of women) 11, 15, 22, 24
nyūbu 入峰 (also pronounced *mineiri*, mountain-entry rituals) 1, 9, 115, 133

oi 笈 (portable altar) 24
Okamoto Tarō 岡本太郎 (1911–96) 20–2
Okinawa 沖縄 19–20
Okugake 奥駈け (alt. Okugake no michi 奥駈けの道) 56, 127–9, 132, 245n13
Ōmine 大峯山, Mt. 10, 14–15, 24, 43, 107, 116, 168

Ōminesan nyonin kinsei no kaihō wo motomeru kai 大峰山女人禁制の開放を求める会 (Association for Lifting the Rule of Exclusion of Women from Mt. Ōmine) 24
ominuki 御身抜 (ascetic drawings) 28, 200–1, 203–4
Onjōji 園城寺 8, 71–73, 130, 139, 244n8
Onmyōdō 陰陽道 (the Way of Yin and Yang) 5, 25, 245n2
Ontake, Mt. 御嶽山 55, 115
Ontsuka Gongen 御塚権現 (August mound Gongen) 207
ordeals and truth 223–4
oshi 御師 (itinerant preachers) 5, 38, 55, 189–90, 249n12
Otake Dainichi Nyorai お竹大日如来 27, 87–102
Otake Dainichi Nyorai engi emaki (1849) お竹大日如来縁起絵巻 91–2, 94
Ōuchi Fumi 大内曲 15
Ōyama, Mt. 大山 15

Padoan, Tatsuma 14
Pfoundes, Charles (1840–1907) 12
pilgrimage 37, 55, 115, 187–99, 203
poetry, Chinese-style (*kanshibun* 漢詩文) 145–52
primitivism (and Japanese cultural identity) 19
Pu Songling 蒲松齢 (1640–1715) 163

Rambelli, Fabio 22, 253 n. 6
Renondeau, Gaston (1879–1967) 13
Rikamatsu jiken 離加末事件 (incident of the "separation from the main temple") 104, 106–8
Rinnōji 輪王寺 (Nikkō, Mt. 日光山) 79
Rotermund, Hartmut O. 12, 13
Roth, Carina 14
Ryōjin hishō 梁塵秘抄 (twelfth century) 66, 67
Ryūju Bosatsu 龍樹菩薩 (Nāgārjuna) 27, 107, 117

sacred geography 6, 14, 167–8. *See also individual mountains*
Saichō 最澄 45, 111

saitō goma 柴燈護摩 (outdoor fire ritual) 132
Sakurai Tokutarō 櫻井德太郎 (1917–2007) 46, 53
Sakuramoto-bō 桜本坊 15
sangaku shinkō 山岳信仰 (mountain beliefs) 33, 43, 55, 59
Sangaku Shugen Gakkai 山岳修験学会 (Association for the Study of Japanese Mountain Religion) 53
Sangaku shūkyōshi kenkyū sōsho 山岳宗教研究叢書 (1984) 15, 53
Sanjōgatake, Mt. 山上ヶ岳 43, 168
sankei mandara 参詣曼荼羅 (pilgrimage mandalas) 28, 191, 197–9
sanrin bukkyō 山林仏教 (Buddhism of mountain asceticism) 6, 65
  as asceticism 44
sanrō 山籠 (mountain seclusion) 5, 6
Sanzon kuson zu 三尊九尊図 195–7, 200
Sasaguri 篠栗 16
Sawada, Janine, 15
Schurhammer, Georg (1882–1971) 13
Seiyaku kyōkai 聖役協会 (Seiyaku publishing organization) 108–9
Sekiguchi Makiko 関口眞規子 9–10, 65
Sekimori, Gaynor 15
sekkō 石工 (stone-engravers) 214, 216
sendatsu 先達 (alt. *sendachi*) 9–10, 55, 72, 75, 78, 111, 188, 288n3. *See also* Kumano *sendatsu*
sendatsu shū 先達衆 (groups of leaders) 5, 10
Sengen 浅間 (also 仙元, Mt. Fuji deity) 189. *See also* Moto no chichihaha
sennichigyō 千日行 (three years and three months ascetic retreat) 213
shakujō 錫杖 (staff used by *shugenja*) 133, 154, 234n33
Shasekishū 沙石集 (1283) 45, 70
shashin 捨身 (to cast away one's body) 13, 128
shenxian 神仙 (Jp. *shinsen*, Daoist immortals) 44
Shichi tengu'e 七天狗絵 (1296) 139, 141, 143
shidosō 私度僧 (privately ordained monks) 41

Shigi 子義 79
Shijū hyaku innenshū 私聚百因縁集 (1257) 69, 138, 139
Shin Chomonjū 新著聞集 (1749) 91, 92, 99
shinbutsu bunri 神仏分離 (separation of *kami* and buddhas) 2, 3, 34, 36–40, 55, 129. *See also shinbutsu hanzenrei, haibutsu kishaku*
shinbutsu shūgō 神仏習合 (combinatory system between *kami* and buddhas) 17, 33, 38–40, 233n16, 234–5n17
Shingi Shingonshū 新義真言宗 (Shingi branch of the Shingon school) 104, 106–9, 244n2
Shingonden 真言伝 (1325) 141–4, 147, 246n1
shingonshi 真言師 (master in incantations) 66–7
Shingū Yamabiko Group 新宮山彦グループ 129, 132
Shingū 新宮 8, 24. *See also* Kumano Sanzan
Shinsarugakuki 新猿楽記 (also *Shinsarugōki, Shinsarugakki*, eleventh century) 66, 67, 68, 70, 137
shintaizan 神体山 (the mountain itself as the abode of the *kami*) 38
Shinto 神道 11, 39–40
shinzō 神像 (wooden statues of *kami*) 24, 34
Shō Nei 尚寧 (1564–1620), King of the Ryūkyū 226–7
Shōbō 聖宝 (833–909) 10, 107, 172, 176
Shōgoin 聖護院 8–9, 16, 24, 79, 116, 124, 129–30, 135, 187
Shoku Nihongi 続日本紀 (797) 44, 45, 123
Shōtoku Taishi 聖徳太子 (574–622) 110, 123–4, 245n12
Shozan engi 諸山縁起 (end of the twelfth century) 11, 14, 66–8, 83, 126, 134, 139, 170, 232n17, 254n1
Shudaeten 須陀会天 212
shugen 修験 (as a skill, practice or training) 7, 66–73
  as anti-state 19–20

as culture 17
and Daoism 83–5, 220. *See also* Way of Celestial Masters
as doctrinal teaching (Shugendō kyōgaku 修験道教学) 109
and early modern popular culture 76, 101
as ethnic culture (*minzoku bunka* 民族文化) 26, 46
as ethnic or folk religion (*minzoku shūkyō* 民族宗教) 26, 46, 48–50, 64, 134, 238–9n73
as ethnic spirit (*minzoku seishin* 民族精神) 47
and ethnology (*minzokugaku* 民族学) 4, 40, 117
and folklore studies (*minzokugaku* 民俗学) 2, 4, 40, 117, 119
as fundamental culture (*kisōbunka* 基層文化) 46, 50
and gender 22–3
as Japanese Buddhism 111
and Japanese fascism 52–4
and Meiji period 3, 36–8, 103–4, 115
and mountain climbing 55–6
as mountain religion 134
as national Buddhism (*kokuminteki bukkyō* 国民的仏教) 119
and national thought (*kokumin shisō* 国民思想) 116
and other Japanese religions 25
as popular beliefs (*minkan shinkō* 民間信仰) 52
and popular religions 2
and popular understanding 18–22
as proto-Shugendō 1
and sexuality 24–5
and shamanism 20–1
as Shugen school 修験宗 112
Shugendō 修験道, definitions 1, 7, 45. *See also* shugen
and UNESCO World Heritage Program 56–7
as universal religion (*fuhen shūkyō* 普遍宗教) 110, 117–18
as Vehicle of Supernatural Powers (Genjō 験乗) 110

as "village Shugendō" (*sato shugen* 里修験) 5
Shugen kenkyū 修験研究 (1921–23) 4, 109–10, 115–16
Shugen mondō 修験問答 (1561) 78–9
Shugendō girei no kenkyū 修験道儀礼の研究 (1971) 53
Shugendō hatto 修験道法度 (1613) 75, 95
Shugendō no hattatsu 修験道の発達 (1943) 51
Shugendō shōso 修験道章疏 (1916–19) 4, 109–10
Shugendō studies 2–26, 49, 53–4, 63–4, 104, 115–20, 124
Shugendōshi kenkyū 修験道史研究 (1943) 50
shugenja 修験者 (Shugendō practitioner) 1, 2, 5–10, 21–5, 36–7, 66, 88, 103–19, 129–33, 153–64, 177, 199, 206–8, 213, 244n3, 247n1. *See also* yamabushi
  as ascetic groups (*shūdan* 集団) 7
  as "confraternities of ascetics" (*gyōja kō* 行者講) 8
  as mountain guides (*yama sendatsu* 山先達, alt. *sendatsu*) 9, 55, 112
  as sectarian organizations (*kyōdan* 教団) 7
  as spies 25
  as un-affiliated *shugenja* (*mappa shugenja* 末派修験者) 9
  as village *shugenja* (*sato shugenja* 里修験) 5
shugojin 守護神 (protector *kami*) 205
shugyō 修行 (ascetic practices) 6. *See also* yamabushi shugyō
Shuihu zhuan 水滸伝 (Jp. *Suikoden*, fourteenth century) 157–9
shuku 宿 (lodge, station) 66, 68, 127ff
shukubō 宿坊 (lodgings) 55
shuryōmin 狩猟民 (hunting population of the mountains) 6
Shutara Ryōen 修多羅亮延 (1842–1917) 39
sokushin jōbutsu 即身成仏 (attaining buddhahood in this body) 36
Sonshō mandara 尊勝曼荼羅 (Victorious One Mandala) 210–12
Steineck, Raji 16
Sueki Fumihiko 末木文美士 19

Sumeru, Mt. 須弥山 167
Suzuki Masataka 鈴木正崇 10-11, 22-3, 56
Suzuki Shōei 鈴木昭英 5, 231n3
Swanson, Paul 14, 16-7

Taizōkai mandara 胎蔵界曼荼羅 (Womb Realm Mandala) 189, 205, 210-11
Takeda Shingen 武田信玄 (1521-75) 228
tengu 天狗 37, 139
Tengu zōshi 天狗草子 (1296) 71
Tenkai 天海 (1536?-1643) 80, 97
Theosophy 21, 232 n. 13
Thomas, Jolyon 22
tō 塔 (votive stelae) 206, 213-14, 216. See also *fujiki kuyō*
Tōdaiji 東大寺 43, 45, 139-43, 167, 172-6
Togakushi, Mt. 戸隠山 26, 42, 75-86
Togakushisan daigongen engi 戸隠山大権現縁起 (ca. 1736) 80, 82-3
tōgyō 当行 (self-seclusion retreat on Mount Kasuga) 9
Tohoku Triple Disaster of March 11, 2001 19
Tōji 東寺 73, 139-42, 221
Tokugawa Ieyasu 徳川家康 (1542-1616) 212
Tokunaga Seiko 徳永誓子 7, 45, 65
Tosaka Jun 戸坂潤 (1900-45) 52
tosō 抖擻 (mountain asceticism) 46, 50, 66, 68, 168
Towazugatari とはずがたり (ca. 1307) 227-8
Tōzan-ha 当山派 (Shingon-style Shugendō) 4, 79, 103, 107
Tōzan-kata 当山方 (self-administered groups of ascetics affiliated with Kōfukuji) 9
Tōzan-kata *sendatsu* 当山方先達 (Tōzan-kata leaders) 10
Tsuga Teishō 都賀庭鐘 (1718-c.1794) 156
Tsuji Zennosuke 辻善之助 (1877-1955) 39
tsuka 塚 (sacred mounds) 206-7, 217. See also *bontenzuka*, *gyōninzuka*, Ontsuka Gongen
Tsukuba, Mt. 筑波山 213
Tyler, Royall 14, 16-7

ubasoku 優婆塞 (unordained practitioners) 41, 80, 138
Ueda Akinari 上田秋成 (1734-1809) 155, 160-2, 164
Umiura Gikan 海浦議観 (1855-1921) 3, 109, 120
Uno Enkū 宇野圓空 (1885-1949) 4, 40, 46-9, 118-19
Usa Hachiman 宇佐八幡 19

visual culture 28, 189-90, 220. See also specific items

Wakamori Tarō 和歌森太郎 (1915-77) 4, 50-3, 85, 231n1
Wakan sansai zue 和漢三才図会 (1712) 76
Way of Celestial Masters (Tianshi dao 天師道) 83-4

yama no hi 山の日 (Mountain Day) 58
yamabushi 山伏 (Shugendō practitioners) 2, 6, 8, 9, 11-13, 21, 36, 45, 65-73, 118, 137, 139, 153-7. See also *shugenja*
yamabushi shugyō 山伏修行 (mountain practices performed by specialized ascetics) 7, 66-8
Yanagita Kunio 柳田國男 (1875-1962) 4, 5, 40, 51-2, 103-4, 118, 120, 236-7n50
yomihon 読本 (short-form historical narratives) 28, 154-64
yorigitō 憑祈禱 (exorcisms) 7
Yudono, Mt. 湯殿山 15, 29, 88-9, 95-6, 205
Yudono Gongen 湯殿権現 29, 205-9, 211, 213-14, 216
 Yudono Gongen shū 湯殿権現衆 (sorority of Yudono Gongen) 215

Zaō Gongen 蔵王権現 11, 28, 45, 57, 126, 168-83
zenji 禅師 (shamanistic religious specialists, meditation masters) 41
zenjō 禅定 (meditation) 6, 44
 zenjō no zu 禅定の図 (*samādhi* pictures) 197

www.ingramcontent.com/pod-product-compliance
Lightning Source LLC
Chambersburg PA
CBHW052112010526
44111CB00036B/1783